FÊTING THE
QUEEN

A VOLUME IN THE SERIES

Massachusetts Studies in Early Modern Culture

EDITED BY
Arthur Kinney

FÊTING THE
QUEEN

Civic Entertainments
and the
Elizabethan Progress

JOHN M. ADRIAN

University of Massachusetts Press
Amherst and Boston

ISBN 978-1-62534-629-2 (paper); 628-5 (hardcover)

Designed by Sally Nichols
Set in Perpetua
Printed and bound by Books International, Inc.

Cover design by Rebecca Neimark, Twenty-Six Letters
Cover art by T. Allon, detail of *The Festivities at Kenilworth in Honour of
Queen Elizabeth*, c. 1575. From the publication *Warwick Castle and Its Earls: From
Saxon Times to the Present Day*, by Frances Evelyn Maynard Greville,
published by E.P. Dutton, 1903. Flickr/Wikimedia Commons.

Library of Congress Cataloging-in-Publication Data
Names: Adrian, John M., 1975–author.
Title: Fêting the queen : civic entertainments and the
Elizabethan
progress / John M. Adrian.
Description: Amherst ; Boston : University of Massachusetts
Press, [2021] |
Series: Massachusetts studies in early modern culture | Includes
bibliographical references and index.
Identifiers: LCCN 2021016897 (print) | LCCN 2021016898
(ebook) | ISBN
9781625346285 (hardcover) | ISBN 9781625346292 (paperback) | ISBN
9781613769058 (ebook) | ISBN 9781613769041 (ebook)
Subjects: LCSH: Elizabeth I, Queen of England,
1533–1603—Travel—England.
| Great Britain—History—Elizabeth, 1558–1603. | England—Social life
and customs—16th century. | Processions—England—History—16th
century. | Festivals—England—History—16th century. |
Hospitality—England—History—16th century. | Visits of
state—England—History—16th century.
Classification: LCC DA356 .A37 2021 (print) | LCC
DA356 (ebook) | DDC
942.05/5—dc23
LC record available at https://lccn.loc.gov/2021016897
LC ebook record available at https://lccn.loc.gov/2021016898

British Library Cataloguing-in-Publication Data
A catalog record for this book is available from the British Library.

Chapter 2 was previously published as "'A supplicacion for the Havon': Sandwich, Civic Pageantry, and
Queen Elizabeth I's Visit of 1573," in *Explorations in Renaissance Culture*, 43, no. 1 (May 2017): 30–55.
Chapter 4 was previously published as "'Warlike pastimes' and the 'sottell Snaek' of Rebellion: Bristol,
Queen Elizabeth, and the Entertainments of 1574" in *Studies in Philology*, 111, no. 4 (Fall 2014): 720–37.
Used by permission.

To my girls, Wendy and Isabella

CONTENTS

PREFACE

Queen Elizabeth I's annual progresses are among the most captivating events of her long and illustrious reign. In late summer, the Queen and her considerable retinue would leave London and spend several weeks progressing through the realm via a predetermined but always highly varied itinerary. She visited courtiers, attended banquets, entered cities, inspected coastal defenses, and traversed the verdant English countryside. Everywhere she went, Elizabeth's subjects put their best foot forward. They cheered her arrival, showered her with gifts, arranged lavish accommodations, devised elaborate entertainments, and lamented her departure. It is no wonder that these royal peregrinations have become so closely associated with the pageantry and pomp of the Elizabethan age. But the Queen didn't merely undertake progress visits as a summer recreation. Rather, she employed these occasions as public relations tools to display power, cultivate affection, and inspire loyalty among her people. These strategies are given vivid representation in Thomas Allom's later—and somewhat romanticized—depiction of *The Festivities at Kenilworth in Honour of Queen Elizabeth* (see cover image). As she approaches Kenilworth Castle in Warwickshire, Elizabeth sits majestically on her horse and gazes down at her adoring subjects. In her luminous white gown and intricate hairstyle, she is the living embodiment of Gloriana, the Virgin Queen. At the same time, the intimacy of the encounter—only a few feet separate her from the common people—also imbues her with the accessibility and humanity of Good Queen Bess.

Such monarchical readings of the Elizabethan progress are common, and typify the extent to which these events are generally seen as instances of royal performance that served the political objectives of the monarchy. While this is certainly a fruitful approach—Elizabeth *was* a savvy politician and consummate actor—it tends to overlook the agency that progress visits afforded to the

Queen's hosts. While the Queen was within their walls, hosts enjoyed direct access to the reigning monarch and were in a position to fashion a particular image of themselves to their royal visitors. In recent decades, scholars have begun to explore the responses of individuals—nobles, gentry, councilors, courtiers—to the opportunity of hosting the Queen. Yet a significant number of progress hosts were not private individuals, but rather urban communities. On almost every progress, the Queen visited cities like Rochester, Salisbury, Bath, Winchester, Norwich, Bristol, and Canterbury—often staying up to a week in each place. These royal visits were enormous opportunities for English cities, which were growing in both autonomy and importance over the course of the sixteenth century. Urban leaders may have welcomed the Queen by singing her praises and professing their undying loyalty to her government, but that is not all they did. They also used the occasion of the Queen's visit to subtly broach local needs and concerns, influence crown policies, and cultivate potential patrons who could give them much-needed channels of access to the center.

Look again at Allom's *Festivities*. As the Queen moves through the urban area outside the castle, she is not only projecting her authority over the city, she is also an observer who is experiencing the city. She is traversing its distinctive topography, forming impressions of its built environment, seeing banners, hearing music, and interacting with its citizens, who smile, laugh, shout, and hold torches aloft. In other words, Elizabeth is imbibing a particular vision of the city that is being carefully crafted by her hosts. Later, she will hear speeches, see pageant devices, enter buildings, eat local delicacies, and talk with corporation officers. As the image suggests, progress visits were not one-way projections of royal authority but dynamic opportunities for cities to influence the Queen.

This book examines the progress entertainments that English cities created when hosting Queen Elizabeth I in the middle years of her reign. Each of my chapters focuses on a specific progress visit to a particular city: Oxford in 1566, Sandwich in 1573, Canterbury in 1573, Bristol in 1574, Worcester in 1575, and Norwich in 1578. My aim is to establish the precise local contexts of each visit—what problems or challenges mattered most to each city in the year that it hosted the Queen?—and then provide a careful analysis of the entertainments that town leaders devised to "speak to" and influence their royal visitors. My close readings consider the pageant devices and orations of the formal entertainments as well as the ways in which they were framed and experienced, including the city's use of space, movement, color, costume, sound, and architecture. I also explore a range of printed and archival sources to examine the less formal aspects of the week—where the Queen lodged, what she ate, whom she interacted with, and what excursions she took— and how these (oft-overlooked) elements augmented the broader themes of the visit. My goal is to understand how each urban community deployed the highly nuanced features of early modern civic pageantry to craft a particular self-image that reflected how it wanted to be seen and valued by the center. In doing so, I also shed light on the distinctively English adaptations of European festival practices in the very decades (1560s and 1570s) in which the Elizabethan progress peaked. At the same time, my in-depth analyses of these cities function as case studies of key Tudor domestic issues (education, immigration, economy, defense, poverty, trade, militia) that are frequently overshadowed by foreign affairs and religion in treatments of the mid-Elizabethan period. Together, my chapters suggest how these crucial national issues played out on the local level.

ACKNOWLEDGMENTS

Like an Elizabethan progress, my work on this book has wound its way through a great many places and been bolstered by throngs of supportive people. First and foremost, I am appreciative of the time I was able to spend in each of the six cities that this book chronicles: Oxford, Sandwich, Canterbury, Bristol, Worcester, and Norwich. While abroad, I was assisted in conducting research at a number of libraries and archives, including the Norfolk and Norwich Millennium Library, Norfolk Record Office, Bristol Archives, Worcestershire Archive and Archaeology Service (at The Hive), Kent History and Library Centre, Canterbury Cathedral Archive, Bodleian Library, and the British Library. At each of these stops, I was given ready access to resources and assisted by cheerful staff. In addition, my queries profited from the warm hospitality and perceptive insights of local scholars evincing an almost unlimited knowledge of the cities they love. In particular, I would like to thank Karen Brayshaw and Margaret Sparks (Canterbury), David Clark and Peter Ockman (Bristol), and Nicholas Groves (Norwich) for sharing their time and expertise. I am also indebted to the numerous guides and docents who conversed with me at the cathedrals, civic buildings, museums, and historical sites that I visited. Their work helps ensure that the palpable associations of place can continue to inform our understanding of those who came before us.

Aside from these research forays, I have been helped by a number of professional organizations whose conferences and seminars gave me opportunities to present my ideas and garner valuable feedback. I would therefore like to thank the Southeastern Renaissance Conference, Renaissance Society of America, Early Modern Studies Conference, the University of Virginia's (UVA) College at Wise Medieval/Renaissance Conference, and the Society for Renaissance Studies. I am especially grateful for the chance to participate in the 2016 Huntington Seminar on Early Modern Literary Geographies.

At UVA Wise, my scholarly endeavors have benefitted greatly from a gener-ous administration, thoughtful colleagues, and enthusiastic students. Sanders Huguenin, Amelia Harris, John Cull, Trisha Folds-Bennett, the Academic Enhancement Committee, and the Faculty Development Committee have supported my research in the form of travel grants, course releases, summer stipends, and a 2015 research sabbatical. Other colleagues read portions of my work or otherwise facilitated my research, including Ken Tiller, Brian McKnight, Mark Clark, Lucian Undreiu, and Chris Hill. I would also like to acknowledge the active assistance of the UVA Wise library staff. Robin Benke, Kim Marshall, Carolea Newsome, Amelia VanGundy, Angie Harvey, David Locke, and Angela West all had a hand in helping me access scholarly resources and in giving me a tranquil space in which to make progress on the book.

I would especially like to thank Mary Dougherty for her initial interest in the manuscript and for her invaluable help and support throughout the pro-cess, Rachael DeShano and Julie Shilling for their painstaking editing and pro-duction work, and Sally Nichols for her assistance with the maps. An earlier version of the Sandwich chapter appeared in *Explorations in Renaissance Culture* 43:1 (2017) and of the Bristol chapter in Brill and *Studies in Philology* 111:4 (Fall 2014); I am grateful to Brill and *Studies in Philology*, respectively, for per-mission to reproduce this material.

Finally, my wife, Wendy, and daughter Isabella have accompanied me on each step of these meandering progress journeys. They have willingly traveled to distant realms, listened to my orations, and proffered much-needed advice. Above all, they have understood the lure of the intellectual peregrinations that animate scholarship, and they have given me the space, time, and support to pursue them.

ABBREVIATIONS

The following works are abbreviated in citations in the text and the notes.

*JN*1   Elizabeth Goldring, Jayne Elisabeth Archer, Elizabeth Clarke, eds. *John Nichols's "The Progresses and Public Processions of Queen Elizabeth I: A New Edition of the Early Modern Sources,"* vol. 1. Oxford: Oxford University Press, 2014.

*JN*2   Elizabeth Goldring, Jayne Elisabeth Archer, Elizabeth Clarke, eds. *John Nichols's "The Progresses and Public Processions of Queen Elizabeth I: A New Edition of the Early Modern Sources,"* vol. 2. Oxford: Oxford University Press, 2014.

*K*2   James M. Gibson, ed. *Records of Early English Drama: Kent,* vol. 2. Toronto: University of Toronto Press, 2002.

ES   Martin Luther. *An Exposition of Salomons Booke, called Ecclesiastes or the Preacher.* Translator unknown. London: John Day, 1573.

RB   Mark C. Pilkinton, ed. *Records of Early English Drama: Bristol.* Toronto: University of Toronto Press, 1997.

Scotland

Map of
ENGLAND

Norwich●

Worcester●

Wales

Oxford●

●Bristol

London●

Canterbury—●
Sandwich

Map reproduced by Coni Porter. Reproduced from "England and Wales: principal cities and towns,"
in Penry Williams, *The Later Tudors: England, 1547–1603* (Oxford: Oxford University Press, 1995).
© Penry Williams 1995. Reproduced with permission of the Licensor through PLSclear.

FÊTING THE
QUEEN

INTRODUCTION

Rochester Bridge was falling down. By 1570, the bridge's maintenance had been neglected for decades so that "the woorke declined daily to more and more decaie."[1] Help arrived when Queen Elizabeth I visited Rochester during her 1573 progress through Kent. After being informed of the bridge's poor condition, the Queen promptly established a commission of local stakeholders to examine the causes and possible remedies. Three years later, Parliament passed *An Acte for the perpetuall mayntenaunce of Rochestre Bridge*.[2] William Lambarde credits "the princely care of the Queenes Majestie" with saving the bridge, asserting that without her efforts "it was to be justly feared, that in short time there would have been no Bridge at all."[3]

The bridge's salvation is surely linked to the royal progress of 1573, but it would be a mistake to attribute it solely to the Queen's spontaneous aegis. For their part, the citizens of Rochester recognized that their bridge over the Medway was both "a beautiful ornament" and a "a moste serviceable commoditie," and they used the progress visit to actively solicit the Crown's assistance.[4] Hosting the Queen gave the city corporation and local gentry direct access to the reigning monarch, and they no doubt used this entrée to acquaint Elizabeth with the scope and extent of their local crisis. Indeed, many of the individuals who would have played a role in hosting the Queen—including the mayor of Rochester, the dean of Rochester Cathedral, Richard Watts, Sir Walter Mildmay, and William Brooke, Lord Cobham—were subsequently appointed to the commission.[5] City officials also made sure that the Queen spent time in close proximity to Rochester Bridge. Not only was the Queen given a "personal inspection" of the bridge, she was also lodged in the Crown Inn—just a few feet away from the southern end of the structure.[6] During her four-night stay, she would have been well-positioned to witness the bridge's condition firsthand. At the same time, the inn's central location just below the city's massive castle and adjacent to its beautiful cathedral would have helped remind the Queen that Rochester was an important political, religious, and commercial center—and thus worthy of her assistance. Finally, the city used pageantry as part of its appeal for aid. On the last night of the Queen's visit, there was a "triumphe [on] the water by nighte at Rochester."[7] Although we do not know the content of this entertainment, it is unusual and significant that it occurred on the water. This setting would seem to underscore the importance of the Medway (and thus the bridge that spanned it) for both Rochester's self-definition and for its continuing prosperity.[8] Thus, even as the city proffered hospitality to the visiting monarch, it used a combination of personal appeal, topography, and pageantry to proactively seek a means of repairing the bridge.

Too often, royal progresses are seen solely in terms of the motives and goals of the sovereign. There is no doubt that progresses were public relations tools that Elizabeth wielded with considerable skill, but they were also two-way streets. Hosting the reigning monarch was a momentous opportunity for Rochester, Norwich, Worcester, and dozens of other urban communities. Their citizens may have sung the Queen's praises and affirmed their undying loyalty, but they also used progress visits to subtly speak to their monarch. They presented particular images of themselves, articulated and sought assistance with specific needs and concerns, and tried to influence royal policies. As we shall see, they pursued these aims primarily through the civic pageantry that they devised to welcome and entertain the Queen and her entourage.

This book will examine Queen Elizabeth's progress visits to six English towns in the 1560s and 1570s. Scholars writing about Elizabethan progresses have tended to focus on private hosts—at Kenilworth, Elvetham, Cowdray, Bisham, Harefield, Rycote, Ditchley, and so forth—at the expense of civic visits.[9] Yet Queen Elizabeth made some 83 visits to over 50 towns during her reign.[10] Of the 23 progresses that she embarked upon, 20 included visits to towns.[11] Her civic destinations included many of the main urban centers of the midlands, south, and eastern parts of the realm. Elizabeth also spent a relatively large amount of progress time in towns. For instance, the 1573 progress lasted 75 nights, 35 of which were spent in the towns of Canterbury, Dover, Faversham, Rochester, Rye, Sandwich, and Winchelsea. In 1574, the proportion was lower (23 out of 100 nights), but still included multi-night visits to Reading, Bath, Bristol, Salisbury, and Winchester.[12] It is clear that Elizabeth made frequent visits to provincial towns and that they were a priority for her while on progress.

Sixteenth-Century Towns

English provincial towns are often overlooked in the sixteenth century because of the size and importance of early modern London. By 1603, London had an estimated population of 200,000, while the next largest city, Norwich, hovered around 15,000 people.[13] Yet these smaller urban areas were numerous. Robert Tittler reports that there were somewhere between 600 and 700 English towns in the sixteenth century.[14] The vast majority of these were small market towns with populations between 800 and 1,500 residents.[15] According to Peter Clark, "despite their rural aspect and absence of walls . . . [these smaller towns] were much bigger and more economically advanced than villages and had an extensive role in provincial society."[16] In the next tier were regional centers like Oxford, Great Yarmouth, Chester, Canterbury, and Shrewsbury.[17] There were about 100 of these, each with a population of 1,500 to 5,000.[18] These towns were not only distinguished by their larger sizes, but by their greater economic and political complexity.[19] Finally, at the apex of the provincial town hierarchy were the provincial centers. This was a much smaller group of five to seven cities comprised of Norwich, Bristol, York, Exeter, Newcastle, and possibly Salisbury and Coventry.[20] In 1603, their populations ranged from 7,000 to 15,000.[21] Clark calls them "provincial capitals" and characterizes them as "significant regional cities with extensive trading connections and elaborate civic privileges."[22]

Not only were provincial towns numerous and complex, they were also growing in importance over the course of the sixteenth century. In terms of population, there was an overall trajectory of urban growth over the course of the sixteenth and seventeenth centuries. In 1500, only 15 towns had populations of over 4,000; by 1700, 30 towns had populations of over 5,000.[23] Moreover, between 1525 and 1600, the "total population of the leading 17 provincial towns rose from about 85,000 to about 130,000."[24] Finally, there was an overall increase in the percentage of the total English population that lived in towns. According to Clark, this figure rose from 5 percent of the population in 1540 to 8 percent of the population in 1600.[25]

Many towns were also experiencing economic growth. The general consensus among historians is that numerous towns suffered economic decay in the first half of the sixteenth century, only to rebound in the second half.[26] This economic downturn seems to have been caused by a number of factors, including the "troubled cloth industry," competition with and "diversion of trade to London," disease and mortality, and royal taxation.[27] The result was that "to a greater or lesser extent these damaging processes eroded the population, wealth, and morale" of provincial towns.[28] But from the middle of the sixteenth century, an economic turnaround was created by compensating factors, including a heightened demand for urban services, the diversification of urban economies, the expansion of Baltic and Atlantic trade, the arrival of the manufacturing of lighter fabrics known as the "new draperies," freedom from major epidemics, and immigration from the countryside.[29] At any rate, A. L. Rowse and others see a clear "contrast between depression and decline in the earlier part of the century and the recovery and increasing wealth of Elizabeth's reign."[30] Of course, the accuracy of this view varied in relation to individual towns and is certainly not without exception.[31] Nevertheless, the larger picture is of population growth and economic recovery as we move into Elizabeth's reign.

At the same time, towns were also becoming more autonomous. As Tittler explains, the 1540s to the 1560s were watershed decades for English towns.[32] The Dissolution made local church lands and buildings available, which town corporations then moved to acquire. The Reformation thus made towns wealthier and also removed much of the "ecclesiastical lordship" that had rivaled urban authority.[33] In the decades that followed, many towns seized the initiative to legally formalize their growing authority via "a variety of legal and constitutional devices," including litigation, incorporation, and enfeoffment.[34] Indeed, Catherine Patterson refers to these years as a "great wave of town incorporation."[35] From 1485 to 1540, there were thirteen borough incorporations; from 1540 to 1558, there were forty-five—a "geometric rate of increase."[36] The trend continued into Elizabeth's reign, with fifty-three more incorporations.[37] The charters that accompanied these incorporations spelled out the legal privileges of the town, including the corporation's right to elect officers, regulate trade, hold courts, maintain defenses, levy taxes, enforce laws, maintain order, and settle disputes.[38] Overall, these decades resulted in a net increase in the "degree of self government" for towns, both internally and also from rival external authorities like the church, manor, county, and other seigneurial authorities.[39]

This process was actually aided by the Crown. Again, the Reformation had created something of a vacuum in local authority, as traditional structures for dispensing charity and maintaining order and deference were swept away.[40] At the same time, the 1530s and 1540s were marked by a host of social problems and disorders, including disease, inflation, crime, rootlessness, and unrest.[41] The central government looked to partner with town corporations to fill this void and ensure that law and order were maintained. To do so, it increased urban privileges, granted powers of "social and economic regulation," and protected towns from rural economic competition.[42] In other words, the Crown "happily complied" in the process of borough incorporation and increased autonomy because it became a "medium through which authority and civilisation could be imposed."[43]

Population growth, economic development, and increased autonomy also created problems and challenges for evolving towns. Internally, as town corporations consolidated their new power, they also needed to create a new political culture. Throughout the Middle Ages, "Catholic belief and practice had come to form an essential underpinning . . . for the goals of hierarchy, order, and discipline, which were essential to a well-ordered society at every level."[44] But the Reformation—though it created the opportunity for town governments to carve out more wealth, privileges, and authority—also left town officials "without their accustomed means of engendering loyalty, deference, and obedience."[45] This problem was intensified by the fact that town leaders—unlike local gentry or ecclesiastical officials—could not naturally inspire the kind of deference that would support their authority; they had "no titles, no hereditary status in a fixed social hierarchy, no regional base of support, and no statutory right to legal or social distinction."[46] Thus, from the 1560s, they self-consciously set about creating a political culture "of order and deference" that would validate and legitimize increasingly oligarchic town governments.[47] One of their main tools for constructing this culture was civic ritual. Mayoral processions were used to underscore hierarchy, civic regalia helped define authority, and secular mythology (i.e. the replacement of patron saints with mythological founders) assisted in forging "civic memory" that helped create a shared identity.[48]

Another challenge was external: working out the relationship of the town to the center. This challenge was not an entirely new one. As Lorraine Attreed explains, fourteenth- and fifteenth-century boroughs had tried to forge a "delicate balance between relying upon the royal government, the source of one's privileges, and making independent decisions based on self-defined needs . . . They needed to acknowledge their gratitude without impairing their freedom to determine and exercise their own governing abilities."[49] This paradox only intensified in the sixteenth century, as towns came to be more in the orbit of the center. Corporations looked to the Crown "to consolidate their authority over the inhabitants and remove themselves from the jurisdiction of their former manorial overlords," but this process also "strengthened royal control over boroughs by specifically defining the rights of town governments and by making the chief officer of a corporation (usually the mayor) a royal official."[50] Even though they partnered with the Crown to pursue mutually beneficial goals like order, stability, and defense, towns nonetheless evolved independently. This divergence could lead to friction. Sybil Jack notes a "distinct tension between the contradictory faces of town life: between its drive for autonomy and its responsibility to king and kingdom."[51] In some ways, town oligarchies had secured their own authority within the town at the expense of wider civic autonomy; urban privileges had been granted by the Crown and so could theoretically be withdrawn at the pleasure of the monarch.[52] At the same time, towns could leverage their relationships with the center. As Ian Archer points out, "Because the crown was the arbiter of the privileges on which urban autonomy rested, the power of the centre could be invoked to secure benefits for towns or for groups within them."[53]

Urban Patronage

One of the ways that towns navigated their relationship with the center was through urban patronage. As Patterson explains, patronage was "a network of personal relationships which . . . overlay the institutions of government." Since direct access to the monarch was rare, those who held office or were influential were expected to not only discharge their duties, but "provide favor to others, assisting in administrative procedure and putting suitors on the way toward office or favor or benefit from the crown."[54] Thus, towns, like individuals, needed to cultivate influential patrons in order to gain access to the center and secure benefits. Patterson argues that rather than attempting to jettison outside influences that might interfere with their drive for autonomy, towns actively "sought out connections as a means to strengthen their own position by gaining access to the center."[55] Towns regularly sought grants and assistance from the center for a variety of purposes, including trade and commerce, land acquisition, taxation, militia, and charter confirmation.[56] Sometimes towns made positive appeals in these areas; other times they merely tried to mitigate the demands of central government for "purveyance, military service, taxation, and other financial exactions."[57] These negotiations with the center required patrons at every step of the way. For instance, a new charter would require local advisors to consult on legal issues and the best method for proceeding; advocates to further the suit and bring it "to the attention of the decision-makers at Court"; and influential people at court to actually back the petition, reassure the Crown of its legitimacy, and see it acted upon.[58] Patrons thus served as mediators between urban elites and the center; a patron would not only support the town but also help it navigate the complexities and nuances of the political system.

Not surprisingly, towns cast a wide net for potential patrons. Many towns looked to influential gentry and nobles who owned property (and thus had a natural power base) in their region. Cathedral cities might enlist the aid of their bishop, while ports could turn to an influential maritime officer.[59] Still others might call on manorial lords or royal officials like the wardens or constables of nearby royal castles.[60] Lawyers with local ties were especially useful, not just for legal counsel but for the myriad contacts that they could offer.[61] Indeed, the relationship of towns to lawyers was often formalized in the civic office of the recorder. All of these urban patrons offered channels of access to the center.

Towns might also appeal more directly to individuals associated with key royal institutions. The Privy Council was "the central organ of state" and had wide-ranging functions from foreign policy to finance.[62] It also had—at least theoretically—a monopoly on offering counsel to the sovereign, and its advice was more often than not heeded by the Queen.[63] A privy councilor could thus be a powerful ally for a town. The royal court also played an important role in the distribution of patronage. It "created non-stop opportunities," points out Christopher Haigh, "for private lobbying and personal relationships which could be pressed into political service."[64] On a more practical level, it was the place where affairs were discussed, petitions were presented, and decisions were made.[65] For all of these reasons, it was a "crucial link between the crown and the regions."[66] Not surprisingly, towns sought out courtiers who could advance their interests in this turbulent but vital arena. At court, those in closest physical proximity to the monarch were the officers and servants of the Privy Chamber. These included the Lord Chamberlain, Vice Chamberlain, Treasurer of the Chamber, ladies of the bedchamber, and yeomen of the guard. Since these individuals controlled access to the Queen, they too played a key role in politics and patronage. The twenty or so maids and ladies of the bedchamber and privy chamber were constant companions of the Queen. They therefore were privy to political secrets, provided important information about the Queen to would-be suitors (including her mood), and could even influence the Queen's political views.[67] Naturally, towns attempted to make use of those in the royal household who had local ties.[68]

Some relationships that towns cultivated with urban patrons were formalized in particular offices. In the second half of the sixteenth century, many towns gave the honorary title of High Steward to a nobleman (typically with local or regional ties) who "provided the corporation with links to the center and promised protection and support for the town and its inhabitants."[69] Beginning in the fifteenth century, towns commonly used their parliamentary seats to cultivate patronage—either by offering them to outsiders (like local gentlemen and lawyers) whose favor they wanted to curry or by giving the power of nomination to an aristocratic benefactor.[70] By the sixteenth century, it was also common for towns to fill the position of recorder—the town's official legal adviser—with an outsider.[71]

Other patronage relationships were less formal. In some cases, they "rested upon long-term ties between a town and a local magnate's family living in close proximity," and thus continued a much older tradition of "good lordship."[72] In other cases, they might be more temporary and situational. Patronage assistance might be cultivated for some short-term goal with "anyone who might be able to provide inside information, hurry along some paperwork, or slip a petition to an important courtier."[73]

Regardless of the longevity or nature of the relationship, towns needed to choose their patrons carefully. They were not so indiscriminate as to seek any help they could get. This is because many of the people to whom towns might naturally appeal—including local gentry and the church—had a vested interest in the town; they "both needed the town and sought to control it."[74] In exchange for their patronage, some individuals might expect to wield influence in the political, economic, and religious affairs of the town. As a result, many towns had what Jack refers to as a "love/hate relationship" with local lords and gentry.[75]

Once patrons were identified, towns set about wooing them and cultivating their assistance. Once again, towns turned to civic ritual, though in this case as an expression of hospitality. When magnates, bishops, judges, country gentlemen, privy councilors, and other dignitaries visited a town, urban hospitality typically took the form of "elaborate welcomes," gift-giving, "ceremonial organization and display," lodging accommodation, feasting, and even formal entertainments.[76] These rituals were a way of honoring a guest, showing respect, and cultivating favor. As Attreed puts it, these elaborate welcomes helped towns "establish peaceful relations," "interest [potential patrons] in a town's welfare," and "convince them to assist . . . and act sympathetically toward" urban needs.[77] But they were not just one-sided appeals. As Daryl Palmer points out, the exercise of early modern hospitality was also a way of creating "codes of exchange" and inviting reciprocity.[78] Gifts were especially useful in this regard, so visiting dignitaries were routinely presented with offerings of wine, cheese, fowl, marmalade, and, especially, sugar loaves.[79] As Patterson explains, such gifts "symbolized the respect of the giver toward the recipient, as well as the acceptance by the recipient of the obligation it conveyed."[80] Other gestures like ritual feasting or painting the heraldic arms of a nobleman throughout the town were made in the same spirit. The goal of such hospitality was to attract and inspire potential patronage. As Attreed says, "All urban subjects lived in hope that the right amount of wine, fish, processions, and entertainments would convince a guest to take municipal interests to heart."[81]

As we shall see, royal progress visits to towns were marked by many of the same features: processional entries, lodging accommodation, feasting, gift-giving, and entertainment. Obviously, the stakes were much higher and the ceremonies more elaborate, but the practice of hospitality was essentially the same. Indeed, a key aspect of my approach to civic pageantry in this book is that it should be seen first and foremost as an exercise in hospitality—with the same goal of cultivating urban patronage. From the town corporation's perspective, one of the most exciting facets of a royal visit was that it provided direct access to the center. Cole asserts that progress hosts "briefly became part of [the Queen's] court"—so that the typical barriers of access were temporarily removed and they could appeal directly to the monarch.[82] Indeed, a royal progress was one of the few occasions in which Elizabeth routinely interacted with those below the rank of a gentleman.[83] These interactions not only characterized the formal parts of the visit—such as when the Queen heard a speech by the mayor or responded to the acclamations of the thronging townspeople—but also the less formal moments. At Rochester and Bristol, the Queen lodged in the homes of prominent townspeople. In Sandwich, she dined with the principal women of the town at the local grammar school. In Warwick, after returning from a visit to nearby Kenilworth Castle, she "sodenly went into master Thomas Fishers house . . . who at that time was grevously vexid with the gowt" (*JN2*, 39). Since Fisher—the son of a fishmonger who had risen to prominence in Warwick—could not come to her, the Queen visited him, and "with most gracious woordes comfotid him" (*JN2*, 39). Not only did such incidents provide access to the reigning monarch, they also revolved around the exercise of hospitality that attempted to "entangle the Queen within a relationship of mutual obligations."[84] The short-term hope was that the Queen would look favorably on any of the town's active requests, concerns, or petitions. In the long term, the town would have built up some good will "capital" that might be of use in the future.

At the same time, a royal progress was also an opportunity for the town to cultivate other patrons that might be in the royal entourage. On a typical progress, the Queen was accompanied by up to 350 people.[85] This number would have included courtiers, nobles, privy councilors, household officers, ladies and gentlemen of the privy chamber, court physicians, foreign ambassadors, musicians, heralds-at-arms, and a large train of servants for feeding and clothing the itinerant court. In other words, the Queen's retinue would have included many of the very people whose patronage the towns were keen to cultivate. Since the Queen would leave the town in a few days—in most cases, never to return— these individuals represented the possibility of longer-term channels of access to the center. This is why, at Worcester, a delegation of town officials made separate visits to the lodgings of Sir James Croft, Lord Burghley, and the earls of Leicester, Warwick, and Sussex, and presented them with gifts of spiced wine and (for Croft) a tankard. It is also why, at Oxford, thirteen men—including nobles, privy councilors, and household officers—were presented with honorary degrees at the end of the week. The servants of the royal household were also courted. Civic records in Norwich, Canterbury, Lichfield, Worcester, and Saffron Walden record generous gifts to the Queen's porters, sergeant of arms, footmen, musicians, cooks, and gentlemen ushers. As we have seen, these individuals were important presences in the inner circle of the court, and their good opinion or future cooperation might just prove invaluable.

Royal progresses could even be used to shore up existing urban patronage. The Earl of Warwick naturally accompanied the Queen to Warwick in 1572; while he was there, the town presented him with a fat ox and ten sheep. The Earl was reportedly pleased, and before he departed he arranged for four deer "to be geven & deliuered to the bailief & townes men to make myrry withall."[86] In honoring the Earl in front of his peers and the Queen, the town engaged in an exchange of gifts that helped maintain an existing patronage relationship. Since so much of Elizabethan politics came down to "personal relations" and "personalities," perhaps the biggest boon that royal visits afforded to towns was the opportunity to build relationships with people outside of the urban sphere.[87]

Although some accounts of Elizabethan progresses present towns as naïve, obsequious, and blinded by the glare of the incandescent court, most towns were well-equipped to take advantage of the possibilities of a royal visit.[88] Corporation minutes and account books suggest that town leaders responded purposefully and effectively to the news that the Queen would visit. Within a couple of months, they raised money, refurbished streets, painted houses, repaired walls, bought a suitable gift for the Queen, purchased new robes and regalia, wrote speeches, and devised entertainments. Moreover, the medium of civic pageantry was one that they were both familiar with and adept at. Most towns had a long tradition of civic ritual that included medieval religious processions (like Corpus Christi) as well as secular events like mayoral processions. As we have seen, secular rituals had taken on even greater prominence in the post-Reformation town, as civic leaders had leaned on them heavily in creating the new political culture of order and deference. And, of course, towns were used to welcoming and wooing outside guests using many of the same conventions that characterized royal receptions.

It is therefore surprising that so many critics approach Elizabethan progresses primarily from the Queen's perspective. Much has been written on Elizabeth's goals and motives for going on progress: to show herself to the common people, build rapport, cultivate affection, win hearts, and inspire loyalty.[89] From this perspective, Elizabeth emerges as a shrewd politician and consummate actor. No doubt she was. But this preoccupation has caused critics to see progresses primarily as occasions of royal performance. For example, Jean Wilson characterizes the Elizabethan progress as an "exercise in public relations" that used the "spectacle" of royal splendor to awe the local inhabitants.[90] According to Felicity Heal, "Elizabeth's journeys have been read as social drama, enacting the monarch's symbolic and physical possession of her realm."[91] This monarchical lens has also been applied to civic visits. In his seminal *English Civic Pageantry: 1558–1642*, David Bergeron treats the sovereign's entry into a city primarily as an occasion that "help[ed] ratify the monarch's claim to the throne and define the city's response to such claims by honoring and celebrating the monarch."[92]

However, there has been a recent turn toward the perspectives of those who hosted or participated in royal progresses. Mary Hill Cole in particular has alerted us to how English towns used these occasions to engage in "ceremonial dialogues" with the Queen and make requests or other petitions.[93] Scholars are now beginning to recognize that progresses were two-way streets and that they were opportunities for civic hosts to actively fashion and project particular images of themselves to the reigning monarch. A couple of recent collections include articles that explore this dynamic, including Jayne Archer, Elizabeth Goldring, and Sarah Knight's *The Progresses, Pageants, and Entertainments of Queen Elizabeth I.*[94]

Scholars of Continental pageants have been more attuned to the strategies and responses of urban elites. Peter Arnade and Margit Thøfner have produced book-length studies of Low Country ducal entries for the cities of Ghent, Antwerp, and Brussels.[95] Meanwhile, Neil Murphy and Michael Wintroub have done similar work on royal entries into Rouen and other French cities in the late medieval and early modern periods.[96] Many of these readings have been based on reconstructing the cultural world of these urban centers and on examining the "production, meaning, and use" (in Wintroub's phrasing) of these rituals for civic elites.[97]

This book endeavors to apply this focus and methodology to the progress receptions of English towns. Like their Continental counterparts, English towns responded to royal progresses in more complex ways than simply hosting the sovereign and celebrating the monarchy. Instead, they recognized that a royal visit was not just an honor, but an opportunity for the town. They therefore sought to craft a civic image that reflected how they wanted to be seen— and valued—by the center. At the same time, towns frequently used the visit to broach a particular need, concern, or request—though not always in the form of an actual petition. Finally, towns used a combination of hospitality, ritual, and pageant entertainment to generate goodwill and cultivate patrons—targeting both the Queen and those in her retinue—who might assist the town.

Civic Pageantry

What did these receptions look like? It would probably be useful to start with some of their formal features. The Queen's visit was almost always marked by an elaborate royal entry. A delegation of city officers would meet the incoming royal retinue at the farthest limits of the town liberties. This initial encounter was highly ritualized and involved the ceremonial surrender of the town mace to the Queen, who then duly returned it to the mayor. The Queen was then treated to a formal welcome oration, often delivered by the town recorder. Afterward, the Queen was presented with a gift, typically in the form of a silver cup or a purse full of money. The Queen and her attendants—escorted by the town officers—would then enter the city gates and process through the town. Along the route the cavalcade might pause periodically for pageant devices and additional speeches. The procession would typically end either at the Queen's lodging or at the cathedral, where a special service would be held. Many of these performative elements were not new; as we have seen, towns had long used modified versions in religious and secular processionals, including the welcoming of outside visitors.[98] We also find some of these conventions in earlier royal entries to towns going back to the late fourteenth century.[99] However, these ritual performances were becoming richer and more elaborate by the second half of the sixteenth century.

One of the main catalysts was Queen Elizabeth's 1559 coronation entry into London. Though there had been relatively little royal pageantry in the reigns of Edward VI and Mary Tudor, the accession of Elizabeth seemed to spur civic pageantry in all its forms.[100] Elizabeth's coronation featured a long procession from the Tower of London to Temple Bar. Along the way seven pageant devices were set up at key locations within the city, including at Fenchurch Street, Cornhill, Soper Lane, and Cheapside. All of these devices featured scaffolds, on top of which were depicted allegorical tableaux drawn from biblical and mythological subjects. For example, the pageant in Cornhill portrayed four virtues treading on four vices: Pure Religion upon Superstition and Ignorance, Love of Subjects upon Rebellion and Insolence, Wisdom upon Folly and Vainglory, and Justice upon Adulation and Bribery. At Temple Bar, the device included representations of the ancient British giants Gogmagog and Corineus. A number of these elements featured in the Queen's 1559 entry would be seen in later Elizabethan pageantry in provincial towns: a carefully chosen processional route, temporary stages, triumphal arches, allegorical devices, formal speeches, gift-giving, music, and thronging crowds. Indeed, Bergeron sees the 1559 entry as setting the "basic pattern" and "epitomizing the chief characteristics to be found" in subsequent Elizabethan entries.[101] This London entry was no doubt especially influential because it was disseminated in a popular pamphlet authored by Richard Mulcaster and printed in 1559.[102]

Another key influence on provincial pageantry was the London Lord Mayors' Show. Unlike the coronation entry, it was an annual event. Every October 29, the newly elected mayor of London would process to Westminster to take his oath of office and then return to the Guildhall in the city. Along the way, the guild from which the new mayor had been elected would present "its dramatic show, consisting generally of various dramatic tableaux stationed along the route."[103] These shows had only emerged in the mid-sixteenth century, but already they were becoming more elaborate as the competing guilds attempted to outdo one another.[104] According to guild records and spectator accounts, these shows featured temporary (and sometimes portable) scaffolds, brightly painted canvas and wood, historical personages and allegorical figures, speeches, colorful costumes, live animals, visual and textual allusions to trade guilds, and puns on the new mayor's name.[105] For example, the 1561 pageant for Sir William Harper (put on by the Merchant Taylors) made use of the mayor's last name to create a pageant that revolved around musical associations.[106] It depicted five personages with musical links (David, Orpheus, Amphion, Arion, and Topas) on a stage with their stories painted behind them. It also included a device on Psalm 150 (Praise the Lord "with the sound of the trumpet: praise him with psaltery and harp") and an accompanying children's choir that played and sang. These annual shows exhibited many of the same elements found in royal entries, so it is likely that they were both influenced by and contributed to the genre. Accounts of the Lord Mayors' Shows do not seem to have circulated as printed texts before 1585, but it is likely—given the centrality of London and the annual recurrence of the shows—that many people from provincial towns had seen one or more first-hand. At any rate, town leaders would have had a rich native tradition of pageantry to draw from as they made preparations to host the Queen.

Towns may also have looked to their sister cities on the Continent for inspiration. Urban pageantry and spectacle were well-established throughout Europe by the fifteenth century.[107] Indeed, J. R. Mulryne describes the pageantry of the period as possessing a shared "lexicon . . . with a wide range of recognisably common elements across national boundaries."[108] In France, royal visits to cities were especially prevalent, because each new monarch would begin his reign by visiting all of the major cities in the realm.[109] For example, in the 1560s the young Charles IX visited over one hundred French towns in a twenty-seven-month period.[110] Over the course of the sixteenth century, French entries evolved to become more secular (and less religious), more magnificent, and more political.[111] French entries also exhibit many of the same conventions found in England. They too feature a procession through the city along a predetermined route, a welcome speech and gift to the monarch, and elaborate decorations and pageant devices that blend symbolism, allegory, history, and myth.[112] French pageantry of the 1550s and 1560s is often militaristic, just like that of Sandwich and Bristol in the 1570s.[113] However, French entries differ from their English counterparts in their emphasis on banqueting, the Te Deum service, and the oath-taking of the monarch as well as in their inclusion of holy objects and the symbolic keys of the city.[114] France developed a tradition of "lavishly illustrated festival books," so accounts of many French entries were printed, translated, and disseminated throughout Europe.[115] Among them are particularly elaborate versions of royal entries into Lyon (1548), Paris (1549), and Rouen (1551) that may have influenced English pageantry.[116] A few Englishmen and women witnessed French entries firsthand. For example, the English ambassador Sir John Mason was present at Henry II's entry into Rouen in 1551.[117]

Meanwhile, in the Low Countries, cities like Antwerp and Brussels had "well-established ceremonial traditions" in the sixteenth century.[118] Two of these ceremonies were the annual *ommegangen* (a civic/religious procession) and the more occasional Joyous Entry (at the accession of a new ducal ruler).[119] The latter featured elaborate decorations, triumphal arches, allegorical tableaux, and the participation of civic militiamen. The former was especially renowned for its stationary floats. A 1571 Antwerp inventory gives vivid descriptions of the floats for that year, which included classical, secular, and local mythological figures.[120] Moreover, some of these floats had a "topical element" and would be used to comment on and "address current affairs."[121] As in France, some of these accounts were printed—though in the form of "booklets or souvenir guides" rather than lavishly illustrated tomes— including ommegangen descriptions from 1559, 1561, 1562, 1564, and 1566. It is also likely that a number of English visitors experienced these ceremonies firsthand. Up until 1569, Antwerp was the center of the Continental wool market, thus there was a strong English mercantile presence in the city. It is therefore likely that Continental practices provided additional models that English towns could draw from.

Aside from the actual practices and conventions of civic ritual, towns could also convey particular themes and messages by appealing to shared iconographical traditions that were common across Europe. A good example of this shared visual culture is Cesare Ripa's *Iconologia* (1593), a compendium of allegorical, mythological, and religious meanings and their symbolic representations. Such an iconographical "vocabulary" is especially useful to pageantry;

just by looking at the clothing, gestures, or props associated with a particular figure, audiences could instantly recognize the visual portrayal of an abstract virtue, vice, or idea. As a consequence, pageant devisers could convey complex ideas clearly and efficiently. They could also be reasonably certain that audiences would understand what they were seeing. Gordon Kipling has written about "the importance of signs to the Renaissance mind."[122] Unlike their modern counterparts, sixteenth-century men and women were well practiced in reading allegory, symbol, and emblem, and were particularly attuned to the interplay between word and image.[123] As Bergeron puts it, early modern England was "an aesthetic climate that readily embrace[d] symbolic, emblematic, and iconographical art" and was therefore "a world rich in metaphorical possibilities and understanding."[124] In other words, audiences would have been highly attuned to and skilled at reading civic pageantry.

Even though the form, conventions, and vocabulary of civic pageantry transcended national boundaries, there are some differences worth noting between Continental and English practices. For one thing, English pageantry was less elaborate and on a "lesser scale."[125] Henry II's 1551 entry into Rouen "included 50 Norman knights, horse-drawn chariots for the figures of Fame, Religion, Majesty, Virtue, and Good Fortune; 57 armored men representing the historical kings of France, musicians, military and regional groups parading en masse, 6 elephants and a band of slaves and captives, all of whom moved through a Roman Arch of Triumph."[126] The coronation entry of Pope Leo X into Rome in 1513 featured "the creation of 'an outdoor museum of [antique] sculpture' within the processional route."[127] There is nothing to match this kind of grandeur and magnificence in English royal entries. Although, as we shall see, this need not be taken to mean that English pageantry was less complex in iconography or meaning.

A related difference is that English towns tended to use existing architecture rather than creating elaborate temporary structures. As French entries became more magnificent, they invested heavily in "architectural constructions such as triumphal arches, obelisks, porticos, and perspectives in trompe-l'oeil."[128] Not only were these pieces large and ornate, they were also thoroughly classical insofar as careful "[a]ttention was paid to perspective and correct orders of architecture."[129] In Maximilian II's 1563 entry into Vienna, the city used these motifs precisely in order to "boost the city's self-image by linking it with a classical past."[130] Other Continental cities, like Rome, invested heavily in "elaborate temporary structures" to modify and change the cityscape during royal entries.[131] English cities did not follow this trend. Other than the occasional use of triumphal arches—mainly in London—English pageantry utilized relatively simple scaffolds as stages for pageant devices.[132] They certainly did not transform the architectural appearance of the town. This difference has probably led modern scholars to underestimate the role of architecture in English entries. As I will argue, the permanent architecture of host towns did play a key role in their receptions of the Queen. These buildings are easy to overlook precisely because they are a permanent part of the built environment and did not obviously convey meaning in the way that something specially constructed for the occasion would. Yet, English buildings were not only important backdrops for pageantry; they were consciously used by town hosts in their ceremonial dialogues with the Queen. As such, they deserve careful study.

Finally, English pageantry differs from Continental pageantry in its investment in the written and spoken word. Bergeron notes the relative absence of speeches in Low Country pageants, which instead exhibit a "heavy reliance on painted figures or 'images' and painted scenes as opposed to live actors."[133] In contrast, English pageantry is less pictorial and more verbal. This difference may have arisen as an English response to a potential weakness of pageantry: clarity of meaning. As Janette Dillon reminds us, it is "clear that some spectators regularly failed to understand the often complex allegorical intentions of pageants."[134] In France, the tendency toward dense symbolism and complex iconography created a situation where even "many kings understood little of the thematic content."[135] This difficulty was perhaps heightened by the fact that the monarch was in processional motion and was being exposed to a number of other visual stimuli that competed with a careful "reading" of the pageant. Regardless, such a situation would undercut a town's goal of using pageantry to communicate with the visiting monarch. English entries self-consciously attempted to avoid such confusion and misinterpretation by investing in the spoken and written word. As we have seen, most entries featured a welcome speech at the beginning of the entry that not only greeted the monarch, but also painted a particular picture of the city, including its history, privileges, and strengths—as well as any particular challenges it might be facing. At Bristol and Worcester, the welcome speech even provided instructive context for how to "read" the coming entertainments. Many English towns also provided explanatory speeches later in the procession. When the Queen visited Coventry in 1566, each of the four pageant devices was accompanied by an orator who explained the content and meaning of the visual depiction. For example, in the third pageant "were certen personages representyng the sacred counsel of Sion gathered together where vnto her grace was maid an other oration declaryng the effecte and meanyng of the same" (*JN*1, 463). Written text might also be affixed to the front of a scaffold—as at Norwich—to help audiences understand what was being depicted. Finally, as at Bristol, the Queen might be presented with a permanent written account of the pageants she had just witnessed and speeches she had just heard. All of these measures suggest that for English towns, the meaning—and not just the visual spectacle—was of utmost importance.

But if the provincial pageantry that I will examine is different from Continental pageantry, it is also different from the Queen's 1559 entry into London or the annual Lord Mayors' Shows. I would like to emphasize the uniqueness of these provincial towns and their hosting of the monarch. Unlike London and Continental cities like Antwerp, Brussels, Rome, and Rouen, most of these English towns only got one shot at hosting what was otherwise a rather distant monarch. That distance is an important part of the dynamic, because it meant that the Queen journeyed from relatively far away and had little experience with—and fewer pre-conceptions about—the town that she was visiting. It also meant that the Queen tended to spend several days in the town. Whereas she might only stay a night or two with a private host, Elizabeth might lodge in a single town for as long as a week—and even two weeks in the case of Canterbury.

Because of the lengths of these urban visits, I would like to focus not only on the pageantry of the royal entry (which was limited to the day the Queen arrived), but also on the other activities that filled the week of a royal visit. Bergeron divides royal progress pageantry into two sub-categories: *royal entries,* which he says occurred "when the sovereign made an official procession through city streets with dramatic scenes enacted along the route," and *progress entertainments,* which were "outdoor dramatic shows presented . . . on the private estates of noblemen being visited by the sovereign."[136] This is a useful distinction, though like most acts of categorization, it is liable to exceptions. In the first place, not all royal entries involved dramatic scenes or pageant devices. At Oxford, for example, the large formal procession was punctuated by no fewer than seven speeches—but no dramatic devices or tableaux. In addition, Bergeron's binary tends to associate royal entries with towns and progress entertainments with private hosts, yet (as Bergeron later acknowledges) some towns—like Bristol—did feature "dramatically unified entertainments" later in the week.[137] But even this acknowledgement tends to privilege the formal entertainments that took place in towns. While the Queen was lodged in the castle during a 1572 visit to Warwick, the "[c]ountrey people" turned up to "Daunce in the Court of the Castell her maiesty beholding them out of her Chamber wyndowe" (*JN2*, 39). This is not exactly the sort of formal entertainment that Bergeron has in mind, but it seems a significant interaction between the monarch and the local people—and much of its charm derives from its seeming spontaneity.

At any rate, many other events occurred in the days following the royal entry, and most of them defy easy categorization. If the Queen was in town on a Sunday, she might attend divine service at the cathedral or another prominent church. On other days, she might make short excursions within the town to visit a prison (Norwich), stop by the local grammar school (Coventry), or tour port facilities (Bristol). In Sandwich, she was invited to a banquet of 160 dishes by the jurats' wives. At Oxford, she attended three days of academic disputations. The Queen might also take day trips beyond the town walls to visit the houses of nearby gentry, where her pastimes might include dining (Norwich) and hunting (Worcester). When she returned to the town, urban leaders might use the occasion to "perform" a secondary entry, complete with orations and even other pageant devices (Norwich). In the evenings, she might enjoy fireworks (Warwick), attend a play (Cambridge), or observe a waterborne pageant (Rochester). Finally, town visits almost always terminated with a carefully staged departure. Like royal entries, these were elaborate processionals with formal speeches, colorful clothing, and intricate decorations. However, they were more muted in tone (the jubilation of entry being replaced by the lamentation of departure) and typically did not include pageant devices. Some of these varied events are what Bergeron might classify as formal pageant entertainments—the evening masque at Norwich and the mock battles at Bristol and Sandwich. But many of them were informal, and some of them do not even seem to be entertainments at all—such as the Queen's presence at a cathedral service. Yet I hope to show that all of these interactions were important, that they were usually a deliberate part of the town's reception of the Queen, and that they often helped further the way in which they hoped to speak to the Queen. The few scholars who have assessed royal progress pageantry from the town's perspective tend to emphasize formal petitions made by the town.[138] But English towns "rarely presented direct requests."[139] They might talk about the decayed state of the town (Worcester) or stage a three-day mock battle using their own militia (Bristol), but their appeals of economic assistance and military autonomy are implied rather than publicly stated.[140] It is therefore especially important to consider the nuances of towns' interactions with the monarch. One of my goals is to broaden the field of inquiry beyond just entries and formal entertainments to consider other episodes throughout the week.

I hope to examine not just the substance of these activities, but the ways in which they were framed and experienced. While I will be looking closely at the words and meanings of an oration, for instance, I will also consider who uttered it, what they were wearing, where it was delivered, and how the participants were arranged. In other words, I want to consider complementary realms like space, movement, color, costume, sound, and architecture. As recent scholars have emphasized, early modern civic pageantry was highly nuanced. Kathleen Ashley describes it as a complex fusion of narrative, sound, image, and movement.[141] For Cole, its complex ritual elements can be thought of as a kind of rhetoric.[142] We should therefore be attentive not only to the part of the pageant making an intellectual appeal, but also to its "sensory impact": its "soundscape, landscape, colors, and sights."[143] Indeed, it is this very "multidimensionality" that allows pageantry and processional performance to produce such a powerful "unity of meaning."[144] Whereas past scholars have tended to focus on the more straightforward features of pageantry—speeches, allegorical devices, gift exchange—contemporary scholars are beginning to probe these supplementary dimensions. Pageantry itself is highly interdisciplinary, so it is no surprise that scholars from the fields of music, architecture, literature, political science, cultural studies, art, anthropology, and performance studies are all finding it to be fertile ground.[145] I hope to use the fruits of these inquiries to gain a better understanding of English pageantry.

One of the key areas that I would like to examine is space. In *The Language of Space in Court Performance,* Janette Dillon has shown that early modern culture was especially sensitive to how space was constructed, occupied, and moved through—and that these elements could generate a rich panoply of meaning.[146] Dillon naturally extends such courtly performances to royal progresses, though she tends to emphasize the monarch's ability to "[transform] the spaces he or she entered and the lives of the subjects who inhabited them."[147] But towns were also aware of the performative potential of their own urban spaces. This dynamic is possible, in part, because urban spaces are already resonant with meaning. Urban environments are "historically constituted" and their streets, buildings, and monuments are already inscribed with historical associations and collective memory.[148]

And if court space was becoming more defined, more hierarchical, and more complex over the course of the sixteenth century, as Malcolm Smuts suggests, so too was urban space.[149] As English towns sought to create new political cultures in the 1560s, they set about constructing and reorganizing urban spaces. Not only did they build town halls as symbols of their own authority, they also carefully organized the spaces within, including furnishings, seating arrangements, and rooms with specialized functions.[150] Town corporations were thus conscious of and attuned to the possibilities of space, and they could appropriate this form of courtly "discourse" in influencing the monarch. It is therefore important to consider space when examining civic pageantry. After all, royal entries "derived meanings from the space of the city" since they were "necessarily created by, within and for a particular space."[151] Thus, studying the associations and deployment of that space can allow us to, as Smuts puts it, "decode" political messages and penetrate into "webs of meaning."[152] Thus, space offers us a useful lens for examining how towns spoke to the Queen.

Moreover, royal progress visits provided unique spatial opportunities for towns. By going on progress, the Queen was leaving the carefully controlled spaces of her royal residences. As we have noted, this gave towns greater access to the person of the monarch. At court, access was controlled by a variety of spatial barriers. Palaces were structured so that various presence chambers grew progressively more private; only the most privileged could penetrate into these inner recesses. Yet when the Queen left the court and went on progress, the spaces around her were less controlled and more permeable. This was especially true during royal visits to towns. When the Queen stayed with a private host, their stately home might have a special suite of rooms that essentially replicated the controlled courtly space that the Queen was used to. But the arrangements in towns were decidedly more ad-hoc. Elizabeth might lodge in a bishop's palace (Worcester) or an earl's castle (Warwick), but she might also stay in the more humble house of a local dignitary (Sandwich), or even in an inn (Rochester). From the town's perspective, heightened physical access to the Queen might auger heightened metaphorical access, and thus embolden their hopes of a sympathetic hearing.

Towns not only enjoyed increased access, they were also in a position to shape the spaces that the Queen occupied and moved through. Since the town was hosting the Queen, its leaders determined how she experienced the town and, to some extent, how she spent her time during the week. For the most part, town leaders decided what route Elizabeth took through the town, where she lodged, what she ate, where she sat, and, by extension, who she spoke to. Obviously, the town was not in a position to dictate these things, but hosting the Queen did give them agency. By presenting the Queen with an oration, they could compel her to pause in a particular place and listen to a particular message. By planning a special cathedral service in her honor, they could seek her tacit endorsement of a particular style of worship. Even the Queen's lodging could be useful. In Sandwich, Elizabeth was provided with a particular view of the town's harbor that laid the groundwork for an economic appeal. Such dynamic uses of space helped towns craft messages that could be more than just verbal.

A related lens is processional movement. In being attuned to where events occurred and how space was organized, we should also examine the movements of participants. Civic ritual was highly performative and might draw from the subtleties of motion, stance, and gesture.[153] These movements could be used to express meaning, reflect hierarchies, and signal relationships. Ashley writes that the processional mode is "a privileged vehicle for articulation" and that it performs all sorts of important cultural work.[154] In terms of royal entries, one of the key aspects of movement is the processional route. It determined where the monarch entered into and departed from the city, which streets were seen (and not seen), which landmarks and buildings were passed by, and where the procession lingered for pageant devices and orations. As Mulryne explains, the processional route could offer "mute commentary" on the identity, values, and power structures of a city.[155] Thus, towns could use processional routes to shape their visitors' perceptions and frame the messages that they sought to impart.

Not surprisingly, many surviving English accounts take pains to record the size and order of processionals, the speed at which they moved, whether any of the participants were on horseback, and where and when processionals paused.[156] Processional routes, in particular, are recorded in great detail. For example, Coventry's 1566 account of the Queen's visit specifies that she was met "at the vttermoste parte of the Liberties of the citie of Coventry betwene Shulton and Barnacle"; that she then "passed thorowe folloshull and ouer Folleshull heithe . . . to a place called the Arbour vpon Folleshull," where she heard a welcome oration and was given a gift; that she then went from "thence toward the citie," though "when her grace came to Steiple feildes . . . she alighted and changed her horse"; that she next paused "at a place called the

Barne yard . . . [where] the Erle of huntingdon tooke her graces sword oute of the case and bare it from thence thorowe the citie"; that she finally "entered in at the Bishoppes gate . . . and rode downe the Bishoppe strete" (*JN*1, 454, 462). Other progress accounts exhibit a similar attention to the minutiae of places and topography. As we shall see, processional routes are particularly important for Sandwich and Norwich, where they serve to underscore key pageant themes.

As recent scholars have shown, ceremonial meaning could also be augmented by the "soundscape," or various auditory elements that accompanied an entry or an entertainment. In early modern pageantry, these might include singing, playing musical instruments, firing cannons, ringing bells, and even the joyful shouting of crowds. Though frequently in the background, these sounds nevertheless "communicat[ed] . . . messages about the event and its various participants."[157] Sometimes, special music was written for the occasion, which "serve[d] crucial thematic purposes in the entertainments."[158] For example, Iain Fenlon discusses the importance of instrumental and vocal music in sixteenth-century Florentine ducal entries, arguing that they created an "iconography of sound" that shaped experience and meaning for the spectators.[159]

The soundscape that accompanied civic pageantry gets less attention in surviving English accounts, though it clearly played a role. The most common sounds recorded are of ringing church bells and celebratory cannon fire. As we shall see, the latter is particularly relevant to pageant themes at Bristol and Sandwich, where it creates a suitably militaristic soundtrack. Some English progress receptions do feature formal music. During the Queen's entry into Coventry, each of the four pageants was augmented by songs sung by the choristers of Lichfield Cathedral. As we shall see, at Norwich and Canterbury music is particularly prominent.

Finally, I would like to look closely at the role of architecture in civic pageantry. As noted above, both permanent and ephemeral architecture could play a prominent role in town receptions. The recent collection *Architectures of Festival in Early Modern Europe* attests to the growing interest among scholars in how architecture intersects "with the historical, political and performance concerns of students of festival."[160] As these essays demonstrate, some buildings have existing meanings that can be brought to bear on festival meanings.[161] In other cases, buildings might be given new meanings and associations through their participation in festival.[162] Finally, temporary festival architecture can be used alongside permanent architecture to help imbue the latter with temporary meanings.[163] However, many of these meanings are subtle and not self-evident. In her account of the Duke of Anjou's 1582 entry into Antwerp, Thøfner writes evocatively of the city's careful placement of a triumphal arch.[164] On the one hand, it served as an "elegant compliment to the Duke." On the other hand, its form and placement on the exact spot of a recently demolished city gate allowed it to speak to ordinary citizens and serve "as a vehicle for recalling and reflecting on the history and nature of the urban fabric." In this way, "it provided something for everybody." Such a reading helps validate my claim that towns did indeed plan carefully and that they used the associations of architecture and topography to shape meaning. Yet as Thøfner herself points out, such subtleties of architecture and space are not obvious and "can only be recovered by paying careful attention to materiality . . . and [the] topographical aspects of festive pageantry."[165]

As noted, English towns were more likely to use existing buildings in their receptions, which is one of the reasons why this aspect of English pageantry has been understudied. Yet the built environment did play a key role in their receptions of the Queen. In the mid-sixteenth century, the growing importance of a town's physical fabric was registered by travelers like John Leland, who often notes the general appearance of a town as well as its prominent individual buildings.[166] Urban architectural features were also beginning to be described in the chorographic works that proliferated from the 1570s. For example, William Lambarde notes the prominent castles, churches, bridges, residences, and civic buildings that he encounters in his A Perambulation of Kent (1570). Tittler has shown that towns were investing more in their own physical fabrics in the 1560s and 1570s. As with space, town leaders used buildings as an expression of power and as a way to construct new political cultures. In these decades, towns were actively engaged in constructing and modifying schools, prisons, workhouses, markets, almshouses, and especially town halls.[167] These purpose-built structures addressed existing needs, but they also served to express the corporation's power, authority, and values. As Tittler suggests, town leaders and citizens alike understood that a building was a "semiotic object."[168] Not surprisingly, towns that hosted the Queen often featured and drew attention to these same buildings as they engaged in ceremonial discourse with Elizabeth.

When towns added the rhetorical possibilities of space, movement, sound, and architecture to the more straightforward modes of word and pictorial image, the result was a powerful and integrated performance. Indeed, Thøfner sees urban ceremonial and procession as "a form of self-portraiture" that is the fullest expression of urban identity—"formalized, socialized, and commemorative."[169] As I will argue, civic pageantry not only functions to construct internal identity, it is also a powerful tool for "negotiating . . . relationships with other secular and religious authorities"—including the Crown.[170]

The 1560s and 1570s

Given these rich possibilities, what sorts of receptions did English towns devise? I would like to begin my examination by noting that there have not been many in-depth treatments of individual English towns outside of London.[171] Moreover, existing treatments of royal visits are typically not from the perspective of the town and do not take into account the full range of possibilities afforded by civic pageantry (including those just mentioned above). I propose to closely examine royal visits to the following six towns: Oxford (1566), Sandwich (1573), Canterbury (1573), Bristol (1574), Worcester (1575), and Norwich (1578). My objective is to provide in-depth close readings of each visit. What local and national issues mattered most to each town in the year of the royal visit? How did town leaders design pageantry—including the entry, but also the various entertainments throughout the week—to articulate these needs? And what was the result? For each of these urban centers, I will begin by painstakingly recreating the local context for each visit. As Mulryne reminds us, ceremonial is "flexibly adapted to the political and social circumstances of the moment it addresses"; though often overlooked, such context is "vital to its suasive role."[172] I am particularly interested in identifying the problems or challenges that each town was facing, as these issues largely determined the way in which the town attempted to influence the center. In the cases of Oxford and Canterbury, I will focus on the responses of the University and the Archbishop of Canterbury, respectively, since it was they—rather than the town corporations—who fulfilled the role of host during the Queen's visit.

The six royal visits that I will examine are all clustered in the same twelve-year period from 1566 to 1578. In many ways, this was a key decade for English towns. As we have seen, the Dissolution benefitted towns both in the form of added wealth and in the elimination of rival ecclesiastical lordship. From circa 1540 to 1560, town leaders consolidated these gains and sought to legally formalize them via incorporation. Beginning around 1560, they set about using civic ritual to create a new political culture of order and deference that would validate and legitimize their increasingly oligarchic corporations. At the same time, town leaders were busy looking beyond the town as they negotiated their changing relationship to the Crown and sought urban patronage. Thus, in the 1560s and 1570s, towns were heavily engaged in the possibilities of civic ritual and eager to make wider connections. A royal visit gave them the chance to take a familiar medium and turn it outward to shape how the Queen and potential patrons saw them.

At the same time, circa 1566 to 1578 was also a key decade for the Crown. Elizabeth's throne had been unsettled in 1558, but by 1563 "the immediate threats which had faced Elizabeth at her accession had been removed or at least diminished."[173] By the mid-1560s, the religious, political, and foreign policy situations had all improved, England was at peace, and the Queen's reign was more firmly established. Even though the crisis of 1568 to 1572 (involving the Duke of Norfolk, Mary Stuart, the Northern Rebellion, and the Ridolfi Plot) proved an exception, things had largely stabilized again by 1572.[174] In any case, these tumultuous events came after the Oxford visit of 1566 and before Elizabeth's visits to the other five towns (during 1573 to 1578) that I will examine. It is thus possible to think of the years of these royal visits as relatively peaceful and stable. Indeed, Randell refers to 1573 as the beginning of the period of "Mid-Elizabethan Stability," which he sees as an era of relative cooperation at Court.[175] In these years, the Queen was interested in building consensus and cultivating the devotion of her people. That is why the 1570s saw some of her longest and most ambitious progresses. The alarms of the 1580s—and the Queen's concomitant desire to stay near London—were in the future. Later in her reign, "Elizabeth became a much less public queen" and when she resumed her progresses in the 1590s, "she travelled short distances, kept away from towns, and made no real attempt to mix with her people."[176] But in these middle years of her reign, Elizabeth did go among her people, and she invested in royal progresses for all sorts of reasons, ranging from cultivating loyalty and affection to ensuring religious conformity to inspecting defenses.

If the years 1566 to 1578 were important for the towns and the monarchy individually, they were also a key moment for the two in relation to one another. As we have seen, after the Reformation, the Crown increasingly looked to towns to maintain law and order. In order to achieve this goal, the Crown affirmed charters, helped liberate towns from rival authorities, and granted a greater degree of self-government. A royal visit was a way to ensure that this charge was being carried out. It allowed the Queen to both inspect the town on the ground level and also validate the ruling oligarchy (with the mayor as a de facto royal official) in front of the townspeople and affirm their authority. From the town's perspective, a royal visit was a chance to assure the monarch of their loyalty and showcase the good job they were doing. At the same time, hosting the Queen provided an opportunity for town leaders to leverage that relationship in order to pursue additional benefits for the town. Progresses were thus of immense value to both sides in affirming their partnership and also in continuing to work out its terms. In France, royal entries were becoming merely a tool for "the consolidation of monarchical rule"; as the sixteenth century progressed, they "took less the form of a dialogue between the king and his subjects . . . than that of an encomiastic discourse, praising the glory of the sovereign."[177] In England, however, royal entries were still two-way streets in which town and Crown might negotiate their relationship.

Looking at town visits during these years will shed light on particular local and national issues of the 1560s and 1570s. In general, this period of Elizabethan history tends to be understudied. Natalie Mears even refers to it as the "much neglected mid-Elizabethan" period.[178] One reason for its neglect may be the aforementioned idea of "mid-Elizabethan stability." Though revisionist historians have sought to complicate this picture, these decades have probably proven less interesting to historians than the turbulent years at the beginning and end of Elizabeth's reign. Those who do write about the 1570s tend to focus on foreign affairs.[179] Indeed, Wallace T. MacCaffrey asserts that "from about 1572 to about 1577, men's attention was largely drawn to the scene abroad—to Holland and to France," and how events there might affect England.[180] While it is true that towns like Worcester were keenly interested in, say, the viability of the wool market at Antwerp, such an approach tends to overlook domestic concerns that were much closer to home.

When a domestic lens is applied to the 1570s, it is typically done so in the service of religion. Certainly there were momentous developments in this decade, sufficiently amounting to what MacCaffrey calls a "domestic religious crisis."[181] The publication of John Field and Thomas Wilcox's *Admonition to Parliament* (1572) galvanized nascent Puritanism and led to more strenuous attempts at enforcing religious conformity. Meanwhile, in the wake of the Northern Rebellion (1569), the papal bull (1570), the St. Bartholomew's Day Massacre (1572), and the arrival of Catholic missionaries from Douai (1574), religious policy began to harden against Catholic recusants. Other commonly discussed domestic concerns of the 1570s include the related issues of the Queen's marriage and succession and the ongoing "problem" of Mary Stuart.[182]

Still, even these issues have something of an international flavor and would have been of greater import at court than among provincial subjects.

In the chapters that follow, I hope to illuminate some of the more local domestic issues of these years, including education, immigration, economic stagnation, defense, poverty, local political rivalries, militia, and trade. Such issues are more quotidian, yet they would have resonated deeply with town leaders and residents. Of course, many of these local issues can be connected to the larger national issues of the 1570s. The state of Sandwich's harbor might well be relevant to the possibility of a Spanish invasion, even if most residents were concerned about harbor silt primarily because "the havon" was the economic lifeblood of the town. My case studies of these six towns will shed light on many of the overlooked day to day concerns that did loom large for urban communities. At the same time, I will endeavor to show how national issues filtered down to and were negotiated on the local level.

In many ways, the years that I will be looking at are the high water mark for a genre that peaked during Elizabethan times. Cole identifies the 1570s as a key decade for Elizabeth's progress activities.[183] In these years, her progresses were more frequent (nine out of ten years), lasted for longer durations, and took her farther from London than in any other decade.[184] It was also a key decade for the Queen's visits to towns. According to Cole's painstaking recreation of the Queen's various progress itineraries, her eighty-three civic visits can be broken down into the following decades:[185]

1550s: 1
1560s: 21
1570s: 39
1580s: 9
1590s: 12
1600s: 1

Elizabeth's progress visits to towns clearly peak in the 1570s, with the 1560s being the next most significant decade. By focusing on six visits that occur in these two decades, I should be well positioned to say something about the genre as a whole in the very years when it was most dynamic. In fact, almost all of the surviving accounts of civic visits belong to these years. Of the eight-three civic visits, there are detailed records for only ten. I will be looking at six: Oxford (1566), Sandwich (1573), Canterbury (1573), Bristol (1574), Worcester (1575), and Norwich (1578). The other four—which I make occasional references to—are Cambridge (1564), Coventry (1566), Warwick (1572), and Oxford (1592). All but the second Oxford visit fall within the twelve-year period that I will be examining. Again, this book should be well positioned to assess how English towns responded—both collectively but also individually—to a similar historical moment.

Despite this relatively concentrated span of years, the six towns that I will focus on comprise an impressive variety. Bristol and Norwich were provincial centers, and thus among the five to seven most important urban areas outside of London. Meanwhile, Worcester, Oxford, and Canterbury fall firmly within the list of the hundred or so regional centers. Finally, the chapter on Sandwich will provide a look at a smaller, less significant town.[186] These six towns provide insights into a diverse range of local issues. Though some issues adhere to Cole's emphasis on economic concerns (Worcester, Sandwich), other issues provide a window into local negotiations regarding education, immigration, foreign policy, and religion. The entertainments that these towns devised were similarly varied, ranging from allegorical devices to mock battles to formal masques to humanist orations. Most of these towns drew from the established conventions of royal entries, including the ceremonial exchange of the mace, the welcome speech, and the presentation of a gift. Yet, as I will show, towns could be very savvy in the way that they modified pageant conventions in order to suit their specific purposes.[187]

Indeed, one of the things that accounts for such subtle tailoring is the fact that town leaders had a fair amount of control over the festivities. When they got word that the Queen was likely to visit them on progress, they usually only had a couple of months to plan. In that brief time, there would be a flurry of activities in the town records, as towns collected money, beautified the urban environment, and organized the logistics of hosting the reigning monarch. As the Queen's visit drew near, town leaders would have contact with royal officials who came ahead of the Queen to "ensure that all of the necessary arrangements had been made"—that the roads were passable, the welcome would be well-attended, her majesty's lodging suitable, and above all that the Queen's safety was assured.[188] But one of the most important preparations—and one that was largely left to the town leaders—was the devising of entertainments. Along with gift-giving and readying the physical fabric of the town, welcome and entertainment was the town's main hosting expense.[189] Cole notes that towns were different from private hosts in that they were freed from expenses like lodging and feeding the Queen and her court; instead, "town officials could concentrate their energies and finances on arranging the ceremonial structure of Elizabeth's visit."[190] Thus, towns could spend substantial time and effort on building scaffolds, making costumes, writing speeches, planning mock battles, and devising dramatic interludes. The corporation relied mostly on its own citizens—skilled craftsmen to build the physical components of pageant devices, the local schoolmaster and other "intellectuals" for the text and substance of the pageant. In Bristol and Worcester, payments to local individuals for many of these services are noted in the records.

However, town corporations might also hire outsiders to help prepare the entertainments. Both Bristol and Norwich called in Thomas Churchyard, presumably because they thought that his knowledge of the court would help them entertain the royal visitors and speak to them in their own language. But even here, corporations retained some creative control. Churchyard records that he "came to Norwiche aboute that businesse, and remayned there three long weekes before the Courte came thyther, deuising and studying the best I coulde for the Citie" (JN2, 721). Thus, he presumably worked closely with city leaders to create pageantry on their behalf. This is consistent with what we see on the Continent, where civic leaders had "considerable control" over funding, designing, and producing civic pageantry for ducal visits.[191] In England, town leaders had similar control over the form and message of the entertainments they devised. This was also true at Oxford and Canterbury, where university and ecclesiastical leaders made similar preparations and had similar control over the festivities. It is thus entirely within reason to listen for their voices and hear what they might be saying to the Queen. It is worth acknowledging, however, that towns were not monolithic entities and that even those in the inner circle of town government did not always speak with one voice.[192] Nevertheless, as Cole asserts, townsfolk did tend to put aside their differences and "preserve a corporate image of communal solidarity" during a royal visit.[193]

Approaches and Sources

In order to analyze what towns did say to the Queen, we need to consider the ways in which that message has come down to us. In the cases of Bristol and Norwich, events were reported in contemporary printed versions that enjoyed wide circulation. For most other towns, official accounts of the royal visit were preserved in the city records. As many critics have rightly pointed out, both kinds of formal accounts should be used with caution because they are inherently subjective and idealized. As Dillon suggests, these performance narratives are "not neutral" but rather "produced for particular purposes" that tend to serve the dominant hierarchies that are producing them.[194] Though these accounts seem to merely record the events of the Queen's visit, they are actually "secondary shapings" that provide subtle commentary and interpretations.[195] Murphy is more blunt about French festival books, which he describes as "regularly distort[ing] or manipulat[ing] their material."[196] Yet this very subjectivity is also useful insofar as it allows us to see how towns perceived a royal visit and what they chose to emphasize as being important or significant. If, as Palmer asserts, "pageants foreground their own social functions" and speak to their own "aims," this is surely an illuminating kind of bias—one that allows us to recover the subtle ways in which towns hoped to speak to the Queen.[197] For example, Worcester's account of its royal visit reflects the premium that city leaders put on their own acts of hospitality. It provides detailed descriptions of lodging arrangements, gift-giving, escort delegations, and even the care of visitors' horses. The account also frequently registers the effusive responses of the Queen and other guests to this hospitality. Yet it provides scant details about pageant devices, only noting that during the Queen's entry, stages were set up at the Grass Cross and in front of St. Helen's church. The records do not indicate what these stages looked like, what historical or mythological figures they contained, or what spoken or acted messages they conveyed.[198] The implication is that for Worcester, acts of hospitality were more integral to their ceremonial dialogue than pageant devices.

Formal written accounts of this type also illuminate by the additions that they make. Sometimes they highlight or interpret a small detail in order to make a covert meaning more overt. Other times, they record a device or speech that was intended but never actually executed because of bad weather or insufficient time. During the Queen's 1578 entry into Norwich, a poetic oration by King Gurgunt, the mythical founder of the city, was "by reason of a showre of raine . . . not vttered," but Bernard Garter's printed text includes the forty-four-line speech in its entirety (JN2, 790–92).[199] Such an addition may increase the "gap between the printed text and the actual performance," but it also gives a fuller sense of the town's intention.[200] Even if the Queen did not hear this oration, it was a vital part of the town's message—and important enough to be included in the official record of her visit.

In addition to scrutinizing formal accounts, I have also paid close attention to other primary sources relating to royal receptions, including town council minutes and records of financial expenditure.[201] As Murphy suggests, these sources can give valuable insights into "what urban elites hoped to achieve" as they prepared to host the monarch.[202] By examining the nature of a town's preparations or the relative amounts that were spent on different parts of the entertainment, we can gain a clearer picture of its goals and priorities.

Not surprisingly, both formal accounts and archival sources related to the Queen's visit have been reproduced in print. After all, a royal entry was among the most celebrated events in the life of a town. From the late eighteenth century, local historians like William Boys and Valentine Green scoured city archives and published their discoveries.[203] John Nichols took an even wider aim in the 1820s, when he synthesized many of these scattered sources into his three-volume *The Progresses and Public Processions of Queen Elizabeth I*.[204] As its full title suggests, the work is a treasure trove of documents related to Elizabeth's progress visits. Later scholarly source books have drawn from and added to Nichols's work, including the Records in Early English Drama series—with individual volumes devoted to the performance history (including progress receptions) of English counties and towns. In 2014, a team of scholars brought out a much-needed modern edition of John Nichols's work. This volume, aptly titled *John Nichols's "The Progresses and Public Processions of Queen Elizabeth I": A New Edition of the Early Modern Sources,* contains extensive explanatory notes and also contributes new source material, including personal letters, diaries, and spectator accounts.[205] As we shall see, the latter is particularly useful for re-creating Elizabeth's visit to Oxford. What all of this means is that the civic receptions for Elizabethan progresses are particularly well-documented. My goal, then, has not been to find and analyze heretofore unknown sources, but rather to look at existing documents with fresh eyes and a new perspective. Instead of mining these primary accounts for what they reveal about the monarch and her court, I have focused on the town's perspective. By foregrounding the particular needs and priorities that animated each town in the year of the Queen's visit, we can then use these documents to see the nuanced ways in which civic hosts attempted to influence their royal visitors.

For all scholars interested in civic pageantry—and especially those located on the west side of the Atlantic—these edited compilations of primary sources are a boon. Nevertheless, my work has also benefitted from visiting each of the six cities featured in this book. By combing through city and county archives, I located additional documents that I could bring to bear on each of my case studies. These discoveries include an early map, a household inventory for one of the Queen's lodgings, correspondence tracing a local economic concern, and a roster of guild members.[206] While these sources do not describe royal receptions per se, they are valuable supplements for my focus on the local contexts of each visit. One of my biggest archival finds was a document entitled "The Proporcion of Sandwich Haven 1574." This three-page manuscript suggests that Sandwich's 1573 entertainments did bear fruit in the form of a royal commission (to which the "Proporcion" presumably responds). There are no doubt other archival sources that might augment our understanding of particular Elizabethan progress visits.

During my sojourn in each city, I also profited from the wealth of secondary sources that I found in the local history sections of public libraries. These sources provided valuable information about population figures, demographic data, economic trends, religious sympathies, and political factions, enabling me to re-create the mid-Elizabethan context of each city as minutely as possible. I was particularly interested in the physical landscape of each city in the 1560s and 1570s, so I needed to know about street patterns and public spaces as well as the appearances and functions of particular buildings. In Norwich, where the built environment played an especially prominent role in the royal reception, I was able to find locally printed books devoted to the city's market, hospital, and ancient monastery.[207] Even though such specialized sources are in print, they do not have a wide circulation and are therefore unknown to most scholars. Indeed, some are so narrowly focused that they are little more than pamphlets. At Norwich, I found individual works devoted to *The Plains [or open spaces] of Norwich, The [musical] Waits of the City of Norwich,* and *The Mayors of Norwich: 1403 to 1835.* All were extremely useful for my purposes. In addition to combing through libraries, I read historical signboards, visited museums, interrogated cathedral guides, and interviewed local scholars who had studied their native cities for decades.[208]

I also made a point of familiarizing myself with the physical layout of each city. I walked city walls, visited churches, explored civic buildings, stood in public spaces, and, of course, retraced Elizabeth's processional routes. I do not want to romanticize the experience of "being there" as a prerequisite for understanding civic pageantry, yet my peregrinations did yield insights that I would not have otherwise had. In coming to understand each city spatially, I found that I had a better handle on the ways that urban hosts deployed different spaces. After walking city streets and experiencing local topography, I gained insights into why certain processional routes were chosen (and others avoided). After visiting lodging sites in Sandwich and Canterbury—and seeing the panoramic views of the city that they afforded—I understood why they were chosen in the first place. After venturing inside guildhalls, grammar schools, bishop's palaces, hospitals, and great halls, I apprehended how their architecture and interior decoration likely enhanced the impressions that hosts sought to convey. Together, these experiences aided my understanding of the many ways in which these cities utilized their physical environments to speak to the Queen.

Finally, my physical presence in each city allowed me to discover and conduct "readings" of less traditional primary sources like tombs, maps, furniture, clothing, statues, gifts, and regalia. Many of these surviving bits of material culture were vital components of the Queen's visit. At Bristol, I was able to study a piece of civic regalia that had been newly made for the royal reception. At Worcester, a tomb inscription helped reveal the motives of a civic host. At Canterbury, I examined an ancient chair that featured prominently in Elizabeth's birthday feast. In other cities, I scrutinized statues that were deliberately placed in the Queen's field of vision and perused presentation copies of books that were given to her. Many of these objects were serendipitous discoveries, but all of them provided useful insights into how cities used material culture to augment and enrich the ceremonial dialogues in which they were engaging.

In considering all of these sources, my goal has been not only to look at how towns spoke to the Queen, but also how they targeted the various secondary audiences who accompanied her. In a number of towns, civic leaders tried to cultivate urban patronage via interactions with powerful and influential people in the royal entourage, including privy councilors, courtiers, household officers, clergymen, and women. Privy councilors were an especially important audience, and they were actively courted in all six of my urban case studies. As we have already noted, the Privy Council was "the central organ of state" and had wide-ranging administrative functions. Its members were active in regulating commerce, creating foreign policy, serving as diplomats, suppressing sedition, shaping ecclesiastical affairs, intervening in legal proceedings, overseeing militia, and setting budgetary priorities.[209] Given the Privy Council's wide scope, it is not surprising that towns would seek to influence them on a number of matters. As Michael Pulman suggests, the Council was also seen as something of a problem-solver for localities outside London.[210] Throughout the 1570s and 1580s, it stepped in to repair harbors (at Dover), fix roads (in Suffolk), and cleanse and scour rivers (in Ely and Carlisle). As a central institution, it could serve as an "organizing force" for various stakeholders and authorities, as in 1583, when it coordinated relief efforts after a devastating fire in Nantwich. Because of such involvement, local leaders "clearly regard[ed] the council as being the natural place to turn to for assistance when their own nearby resources failed them."

Privy Council members were also a key secondary audience because they gave formal advice to the monarch. Though we know that other courtiers and household officials could and did influence the Queen, the Council at least in theory had a monopoly on this advice-giving function.[211] Indeed, the Elizabethan Privy Council gave advice freely to the Queen—even when its policy views differed from hers—and its advice was often heeded.[212] And if it did not always succeed in convincing the Queen outright, Haigh has shown how the Council could influence, manipulate, and occasionally outmaneuver Elizabeth.[213] For all of these reasons, towns saw the Privy Council as a promising secondary audience to which they might appeal. That many Privy Councilors accompanied the Queen on progress and held regular meetings while on the road would have lent a particular immediacy to town hopes that it might adopt a particular policy position.[214]

In the early 1570s, there had been a flurry of new Privy Council appointments, including Thomas Radcliffe, 3rd Earl of Sussex (1570), Sir Thomas Smith(1571), George Talbot, 6th Earl of Shrewsbury (1571), Francis Walsingham (1573), and Ambrose Dudley, 3rd Earl of Warwick (1573).[215] Despite this turnover, the Council was relatively stable—particularly after 1572—and it tended to be unified in its policy positions.[216] Though there were some nineteen privy councilors in 1570, many of the great landowners were absentee members; only a core group of seven to ten people were in regular attendance at meetings.[217] These included "the Lord Treasurer [Burghley], Lord Chamberlain [Sussex], Lord Admiral [Lincoln], Secretary [Walsingham], the Treasurer and Comptroller of the Household [Sir Francis Knollys, Sir James Croft], and the Earl of Leicester."[218] Of these, the most important players in the 1570s were Burghley, Leicester, and Walsingham, with Hatton emerging in the middle of the decade.[219] Burghley and Leicester played particularly important roles in patronage. Burghley was Lord Treasurer and Master of Wards—"the biggest reward-giving institutions"—while Leicester "had his finger in every pie," and his patronage was especially valuable for the church, university, and diplomatic service.[220] Leicester was also known as something of a friend to towns; an unusually high number of them had bestowed upon him the office of High

Steward and "counted on him to back them in their quarrels or their ambitions, especially when they had to seek the favors of the Crown."[221]

Of course, not all Privy Council members went on every progress, and even those who did might join up for only part of the itinerary. Still, this body gave towns an attractive secondary audience that they might target either as a collective or by singling out individual councilors. If pursuing the latter strategy, towns might naturally consider the geographical ties of individual members. According to Pulman, all Privy Councilors had geographical power bases that they needed to cultivate and thus had "intimate knowledge of local people and conditions."[222] Thus, it is not surprising to find Oxford looking to Sir Francis Knollys and Worcester trying to strengthen patronage bonds with Sir James Croft; both men owned estates in these respective areas and were active in local politics. Towns might also consider the particular offices, titles, or realms of influence of a particular councilor. In 1574, Bristol was eager to demonstrate that it had a strong militia and was able to maintain order in the west. This made the Earl of Lincoln (Edward Clinton) a particularly important progress visitor. Lincoln had been Lord High Admiral for the entirety of Elizabeth's reign, which made him (in a country with no standing army) the chief military officer of the realm.[223] As we shall see, Bristol took special pains to accommodate the admiral.

As might be expected, the particular targets and strategies varied from town to town. Moreover, cultivating the patronage of specific individuals was balanced by the desire to cast as wide a net as possible. Even if a town had a particular policy issue in mind, it also hoped to cultivate a positive civic image and aura of goodwill in general, as these things would promote its overall reputation and would be of great service in future dealings with the center. The imaginative ways in which towns used the features of pageant entertainment to construct civic identity, broach particular needs and concerns, and cultivate patronage will be the subject of the next six chapters.

The first chapter will focus on the Queen's visit to Oxford in 1566. She arrived with an unusually large train of nobles. Though this group was generally supportive of the new learning, most of its members had not attended university and were not necessarily convinced that they were centers of humanist learning. Throughout the week, Oxford students, professors, and administrators used a variety of literary and academic forms (Latin dramas, declamations, dialogues, classical poetry, disputations) to define and showcase the institution's humanist values. Indeed, I argue that the university's entertainments actually exaggerate the presence of the new learning at Oxford (and run counter to its own rather conservative curricular statutes of 1565) for the benefit of its courtly audience. Oxford's entertainments also emphasize the *practicality* of university education and seek to celebrate and defend a particular concept of gentility that (it argues) arises from university education. Oxford's goal throughout the week was to solicit the good will and support of its visitors in the form of financial backing (foundations, endowments, professorships, building projects) and protection for its hard-won liberties and privileges (particularly against town incursions). Since many of the visiting nobles had young sons, the university also hoped to inspire them to someday send their offspring and heirs to Oxford as gentlemen commoners (a practice that was just beginning in the 1560s). By lodging most of the visitors at the unfinished Christ Church College and awarding honorary degrees to thirteen noblemen, Oxford creatively deployed architecture and academic exercises to pursue these aims. However, in trying to forge closer connections with the Queen and the leading families of the realm, Oxford was also wary of inviting outside interference. It thus used some of the same performative moments to discourage overly prescriptive interference, the micromanaging of its affairs, religious scrutiny, and undue lay influence. Throughout the week, Oxford fashioned an image of itself as a well-ordered place with effective internal governance; presented academia as a specialized and rarified world; and idealized a particular model of hands-off patronage. Through a combination of literary, performative, and academic activities, Oxford posited a particular kind of relationship to the state that invited protection and largesse but discouraged interference.

Chapter two examines Queen Elizabeth's three-day visit to Sandwich during her 1573 progress through Kent. In the late Middle Ages, Sandwich had been a thriving commercial port, a gathering point for English warships, and a key point of embarkation for the Continent; however, it had been in precipitous decline from the late fifteenth century onward due to the silting up of its harbor. Not surprisingly, town leaders used the Queen's visit to craft a plea for royal aid. However, instead of emphasizing its decline, Sandwich projected an image of strength and vitality, presenting itself not as a declining backwater that desperately needed the Queen's intervention but as an important port—still militarily and commercially vibrant—that could continue to be so with a little help from the Queen. To this end, it created a spatial and topographical performance that relied on its physical fabric to an unusual degree. It asserted its continuing strategic importance by creating a processional itinerary whereby Elizabeth would pass through and by a series of formidable defensive structures (ramparts, gates, wall, artillery fortification) that had been carefully refurbished in the weeks leading up to visit. It played up its remaining wealth and prosperity by presenting an unusually lavish gift to the monarch and by prominently featuring its surviving timber-framed merchants' houses. Above all, Sandwich kept the Queen in close proximity to its harbor (via her lodging and excursion destinations) and used pageant devices (including a mock battle) to comment on and mythologize the harbor's military and commercial importance to the town. Finally, a feast at the grammar school allowed town leaders to use that building as an emblem of collaboration between the center and the town that the latter hoped to forge anew in addressing the problem of the harbor. All of these spatial, topographical, and architectural elements allowed Sandwich to lay the groundwork for the town to formally request royal aid at the end of the visit. Indeed, as a surviving archival document attests, Sandwich's strategy was effective enough to get the Queen to take a closer look at repairing its harbor.

Chapter three explores the Queen's 1573 visit to Canterbury, where she spent two weeks as the guest of Archbishop Matthew Parker. Her visit came at a pivotal moment for Parker and the English Church, which was under Puritan attack for its "worldliness and pomp"; indeed, the Admonition Controversy of the previous year had called for the abolition of the episcopal hierarchy. Meanwhile, the Queen and Privy Council had been slow to respond to nonconformity and were lukewarm in support of the bishops. This chapter argues that Parker used the opportunity of the Queen's visit to assert the authority, continuity, dignity, and effectiveness of the ecclesiastical hierarchy. The main way he did this was through lavish hospitality and displays of clerical magnificence—one of the very things that the Puritans were critical of. But far from mere ostentation, Parker's approach was intended to show that clerical magnificence was itself an effective tool that could serve social, religious, and political ends. Among other things, it could be used to shape public opinion, partner with local leaders, interpret and appropriate scripture, ensure obedience and uniformity, aid in diplomacy, cultivate learning, and defend the monarchy. Parker made these points through traditional forms of hospitality (open house, birthday feast, gift-giving), but also through his careful deployment of books and places. In advance of the progress, Parker sent four religious and antiquarian texts to Burghley (including a lavish edition of the archbishop's own *De Antiquitate Britannicae Ecclesiae,* 1572); at its conclusion, he gave three

other religious/polemical texts to departing courtiers and councilors. I consider the import of such texts as well as their depictions of the episcopacy. The
other strategy that I draw attention to is Parker's immersion of the Queen in
the magnificent architectural spaces of Canterbury: he made sure that the
Queen lodged near the spectacular ruins of St. Augustine's Abbey, he invited
her to a lavish birthday feast at the eleventh-century Archbishop's Palace, and
he presided over her worship at Canterbury Cathedral. I combine close readings of these ceremonies with a careful consideration of the three buildings in
which they were staged. Overall, I illuminate how Parker used the Queen's
two-week visit to defend clerical wealth and rehabilitate clerical magnificence
in an attempt to inspire greater public support from both Crown and Council.

Chapter four focuses on the Queen's 1574 stay in Bristol. Although Bristol
was the realm's third largest city, its civic and diocesan charters were recent
(1542) and its leaders had endured repeated challenges to their authority. The
bishops of Bristol, the surrounding landed gentry, the Gloucestershire county
commissioners, the Council of the Marches, and the Court of Admiralty, had
all impinged on the corporation's jurisdiction—usually under the pretense of
stabilizing this potentially volatile region. These rivalries were exacerbated by
the Northern Rebellion of 1569, which created a heightened concern with
domestic order and a fixation on the effectiveness of local militias. I argue that
these contexts help explain the thoroughly militaristic nature of Bristol's 1574
pageants. Even though the city's prosperity and reputation were founded on
trade, it entertained the Queen with an elaborate three-day mock battle that
included hundreds of uniformed soldiers, exploding gunpowder, a mock fort
razed to the ground, and a naval engagement on the nearby River Avon. These
dramatic military maneuvers were intended to demonstrate the martial prowess of Bristol's citizen militia and to underscore the city's ability to prevent
rebellion in the west. Bristol's warlike themes were supplemented and developed by other festival practices, including the remaking of urban spaces, the
creation of a bellicose soundscape, and the investment in new civic regalia and
militia uniforms. But above all, these themes were given an extended intellectual treatment via speeches that accompanied the mock battle and that grapple
with the complexities of war and peace. In one key moment, Dissension objects
that strong military values are incompatible with a peaceful, trading city like
Bristol (which probably reflected an actual perception of the city in the 1570s
because of the corporation's frequent clashes with unruly soldiers headed for
the Irish wars). Ultimately, an allegorical representation of the City argues that

Bristol can be devoted to peace and yet still ready and willing to use force to maintain it. Indeed, Bristol emerges as an ideal peacekeeper because—unlike the bloodthirsty and reckless soldier—its pre-existing commitment to trade and civil life ensure that it will use force to create stability and not disorder.

Chapter five examines the 1575 visit to Worcester. In the sixteenth century, the city produced more cloth than any other town in England, and its broadcloths were famous throughout Europe. Because they dominated the city oligarchy, clothiers were able to carefully regulate the wool industry, assure quality control, and stifle local competition in the surrounding countryside. Yet Worcester broadcloths were made almost exclusively for the Antwerp market, which meant that the health of Worcester's main industry was subject to the practices of London merchants, the foreign policies of the Crown, and the fluctuations of the European market. This city of only five thousand people needed strong national advocates. During the Queen's weeklong visit in 1575, Worcester used its welcome oration to assert its anxieties about both the vicissitudes of the cloth market and its own inability to control the national and international factors that were affecting it in the 1570s. Worcester then used the rest of the week to solicit help from both the Queen and the Privy Councilors who had accompanied her. The city based its appeal on the claims of early modern hospitality, which could create both access and agency for the host. Worcester relied on ceremonial display, guest services, and other reputation-enhancing gestures to show that it was vibrant, generous, honorable—and worth helping. In turn, the royal visitors' consumption of this hospitality created a social bond that theoretically entailed an obligation of future reciprocity. To strengthen this claim of reciprocity, Worcester highlighted its past support of the Queen, cultivated a neighborly dynamism between Queen and people, painted the royal arms throughout the city, and engaged in lavish gift-giving. Finally, Worcester used its cathedral—which housed the richly decorated royal tombs of King John and Elizabeth's uncle Arthur Tudor—to dramatically depict a pre-existing and mutually beneficial relationship between the city and the monarchy. The implied logic was that since Worcester had long been and would continue to be hospitable to the Crown, the Queen should respond reciprocally by safeguarding its broadcloth industry.

The chapters conclude with the Queen's 1578 visit to Norwich, the largest and wealthiest provincial city outside of London. Norwich welcomed the Queen warmly and proffered a variety of entertainments throughout the week. However, my emphasis in this chapter will be on how the city corporation used the occasion of the Queen's visit to speak to its own citizens and construct a shared urban identity. In 1565, the mayor of Norwich had invited religious refugees from the Low Countries—men who specialized in the weaving of the new draperies—to settle in Norwich and help revive the local textile economy. By 1578, the strangers (as they were known locally) comprised over a third (6,000) of the city's total population (16,000). Yet because of economic competition, linguistic and cultural barriers, and religious differences, they were regarded with deep suspicion and even active resentment by the general populace. Though ostensibly supported by the city leaders, the strangers were subject to economic restrictions and social control throughout the 1570s, and were effectively second-class citizens. In this chapter, I argue that the mayor and aldermen who commissioned the pageants used the Queen's visit as an opportunity to forge unity between native residents and recent immigrants. The strangers' direct participation in the entertainments (in both pageants devices and orations) was designed to convince a skeptical local audience of their value to the city and their worthiness to enter fully into its life. At the same time, other pageant elements (like a speech by King Gurgunt, the city's mythical founder) created a more traditional type of Norwich identity that may well have been intended to educate and assimilate the strangers into their adopted home. Finally, civic leaders deployed a range of other festival devices—biblical allusions, broken music, an engraved cup, the Tudor rose—to set forth a particular vision of unity comprised of equal parts empathy, diversity, and friendship. Although these virtues were ostensibly applied to Elizabeth, presenting her in this light allowed the Queen to serve as both a model for this imagined unity and a locus around which it might cohere.

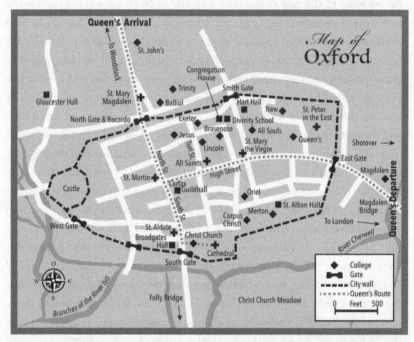

Map reproduced by Coni Porter. Reproduced from Nigel James's "Oxford, in the second half of the 16th c.," in *John Nichols's "The Progresses and Public Processions of Queen Elizabeth I: A New Edition of the Early Modern Sources,"* ed. Elizabeth Goldring, Faith Eales, Elizabeth Clarke, and Jayne Elisabeth Archer, vol. 1, 1533–1571 (Oxford: Oxford University Press, 2014). © in the editorial matter and arrangement Elizabeth Goldring, Faith Eales, Elizabeth Clarke, and Jayne Elisabeth Archer 2014. Reproduced with permission of the Licensor through PLSclear.

CHAPTER ONE
OXFORD, 1566

The first royal progress to consider is the Queen's visit to Oxford. By 1566, Elizabeth had been on the throne for eight years and her regime had entered a period of relative stability and peace.[1] It was thus an opportune time for the Queen to abandon the confines of London and go out amongst her people. Indeed, the 1566 progress was the Queen's most wide-ranging (and one of her longest) progresses to date.[2] It lasted for sixty-one days. She departed London on July 8, visited private hosts in Hertfordshire and Bedfordshire, travelled north as far as Lincolnshire, and then circled west through Northamptonshire, Warwickshire, and Oxfordshire. She thus arrived at Oxford near the end of the progress, on August 31. The Queen remained in Oxford for six nights, departing on September 6 to head back toward London.

When she arrived at the outskirts of town on Saturday, Elizabeth was met by both university and civic delegations, who accompanied her on her formal entry into the town. The procession came in through the Northgate and passed by Carfax before arriving at Christ Church college, where the Queen was shown to her lodging. Along the way, the royal visitors were welcomed with a number of formal orations. During the remainder of the week, the Queen heard formal academic disputes at St. Mary's Church during the day. At night, she was entertained by plays written by Oxford alums and staged in the great hall at Christ Church. At various points throughout the week, she was presented with gifts, ushered through gardens, showered with poetic offerings, and treated to additional orations in Greek, Latin, and Hebrew (and even delivered a Latin oration herself). On Friday, the Queen and her retinue departed with great fanfare out the Eastgate and across Magdalen Bridge.

The entertainments at Oxford were among the most varied and learned of all of the Queen's progress visits. In order to understand and interpret their significance (particularly for the university that devised them), we must start by taking the pulse of the university at the moment of the Queen's 1566 visit. The previous few decades had been an era of great change at Oxford. Not only had the university been dramatically affected by the Reformation (and its continuing reverberations), it was also undergoing a number of institutional changes. Its scholastic curriculum was being challenged by the new learning of humanism. Its enrollment figures were declining, and it needed to attract a broader cohort of students. Further, the university's relationship to central government was contracting, and it was increasingly subject to outside interference. With many of its traditional features under threat, mid-century Oxford needed to redefine its institutional identity and assert control over the changes that were affecting it. The 1566 royal reception provided just such an opportunity. As we shall see, Oxford used its entertainments to craft a particular image of the university that would appeal to its visiting courtly audience. In doing so, its leaders attempted to cultivate patrons who would assist Oxford in meeting its challenges while also allowing it to maintain some measure of autonomy.

Sixteenth-Century Oxford

Oxford was advantageously sited at a shallow ford at the confluence of the River Thames and the River Cherwell. It enjoyed road and river networks to both London and the sea. Although there was no Roman predecessor on the site, it had become a regionally important center for trade even before the twelfth century. By that time, "Oxford's central location and thriving commerce [made] it an attractive venue for the establishment of the institutions that would radically change the direction of the town's development."[3] Early in the twelfth century, two Augustinian priories were founded on the outskirts of the town. The Augustinians were followed by other religious groups—including Cistercians, Dominicans, Franciscans, Carmelites, and Austin friars—all of whom had established religious houses in Oxford by the mid-fourteenth century.[4] Indeed, Barrie Dobson asserts that Oxford possessed "an agglomeration of varied monastic and mendicant settlement unsurpassed elsewhere in England."[5] The presence of such institutions likely attracted scholar teachers from the newly established universities at Paris and Bologna in the late twelfth century. Since Oxford had become "a centre for the trying of ecclesiastical court cases," it "afford[ed] masters and students the opportunity of studying both the theory and practice of canon and Roman law."[6] The fledgling university was eventually incorporated in 1231 and given a royal charter (by Henry III) in 1248. In the centuries that followed, the university developed alongside but separate from the town. The university was the smaller of the two, comprising only about 28 percent of the town population during term time.[7] However, the university exercised a disproportionate amount of influence. It continued to accumulate commercial, legal, and judicial privileges throughout the medieval period, often at the expense of the rights of the town; in addition, "the scholars were all in minor orders and so subject not to the civil courts but to the ecclesiastical courts."[8] As a result, there were rising tensions and occasional riots between town and gown, culminating in the infamous St. Scholastica's Day riot of 1355. Relations had improved by the early sixteenth century. Despite some lingering tensions, there was a growing mutualism between the two.[9]

At the dawn of the sixteenth century, the university was both stable and flourishing. It had been in existence for upward of three hundred years. Its enrollment of approximately 1,700 was on the high side compared to other European universities.[10] To its original three endowed colleges of the thirteenth century (University, Balliol, Merton) had been added seven others (Exeter, Oriel, Queen's, New, Lincoln, All Soul's, and Magdalen). The institution would add a further three foundations in the early sixteenth century: Brasenose (1513), Corpus Christi (1516), and Cardinal College (1529). This growth was accompanied by architectural improvements. Magdalen had set a "new standard of size and grandeur" in the 1480s, which the new sixteenth-century foundations sought to emulate and exceed.[11] During the last quarter of the fifteenth century, many of the university-wide buildings—the theology school, canon law school, library, and university church of St. Mary's— were all renovated and beautified.[12] Moreover, the academic reputation of Oxford was high. At the close of the fifteenth century, many of the texts that were studied in universities across Europe—particularly in logic and natural philosophy—were written by earlier Oxford masters and recent alums like John Duns Scotus, William of Ockham, and Walter Burley.[13] The study of theology also flourished within Oxford's walls, and it produced a large number of clergymen—neither of which was surprising given the medieval university's close ties to the church. But in many ways Oxford was a secular as well as religious institution, and it drew students bound for careers in fields like medicine and law. Indeed, Oxford's continued association with the ecclesiastical courts made it a center for the study of canon law. To a large extent, pre-Reformation

Oxford was a "self-governing institution."[14] It was presided over by assemblies of regent masters (congregation and convocation) as well as the officials (chancellor, vice chancellor, proctors, and so forth) that these bodies elected.[15]

But the university was subject to dramatic changes over the course of the sixteenth century. Its people, buildings, curriculum, and institutions were all affected by the Reformation. The Dissolution closed monastic foundations in the suburbs; some buildings were demolished while others provided new sites and building materials for existing colleges.[16] Monastic colleges—including Canterbury, St. Bernard's, Durham, Gloucester, and St. Mary's—were closed in the 1540s, though some were repurposed: "the quadrangles of Durham, St. Bernard's and Canterbury Colleges surviv[ed] to a new use in the post-reformation university."[17] Despite the loss of the monks and monastic orders that had played such a large role in the university's history, Oxford would play a prominent role in the new state church. In the Middle Ages, Oxford had been part of the diocese of Lincoln, but in 1542 it became the seat of the new diocese of Oxford—with its cathedral housed within the Oxford college of Christ Church. The Reformation also brought academic and curricular changes. With the break from Rome, the study of canon law was abolished at Oxford in 1535. This, along with "the removal at the Reformation of the monks and friars who had swelled the theology faculty," helped fuel the increased prominence of the arts curriculum.[18] Religious changes also set in motion the same vicissitudes that the nation was subject to during the successive reigns of Henry VIII, Edward VI, and Mary I. In 1535, 1548, 1556, and 1559, Oxford received formal visitations from royal commissioners who were intent on making sure that Oxford and its colleges were "religiously sound" and did not harbor "the religiously and politically disaffected."[19] Despite complying with each of these visitations in turn, Oxford tended to be pretty conservative overall. Whereas Cambridge became associated to a greater degree with radical reformers, Oxford housed Catholic recusants well into Elizabeth's reign.[20] Aside from religion, the university itself—as an institution of higher learning—was also transformed over the course of the sixteenth century. Historians of the university have outlined a number of important developments, including the rise of individual colleges, the proliferation of undergraduates, the influx of commoners, the expansion of curriculum, the primacy of the arts, and the increasingly oligarchic nature of internal governance.[21] I want to focus in on the changes in two particular areas—curriculum and enrollment—as both are of particular relevance to the 1566 entertainments.

Curriculum

From the late fifteenth century, humanist educational ideas spread from Italy across Europe. They differed markedly from the late medieval focus on scholasticism and metaphysics. Since these humanists looked to classical writers for inspiration and models, their educational program emphasized Greek and Roman texts. Not only did they draw from classical works of logic and rhetoric, they also invested heavily in more "humane" fields of literature, history, geography, and moral philosophy. Their goal was to produce well-rounded individuals who could pursue virtue in the service of the state. Thus, they put a premium on the "importance of 'polished' writing and speech . . . which they believed necessary for the success of the civic humanist."[22] In England, the new learning came in via men like John Colet, Erasmus, and Thomas More, and eventually found a ready audience at the court of Henry VIII—especially among those sympathetic to religious reform. Erasmus's endorsement of *bonae literae* represented a distinct challenge to monastic erudition. He "followed Lorenzo Valla in his call for setting aside the scholastic theology of the Middle Ages, formed in a University culture dominated by Aristotelian logic."[23] Erasmus proposed instead the study of "good letters"—the poetry, literature, and philosophy of the ancients—as a pathway to the cultivation of Christian virtue that could then be deployed in a life of active public service.

But what was the nature of the new learning's impact at Oxford? Colet had been educated at Oxford; after travelling on the Continent, he returned to Oxford in 1496 as a lecturer. He invited Erasmus to visit Oxford in 1499, where the latter also taught briefly. Richard Foxe, Bishop of Winchester, belonged to this same humanist circle; when he founded Corpus Christi in 1517, it "brought with it a commitment to humane studies and a degree of discipline which set an entirely new style."[24] Soon afterward, Cardinal Thomas Wolsey's foundation of Cardinal College in 1524 and 1525 also reflected the "influence of the humanistic programme" in its stipulation of daily lectures on Latin and Greek authors.[25] In 1535, Thomas Cromwell and other religious reformers sought not only to ensure Oxford's acceptance of the break with Rome, but also to "put the new learning on a solid footing."[26] To that end, they established Latin and Greek lectureships at five different colleges, reporting that John Duns Scotus—and the scholastic approach that he represented—had "been banished from the University forever."[27] Thus, at Oxford there was something of a shift toward the new learning in the first few decades of the sixteenth century—a shift that actually spanned the Reformation rather than being caused by it.[28]

In terms of the curriculum, the new learning had the most impact on grammar, rhetoric, and logic. In grammar and rhetoric, "the new, humanistic texts ousted the earlier books," while in logic, the removal of the "superstructure of 'sophistry'" allowed for a return to Aristotelian logic in the manner advocated by Salutati and Erasmus.[29] In the 1540s, the declamation—"one of the standard teaching devices of the orators of ancient Rome"—was introduced "as a teaching tool to supplement the older disputation."[30] In terms of individual colleges, the humanist impact was clearly discernable at Exeter, Merton, Corpus Christi, and at the newly founded Trinity College (1555).[31]

Yet the inroads made by the new learning were nowhere as thorough or dramatic as they might have been. Throughout the sixteenth century, the BA and MA curriculum was still organized around the seven traditional liberal arts: the medieval trivium (grammar, logic, rhetoric) and quadrivium (arithmetic, geometry, music, and astronomy). Moreover, the new learning made surprisingly little impact on curricular statutes. We do not find allowances to incorporate the "new" humanist fields of history, literature, geography, and moral philosophy into the university curriculum. In fact, the Tudor masters "appear more concerned to enforce and strengthen the old statutes than to introduce any important innovations: modifications are accompanied by phrases that emphasize the validity of the old statutes and their continuing relevance to the contemporary situation."[32] At Oxford, the new learning was certainly endorsed less enthusiastically than at other Protestant universities like Basel, Tübingen, and Glasgow, all of whom "revised their statutory regulations drastically."[33] Even Cambridge was more hospitable; as early as 1488, it had exchanged some of its prescribed logic and natural philosophy for "two years' study of humane letters."[34] Oxford seems to have exhibited more intellectual conservatism. According to J. M. Fletcher, Oxford faculty appear not to have been convinced of the value of the humanist approach in fields other than grammar and rhetoric.[35] Their hesitation may also have had something to do with religious conservatism: "The Oxford masters, proud of their own past, were suspicious of the value of many of the changes urged on them by renaissance scholars, influenced mainly by continental reformers."[36]

Thus, the humanist impact largely proceeded through unofficial channels. In practice, the curriculum was "filled out and brought up to date by the addition of authors and commentators and even of disciplines not mentioned in the statutes."[37] The content of traditional curriculum could be and was supplemented by college lecturers, private teaching, and the guidance of tutors.[38] Surviving book inventories and student notebooks do reflect the informal infusion of the new learning at Oxford.[39] Though the statutes remained largely static, there was some movement in the direction of the humanities, the arts of rhetoric and persuasion, and the emphasis on service to the state.[40] Despite disagreement amongst historians over how much movement, it seems fair to say that Oxford's mid-century curriculum was a mix of old and new that "combine[d] much of the best of both the medieval and the humanist views of the character of higher education."[41]

Enrollment

Another key dynamic in Tudor Oxford was a shift in student enrollment. Over the course of the sixteenth century, enrollment increased from around 1,700 students in the late fifteenth century to 2,920 by 1612.[42] In large part, this growth is accounted for by a surge in the number of undergraduates; Oxford was well on its way to becoming an undergraduate institution.[43] There was also a demographic change in the social strata of the average Oxford student. The university had traditionally been a training ground for clerics (and so often attracted those of a relatively humble background); in the sixteenth century it began to attract the sons of the landed elite. These students were typically not bound for the clergy but for secular careers as courtiers, lawyers, and owners of landed estates.[44] Indeed, many of them were not seeking a degree so much as a "veneer of polish and learning" that would qualify them for government service and give them the cultivated refinement that would allow them to move easily among the social elites.[45] These students (and their fathers) tended to gravitate more toward the new learning—"instruction in the broader classical humanities"—rather than the traditional university curriculum.[46] At the heart of this trend was "a new concept of gentility, promoted by Renaissance humanists." Rather than locating gentility in "military prowess and chivalric conduct," humanists like Erasmus "argued that true nobility came from imbibing the virtues of civility and charity embodied in classical literature and holy writ, and was only properly accessible to those who could read the texts in their original tongue." This argument found particularly fertile ground in England, where the landed elite began to send their sons to university at a much higher rate than on the Continent.[47]

However, since many of these students were not taking a degree and might only be at Oxford a year or two, they weren't bound by the full range of statutory requirements and regulations. As a result, their studies evolved into what was essentially a secondary educational track.[48] These upper-class students would still attend lectures and were involved in college life, but they were also "free, to some extent, from the constant round of lectures and disputations which formed the kernel of the [typical] student day."[49] Their pursuits tended to be more varied, more humanistic, and more practical. Along with imbibing the typical subjects of the seven liberal arts, these students might learn modern languages like Italian and French, study geography, government, and the scientific arts, "become proficient on a musical instrument . . . [or] improve their dancing, fencing and equestrian skills."[50] This broader education was facilitated by the rise of the college tutor: an individual associated with the college who was paid by well-to-do fathers to keep an eye on their sons, set their course of study, and provide personal instruction.[51] The tutor could oversee his student's participation in university instruction, but also supplement it accordingly. He was something of a "director of studies," whose varied roles might include "finding private tutors where needed, suggesting books his charges could read, and increasingly taking his pupils singly or in small groups to quiz them on their personal studies and to give them direct instruction."[52]

Somewhat surprisingly, these developments were embraced by the university. By 1552, enrollment at Oxford had dropped from a healthy 1,700 pupils down to around 1,100.[53] Oxford needed students, and the sons of the wealthy were particularly appealing. Whereas a high number of students had traditionally been "on the foundation," these students came in as fee-paying commoners. Known as "gentlemen commoners," they paid higher entrance fees than other commoners and were even expected to present their colleges with a silver cup or bowl.[54] Not only were such students a financial boon, they also allowed the university to associate with important people and expand its area of influence. Thus, from the mid-sixteenth century, Oxford colleges began to actively recruit and cater to the sons of the elite.[55] How extensive was this influx? The numbers are hard to gauge in the middle part of the century because Oxford students did not have to formally matriculate until 1581, and many gentlemen commoners were only nominally associated with particular colleges. But by the end of the sixteenth century, surviving records indicate that somewhere between a third and a half of all Oxford students came from the gentry class and were headed for secular careers.[56] A substantial number of these were non-degree-seeking students.[57]

For my purposes, the timing of this influx is important. To be sure, some upper-class boys did begin to attend Oxford earlier in the century. The foundation statutes of Corpus Christi College (1518) made allowances for gentlemen, and Sir Thomas Elyot's *The Governour* (1531) touts the value of university education for the gentry.[58] By the 1540s and 1550s there was a noticeable stream of such students.[59] Nevertheless, it was in the early 1570s that the trend began "in earnest."[60] It was not until that decade that "well-born lay students . . . came for the first time in any numbers to the universities to obtain the humanistic education now thought appropriate for their role as governors of the realm."[61] For example, Henry Stanley, 4th Earl of Derby, sent his eldest son, Ferdinando, to St. John's College, Oxford for a year in 1572. Meanwhile, Sir Nicholas Bacon, Lord Keeper of the Great Seal, sent his two sons Anthony (in the early 1570s) and Francis (during 1573 to 1576) to Trinity College, Cambridge.[62] The timing of this trend meant that it was far from an established practice in 1566. Indeed, L. W. B. Brockliss reports that humanist education didn't have full buy-in from all the leading families of England until the late sixteenth century, and Lawrence Stone reminds us that "University education never became the *sine qua non* [absolutely essential quality] of the cultivated nobleman."[63] This hesitation can be seen in no less a work than *The Courtier* (1527), in which Baldassare Castiglione has to self-consciously justify the study of letters alongside the pursuit of military arts. Even those mid-century nobles who saw the value of humanist education were not necessarily sure that the university was the best place to get it. After all, they had imbibed the classics via private tutors. With a few exceptions, the most influential people at the early Elizabethan court—including the Queen herself—had not been to university. By the 1560s, some were starting to send their sons to university, but these were a minority. The majority would need to be convinced of the relevance and importance of Oxford.

Outside Interference

The final mid-sixteenth-century trend that I want to focus on is the increase of outside interference at Oxford. In addition to the other ways in which Oxford developed as an educational institution, it also came to be more in the orbit of the state. The course of the sixteenth century saw a "vast enlargement of royal authority" that was related directly to the emergence of a new state church and the Tudor emphasis on political centralization.[64] The universities were a key aspect of both trends, since they trained the clergy and (as we have seen) were taking on an increased role in preparing laymen for secular careers in the state. Thus, the century witnessed "frequent bursts of state interference" in order to maintain religious and political stability.[65] At Oxford, this interference included ecclesiastical visitations (in 1535, 1548, 1556, and 1559) as well as actual royal visits (in 1566 and 1592). Even when the Crown and its representatives were not physically present, they left behind college visitors—ecclesiastics "task[ed] [with] keeping a college or hall on the straight and narrow"—and worked to modify university governance so that it would be more oligarchic and more responsive to the center.[66] The Crown and Privy Council also issued a stream of admonitions from Whitehall and were particularly keen to control the dress and discipline of university students.[67] Increased outside influence is evident even before the Reformation, when university patrons like Archbishop William Warham and Cardinal Wolsey "wielded considerable influence over the university."[68] Scrutiny only intensified during the Reformation. In 1530, Oxford drug its feet on supporting Henry VIII's divorce, "bringing upon the university a closer royal supervision than ever before."[69] Though the university was more docile after that, each change in the religious situation through the reigns of Edward VI, Mary, and Elizabeth brought fresh scrutiny in ensuring conformity. Over the course of the sixteenth century, not just the Crown, but secular officials, courtiers, and landowners began to acquire a growing influence over the university. Penry Williams talks about the influence they brought to bear in the election of heads of houses, the dispensing of fellowships, and even the disposal of college leases.[70] The most influential laymen included the likes of Robert Dudley, William Cecil, Robert Cecil, Francis Walsingham, and Robert Devereux, though there were numerous other lay patrons.[71]

In some ways, such external connections were desirable. In fact, Oxford was looking more and more to the state for protection, support, and benefits. In the first place, institutional finances were not robust, with the university operating on what was essentially "a shoestring" budget.[72] While most college endowments covered basic operational expenses and fellowships, very little money was available for extra things like building projects.[73] In fact, there was no new, large-scale building at Oxford in the second half of the sixteenth century. Instead, the colleges followed a "make-do and mend" approach, which included using the former monastic land and buildings that became available after the Reformation.[74] However, the founding of two new colleges in the 1550s and rising enrollments in the 1560s meant that most of this available space had been absorbed.[75] Thus, if colleges were going to improve their physical fabric—and construct newer, more spacious buildings to cater to the incoming elite—then they would need to attract outside benefactors.[76]

Second, the Tudor university needed outside assistance in maintaining its privileges. Earlier in the century, the university "feared its long-standing privileges would be eroded by a reinvigorated town government."[77] They had successfully petitioned Wolsey for help, but after the cardinal's fall, Thomas Cromwell used these local tensions—and the threat of revoking university privileges—as leverage for getting the university to affirm the king's divorce.[78] In this way, the university was made to look to the center for protection and become more dependent on the Crown. This dynamic was formalized in the 1530s, when the Privy Council emerged as the primary arbiter of town/gown disputes. In many ways, this development was an improvement—as "regular institutional supervision" proved to be more desirable than "sporadic, direct intervention by the sovereign in reaction to a crisis"—but it drew Oxford ever closer to the center.[79] In 1543, the university's privileges were reconfirmed and it once again had the upper hand over the town, but the university was naturally wary, and it would need to ensure its future influence at court. This was probably one of the reasons that convocation so willingly elected Robert Dudley, Earl of Leicester as chancellor in 1564.

While such external connections could be beneficial, Oxford recognized that they might bring increased interference and decreased autonomy. For example, the religious environment at Oxford changed markedly over the course of Elizabeth's reign. The visitation of 1559 administered the Oath of Supremacy to root out "the most uncompromising catholics," but the Queen moved slowly and "there was no government witch hunt."[80] In the 1560s and 1570s, there were numerous recusants—as well as some radical Protestants—in the colleges and halls of Oxford.[81] But beginning in 1581, the scope of religious possibilities narrowed considerably. In that year, Leicester "ordered a crackdown" and the university promulgated a matriculation statute that required all incoming students to take the Oath of Supremacy and also subscribe to the 1563 Articles of Religion.[82] This new statute "effectively closed the university to students with Catholic sympathies."[83]

Another area of decreased autonomy was self-governance. The authority of congregation and convocation—the two governing bodies of resident masters—was "gradually eroded" over the course of the century.[84] Instead, power became concentrated in the hands of the vice-chancellor and the college heads, who were more answerable to the chancellor and the Crown.[85] Brockliss characterizes this shift as the imposition of a "senior management structure . . . to police the corporation of masters and scholars."[86] A big part of this shift rested in the growing power of the chancellor. Early chancellors had been chosen by the university from among its resident masters, but after the Reformation the chancellor was effectively appointed by the monarch.[87] Though not involved in day-to-day activities, the chancellor was the chief officer of the university. By Elizabeth's reign, the chancellor was "a lay grandee, capable of bringing to bear considerable pressure on the university but able in exchange to provide patronage and favour."[88] Leicester occupied this position from 1564 until his death in 1588, and over that long period he took an active role and expanded the powers of the office. He approved new curricular statutes in 1565, moved to streamline convocation in 1569, and took over the nominating of vice chancellor candidates (who did run the day-to-day university) in 1570. Leicester's correspondence from the period reflects his active role in "reprimanding, ordering, and advising" the university on "a wide range of affairs." Overall, Leicester "took a close and continuous interest" in the university and—though a non-resident—was "the single most important figure in Elizabethan Oxford." His prominence was yet another symptom of the increase in state influence. It is no wonder that Penry Williams has referred to the combined effects of royal influence and lay patronage in this period of Oxford's history as "the University Subdued." By the end of the sixteenth century, "the university had . . . come to rely upon external support and lay open to state influence." Or, as Claire Cross puts it, "To a quite unprecedented degree Oxford . . . had capitulated to state control."[89]

But as even Williams is quick to point out, "the impact of the governmental machinery . . . was not rapid . . . the colleges were sometimes capable of resisting encroachment . . . [and] the university never entirely subservient."[90] Moreover, the process of state encroachment "was probably not, on balance, seriously damaging . . . until the end of the sixteenth century."[91] Even if this were the future trajectory, Oxford was not there yet in 1566. Elizabeth had only been on the throne eight years, and she was proceeding slowly and cautiously. Leicester had only been the chancellor of Oxford for two years and had not yet begun to flex his muscle. Indeed, he had only visited the university once as chancellor prior to the Queen's 1566 progress visit, and his aforementioned interferences into the nomination of the vice chancellor, the activities of convocation, and the election of proctors were still in the future. It wasn't until 1568 that he "issued the first of many thunderous complaints about the conduct of the university's affairs."[92] In the Oxford of 1566, students did not yet have to formally matriculate, did not have to take the Oath of Supremacy, and did not have to subscribe to the Articles of Religion. The situation was much more fluid. The university no doubt sensed that it was being drawn into the wider orbit of the state and even that it would need those external partners to thrive, but it probably felt as though it could still try to determine the terms under which that happened. It sought a particular kind of relationship with the center wherein it could maximize the state's support and protection but minimize its interference in university affairs.

Oxford's Response

The Queen's 1566 visit to Oxford was an unparalleled opportunity for the university to negotiate and construct an advantageous relationship. Not only was the Queen in attendance, but she was joined by a large train of nobles, courtiers, privy councilors, and domestic officials. Here was the very collection of people the university hoped to impress and gain the support of. Though this group was generally supportive of humanism and the new learning, most of its members had not been to university and were not necessarily convinced that universities were the centers of humanist learning. This week gave Oxford the opportunity to use its entertainments to showcase its humanist values and dramatically display what it had to offer. As I will argue, the university's entertainments actually exaggerated the presence of the new learning at Oxford (and ran counter to its own rather conservative curricular statutes of 1565) for the benefit of its courtly audience. The university entertainments also went out of their way to emphasize the *practicality* of university education—another key consideration for this audience. In emphasizing the practicality of humanism, Oxford sought to demonstrate, celebrate, and defend a particular concept of gentility that (it argued) arises from university education. Oxford's goal throughout the week was to solicit the good will and support of its visitors in the form of future protection, support, and financial backing. Since many in the royal entourage had young sons, the university also hoped to inspire them to someday send their sons and heirs to Oxford as gentlemen commoners. In other words, to turn the steady flow of such men into a flood.

Yet as it tried to forge closer connections with—and extract benefits from—the Queen and the leading families of the realm, Oxford was also wary of increasing outside interference. Thus, it hoped to use its pageants to posit a particular type of relationship that would be most beneficial to the university. It would make the case for outside protection, financial support, self-governance, the defense of university privileges, and the professional advancement of its graduates. At the same time, it would use these performative moments to discourage overly prescriptive interference, the micromanaging of affairs, religious scrutiny, and undue lay influence. Throughout the week, Oxford fashions an image of itself as a well ordered place with effective internal governance (that does not need policing); plays up its financial and building needs; presents academia as a specialized and rarified world; and idealizes a particular model of hands-off patronage. Through a combination of literary, performative, and academic activities, Oxford posited a particular kind of relationship to the state that was serviceable to its historical moment.

Such an approach to the Queen's 1566 visit to Oxford runs counter to other critical approaches. Most critics view the week through a monarchical lens. That is, they seek to uncover the Queen's motives for coming to Oxford and assess how the visit was useful to her. Thus, Eleanor Rosenberg and James Binns both write about the Queen's desire to encourage learning at the universities in order to "mobilise the nation's academics in the service of the state."[93] Meanwhile, Mary Hill Cole reads the visit in terms of Elizabeth's desire to enforce religious conformity, particularly in light of recent church controversies on the wearing of vestments.[94] Linda Shenk also adopts a religious approach, though she argues that the Queen was more interested in forging consensus by sidestepping controversy and striking a note of inclusivity to both Catholics and radical Protestants.[95] Others, like Siobhan Keenan do examine how the university used the occasion of the Queen's visit, though Keenan mainly reads the plays and disputations as veiled attempts to offer the Queen counsel about marriage and the royal succession.[96] But in my view, the primary goal of the Oxford entertainments was not to offer commentary on these national topics.

Given the newness of the Elizabethan Settlement and the fluidity of the 1560s, religion would seem to resonate the most inside the walls and quadrangles of Oxford. Though as discussed above, the university contained within itself a relatively broad scope of religious belief, and the Crown (at this early stage) was moving cautiously. That 1560s Oxford could accommodate the likes of both Edmund Campion and Laurence Humphrey is pretty revealing.[97]

More importantly, the pageants themselves seem to consciously avoid religious topics. Unlike some of the reform-minded shows at Cambridge in 1564, "the [Oxford] scholars generally avoided the issue of religion."[98] This avoidance is in keeping with my claim about Oxford not wanting to invite undue outside interference. At Oxford, the religious status quo was relatively stable and there were fewer radical Protestants calling for reform: "Throughout the first two decades of Elizabeth's reign, then, most of the intellectual talent of the university was involved either in discreet self-preservation or the defence of the 1559 settlement against catholic jibes [from former colleagues now in exile], not in discussion of further radical alteration of the church."[99] As a result, there was little impetus at Oxford to partner with the Crown to establish a particular religious vision—especially if invoking central authority would invite scrutiny that might easily spill into other areas. Thus, religion was not really the central issue of the 1566 entertainments at Oxford. Instead, the university's focus was on something larger and more overarching: its relationship to the state.

There is no official university account of the 1566 visit that would enable us to see this focus. Instead, there is something that is even more useful: a number of different primary accounts written by a range of students, faculty, heads of houses, tutors, and visiting scholars, some of whom participated directly in the festivities. Manuscript accounts survive from Miles Windsor, fellow of Corpus Christi and actor in the evening plays; Nicholas Robinson, Cambridge graduate and Bishop of Bangor, who was in attendance; John Bereblock, fellow of Exeter; and Richard Stephens, who would enter Corpus Christi the following year. All of these men wrote first-person descriptions of the events, although they were not intended to be produced for publication at that time. Other sources actually formed part of the welcome and entertainment. Thomas Neale, regius professor of Hebrew, presented to the Queen the *Topographica Delineatio,* a verbal tour of Oxford framed as a fictional dialogue between Queen Elizabeth and the Earl of Leicester. Another valuable source for the Queen's visit is the collection of speeches and poems presented to her by university members, including Laurence Humphrey (president of Magdalen), Thomas Kingsmill (public orator), Thomas Cooper (Latin dictionary author), Henry Bust (debate participant), and other fellows. Together, these documents provide a varied collection of sources that tell us much about how contemporaries perceived the image of Oxford that was being projected to the royal court as well as the imagined effects of these events and entertainments. In some cases, these sources provide parallel descriptions that underscore key moments or effects.

At other times, they exhibit differences in focus and emphasis. Yet these differences are instructive in showing the varied (and ultimately cohesive) ways in which Oxford sought to speak to the Queen.

Audience

We will begin not by focusing on a particular account, but by considering the audience the university sought to target. As noted above, not only was the Queen in attendance, but she brought with her a large train of nobles, courtiers, councilors, and officials. Nicholas Robinson's account gives a list of nineteen men "who were distinguished for their nobility who were at Oxford."[100] Other sources bring that number to at least twenty-six.[101] This was a much larger number than typically accompanied the Queen on her progresses to other cities in the realm.[102] The retinue at Oxford included a marquis, seven earls, twelve other titled lords, and eight knights. These were some of the most influential men in the realm, including Robert Dudley, William Cecil, Thomas Radcliffe, William Parr, and William Howard. The group included six Privy Councillors (Leicester, Northampton, Howard, Rogers, Cecil, Knollys), the Principal Secretary (Cecil), a recent ambassador to France (Throckmorton), a future lord deputy of Ireland (Grey), and the Master of Ordnance (Warwick). Also present were members of the Queen's inner domestic circle, including the Lord Chamberlain of the Household (Howard), the Vice Chamberlain (Knollys), the Keeper of the Privy Purse (Tamworth), and the Comptroller of the Household (Rogers). In short, it was quite an audience that Oxford might influence.

Robert Dudley, Earl of Leicester, was there as both host and guest. A favorite of the Queen since childhood, Leicester had already been entrusted with high power, having joined the Privy Council in 1562 and been made chancellor of Oxford in 1564. Because of the latter position, he can be seen as the official host of the Queen's visit to Oxford. However, in reality he was something of an outsider at Oxford. He had not attended the university as a student, and he had so far only visited Oxford once in his two-year tenure as chancellor. Moreover, Leicester does not seem to have had a big role in planning Oxford's reception of the Queen.[103] Windsor's account records that Leicester, Cecil, and a few other nobles came to Oxford only two days before the Queen "to see the provision made by the vniversitie for receavinge of her Maiestie" (*JN1*, 469–70). Leicester was welcomed with an oration and dined at Vice Chancellor John Kennall's lodging before he returned to Woodstock (where the Queen was staying) a few hours later. Such formal hospitality suggests that Oxford may well have seen Leicester's arrival as part of the larger royal visit rather than as a preparatory prelude. In fact, university leaders used their audience with Leicester and Cecil to "[enter] into further talke of the Privileges of Oxford" (*JN1, 470*). Thus, Oxford was already engaged in trying to solicit support from would-be patrons, including its own chancellor.

Oxford's reception of the Queen seems to have been mainly orchestrated by its own internal leadership. Keenan notes the formation of a "university delegation" to devise "a programme of entertainments . . . that included orations, sermons, disputations, and plays."[104] This group was most likely led by Vice Chancellor John Kennall, and included the heads of houses of the fifteen colleges. As heads of Christ Church and Magdalen, the two wealthiest colleges, Thomas Godwin and Laurence Humphrey probably played important roles. When the Queen arrived at the edge of town, she was met by just such a cross section of university leadership: "the Earle of Leicester with 4 Doctors in skarlet viz. Doctor Kenall viz. Doctor Vmphrey Doctor Godwyn Doctor Whyte mett the Quens Maiestie with 8 Masters of Arts beinge heds of houses & 3 esquyer Bedels" (*JN1, 471*).[105] Though the university's reception was spearheaded by these men, it also involved other "elected individuals taking charge of the practical arrangements" and relied on wide participation.[106] During the week, doctors participated in disputes, students acted in plays, college orators gave speeches, convocation determined honorary degrees, and individual colleges presented books of honorary verse composed by its members. In other words, Oxford's reception was largely the university's own and thus reflected its particular concerns and goals.

One of the overriding priorities was to reach out to and attempt to forge connections with the train of influential courtiers that had come within its walls. However, as previously suggested, this group did not have a lot of experience with university education in general and Oxford in particular. Most of the courtiers had been educated by private tutors. The Queen, as a woman, had not had the option of attending university, though she nevertheless received an outstanding humanist education under the guidance of John Astley, William Grindal, and Roger Ascham.[107] Similarly, Leicester and his brother Ambrose Dudley (the 3rd Earl of Warwick) had been educated at home in the 1540s by Ascham as well as Thomas Wilson.[108] Also in attendance at Oxford were the Earl of Huntingdon and Lord Strange, both of whom had been educated by the likes of Richard Cox, John Cheke, and Jean Belmain at the English court

alongside the young Edward VI.[109] Meanwhile, Lord Grey and Lord Stafford
had been educated abroad at foreign courts. Finally, there were men in the
Queen's entourage who had followed the traditional practice of serving in a
noble household during their youth. Sir Edward Rogers (b. 1498) had been
attached to the Courtenay family; Thomas Radcliffe, 3rd Earl of Sussex (b.
1525) spent time in the household of Stephen Gardiner, Bishop of Winchester;
and Sir Nicholas Throckmorton (b. 1515) had served as a page in the household
of the Duke of Richmond. A few of the courtiers present did have some level
of exposure to university education. Sir William Cecil and Lord Howard were
educated in the 1520s and 1530s at Cambridge, while the Earl of Huntingdon
spent a year at Oxford in the 1550s. Eighteen-year-old Lord Edward Russell—
eldest son of the 2nd Earl of Bedford—was actually enrolled at University
College, Oxford in 1566. The records are less conclusive about Sir Francis
Knollys, the Earl of Rutland, and the Marquis of Northampton, all of whom
may have spent time at one of the two universities.[110] Still only seven of the
twenty-six noble visitors are likely to have had any experience with university education, and none of these men had taken degrees. Aside from Russell,
Cecil was probably the most committed supporter of university education;
not only had he attended St. John's College, Cambridge, he had been chancellor of Cambridge since 1559. In that year, he had written a memorandum
to Parliament in which he proposed that "the nobility ought to be *required* to
provide a university education for their sons."[111] This memo not only speaks
to Cecil's frustration that many of the leading families had yet to see the value
of university education, but also shows his support for it. Still, when it came
to Oxford, Cecil had much less experience and familiarity there. He was not
alone. Of the twenty-six courtiers present at Oxford in 1566, only two to four
seem to have previously engaged in educational pursuits at Oxford.

Yet Oxford saw the potential for ingrafting these nobles into its educational
mission. Along with Russell, two other members of the Queen's entourage
were actually college-aged: Edward de Vere, 17th Earl of Oxford (age sixteen)
and Edward Manners, 3rd Earl of Rutland (age seventeen).[112] Neither was
attending university, but perhaps Oxford could get them to identify with and
support the institution. Other visiting nobles had young sons that Oxford may
have hoped to recruit. In 1566, the Lords Howard, Strange, Sheffield, Windsor,
Chandos, and Mountjoy had among them some fifteen sons under the age of
ten. Sir Nicholas Throckmorton alone had six sons, five under the age of twenty.
If Oxford made a favorable impression on these fathers, perhaps it could induce

them to send their sons to the university in the near future. At least two of
the visiting fathers had already taken such a step. Cecil's eldest son, Thomas,
had been at Trinity College, Cambridge circa 1558 to 1561, while Sir Francis
Knollys's eldest son, Henry, was at Magdalen College, Oxford in the late 1550s.
Neither had taken a degree, but they had presumably been engaged in acquiring
the learning and polish that would serve them in their public careers.

This is not to suggest that the other nobles were antagonistic to university
education. Not only were the Queen and her nobles highly learned, they also
valued many of the subjects and skills that contemporary Oxford students
were pursuing. As we have seen, many were especially keen on humanism
and the new learning. As a girl in the 1540s, Elizabeth had studied Latin and
mastered Greek under the guidance of Roger Ascham.[113] She was also adept
at learning modern foreign languages like French and Italian. Ascham's correspondence reveals that the Queen's education centered on the Greek and
Roman classics (particularly the orations of Cicero and Isocrates, the histories
of Livy, and the tragedies of Sophocles) and that she approached her studies
with the typical humanist emphasis on rhetoric and style: "From these authors,
I was of opinion, that she would adorn her style with the most elegant diction,
enrich her mind with the most suitable precepts, and frame her high station of
life to every fortune."[114] Similarly, the nobles accompanying the Queen were
educated by tutors whose names form a roll call of some of the most prominent
humanist educators of the sixteenth century: Dee, Ascham, Cheke, Belmain,
Cox, Astley, Grindal, Haddon, and Wilson. Nor did the royal visitors see education simply as an adolescent activity to be mastered and moved beyond. Even
after becoming Queen, Elizabeth's "Greek studies with Ascham continued,
and in her sixties she was still an active translator."[115] Leicester also continued
to pursue learning. Surviving letters from Ascham (1564) and Haddon (1565)
make it clear that Leicester was continuing to work on improving his Latin
and broadening his knowledge of rhetoric, law, philosophy, history, and the
ancient world.[116] Such learning was coming to be valued by the ruling classes
as a part of being educated, cultured, and polished. Because of the premium
that Elizabeth placed on humanist education, it was becoming something of a
requirement for mobility in her court.[117] This was not merely personal preference, but rather the idea that such an education prepared one for public service. The knowledge (and lessons) of antiquity and a broad knowledge of arts
and sciences (and especially the mastery of persuasive rhetoric) were tools that
could be wielded as a part of civic humanism. Thus, perhaps even more so than

its Oxford hosts, this group of nobles and courtiers valued education in terms of its *practical* usefulness. The Queen valued "learning as an accomplishment with some practical use" and "was never what would be called an intellectual, not even especially bookish."[118] The same could be said for Leicester, whose "correspondence displays none of the academic humanism of [his] university-educated contemporaries."[119]

Aware of the particular educational values of its audience, the university went out of its way to equate such practical humanism with an Oxford education. One of the first things that scholars note about Oxford's 1566 entertainments is how closely they followed the festivities at Cambridge in 1564. At Cambridge, the students, masters, and doctors entertained the Queen with Latin orations, formal disputations, academic plays, and poetic verses affixed to the walls and buildings of the town. All of these elements recur at Oxford in 1566. It is not so much that Oxford was being merely derivative, it is that the entertainments had garnered a specific response from the Queen that Oxford was eager to duplicate. At Cambridge, "humanistic literary activity was a very prominent part of the reception" and "Elizabeth explicitly depicts herself as a successful participant in the humanistic tradition of learning."[120] At the same time, the week's activities stress the practical *application* of humanist ideals. Not only did Cambridge seek to entertain, it also sought to "put itself through its paces, so to speak, and demonstrat[e] its prowess in oratory, in acting, in the composition of verses, in the intricacies of learned debates on politics and statecraft, among other matters, in the presence of the Queen and her courtiers."[121] But it was the Queen's response to these Cambridge exercises that would resonate so strongly in Oxford two years later. After the disputations, the Queen delivered a Latin oration in which she affirmed "bonae literae" and "expressed her desire that [it] should be propagated and advanced in the university."[122] These words amounted to an explicit endorsement of the new learning that Erasmus and others had tried to plant in English soil earlier in the century. The Queen went even further in articulating her desire to leave behind "some famous and noteworthy work" at Cambridge—a promise that seemed to refer to the founding of a college or the erection of a monumental building.[123]

Naturally, the Queen's affirmation of *bonae literae* and her promise of financial support were recorded and transmitted to contemporaries. One of the main vehicles was Abraham Hartwell's *Regina Literata*, a Latin verse account of the Queen's visit that was published in London in 1565.[124] A key text for gauging how these events were perceived at Oxford is Thomas Cooper's *Thesaurus*

Linguae Romanae et Britannicae (1565), which was to become "the standard Latin dictionary of Elizabethan England."[125] Cooper, a master of Magdalen College, wrote a lengthy dedication to Leicester that "served as a gloss upon the Queen's speech at Cambridge, clarifying and particularizing the assurances she had given, and reasserting in her name and Leicester's that learning had become the approved road to royal favor and high position."[126] In other words, Cooper actively interpreted the Queen's recent visit to Cambridge and her upcoming visit to Oxford as formalizing her support of the university and its educational mission.[127] However, he "clarifies and particularizes" that support in a specific way; according to Cooper, the Queen's behavior and words at Cambridge show that she will reverse the recent decline in learning at the universities by "restor[ing] the arts to their former glory" so that "skill in languages and the humanistic disciplines might flourish."[128] He then includes an entire section on the practical utility of such learning, not only for the individual but the commonwealth as a whole: "in confirming religion, in cultivating manners, in carrying out diplomatic missions, in expounding the commands of the Prince or Council, in arguing legal matters, in dealing with councils, in public suits, judgments, and all the other activities upon which the administration of the commonwealth depends."[129] Ultimately, Cooper's dedication helped cement the notion that the new learning was both intrinsically valuable and also of great worth in training public servants. More importantly for my argument, Cooper asserts that the Queen herself endorsed such practical humanism, and that she was prepared to liberally support its pursuit. Cooper's dedication helps explain why Oxford's 1566 entertainments were so closely modelled on those at Cambridge two year earlier. Oxford hoped to elicit similar promises from the Queen by showing her that it had similar values—even if, as we have seen, Oxford was notably less devoted to humanism than was its sister institution.

Celebrations of Humanist Learning

Naturally, Oxford's 1566 pageants seek to display and celebrate these humanist values. One of the main ways that they do so is through the prominent use of Latin. At the Queen's entry, she heard Latin orations by Roger Marbeck and Thomas Kingsmill, while the scholars lining the streets cried out "Vivat Regina" in Latin. In the afternoons she observed formal disputations held in Latin, and in the evenings she attended Latin dramas like *Marcus Geminus* and

Progne. During the week, she was presented with special Latin books like Thomas Neale's *Topographica Delineatio,* a verbal and pictorial tour of Oxford's colleges. Finally, as the Queen moved through the actual streets of Oxford, she was surrounded by Latin (and some Greek) verses affixed to the walls and buildings. Though Latin occasionally appeared in the Queen's progress visits to other cities (like Norwich), Latin permeated almost every interaction between the university and the monarch at Oxford. In part, this was simply a way for the university to show its learnedness. As J. W. Binns explains, Latin was "a language of unquestioned prestige" in the period and "[t]he universities . . . [were] one of the focal points of the learned latinate culture of Elizabethan and Jacobean England."[130] Even though the typical Oxford student learned some Latin in grammar school, he devoted his first six terms to mastering Latin grammar and rhetoric.[131] "Essentially, he had to get his reading and speaking knowledge of Latin up to scratch," explains Brockliss, "so that he could follow lectures and take part in debates"—both of which were conducted in Latin.[132] Not only was Latin the language of academic pursuits, students were also required to use Latin when conversing in the dining hall.[133] Thus, the fulsome display of Latin in the 1566 entertainments did reflect institutional realities, but it also served as an indicator of a thriving humanist culture. As Binns explains, "renaissance Latin" was recognizably different from its medieval predecessor in its "greater conformity to classical style, vocabulary, syntax, and usage."[134] In England, this type of Latin emerged circa 1540 and was held in particular esteem at court. The many Latin works produced in this vein can thus be seen, at least in part, as "a manifestation of renaissance humanism." The Latin forms that Oxford featured in its entertainments are meant to illustrate this point, as the particular types of poetry, oration, and drama that we find are all "accoutrements of the emerging humanist culture."

Plays were a particularly prominent part of the week, as theatrical performances were held on four of the six nights that the Queen spent in Oxford. Tobie Matthew's Roman history play *Marcus Geminus* was acted on Sunday. Monday and Wednesday featured parts one and two of Richard Edwards's *Palamon and Arcite,* an English play based on Chaucer's "The Knight's Tale." Finally, on Thursday night, James Calfhill's Latin tragedy *Progne* was performed.[135] All three plays were staged in Christ Church hall—the largest hall in Oxford—which had been temporarily transformed into a theater, complete with stage, tiring houses, and "balconies," "platforms," and "benches" for the spectators (*JN1,* 644). Each night, the hall was filled to capacity with "an infinite and innumerable crowd" of courtly visitors and college officials—so much so that a wall collapsed on Monday night—and the plays lasted until midnight (*JN1*, 647).[136] They were, it seems, a rousing success.

Oxford's investment in theatrical entertainment is not surprising, since the university had a strong tradition of play-acting to draw from. Regular dramatic performances began in the reign of Henry VIII, and by 1566 there is "evidence of a flourishing dramatic tradition" at a number of different colleges.[137] The plays were largely classically inspired Latin dramas, which replaced the medieval interlude (which featured more of a religious focus) over the course of the sixteenth century.[138] At Oxford and Cambridge, these plays were written by, acted by, and largely performed for members of the university community. In fact, Anglo-Latin drama came to be associated almost exclusively with the universities. One of the reasons that Oxford cultivated academic drama is that it was seen as a valuable part of students' rhetorical training in Latin.[139]

In the context of the royal visit, these Latin dramas had many functions. First and foremost, they were meant to entertain their learned visitors. They were also a way of "display[ing] the learning of Oxford's scholars."[140] Not only did the plays show off the student performers' subtle command of Latin, all three playwrights (Matthew, Edwards, and Calfhill) were also contemporary Oxford graduates.[141] Since some of "the Cambridge plays included works by ancient authors . . . [t]his may have been a way of distinguishing the 1566 entertainments from those of 1564 and of suggesting that Oxford was home to native talent comparable with that of the ancients."[142] These Latin plays can also be seen as an expression of the new learning. James McConica says that "the humanist influence was nowhere more strongly felt than here."[143] Plays like *Marcus Geminus* and *Progne* exemplify the humanist conviction that the stories and modes of classical literature might serve as models for engaging with and thinking through contemporary issues. Bereblock's reflection on *Progne* illustrates this approach: "In its wicked actions, the play was an outstanding likeness of the human race, and for the spectators it was, so to speak, an outstanding fable of everyone who indulges too much in love or anger" (*JN1*, 663). Though such drama was not a formal part of the curriculum or a daily academic pursuit, it was nonetheless a part of academic life that Oxford could magnify in order to demonstrate its humanist sympathies.

Another prominent humanist mode of the 1566 entertainments is the declamation. In general terms, a declamation is simply a formal oration. During the Queen's entry into Oxford, she listened patiently to no fewer than five such speeches and was handed written copies of two others.[144] However, these addresses should not be viewed simply as welcome speeches. In fact, they belong to a special genre that was carefully cultivated at Elizabethan Oxford. J. M. Fletcher explains: "Renaissance educationalists were concerned to introduce into the universities one of the standard teaching devices of the orators of ancient Rome, the declamation. Following Quintilian, accepted by Erasmus as the model for all educational reformers, humanists saw the declamation as giving the student an opportunity to practice prose composition based on the standard, classical authorities, and to deliver elegant Latin speeches."[145] In 1566, the declamation was relatively new—it had entered Oxford via the Edwardian statutes—but it was now a formal part of the curriculum.[146] Bachelor students "declaimed" on Fridays, and there were both written and oral components to the exercise.[147] The formal speeches that figured so prominently during the Queen's visit—in her entry, departure, and throughout the week—should be seen as deliberate displays of this form of humanist pedagogy. Not only do these declamations adhere to the forms and rules of classical oratory, they also make frequent allusions to classical authors, events, and personages. The vast majority of these declamations are in Latin, though regius professors Giles Lawrence and Thomas Neale appropriately opt for Greek and Hebrew (respectively) in their addresses to the Queen. As with the plays, delivering sophisticated speeches in classical languages is another way to display learnedness to the royal visitors. Aside from this, they also underscored the connection between university education and rhetorical prowess. One of the reasons that Latin was still the universal language of learned people is that it "was then a more developed language than English, with a greater flexibility of syntax, and an ability to formulate concepts that Elizabethan English lacked . . . [it] was sharp and subtle, and had a ready-made vocabulary to hand."[148] In the sixteenth century, Latin was valued not only by clerics and academics, but also by the new class of secular elites who were just beginning to come to Oxford. They sought the pure, classicizing style as a marker of refinement but also as powerful tool for articulating, influencing, and persuading those around them; it was a means of fashioning their courtly careers. The orations delivered by Oxford scholars, bachelors, and professors are thus a way of demonstrating that an Oxford education cultivates these rhetorical arts at the highest level. The Queen's response to one of these declamations helps validate such a claim. Windsor records that Roger Marbeck's fifteen-minute Latin oration "was verie well lyked of her Majestie sayinge that shee had heard of hym before but nowe we knowe you / the Spanishe Embassador sayde *Hic non pauca multis, sed multa paucis complexus est.* [this man had not explained a few things in many words, but many in a few] The Quene gave hym her hande to kysse & so to the rest of the Doctors" (*JN1*, 471–72). The implication is that not only does polished, succinct Latin create a pleasing effect, it can also open doors for the skillful speaker.

The third humanist mode to feature prominently in the 1566 entertainments was Latin poetry. Accounts of the Queen's visit record that "the entrances and the outer approaches to the colleges were decorated with poems and there were a thousand renditions of the best verses fixed to all of their doors" (*JN1*, 643). The poems decorating Christ Church college and St. Mary's (the university church) garner particular mention. At the former, "Theare weare set vppon the Colledge gates, the haule dore & walls . . . dyvers verses in Lattyn & Greeke" (*JN1*, 474), while at the latter "theare weare dyvers sheetes of verses in Lattyn, Greeke, & Ebrewe sett vppon the doores & walles" (*JN1*, 478). It may well have appeared as though the entire college town was clothed in Latin verse. Nor were these poems merely visual embellishment, as Bereblock reports that the nobles "busied themselves in carefully scrutinizing them; they were wonderfully taken by reading them" (*JN1*, 643). The main subjects of these verses were expressions of praise, good will, and devotion to the visiting monarch (*JN1*, 532, 643), though other verses tackled things like national history and local history and topography (*JN1*, 538). Since these verses were temporarily affixed throughout the city and therefore ephemeral, the Queen was also presented with volumes of bound poetry. According to Robinson, "Each college was said to have written a little book of Latin verses." In addition to describing the students' happiness in welcoming the Queen, the poems also describe the foundations of particular colleges and the "distinguished men who had been nurtured there" (*JN1*, 538). These poetic effusions compliment the Queen's learning and serve as another demonstration of Oxford's humanistic literary culture. Not only are the vast majority of these poems in Latin, they—like the orations—follow specific classical literary models. Some of the most common genres of Anglo-Latin renaissance poetry include acrostics, latticed verses, anagrams, chronograms, shape poems, palindromic verses, riddles, and echo verses.[149] Binns characterizes this type of verse as "public, versatile, formal, fluent, allusive and learned"; it commonly features "countless examples of virtuoso play upon words and letters."[150] Many of these same modes appear in a surviving volume of "verses and orations" that was likely a presentation copy in 1566.[151] In fact, Binns says that the volumes of poetry produced for royal visits to Cambridge and Oxford are among the most representative of Anglo-Latin verse, "where the contributors seem to vie with each other in their mastery of these devices."[152] As with the plays performed throughout the week, writing Latin poetry was not a formal part of the curriculum at Oxford; rather, it was an extension of the broader classical culture that was being cultivated there.

Together, the plays, orations, and poetry generated for the 1566 royal visit were meant to depict the university as a center of classical and humanist learning. In the dedication of his *Topographica Delineatio,* Thomas Neale says that "the University's inhabitants devote themselves to all liberal arts" (*JN1,* 504). But Neale is much more interested in imagining Oxford as the seat of the muses. The word "muse" occurs some nine times in the first thirty-one lines of the dialogue (e.g. Oxford is "the house / Dedicated to the Muses," Leicester is the "Leader of the Muses," and the different colleges are the "fifteen houses of the Muses"). Deriving from Greek mythology, the nine muses are associated with particular human endeavors: poetry (Calliope, Erato, Euterpe), drama (Melpomene, Thalia), music (Polyhymnia, Terpsichore), history (Clio), and astronomy (Urania). In aligning Oxford with the muses rather than with the traditional liberal arts fields (grammar, logic, rhetoric, arithmetic, geometry, music, astronomy), Neale is clearly emphasizing its humanist credentials rather than the fields that were the actual focus of its curriculum. It is another assertion to the visiting nobles that the university is the primary preserve of such learning and should be valued accordingly. Even the buildings of the university are depicted as evoking the magnificence of ancient Rome. Bereblock reports that the hall at Christ Church "had a gilded panelled ceiling, with a roof painted and arched on the inside, and you could say that it imitated the grandeur of the ancient Roman palace in its size and pride, a likeness of antiquity in its splendour" (*JN1,* 643–44). Similarly, the nave of St. Mary's was reconfigured for the disputations so that it appeared as "a huge, spacious, and splendid amphitheatre" (*JN1,* 649).

If part of the entertainments sought to dazzle the visitors with the splendor, beauty, and polish of *bonae literae,* other aspects sought to underscore the hard work and daily regimen that produced such an effect. Bereblock reported that on the Monday following the Queen's arrival, "we go back to the work we have neglected for one day, and pursue the studies we began" (*JN1,* 645).

Stephens also noted the business-as-usual approach, saying that morning lectures and debates "were [all] kept, during the Queenes maiesties aboade in Oxford, as otherwise in full terme" (*JN*1, 667). Of course, this was not an ordinary week at Oxford, and afternoon activities were in fact curtailed, but the point was to show the visitors what Oxford students and faculty did on a daily basis. Bereblock's account takes the reader through the daily schedule: prayer at "an appropriately early hour," then "private" lectures in the colleges and halls, followed by public lectures in Greek, Hebrew, theology, and ten other disciplines, and finally "the schools of rhetoric . . . resound with . . . dispute and debate" (*JN*1, 645–46). Bereblock's account also pauses to explain the practical benefits of each discipline that accrue to students. As a result of this regimen, "the young men have the opportunity to talk correctly through Grammar, to speak elaborately through Rhetoric, to argue incisively through Dialectic, to use numbers efficiently through Arithmetic" (*JN*1, 645). Such skills have an impact that go far beyond the university classroom. Bereblock continues: "We work hard in those subjects as young men, and in them we become used to cutting the difficult and thorny path of learning, beating down the torments of falsehood, shutting off the approach against deceit, setting up obstacles to error, and in the end opening up the way to greater things" (*JN*1, 645). Bereblock thus demonstrates the worthiness and practical application of these common university pursuits that nevertheless might be unfamiliar to many of the visitors. Indeed, Oxford probably adhered to its daily schedule so that the nobles could experience these activities firsthand. According to several accounts, many of the visitors—though not the Queen—attended "ordinary lectures" and "quodlibet debates" on Monday, Tuesday, Wednesday, and Thursday morning. For example, on Monday morning, Leicester accompanied the Spanish ambassador and "other dignitaries of the kingdom" to a lecture in the Divinity School and a debate in the philosophy schools (*JN*1, 533).

Formal Disputations

If these morning activities gave a taste of daily life at Oxford, it was the formal afternoon disputations that showcased the full payoff of a university education. These disputations were held on Tuesday, Wednesday, and Thursday afternoons in the university church of St. Mary's. That they were intended to be the centerpiece of each day's entertainment can be seen in the ceremonial splendor with which they were conducted, the length of time invested in them (four hours each day), and the full participation that they garnered (the Queen was in attendance for all twelve hours). Not surprisingly, they occupy a lot of space in the written accounts of the royal visit.[153] The disputes covered topics in some five different branches of learning: natural philosophy, moral philosophy, law, medicine, and divinity. By and large, these subjects relate to the upper faculties rather than the liberal arts or humanistic fields.[154] The disputations thus showed the specialization and expertise that an undergraduate education might lead to. The participants in these debates were not students but faculty and successful alumni. For instance, the eight disputants on Thursday (in medicine) included Robert Huicke, who had served as a physician to Henry VIII, Katherine Parr, and Edward VI; Thomas Francis, president of the College of Physicians; and Walter Bayley, Regius Professor of Medicine.[155] The debate participants were thus the very brightest and best intellectuals that Oxford had to offer. Both Robinson and Windsor make separate lists of the debate participants, indicating the central role that these distinguished men had in Oxford's reception of the Queen.

Overall, the disputations were less about showcasing individuals and more about demonstrating the admirable skills that were cultivated at the university. Formal disputes were actually an integral part of Oxford's curriculum. During their course of study, students had to participate in a prescribed number of disputations. Undergraduates had to complete one to two exercises *in parviso* and one to two *responsions in determination*.[156] Students who had earned bachelors had to "determine" the following Lent and later participate in both "Austin disputations" and "ordinary disputation" with other students and with faculty.[157] At Tudor Oxford, disputations were regularly held on Monday, Tuesday, Wednesday, and Saturday, so they were an almost daily occurrence.[158] Unlike the declamation, disputations were a traditional part of the medieval curriculum. One of the reasons they persisted is that they required students to combine and practice skills they had been developing separately. As Bereblock indicates above, the disputants would need to "talk correctly" (grammar), "speak elaborately" (rhetoric), "argue incisively" (dialectice), and "use numbers efficiently" (arithmetic) in order to be successful. Making these disputations the centerpiece of the Queen's visit was thus a way of showing all of these different fields operating in harmony. Further, the participating doctors and masters demonstrated how these skills might be applied to practical, real-world questions. The ten questions proposed over the course of these

three days ranged from whether or not "the moon is the cause of incoming
and outgoing tide of the sea" (natural philosophy) to "foods that take long to
digest are preferable to those that are easily digested" (medicine), to "a private
citizen is not allowed to take up arms against the prince, even if he be unjust"
(divinity).[159] Such a broad—and pragmatic—range of application shows how
academic learning can penetrate into every part of life.

Furthermore, these disputations, though they were meant to illustrate the
value of typical, daily pursuits at Oxford, were also heightened in almost every
way. First, the physical setting of the debates was an important part of their
effect. Disputations were typically held in the rather pedestrian building of the
Public Schools, but for the royal visit they were moved to St. Mary the Virgin,
the "official University church from the mid-thirteenth century."[160] This was
the university's "main meeting place," where congregation sat, degree ceremonies were held, and a law court convened.[161] It was also an impressive
building with a magnificent steeple, a newly refurbished nave, a stone pulpit,
and beautiful stained glass windows.[162] The great west window "depicted the
apocryphal early history of the university . . . and its various scholarly grades
and activities."[163] Overall, the space was a physical emblem of the university's
history, authority, and vitality, and it was thus an especially fitting venue for
these disputations.

Moreover, St. Mary's had been specially outfitted for the occasion: "among
the church's columns a huge, spacious, and splendid amphitheatre had . . .
been constructed" (*JN1*, 649). In part, this involved structural alterations in
order to accommodate as many onlookers as possible. Bereblock refers specifically to the many platforms, partitions, stalls, benches, and stools that were
built to create a "vast circle and long enclosure" of seating around the disputants, who were positioned in the center of the nave (*JN1*, 649). These
enclosures differed in elevation, so that "the honoured and more distinguished
men and women could look down most comfortably on the public competi-
tions from their higher vantage point" (*JN1*, 649). These distinctions in rank
were also indicated on the university level, with separate enclosures for the
proctors, doctors, masters, bachelors, and younger scholars. Pains were also
taken to "add majesty to the place" via precious wall hangings and special seats
for the Queen and Chancellor. Elizabeth's seat—located "in the middle of the
platform, in an elevated place"—was "upholstered . . . in gold" and "decorated with precious coverlets" (*JN1*, 649). Leicester's seat—on the south side
of the nave—was "covered in scarlet silk in triumphal manner" (*JN1*, 649).

Together, these additions to St. Mary's made an already impressive space seem even more harmonious, hierarchical, and ornate—"something splendid and magnificent to the onlookers" (*JN1*, 649). It was thus an ideal space for showcasing the spectacle of learning.

Indeed, the disputations were highly performative. Bereblock repeatedly refers to the ecclesiastical space of St. Mary's as a "theatre" and treats the events as intellectual drama rather than dry academic exercises. After describing the splendid setting, Bereblock suddenly launches into the debate proper: "And while everyone's eyes were trained on the figures of the doctors, with close concentration and fixed attention, all at once [Edmund] Campion stepped forward to the respondent's platform, distinguished by his composed expression and movement, and by his handsome costume" (*JN1*, 649–50). Here and elsewhere, Bereblock registers the participants' facial expressions, movements, and attire—and their dramatic effect on the spectators. In fact, Bereblock frequently depicts the debaters as military combatants. Thus, after the proctors "gave the verbal cue for battle," Campion's argument was "strenuously contradicted by [John] Day, who . . . drove hard at, struck, and closed upon his opponent like an assailant, by bringing forward ideas, questioning, and arguing; but he fought with an armed and well-prepared man who could not be easily conquered either by a sudden and fortuitous argument nor by a long and careful speech" (*JN1*, 650–51). After having his say, Day "reluctantly withdrew from combat," to be succeeded by John Meyrick, "as deputy in that task," Richard Bristow, "[who] took up the responsibility and consideration of battle," and Adam Squire, who was "substituted in that same fight" (*JN1*, 651). Even though Campion, Day, Meyrick, Bristow, and Squire were merely debating questions in natural philosophy, they are described as heroic participants in battle. This sort of military metaphor, imagery, and diction continues throughout the account, as the participants "accost," "attack," "strive," "displace," "overthrow," "launch into," and "heap" arguments onto the heads of their respondents (*JN1*, 652–58).

Such depictions not only serve to make the narrative more dramatic and entertaining, they also implicitly address concerns about whether or not such intellectual pursuits are really the proper focus of the nobility and gentry. As we have seen, the nobility had traditionally prioritized the study of military arts over humane letters. Yet Neale's *Topographica Delineatio* has Leicester declare, "It is no less glorious to have governed learning than war, / Both the name of Leader and that of Earl gives me pleasure" (*JN*1, 505). Similarly, Bereblock's account of the disputations is an attempt to put humanist learning on equal footing with martial skill. It does so not by imagining learning as a worthy alternative, but by imagining it as a form of heroic combat. By casting debate in terms of the language and tropes of martial valor, Bereblock suggests that intellectual combat requires the same sort of dexterity, fortitude, and strength as actual battle. It is not unlike Milton's later depiction of intellectual heroism in *Areopagitica*.

Along the way, Bereblock sets up particular individuals as models of intellectual prowess. In Tuesday's debate, it is John Wolley who shows that "nothing is so complex that a philosophically minded man cannot explain it, for so great was Wolley's memory, so great the scope of his attentive care, and almost incredible his consideration of these matters that he could not only reply most suitably to individual questions, but could also comprehensively perceive all objections, judge as he examined, refute as he judged, contradict, and dispel" (*JN*1, 652). Later, Bereblock offers intellectual portraits of Thomas White (*JN*1, 654), Walter Bayley (*JN*1, 658), and Laurence Humphrey (*JN*1, 659). In each case, Bereblock draws attention to the difficulty of their argumentative tasks and celebrates the energy and skill they display. Overall, the pursuit of learning is portrayed not as a retiring, bookish activity but as an active, demanding, dignified, worthy, and heroic quest that has practical applications to many areas of life (and to the state). Within the week-long entertainments, the disputations functioned as a way of demonstrating and justifying the intellectual life and fruits of the university.

At the end of the third and final day of debates, the Queen publicly endorsed this display of learning. After the final question in divinity had been disputed, she rose and delivered an oration—since silence might suggest that she "[held] our labors in contempt and scorn"—to the assembled participants, university members, courtiers, councillors, and other spectators. It is a brilliant, self-deprecating speech in which she bemoans her lack of learning in the form of a spontaneous Latin oration. Nevertheless, the oration affirms the particular vision of learning that Oxford had been laboring to construct. "I praise and think highly of you, who are adorned with all kinds of learning," extols the Queen (*JN*1, 486). She seems to have *bonae literae* in mind, since she uses that particular phrase in referring to her own share in such learning.[164] She also affirms that this type of learning is no mere ornament: "I believe that now I understand the usefulness of learning better" (*JN*1, 487). The Queen draws attention to the value of the academic exercises that she has just witnessed and to the practical applications of such displays of rhetoric. In doing so, she praises a particular type of practical, humanist learning and then associates it firmly with Oxford. These remarks must have been gratifying to the university, as they reflected the same perception of learning that Oxford had been trying to fashion throughout the week. It is no wonder that Richard Stephens's account reports that the entire oration was "to the greate comfort and delectation of" the university (*JN*1, 670).

Elizabeth goes further by also endorsing the particular pedagogy offered by the university. Near the beginning of the oration, she laments the insufficiency of her own educational background. Even though "my father took care, and did so diligently, to bring me up in noble studies, and . . . in a variety of many languages," says Elizabeth, "In relation to my own erudition, I grieve" (*JN*1, 486–87). At other points, she refers to "my inadequacies" and "how clearly unskilled I am in learning" (*JN*1, 486). On the one hand, such self-effacing comments are hard to take at face value, but they might also be read as referring to differences between private tutoring and university education. Shenk draws attention to Elizabeth's focus here on the groups of people who educated her. Even though she praises her tutors, she blames herself for being "unable to make good use of her education."[165] Shenk reads this as attempt to sidestep religious controversy, insofar as it allows Elizabeth to claim the authority of her "Protestant schoolroom connections" while distancing herself from its radicalism.[166] The Queen uses an agricultural metaphor to make her point: "I have applied my effort for some time . . . in learning; however, my teachers have put their effort into barren and unfruitful ground, so that I am not able to . . . show fruit worthy either of my worth or of their labors or of your expectation."[167] Elizabeth seems to imply that the methodology was not as successful as it might have been. Despite the time and effort of both the young princess and her tutors, the results were limited. In contrast, she praises the university for its superior learning: "I have seen many things, I have heard many things, and I have thought highly of everything" (*JN*1, 486). What she had seen and heard throughout the week were the academic forms and exercises associated with university education at Oxford—not only disputations, but lectures, declamations, plays, and poetic creations. These activities were more formal, more active, and more *corporate* than those practices provided by private tutoring, and hence have the potential to bear more robust fruit.

Financial Appeals

During the 1566 visit, Oxford not only sought to convince the Queen and her entourage of the value of university education, it also attempted to garner the active support of its audience. One of its main goals was to inspire financial patronage. Of course, the prospect of an educational institution seeking monetary support from the state is hardly unusual, but, as we have seen, Oxford faced particular financial challenges in the sixteenth century. Early in her reign, the Queen had actually created some of these challenges through "forced exchanges of property" with the Crown, though this policy was discontinued within a few years.[168] Nevertheless, neither university nor college finances allowed for large-scale building projects in the second half of the sixteenth century.[169] Meanwhile, as we have also seen, college enrollments were increasing and most of the available post-Reformation space and buildings had been absorbed by the 1560s.[170] Colleges were now looking to improve their physical fabric in order to attract and cater to the incoming elite. To be sure, Oxford could boast some grandeur—the splendors of Christ Church and Magdalen come to mind—but on the whole it was a far cry from the architectural "mecca" that it would become over the course of the seventeenth century.[171] Before the building boom commenced in the 1590s, many of Oxford's buildings might be described as cramped and "dark, low-ceilinged late medieval buildings often in need of repair."[172] Although some modernizations to interiors were underway—especially with regards to halls, chapels, and lodging quarters—more extensive building projects would require wealthy benefactors.[173]

Traditionally, Oxford had relied on the beneficence of wealthy clerics to found and improve its colleges. Eleven of Oxford's twelve pre-Reformation colleges were founded by clergymen, including the three early sixteenth-century foundations: Brasenose (1513), Corpus Christi (1516), and Cardinal Colleges (1529).[174] The clergy were natural patrons of learning, since they were educated at and typically maintained close ties to the universities, but in the post-Reformation landscape, clerics were both less wealthy and less powerful. Felicity Heal has shown that the real wealth of the episcopacy eroded considerably over the course of the sixteenth century.[175] The clergy also had less political clout. Unlike her predecessors, Elizabeth did not appoint a single cleric to her Privy Council throughout her reign. The leaders of the English Church still maintained close connections to the universities, but by

Elizabeth's reign they were far more likely to bequeath books and manuscripts to college libraries than to found colleges or finance buildings.[176]

The founding of the three most recent Oxford colleges showed that different patterns of patronage were emerging. In 1546, Wolsey's Cardinal College was refounded by Henry VIII as Christ Church. Meanwhile, Trinity (1556) and St. John's Colleges (1557) were established by Sir Thomas Pope and Sir Thomas White, respectively. Pope was an administrator and chancery official, while White was a wealthy merchant who was twice Lord Mayor of London. By the 1560s it seemed that royal and lay patronage had replaced clerical benefactors, and that Oxford would need to look to the Crown and the secular elite for the support it needed.[177] Oxford's leaders were no doubt buoyed by the promises—recorded in Hartwell's *Regina Literata* (1565)—that the Queen had given to Cambridge only two years earlier. As noted previously, Elizabeth had asserted her desire to leave behind "some famous and noteworthy work," whether in erecting a "sumptuous edifice" or founding a college.[178] Oxford was understandably keen to secure a similar promise.

How would it go about broaching the subject? One of the main vehicles was the orations that were ostensibly meant to praise and welcome the Queen. For example, when the Queen arrived at her lodging at Christ Church, Thomas Kingsmill recounted the "generous endowments" and "distinguished privileges" proffered by past monarchs, including Edward III, Richard III, Henry IV, and Henry VII (*JN1, 585*). Kingsmill lingered particularly on what Elizabeth's father (Henry VIII), brother (Edward VI), and sister (Mary) had done for the university. Later, at the Queen's departure, she was addressed in a similar vein by Roger Marbeck. He first thanks her for "our privileges, acquired from your ancestors, increased by your most noble father, continued by your sweetest brother, [and] reinforced by your most renowned sister, and maintained by your distinguished Majesty," before reflecting that "you might think it a small favour compared with what your most venerable mind perhaps plans to bestow in future for the immortal memory of your name" (*JN1, 611*). Marbeck clearly has in mind the Queen's earlier words at Cambridge and is eager to include Oxford within their scope. Both Kingsmill and Marbeck look to establish a tradition of royal patronage at Oxford and then invite the Queen to participate by doing something beneficial for Oxford. That this same pitch occurs both at her entry and departure is a nice way of bookending the visit and underscoring this key theme.

The most detailed and concrete appeal for financial largesse comes from a beautifully illustrated book that was given to the Queen on Thursday as she was en route to the final day of disputations. This book, the above-mentioned *Topographica Delineatio,* was presented by its author, Thomas Neale, Regius Professor of Hebrew.[179] The book is a verbal tour of the buildings of Oxford in Latin verse, contained within a fictional dialogue between Queen Elizabeth and the Earl of Leicester. There are also separate drawings—executed by John Bereblock, fellow of Exeter College—of each of the fifteen colleges, and depictions of the university's Divinity School and Public Schools buildings. Louise Durning's description reveals that the volume is a rich and complex collaboration; not only is it a fruitful mix of verbal and visual rhetoric, it also draws from the contemporary genres of dialogue, emblem book, and chorographic portrait.[180] It is also, I will argue, a carefully calculated appeal for financial beneficence. This purpose is partially masked by the dialogue format, which makes it appear that the insights arrive from the two progress visitors—the Queen and Leicester—rather than as a persuasive document put forward by the university.

In the six lines of Latin verse that Leicester uses to introduce each college to the Queen, he focuses on very specific categories of information: the name of the college, its founder, and the reign in which it was established. For instance, the verses for Oriel College are:

> . . . . Oriel stands as the seventh home
> Of the Muses, O, truly it is called a royal house.
> Venerable in age, those times of Edward witnessed it,
> The king who was the second of that name.
> A certain Adam with the surname Browne built it,
> And he offered its fame to his king. (*JN*1, 506)

Each entry also includes a two- to three-line prose caption beneath the verses. Thus, for Oriel: "Established under Edward II by Master Adam Browne. Almoner of the same Edward, in the year of Our Lord 1323." Sometimes the entry offers additional information about a college's location, buildings, or enrollment, but the founding and founders are always included. Durning notes this emphasis on patronage and goes so far as to characterize the description as "a moralized history, in which each college founder . . . is eulogized as an exemplar of beneficent patronage directed to the advancement of learning."[181]

The college entries do more than just name the founders; they also foreground different aspects related to their foundings. For Lincoln and Queen's, we are given insights into the motives of the founders. In several cases, we are told that the name of the college reflects the particular ideals or values of the founder (such as for Magdalen, All Souls, Trinity, and St. John's). At Exeter, the college name reflects the geographical connections of founder Walter Stapeldon, Bishop of Exeter.[182] Several of the descriptions refer directly to financial aspects of founding: the "wealth, "expense," and "riches" of benefactors are mentioned in relation to St. John's, Christ Church, Corpus Christi, All Souls, Queen's, Brasenose, and Trinity. In other words, there is a thoroughgoing focus on different aspects related to the founding of a college. The entries seem to reflect the hope that the Queen herself might be inspired to found a college at Oxford. Again, the example of Henry VIII looms large, with Christ Church given pride of place in the verbal tour of colleges. Neale has Leicester's character remind the Queen that it had "your father, as patron," and that "it was begun at Thomas Wolsey's expense, / But increased thanks to the wealth of Henry your father" (JN1, 506). Neale also makes much of another supposedly royal foundation, Balliol College. The information that it was established by "John Balliol, born from royal stock" is repeated in the prose caption: "Established under Edward I by John Balliol, King of Scotland. In the year of Our Lord 1265" (JN1, 512). In fact, this "John de Balliol . . . was not . . . king of Scots: Neale confuses him with his fourth and youngest son, also named John de Balliol."[183] Nevertheless, this slippage suggests the extent to which Neale had attempted to establish past instances of royal patronage at Oxford.

Neale's text also casts a wide net in hopes of securing future patronage. For one thing, its organization draws attention to the recent shift from ecclesiastical to secular founders. Rather than allowing chronology or topography to determine the order in which the colleges are discussed, Neale first describes the twelve ecclesiastical foundations, concluding with the three secular foundations.[184] He also has the dialogue speakers consciously register this transition: After Leicester's description of the twelfth college (Exeter), the Queen's character enthusiastically proclaims, "Oh, how devout are the minds of prelates? O blessed age / Which produced such great men from the clergy" (JN1, 510). Leicester's character notes that many of the laity have also benefitted from these clerical foundations, and that they, too, have become actively involved in the propagation of learning.

"Go on, tell me," says the Queen, "how many we possess in the rank of the laity, / Who wished to increase the Muses through their own efforts here" (*JN*1, 511). Then follow the descriptions of Trinity, Balliol, and St. John's. This shift reflects the historical trend that we have already noted, and underscores Oxford's interest in attracting new lay patrons.

In response to the Queen's request to know more about lay patronage, Neale has Leicester single out William Petre as a model of recent beneficence. Petre was a lawyer and former secretary of state who had "endowed seven fellowships at Exeter College in 1566 . . . and consequently gained a reputation as the College's second founder."[185] In the Exeter section of the *Topographica Delineatio,* he shares the limelight with Exeter's early fourteenth-century founder: Walter Stapeldon, Bishop of Exeter. Here, Leicester praises him warmly to the Queen and lauds his contributions to Oxford as a way of giving back to the communities that nurtured him: "Devon your homeland boasts to have produced you, and this city / Rejoices to have educated you with its learning. / And so, thankful for your wealth to both parents, / You give helping hands to both" (*JN*1, 511). Petre's augmentation of Exeter is imagined as a fit legacy and sign of Petre's "glorious" virtue. In singling out Petre, Neale hopes to inspire and instruct others to follow in his footsteps. As Durning remarks, Petre is "presented as the exemplar of the desired moral effect of the dialogue . . . The collective encomium, or praise, of the founders of the past, is an exhortation to future action."[186] Neale's portrayals of the foundations of Oriel College and Queen's College are a reminder that future colleges might also be founded by courtiers as a way of honoring Queen Elizabeth. In the case of the latter, Robert Eglesfield founded Queen's College "as a gift to his Queen" and thus "named this after you (distinguished Philippa)" (*JN*1, 508–9).

The examples of Petre and Eglesfield provide clear models for potential lay patrons to follow. Or, since Queen Elizabeth is the primary recipient of Neale's book, it may be that Neale is appealing to her to help facilitate and arrange lay patronage. Since she expected "public benefaction" from those who received her royal favor, perhaps she might promote university patronage among the wealthy, ambitious, and powerful who gathered at her court.[187] Doing so, suggests Neale, would redound to her glory as well as theirs. Petre's actions, the Queen is told, are "distinguished under your reign, Elizabeth" (*JN*1, 511). Indeed, the prose caption for each college always associates the founder's benevolence with a particular reign. New College was "Established under Richard II by William of Wykeham"; all the other captions begin with the same formulation of "Established under _____ by _____." (*JN1*, 508). Whether or not that monarch actually had any role in the college's founding, he or she still receives some measure of credit. Thus, anything done for Oxford during Elizabeth's reign—regardless of her level of involvement—will reflect positively on her. The implication is that if the Queen did not intend to found a college, she could perhaps encourage others in her stead. Even though the royal entourage would only be in Oxford for a week, it is not a stretch to think that one of these visitors might found a new college. After all, Oxford had been the recipient of five new foundations in the previous fifty years, and those had been brought about by a range of people, including monarchs, clergy, wealthy merchants, and administrators.

I have been emphasizing the founding of colleges, but Neale's text also invites other forms of financial munificence. After the Christ Church entry, Neale has the Queen ask: "How has it come about that although that house could support more, / It is not full, and does not support its own members in all respects?" (*JN1*, 506). Neale's chancellor responds: "That house supports as many as its wealth is equal to keeping. / And would keep more if it increased through more property. / But the untimely death of your father, a death hated by the Muses, / Meant that there could be room here for more" (*JN1*, 506). Here, then, is a clear opportunity for strengthening Christ Church's endowment. Toward the end of the dialogue (in a section called "The Chancellor's Peroration"), Neale has Leicester recount Henry VIII's establishment of five regius professorships at Oxford in the 1540s. He then asks, "May you, his descendent, most similar to your father in quality and greatness, / Continue to support these with generous hand" (*JN1*, 516).

Far more than endowments and professorships, the *Topographica Delineatio* encourages support for new buildings. Neale's verbal tour of Oxford frequently mentions the architecture of both the university and its colleges. He refers to the "high towers" of New College, the "shining roofs" of Magdalen, the handsomeness of University College, and the "splendour" of Hart Hall (*JN1*, 507–9, 514). Neale reserves highest praise for the Divinity School and its spectacular fifteenth-century ceiling: "It rises up into boundless dimensions, with its turreted pinnacles, / Carved in beautiful marble, a four-cornered house. / Its radiant panelled ceilings glow, due to abundant candlelight, / And the stones hanging down gleam through the hand of the craftsmen" (*JN1*, 513). This emphasis on college architecture is heightened by Bereblock's accompanying drawings. Each one captures the main buildings of its college (gatehouse, hall, chapel, lodgings, towers, and so forth), typically clustered around an open quad. The drawings themselves have been referred to as "naïve or as deficient in perspective," and they are sometimes impaired by the plainness of the actual buildings.[188] Nevertheless, Bereblock uses an "additive" approach that creates composite and highly idealized depictions of each college. Durning asserts that the drawings are "visual encomia" that parallel "the literary praise of the founders" in verse; indeed, she sees each building as a "portrait" of its founder, with particular regard for their virtues of "piety and munificence." As such, buildings become another way that the Queen might create a lasting, visual legacy of her patronage.

As elsewhere, Neale offers a particular model that the Queen might follow. This time it is her own sister Mary and the newly renovated Public Schools building. The Public Schools were essentially the university's ten lecture rooms, with each room devoted specifically to the teaching of one of the seven liberal arts or three philosophies. The building had been constructed in 1440 but had become "badly decayed" by the 1550s, at which point it was remodeled during Mary's reign.[189] Neale has Leicester report that "Queen Mary was responsible for the expense, and donated it / So that you can witness these new schools. / Elizabeth, a sister worthy of your sister Mary, / On account of your devotion, you nurture those schools she donated. / So that equal thanks are given to either sister, / For one nurtures these schools which the other donated" (*JN*1, 513). Neale shrewdly makes Elizabeth a partner so that she is not eclipsed by her sister, but it is Mary who is "responsible" for the "donation." And yet Mary's role has also been amplified. For one thing, the buildings were only remodeled in the 1550s rather than rebuilt (as the verse suggests); in addition, the project was funded by "a grant of lands given by the Queen to the university in 1556."[190] Thus, Mary gave the land, but it was seemingly the university that chose to use the revenues for repairing the Public Schools. Neale makes Mary's role seem more active and more dramatic, and he also ties her patronage to a specific building project. In doing so, he creates a concrete model of royal architectural patronage that Elizabeth (perhaps through a dash of sibling rivalry) might be induced to follow.

Oxford's appeal was not only to the Queen to support new building projects; it also targeted the courtiers and councilors in her train. As far as we know, none of them received a book like Neale's *Topographica*. Instead, they were given first-hand experience of the university and its buildings. As at Cambridge, the nobles were lodged in individual colleges. Many of the most prominent men stayed at Christ Church, including Leicester, Cecil, Parr, Warwick, Howard, Throckmorton, Strange, and Oxford.[191] This meant that the visitors got to know one particular college quite intimately; not only did they live in their rooms for a week, they would also likely have dined in the college hall and worshipped in its chapel. University leaders were keen to expose the guests to other colleges as well. During the morning hours, "it was habitual and usual for our Chancellor . . . to lead the ambassador of King Philip of Spain . . . and other of the Queen's noble dignitaries to all of our colleges or at least to the more eminent ones" (*JN1*, 646). Nicholas Robinson provides a detailed account of the Tuesday morning itinerary, which included visits to Merton, Corpus Christi, Oriel, All Souls, University, and Magdalen (*JN1*, 534). At these stops, the delegation was greeted warmly by welcome speeches and then given a tour of the facilities—including halls, gates, libraries, chapels, and gardens. On other days, the visitors attended lectures, sermons, and disputations at various colleges, at the Divinity School, and at the Public Schools.[192] On Wednesday, the Privy Council dined at Magdalen College (*JN1*, 482). The Queen did not participate in these outings, but the members of her entourage must have attained a degree of first-hand familiarity with the physical fabric of the university.

From Oxford's perspective, these excursions helped fill the time and enabled the hosts to entertain and impress their distinguished guests. They may also have been hoping for noble patronage of the sort that Magdalen College, Cambridge had secured in 1564. During that progress visit, "Thomas Howard, Duke of Norfolk, subsequently agreed to give Magdalene forty pounds a year 'till they had builded the quadrant of their College' and promised that 'he would endow them with land for the encrease of their number and studys.'"[193] A 1556 welcome speech delivered to Cecil and Leicester (as chancellors of the two universities) makes this appeal directly: "You will not be unaware of that golden phrase of the Emperor Augustus: I received a Rome of bricks, I am leaving behind a Rome of marble. You should do similarly, and ensure . . . that we have Universities no longer small but very great, no longer average but most flourishing" (*JN1*, 589).

Throughout the week, Christ Church functioned as an example of what such improvements might look like. It was the most magnificent of all of the Oxford colleges. Founded as Cardinal College in 1525, it was Wolsey's inten-

tion for it "to outstrip any other in Oxford and Cambridge in size, architectural grandeur, and academic achievement."[194] For four years, Wolsey poured
money and resources into its construction. Everything was on a palatial scale.
The main quadrangle was 264 by 261 feet, easily the largest in Oxford.[195]
On the south side of the quad, Wolsey installed a "vast and magnificent" hall,
"lit by large Perpendicular traceried windows, separated by pinnacled but-
tresses."[196] Inside, a splendid hammer-beam roof spanned the enormous space
of 115 by 40 feet—the largest at either university.[197] Meanwhile, the college
entrance was an "imposing" two-story gate with flanking turrets and huge
oak doors.[198] It presented a "dramatic skyline of heraldic carvings and battle-
ments on the street front."[199] Even the domestic ranges exceeded other colleges: "The rooms are higher than those in the earlier colleges, and are lit by
square-headed windows with transoms, much larger than the normal collegiate two-light windows, and heated from the beginning by wall fireplaces: a
novel luxury."[200] Cardinal College gained additional prominence when, after
the fall of Wolsey in 1529, it was re-founded by Henry VIII as Christ Church
in 1546. This made it the only royal foundation at Oxford. Henry also chose to
attach three of the five newly created regius professorships to Christ Church.[201]
Mary's reign brought additional financial stability, as "she invested both money
and good will" at Christ Church.[202] In 1566, it remained the largest, wealthiest, and most splendid of the Oxford colleges. For all of these reasons, Christ
Church was chosen to host the Queen and the most prominent members of
her entourage. As a royal foundation, Christ Church naturally had a special
connection with the reigning monarch.[203] This also made the college a convenient setting for Oxford's attempt to encourage further royal beneficence—as
we have already seen in the orations of Kingsmill and Marbeck. Above all,
Christ Church embodied the splendor and magnificence that Oxford hoped
would impress its visitors. Even those not lodging there would have resorted
to Christ Church nightly for plays. They would have entered the magnificent
gate, traversed the spacious quad, and sat in the hall, which "imitated the grandeur of [an] ancient Roman palace in its size and pride" (JN1, 643).

Yet Christ Church was also an unfinished college. At the time of Wolsey's
fall in 1529, the chapel—which was to occupy the entire north side of the
central quad—had not been built. In addition, the gatehouse was incomplete
and the cloister—which was to border the outer perimeter of the quad—
had been barely begun. Nor were these projects completed in the succeeding
decades. Henry died only months after re-founding the college in 1546. After

that, a dearth of resources and students meant that the college made do with what had been completed.[204] No provision had yet been made for a library, so the old medieval refectory fulfilled that function up until the early seventeenth century.[205] But it wasn't just a case of Wolsey's intentions going quietly unrealized; rather, Christ Church was quite obviously an unfinished college. There was a three-hundred-foot-long gap in the north side of the quad where the magnificent chapel was to have been built. In 1529, the footings were in place and the "first layer of decorative stonework evident"; these remnants were still visible well into the seventeenth century, when they were finally removed.[206] Meanwhile, on the three finished sides of the quad, Wolsey had made a start of installing the cloister, in the form of attaching vertical shafts and springers (to support the vault) to the inside walls.[207] These unfinished fragments are still visible today. These were not subtle architectural clues of what might have been, but prominent features that were frequently remarked on by contemporaries. In his account of the 1566 entertainments, Nicholas Robinson notes, "Three parts of this college are almost complete in their construction, but the fourth, that faces north, barely shows that its foundations have been established" (*JN1*, 531–32). In 1603, Sir Roger Wilbraham noted that "I surveyed the chiefest colleges. 1st Christ-church, which was meant to have been a famous monument, but never finished by the founder, Cardinal Wolsey: it was meant to a square of 8 score: 3 parts built, but the church not builded: there I saw the fairest hall with great church windows, and the largest kitchen I ever saw."[208] Wilbraham's reaction is revealing: Christ Church was certainly large, impressive, and among the "chiefest colleges," but it was also incomplete.

There is every indication that Christ Church wanted its distinguished guests to see both aspects. At the main gate into the college "wheare the Quene entred" were affixed "dyvers verses in Lattyn & Greeke," including one that Windsor singles out in his account: "Famous virgin, glory of the female sex, / ornament of your race, and Queen of the British people: / You are most welcome as you come to us, and you carry perfect joys, / As you enter the unfinished monuments of your father" (*JN1*, 474). The last line is particularly striking. The writer draws attention to—rather than glosses over—the incomplete state of the college. Bereblock's drawing of Christ Church in the *Topographica* also adopts this approach. He includes "fragments of the unfinished cloister, on the ground floor of the hall and lodging range."[209] This inclusion is remarkable in consideration of the idealizing and "additive" approach that he adopts elsewhere. The angle of the drawing is also odd. The view is from the missing north side of the quad so that the three completed sides are visible. However, this side angle contrasts with Bereblock's typical views from the fronts of the other colleges' entry gates, so it seems more of an awkward reminder of rather than an "editing out" of the incomplete side of Christ Church.[210] This strategy can be seen as part of Oxford's appeal for financial assistance. For much of the Queen's visit, the architectural splendor of Christ Church is emphasized, yet the visitors are also pointedly reminded that the college is unfinished and is thus crying out for completion. The verses on the college gate implore the Queen to be like her father and complete the monument that he began.

Discouraging Outside Interference

In some ways, then, Oxford is keen to suggest how its visitors might play a role in improving the university. But in other ways, it seeks to fashion an image of self-sufficiency in order to discourage external intervention. Indeed, one of the overriding impressions given by these accounts is that Oxford is an orderly, disciplined, and hierarchical community. Bereblock's account of the Queen's entry emphasizes this deliberate effect: "When she arrived, behold, a new aspect, a new beauty in everything came into view. For everything broken and deteriorated had been repaired, the leaning had been straightened, the old restored, the collapsed rebuilt, even house walls, city walls, window-frames, doorposts, porches, doors, entrances, folding doors, pavements, and everything else seemed to gleam and rejoice at the Queen's arrival as if it had been newly clothed" (*JN*1, 639). The members of the university had been similarly refurbished and set off to good advantage. The scholars, bachelors, masters, and doctors were separately grouped along the entry route, their differing statuses indicated by special clothing and regalia. For instance, the doctors' "clothing, very tidy and decent, implied reverence and authority. For apart from the fact that they were resplendent in scarlet and silk, their more advanced nature and age . . . endowed them with . . . reputation and dignity" (*JN*1, 641). Bereblock's account emphasizes the pomp and ceremony of the entrance, and the gravity with which the university members played their part. As Keenan suggests, "this formalized welcome was intended to impress the monarch with the University's order and scholarship."[211] Hierarchical arrangement was a key feature, not only in the entry (and departure), but also in the carefully constructed seating partitions for the disputations and plays. These, too, "provided a visual display of social order."[212]

Of course, such orderly discipline was far from the daily reality at Oxford. Despite stringent university statutes, assault, defamation, and breaches of the peace were common among both undergraduates and senior members.[213] Indeed, Leicester himself frequently complained about university discipline, evincing "concern over general disorders within the university."[214] The chancellor particularly had fulminated against indecorum in public academic exercises—"negligence and slackness" in lectures and disputations—and the failure of university members to adhere to sumptuary laws.[215] That these complaints were consistent throughout Leicester's twenty-four-year tenure as chancellor suggests that his admonitions were not heeded. Indeed, "he laid the blame upon heads of colleges for their negligence and threatened to visit Oxford soon to see for himself the improvement that he wanted."[216]

Yet throughout the royal visit in 1566, Oxford shone in these very areas. As we have seen, the daily academic disputations were both formal and dignified. Meanwhile, university members dressed appropriately and impeccably. Bereblock remarks that during the visitors' departure, "The entire population of the University, equally distributed on either side of the street, stood most beautifully in the monarch's sight. There it was possible to judge from everyone's dress where each of us stood in status, rank, and honour" (*JN*1, 664). I would argue that Oxford projected an orderly image not just to make a good impression, but also to head off potential outside interference. Since the Queen was worried about religious conformity, Oxford presented itself as fully conforming. Even Laurence Humphrey, who had recently dug in his heels during the Vestiarian Controversy, was resplendent in his doctoral robes (to which the Queen sardonically quipped: "Me thinkes this gowne & habite becommethe you verie well & I mervayle that you ar so straighte laced in this poyntes but I come not nowe to chyde" [*JN*1, 472]). Even the elaborate dinners served to the guests were carefully qualified. Bereblock explained, "I do not wish here to discuss the distinguished preparation of meals or narrate lavish dinners; in this matter grandeur had mainly been considered, so that the dinners would be splendid, but some considerations had also been given to temperance and modesty, so that they should not fall into luxury" (*JN*1, 643). Naturally, the meals were to be lavish extensions of the grandeur that Oxford was trying to project, yet care was taken that they did not cross into intemperance and dissolution. In short, the university did not want to present itself in any light that might provoke oversight, policing, or micro-managing.

Instead, Oxford deployed rhetoric that highlighted its self-sufficiency. Roger Marbeck's departure oration depicts "a University flourishing in its assembly of most learned men . . . strong in its judgments, [and] abundant in its talents" (*JN*1, 610). Earlier in the day, the visitors had gotten a first-hand look at the smooth functioning of the university's internal governance. At dawn, a Convocation was summoned by the proctors and vice chancellor for the purpose of awarding honorary degrees to certain nobles. Then, at 9:00 a.m., a larger Congregation was held to ratify the honorary degrees and admit the noble recipients "by those to whom . . . the administration of our empire and the governance of the city were entrusted" (*JN*1, 664). Thus, the nobles got to see both legislative assemblies in action. And, of course, the carefully planned and smoothly executed events of the week—the entry, accommodations, meals, plays, disputations, and departure—were meant to serve as clear evidence that university leaders knew what they were doing.

Even the way that the entertainments praise Leicester can be seen through this lens. In multiple passages, the chancellor is lauded for his care and sufficiency. Thomas Cooper's welcome speech calls him "the head, root, soul, and life of our University," and says that through his "patronage the dignity of our academy at this time both strongly thrives and flourishes" (*JN*1, 577). Neale refers to him as the "Leader of the Muses" (*JN*1, 505) and the collection of colleges as his "duchy" (*JN*1, 515). Indeed, Durning identifies the praise of Leicester as an important sub-theme of the *Topographica*.[217] Such praise works on a number of different levels. First, it publicly affirms Leicester's leadership and cultivates his future good will and support. At the same time, it also offers subtle instruction. One of Leicester's biographers calls the *Topographica* "a clever piece of propaganda. By giving Leicester the role of defender of Oxford, Neale emphasizes his responsibilities as chancellor and patron of the university." The same approach is taken in the dedication for Cooper's 1565 Latin dictionary, in which Leicester is depicted as a "patron [who] zealously fosters their study and defends it in the royal council and by his authority."[218] In both cases, his primary role is imagined as a defender and a supporter rather than as a superintendent. Finally, by emphasizing Leicester's sufficiency as chancellor, Oxford is effectively discouraging the intervention of others—including the Crown.

At times, Oxford implies that not only does it not require interference, but that outsiders might not really be qualified to intervene. The entertainments do this by presenting Oxford as a highly specialized and rarified world unto itself. Constant references to Oxford's "learnedness" throughout the week contribute to this effect. Moreover, university learning is presented as a difficult and worthy pursuit: "To thrive in intelligence, and to speak many languages clearly is praiseworthy, and it is the outcome of hard work" (*JN*1, 610). University men are further dignified by being "adorned in their robes and scholarly insignia" (*JN*1, 545)—the symbols and pomp of learning. The vehicles for displaying their achievement—declamations, disputations, lectures, Latin plays and poetry—are highly specialized and particular to the university. The disputations are perhaps the fullest expression of the rarefied world of academics. They are highly ceremonial, governed by intricate rules, and extremely competitive. Lasting four hours per day for three days straight, they are also long and arduous. Those who excel in the disputations are portrayed as "heroic" precisely because of the high degree of difficulty. Thus, the goal of these disputes is not just to entertain, but to inspire awe and respect for academic exercises. Bereblock makes a point of recording how some of the welcome orations were received: "With their abundant and polished discourse, these speakers moved the visitors to great admiration for their wisdom and talent" (*JN*1, 646).

The Queen's Latin oration on Thursday shows how such admiration might grow into deference. When she is slow to respond, Bereblock attributes her hesitation to "Womanly shyness," "modesty," "lack [of] confidence," and "a certain noble bashfulness" (*JN*1, 660). A lot of this may have to do with feeling out of her element. Though she shares a love of learning with her hosts, she claims to be comparatively "unskilled . . . in learning," "an ignoramus to the erudite" (*JN*1, 486–87). As noted above, such self-effacement need not be taken at face value. But perhaps what Elizabeth means—given that the speech is being delivered immediately after the conclusion of the third day of disputations—is that she is not steeped in this sort of highly communal and competitive academic environment. In this case, her self-consciousness might be genuine. It may even be the effect that the university was hoping for. If it wanted the Queen and her entourage to admire Oxford, it may well have wanted them to feel a bit like outsiders so that they might adopt a more deferential approach.

Whether or not we take the Queen's words at face value, they do play into what Shenk describes as the leveling and democratizing implications of humanist learning. Elsewhere, the Queen did cultivate a learned persona, and she is repeatedly praised for her learnedness while at Oxford. She is a "learned and well-refined woman" (*JN*1, 592), and, in a rather curious image, we are told that "she does not drink in the Muses superficially, with the edge of her lips, / But swallow[s] books as if with wide-open mouth" (*JN*1, 599). Such praise is complimentary, but it also forges a set of shared values that Oxford can then exploit. As Shenk remarks, "The humanist paradigm presented the educated, absolutist prince with a double-edged sword. Educated status showcased royal authority, but it also threatened to diminish the monarch's exclusive right to that authority."[219] Since anyone might aspire to humanist learning, "education houses a potential to level hierarchies, and when Elizabeth claims a shared academic study with certain university men, the boundary between subject and monarch begins to blur."[220] I would argue that in 1566 Oxford takes this dynamic a step further by then appropriating some of this learned authority for itself. The disputation participants actually debate some of the political principles on which the Queen's authority rests, including whether or not "a prince should be declared by succession [rather than] elections," and if "a private citizen is . . . allowed to take up arms against the prince . . . if he be unjust" (*JN*1, 479, 484). Though the debaters afterward protested that "circumstance, not conviction" dictated some of their otherwise seditious arguments, they still participated in intellectually probing the limits of monarchical authority (*JN*1, 486).[221] In doing so, they also ratified the idea that the theoretical exploration of such questions falls within the purview of the university. By putting the Queen in the role of spectator, the university exalted her as a privileged observer, but it also made her something of an outsider. This seems like a different dynamic than we encounter in some other civic pageants, where the monarch is simply put on a pedestal. The Queen seemed to realize this, because when she returned to Oxford in 1592, she actually cancelled the academic disputes that had been prepared for her. Instead, she gave an oration in which she praises "love [for the sovereign] over learning" and "chastens [university men] 'not to go before the laws but to follow them, nor dispute whether better ones could be prescribed.'"[222] In doing so, the Queen attempts to reclaim the learned authority that she had been partially excluded from in 1566 as her exclusive domain.[223]

The final way that Oxford presents itself as a rarefied world is by drawing attention to the university's special privileges and liberties. The point here is that Oxford is not just a separate realm by virtue of its intellectual pursuits, but that it is also legally set apart. As we have seen, the university began accumulating commercial, legal, and judicial privileges in the Middle Ages. Many of these had come at the expense of the town and had been successfully reasserted after the Reformation (despite a reinvigorated town government). These hard-earned privileges were highlighted at various points throughout the week. During the royal entry, the university delegation met the Queen "at the vttermoste parte of the Vniversitie liberties . . . 2 myles from Oxford" (*JN*1, 471). A full mile later, the monarch was met and greeted by the mayor. Similarly, during the departure, the mayor bid adieu at the far end of Magdalen Bridge, "wheare their liberties endethe," whereas university officials accompanied the Queen "even to Shotover, a myle & somewhat more owte of Oxford wheare the Quene vnderstandinge by the Earle of Leycester . . . that the Vniversitie Liberties ended theare" (*JN*1, 489). In other words, great pains were taken to underscore that Oxford's liberties were both separate from and greater than the town's. The orations given by Kingsmill and Marbeck recount the legal privileges granted and maintained by successive monarchs.

Honorary Degrees

While emphasizing Oxford's separateness, the entertainments also formally invited some of the most prominent nobles to become a part of the university. As noted above, the final morning of the royal visit featured the dispensing of honorary master's degrees to thirteen of the visiting dignitaries.[224] This gesture involved a special ceremony—held at both St. Mary's Church and Christ Church hall—and a formal oath-taking by the recipients. The whole ceremony served to highlight the authority and autonomy of the university. These rites dramatized the university as a separate realm that required special admission even as they extended an invitation of membership. The practice of granting honorary degrees had originated at Oxford in the 1470s as a way to increase the university's "own lustre" (via association with the great) and also "curr[y] favour with . . . the powerful at court."[225] Bereblock calls the thirteen honorary degrees "the greatest and surest indication of our goodwill" and "the University's most generous gifts" (*JN*1, 663). Whereas other royal progress venues might proffer gifts of money, plate, or alcohol, the highest honor that Oxford could bestow was a degree. Such a gift seeks to convey the dignity and importance of learning to an audience that by and large was not university-educated.

The degrees were indeed honorary, but they were also intended to impart ownership and responsibility. Both Windsor and Stephens record the oath taken by the recipients: "ad observandum statuta, libertates, Privilegia, & consuetudines huius universitatis [to observe the statutes, liberties, privileges, and customs of this University]" (*JN*1, 488). If this oath renders the nobles a part of the university, it also secures their support in acknowledging and safeguarding university privileges. As Binns puts it in describing an earlier moment at Cambridge in 1564: "the aristocrats who were given honorary degrees were also bound to its cause."[226]

The university seems to have deliberated carefully about who these thirteen recipients would be. The list was finalized early Friday morning by the vice chancellor, proctors, and heads of houses.[227] Later that morning, degrees were awarded to the earls of Oxford, Warwick, Rutland, and Ormond; the lords Howard, Strange, Sheffield, and Stafford; the knights Cecil, Rogers, Knollys, and Throckmorton; and, finally, John Tamworth, Keeper of the Privy Purse. We have seen that some twenty-six nobles were present at Oxford, so why were these thirteen men selected? Once again, what was done at Cambridge two years before seems to have played a role. Eight of the nobles who had been granted honorary degrees at Cambridge in 1564 were at Oxford in 1566. Oxford awarded degrees to six of those eight: Warwick, Oxford, Rutland, Cecil, Howard, and Knollys. The only two left out were Sussex and Leicester—though the latter was already chancellor and may even have been involved in determining the recipients. These six men might have been chosen because their existing affiliation with Cambridge and their presence at Oxford made them seem particularly likely to support university education. A degree from Oxford might also help foreclose the possibility that they would favor Cambridge over Oxford.

The thirteen recipients also represented a variety of different realms within which Oxford might want influence. Four were members of her majesty's Privy Council: Howard, Cecil, Knollys, and Rogers. Thus, they were ideally positioned to influence policy and protect Oxford's privileges in the political arena. As Principal Secretary, Cecil was especially important in this regard. Other recipients held influential positions in the Queen's household. Howard was Lord Chamberlain, Knollys was Vice Chamberlain, Rogers was Comptroller of the Household, and Tamworth was Keeper of the Privy Purse. Ambrose Dudley, Earl of Warwick, was Leicester's brother, though he may have been chosen primarily because of his military connections. Since he was a professional soldier (and Master of Ordnance), awarding him an honorary degree may have been a way of extending the point that learning and martial skill were not incompatible.

Not all recipients were chosen because of the influence that they currently wielded. The two youngest nobles were the earls of Oxford and Rutland, aged sixteen and seventeen, respectively. Both were awarded degrees, probably as an investment in the future. Even though they were not matriculating at Oxford, they were college-aged, so giving them Oxford degrees was a way of refashioning them into Oxford students. In the future it might be useful to Oxford for them to think of themselves this way. Other honorary degrees were an investment in the next generation. Seven men in the royal entourage had young sons, and six of these men were given honorary degrees: Howard, Strange, Sheffield, Stafford, Cecil, and Throckmorton. Awarding honorary degrees to these fathers might well influence them to someday send their sons to Oxford.

In speculating about these thirteen honorary degrees, I have simplified possible factors into political, domestic, military, and family categories. There is probably a complex combination of reasons for each man. For example, William Cecil was a natural choice because he was already sympathetic to university education, having studied at and sent his eldest son to Cambridge. As we have seen, he also wanted nobles to be required to send their sons to university. However, most of Cecil's ties were to Cambridge, where he had also been chancellor since 1559. Oxford was therefore eager to forge more formal connections with Cecil. As principal secretary, Cecil was the most powerful politician in the realm. Finally, Cecil was master of the Court of Wards, so he held great influence over the early lives of his young charges, including whether or where they attended university. For a variety of reasons, then, Cecil was an important ally for Oxford to cultivate.

Sir Francis Knollys was an equally calculated choice. He, too, was a proponent of education (as we have seen, he may have attended Magdalen College, Oxford, and he did send a son there in the 1950s). He also claimed near kinship to the Queen, was an officer in her household, and had been on the Privy Council since her accession in 1558. Knollys could also be a key local advocate for Oxford. He owned extensive property in the shire and from 1563 had served as High Steward of the town of Oxford—a position for which he "mediated quarrels with the University."[228] Finally, as of 1566, Knollys had six other sons under the age of twenty. For all these reasons, it is not surprising that the university distinguished him with an honorary degree.

Oxford used honorary degrees to not only honor these thirteen individuals, but also to enlist them as advocates and supporters. The degrees instantly gave these men a special connection to the university so that they might see themselves as participants in and furtherers of its educational mission. Just as with Leicester, who was praised as a "patron [who] zealously fosters their study and defends it in the royal council and by his authority," Oxford hoped to forge new connections that would bear similar fruit in the various realms of influence that each man commanded.[229]

Hands-Off Patronage

Oxford had a very specific model of patronage in mind for the new converts. This model was carefully constructed throughout the week in the university's interactions with both the Queen and the visiting nobles. One of its clearest expressions can be found in Thomas Neale's "The Image of Hebrew Learning," a ten-line poem that prefaces the main dialogue of the *Topographica Delineatio*. Neale had been named regius professor of Hebrew in 1559, so the poem is an expression of personal gratitude to his royal benefactor. The "image" in the poem's title refers to an accompanying depiction of a flourishing tree, which the verse then unpacks:

> Do you see how this tree flourishes when its roots are secure?
> How it is enriched by its leaves spreading here and there?
> The tree is an image of Hebrew learning, which rejoices to have
>   had its leaves enriched
> By your financial generosity, Elizabeth.[230]

The passage is dominated by references to monetary support; both the tree and its leaves are "enriched" by the Queen's "financial generosity." The final three lines also emphasize pecuniary matters:

> You, devout Elizabeth, water the roots.
> And so the tree brings forth this fruit appropriate to you,
> Cultivated (O greatest of Princes) by what you have spent.[231]

At the same time, the analogy of the tree makes this munificence both natural and organic. When Elizabeth waters the tree, strong roots, verdant leaves, and fruit result. The analogy also implies a certain kind of patronage that involves the Queen creating ideal conditions so that the tree can flourish. Monetary support is needed, but otherwise her gardening is pretty hands-off. It does not include the active binding, lopping, and uprooting required of Shakespeare's Richard II. Neale has the chancellor reinforce this sentiment in the final speech of the dialogue. If Elizabeth will "strive to moisten with abundant watering," then "God will grant increase" (*JN1*, 516).

This model of hands-off patronage is echoed and extended by other voices throughout the week. Bereblock refers to Elizabeth as "a second Minerva among the Muses" because she inspires, promotes, and protects learning (*JN1*, 640). Henry Bust celebrates her "goodwill toward learned men" and compares her to the Roman matron Cornelia, "the mother of the Gracchi brothers . . . [who] devoted herself to the education of her children" (*JN1*, 587–88).[232] Several speakers depict Elizabeth as a nurse and loving mother: "You are also the mother of learning, / You nurture and watch over liberal arts" (*JN1*, 598). These conceptions emphasize her care, devotion, and encouragement. Other portrayals are more forceful, imagining Elizabeth as an active "protectress of learning," a "guardian" who "looks after" and "defends" the university (*JN1*, 598, 665, 599, 596). All of these conceptions capture the Queen's vigilant care for the university, but they also imply a certain distance. Gardeners, mothers, nurses, and guardians are all benevolent figures, but they are chiefly concerned with the growth and development of their charges. They provide a measure of protection and stability so that learning and learned men can flourish on their own. Kingsmill points to the much wider actions that the Queen has taken: "Since truth lies revealed in the church, peace has been established in the state, and learning revived in the University, we may indeed enjoy some heavenly pleasure in our hearts, without any disaster, or fear of disaster" (*JN1*, 587). Even though the Queen has revived learning, it is not so much her heightened attention to Oxford as her creation of favorable external circumstances in church and state. Above all, she has created a bulwark of security. At the end of the *Topographica,* Neale includes a "Gratulatory Address and Poem."[233] In it, Neale asserts that through Elizabeth, the Lord has "established our borders with peace and removed all cruelty so that your people may live in security." As a result, "your people"—though Neale appears to have Oxford dons like himself in mind—"[have] established their minds in peace with interpretations of understandings to teach the knowledge they are delighted to possess." Neale seems to be describing some sort of academic freedom that allows for multiple interpretations and/or the free flow of knowledge. He then requests that the Queen will "continue now to show goodness to us daily and to give rest and quietness to our teachings." Again, Neale refers to a kind of tranquility generated by a lack of external disturbance. In this address, Neale suggests that the most beneficial thing the Queen can do is maintain such an outer

environment so that teaching and learning can go forward unimpeded. It is
not a call for the Queen's active or shaping involvement in the affairs of the
university.

In this section, I have focused mainly on the Queen, but Oxford seems
to envision a similar patron relationship with Leicester, Cecil, and the other
visiting nobles. As with the Queen, the university wants these dignitaries
to value Oxford as a seat of practical, humanist learning. It wants to forge
connections that will garner support for its educational mission. Above all,
Oxford wants financial backing, particularly in the form of college foundations, building projects, gifts of property, and endowments. The university
also solicits protection for its hard-won liberties and privileges (particularly
against town incursions). It wants friendly faces and policy advocates at court,
in the Privy Council, and in Parliament. It wants the professional advancement of its graduates. It also wants to increase the number of nobility sending
sons to the university, which would swell Oxford's coffers and also increase
its prestige. In other words, it hoped to turn the stream of such students in the
1560s into a flood.

But in trying to forge a closer connection and extract these benefits, Oxford
was also wary of increasing outside interference. The university did not want
to invite overly prescriptive oversight, religious scrutiny, interference with
self-governance, micro-managing of affairs, and undue lay influence. This is
why its leaders took such pains to present the university as a well-ordered place
with effective internal governance. To further discourage undue policing,
they depicted academia as a highly specialized and rarified world. Ultimately,
the 1566 entertainments posit a model of hands-off patronage that invites protection and largesse without interference. At the Queen's departure on Friday,
Bereblock records her final words as expressing that she "so cherished" the
university's words and deeds that "in her heart she would be much more ready
to lose her status or life than to set aside the guardianship of our life or the
memory of our name" (*JN1*, 665). These words—that she would remember
them and continue her guardianship—must have given Oxford hope that it
had largely hit the mark.

Epilogue

It is difficult to assess the long-term effectiveness of the university's carefully
crafted reception. Historians do see the royal visits to Cambridge in 1564 and

Oxford in 1566 as being integral in affirming the importance of university education to the Tudor state. Rosenberg goes so far as to call the visits the "launching of a royal campaign for the encouragement of learning at the universities."[234] If so, Oxford certainly did all it could to lend its cooperation and make this a joint venture. Keenan directly credits the Queen's symbolic support of Oxford with increased enrollments.[235] In the four decades following the Queen's visit, enrollment increased from around 1,764 to around 2,254.[236] There was an even more dramatic rise in the number of students who annually supplicated for degrees: from around 112 in 1566 to 150 in 1570.[237] Meanwhile, "both the number of matriculations and the number of men proceeding to the B.A. continued to increase throughout the reign."[238]

Oxford's entertainments were less successful in soliciting tangible financial benefits from the Queen. She never did follow through on her promise to sponsor "some famous and noteworthy work" at either Cambridge or Oxford. Indeed, her "staying away" from both institutions—she wouldn't visit Oxford again until 1592, and she never returned to Cambridge—may have been due to her "not hav[ing] wished to be reminded of her promised investment in the universities"[239] Perhaps she felt comfortable enough to eventually return to Oxford because she could boast of having done a little bit more there. In 1567, she had reconfirmed—and augmented—the university's privileges.[240] She also lent her name as a founder of the newly formed Jesus College in 1571.[241]

Oxford's pageants were perhaps more successful in eliciting a response from its noble visitors. As we have seen, one of Oxford's main goals was to convince these fathers of the value and importance of a university education so that they would send their sons to Oxford. This strategy paid dividends in at least three of the men who were given honorary degrees. Sir Nicholas Throckmorton's second son, Arthur, matriculated at Magdalen in 1571. Meanwhile, Lord Sheffield's son Edmund began his education at Christ Church in 1574. Finally, Lord Strange, who became the 4th Earl of Derby in 1572, sent all three of his sons to St. John's College in the early 1570s. Together, these prominent sons partook of—and also helped create—a larger trend, for it was in the 1570s that "the influx of upper-class boys . . . [began] in earnest" with the primary goal of "obtain[ing] the humanistic education now thought appropriate for their role as governors of the realm."[242]

In terms of building projects, the payoff was not quite so immediate. There was no new large-scale building at any of the colleges until the turn of the century. However, when expansion did come, it was clear that the colleges "needed outside help," usually relying on the largesse of heads of houses and wealthy alums.[243] The necessity of external funding also held true on the university level. For example, beginning in 1598, it was Sir Thomas Bodley—former diplomat and fellow of Merton College—who financed the extension of the divinity school and the university library that bears his name to this day.[244]

Meanwhile, Christ Church remained unfinished. The north side of the main quad was vacant until 1660. It was then developed in a style to match the other three earlier sides—including the insertion of pillar bases to take the cloister vault, though by then there was no intention of ever installing the cloister. Christ Church did continue to enjoy its associations of royal patronage, and in the 1640s it was chosen by Charles I as his Oxford home during the English Civil War.

Finally, the bigger question of outside interference. As discussed earlier, the trajectory was largely in the direction of increased royal and lay involvement in the university's affairs. In practice, the Queen typically stayed in the background and did not intervene directly; instead, she left the control of Oxford to its university officers and external delegates.[245] Those officers and delegates increased their authority over the course of the century. More and more power became concentrated in the hands of the vice chancellor and college heads, who were more answerable to the chancellor and the Crown. Meanwhile, Leicester's long and active tenure contributed significantly to the growing powers of the chancellor. As we have seen, secular officials, courtiers, and landowners also increased their influence—in the election of heads of houses, dispensing of fellowships, and even the disposal of college leases.

Yet Oxford still maintained some autonomy. Though Penry Williams refers to this period as "the University Subdued," he qualifies that "the impact of the governmental machinery . . . was not rapid," as "the colleges were sometimes capable of resisting encroachment" with "the university never entirely subservient."[246] Even at the end of Elizabeth's reign, Oxford was still in some sense—as it purported to be—a realm unto itself.

Nevertheless, it is hard to conclude that this part of Oxford's 1566 pitch was successful. The university was quite simply a victim of its own success. It had become so important as a recognized training ground for clergy, political office-seekers, and landed gentleman that it had to come under greater scrutiny and control of the Crown and ruling classes. In the end, Oxford could not quite have its cake and eat it, too. Heightened state control was simply the price it paid for its revival and unprecedented growth in the second half of the sixteenth century.

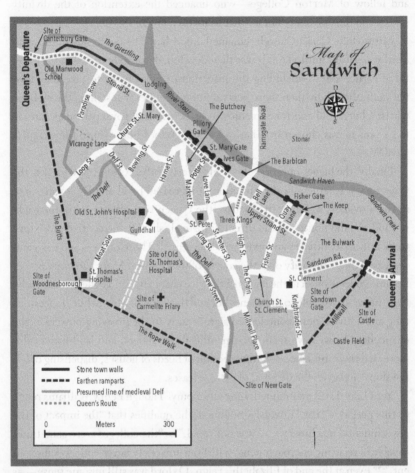

Map reproduced by Coni Porter. Reproduced from Helen Clarke's *Discover Medieval Sandwich: A Guide to Its History and Buildings* (Oxford: Oxbow Books, 2012).

CHAPTER TWO
SANDWICH, 1573

Within two years of the Oxford visit, Elizabeth's regime was enveloped in what one historian has referred to as the "crisis years" of 1568 to 1572.[1] This period featured mounting tensions with Spain in 1568, the arrival of Mary Stuart and the "conspiracy" to have her wed the Duke of Norfolk during 1568 to 1569, the Northern Rebellion of 1569, the Ridolfi plot in 1571, and the eventual execution of Norfolk in 1572. During these years, Elizabeth was naturally cautious. Though she did continue her progresses unabated, the Queen tended to remain close to London.[2] By 1573, however, things had stabilized and she "confidently embarked on the long, elaborate, memorable progresses of the 1570s."[3] In that year, the Queen set out on a seventy-two-day trip through the county of Kent. It was a savvy choice, as Kent was still relatively close to London, and even if the clouds of internal rebellion had been dispersed, there was still a very real fear of foreign invasion. One of the main components of the 1571 Ridolfi plot had been "an invasion of England by the Duke of Alba with papal backing."[4] Even though that particular plot had been thwarted, a formidable Spanish army was still just across the sea in the Low Countries, and the political situation in France was deteriorating. On a practical level, then, a trip to Kent (as opposed to progressing in a more westerly direction) kept Elizabeth between her capital and her foreign enemies; it also afforded a chance to inspect England's coastal defenses. Indeed, one of the main destinations of this progress was the crucial royal fortress of Dover Castle, where Elizabeth spent a week in residence.

The Queen also visited a number of coastal towns in Kent and just across the border in Sussex, including Rye, Winchelsea, Sandwich, and Folkestone. A common problem on the southeast coast during this period was the silting up of local harbors, caused by the "swift and complicated tides of the English

Channel playing upon the sand."[5] Silting damaged the commerce of affected towns, and in some cases threatened to cut them off from the sea entirely. A number of these towns—including Rye, Folkestone, and Sandwich—used the Queen's 1573 progress to petition her for royal aid to rehabilitate their harbors. Of these, only Sandwich has surviving records of any detail. Its reception thus offers a rare chance to see how an Elizabethan town used the occasion of a royal visit to craft a comprehensive plea for economic aid. As we shall see, Sandwich did not only target the reigning monarch; its leaders also solicited the assistance of accompanying Privy Council members, including Burghley, Leicester, Sussex, and Lincoln.[6]

But Sandwich is not only worth examining because it faced a common problem and because its records have survived. Rather, Sandwich is a revealing case study because of both the content and form of its ceremonial message. Instead of playing up its economic challenges and emphasizing its own decline, Sandwich projected an image of strength and prosperity that it did not actually possess. At the same time, the town relied on its physical fabric to an unusual degree. Whereas other towns might speak to the monarchy directly via speeches, scripted exchanges, and allegorical performances, Sandwich's self-fashioning relied largely on spatial and topographical performance. Ultimately, the town was able to both draw from and modify existing civic pageant conventions in order to speak to the particular "political and social circumstances of the moment it addresses."[7]

Sixteenth-Century Sandwich

To fully understand where Sandwich stood in 1573 and why its leaders responded as they did, we must start by revisiting the town's former glories. From its origins, Sandwich owed much to its favorable geographical location on the southeastern coast of England. Because of its position at the mouth of the River Stour, it sat at the "southeastern end of a navigable waterway [that connected] the Outer Thames Estuary to the English Channel."[8] This waterway—known as the Wantsum Channel—could be used "by ships sailing to and from London and the ports of the east coast of England . . . [to] avoid the notoriously dangerous sea passage" around the northeastern tip of Kent.[9] On top of this, Sandwich also boasted an almost perfect natural harbor known as the Haven. Just where the Stour emptied into the sea, a shingle of land jutted outward to form a protective barrier and create a calm pool where ships could safely anchor.

Given these advantages, it is little wonder that a thriving town sprung up here sometime between the mid-fifth and mid-seventh centuries.[10] Sandwich's location made it an ideal stop for trading vessels along the southeast coast, and its sheltered harbor facilitated commerce of all types. In time, the Haven also became a natural gathering point for fleets of warships—as when the Anglo-Saxons assembled naval forces during their ninth and tenth-century campaigns against the Vikings.[11] By at least one estimate, Sandwich had become "the most important port of England" by the time of the Norman Conquest.[12] One reason for its prominence is that it was also a convenient point of embarkation to the Continent. From circa 1150 to 1350, it was a frequent stopover for English monarchs going to and coming from their French territories.[13] And when Thomas à Beckett fled England in 1164 and returned in 1170, he did so via the port of Sandwich. The town also served as the main port for Canterbury, and thus enjoyed close connections to both the cathedral of Christchurch and the monastery of St. Augustine. Another measure of Sandwich's importance can be seen in its designation as a Cinque Port beginning in the eleventh century. Along with four other strategically located coastal towns (Dover, Hastings, New Romney, and Hythe), Sandwich was given the responsibility of providing the king with a certain number of manned ships per year. In exchange, the Cinque Port towns enjoyed special considerations, including tax exemptions, fishing privileges, and specialized courts.[14] The individual towns also accrued the prestige that arose from their special role in defending the most vulnerable coast of England.

Partially as a result of its status as a "liberty," Sandwich enjoyed a well developed town government. In 1213, Sandwich was one of only nine towns in England that had established mayors.[15] It also had a "highly organized" town council of jurats, and—by the 1450s—a common council.[16] By the late Middle Ages, Sandwich had blossomed into a hub of international trade that was routinely visited by great merchant ships from as far away as Genoa and Venice. Each year the Flanders Galleys (the official fleet of the Venetian merchants) visited Sandwich on their way to London and Flanders, and reassembled at the town before sailing back to the Mediterranean.[17] These ships brought luxury goods from the East, including "sugar and molasses, preserved fruit, cotton and silk, coral beads and saltpetre."[18] But Sandwich's most important import cargo was Bordeaux wine, "which was imported for royal, aristocratic and ecclesiastical households, and increasingly for the wealthier members of society."[19] The town's main export was wool, "famed for its high quality and greatly in demand on the continent."[20] In 1378, Sandwich was designated as a "staple"—"a place approved by the King and Parliament for the public sale of wool and other commodities"—which meant that it became something of a clearinghouse for wool from sources all over Kent and beyond.[21]

Sandwich especially benefitted from its role in the Hundred Years' War (circa 1337–1453), since its Haven was a frequent assembly point for the English fleets that transported soldiers and supplies to the battlefields of France.[22] In fact, Henry V's famed longbow archers reputedly practiced at the Butts (an open area on the western edge of town) just prior to embarking for Agincourt. After the English captured Calais in 1347, Sandwich became the main port for sending men and provisions to this military outpost—with obvious economic and political benefits to the town.[23] However, the town's involvement in this conflict was not without danger. On August 28, 1457—probably the darkest day in the town's history—the French attacked and plundered the town and even killed the mayor, John Drury. This attack was, paradoxically, a measure of the wealth and importance that Sandwich had attained by the mid-fifteenth century. Despite this setback, the town bounced back and continued to play a key role in national affairs. During the Wars of the Roses, "fleets and land forces were collected at Sandwich by both sides" and Edward IV visited the town in 1462 and again in 1465.[24] In 1475, "the largest force ever to leave the shores of England assembled in the Haven" and departed for Calais.[25] Sandwich was thus still in a relatively flourishing condition about one hundred years before Queen Elizabeth's visit in 1573.

Those hundred years would see the onset and acceleration of Sandwich's decline. The main culprit was the silting up of the Haven, which began in the second half of the fifteenth century.[26] To some degree, this was due to natural causes: silt from further upstream was gradually deposited by the Stour so that it became shallower and less navigable. Some of this silt was also deposited in the Haven at the mouth of the river. In addition, the thin spit of land that enclosed the Haven collected sand, grew wider each year, and began to encroach into the harbor. The decline of Sandwich harbor can also be tied to specific man-made activities in the area. Throughout the Middle Ages, the marshy land along the edges of the Stour was drained and reclaimed by landowners for agricultural usage. These same owners also constructed weirs and watermills that incrementally began to hinder the free flow—and self-scouring ability—of the river. Sandwich was also a victim of its own coastal trade; visiting ships would sometimes dump ballast into the harbor, which then served as sites around which silt would accrue. Even worse were the occasional shipwrecks in or just beyond the Haven that could collect sand and obstruct shipping lanes. The effect of all these factors—both natural and man-made—is that the river in front of the Sandwich quay became shallower and less navigable, and the broad Haven just downstream began to fill in. As the sixteenth century wore on, larger vessels began to have difficulty accessing first the quay and then the Haven itself. In 1532, the Flanders Fleet made its last recorded visit to Sandwich.[27] Predictably, Sandwich's trade volume began to decrease and its maritime-based economy began to suffer.[28]

Two other events bookended this period of Sandwich's history and further contributed to its economic decline. In 1453, the Hundred Years' War ended and so too did the considerable profits that the town enjoyed as a staging area for English forces. Sandwich would remain the primary supplier for Calais (England's lone remaining Continental possession) for another hundred years, but in 1558 Calais was lost to the French. This, according to Helen Clarke, was the "low point of [Sandwich's] economy."[29] Not only had the town lost some of its traditional sources of income, the silting up of the harbor made it difficult to pursue other commercial options. As a result, the population of Sandwich was steadily declining. It had dropped from around 3,500 in 1471 to 2,700 in 1513 to possibly as low as 1,500 by 1561.[30] Along with the downturn in wealth and population, Sandwich was also losing something more: its relevance. After 1453, the town became less of a focal point for military activities. Sometime in the 1480s, Sandwich Castle—which heretofore had been a "royal administrative centre for the gathering of troops"—was transferred to the town's control, signaling a clear "withdrawal of the royal presence" from Sandwich.[31] Further, though the town had traditionally been an important link in the coastal defensive network, the early sixteenth century saw the construction of other, more "modern defensive structures"—such as Deal, Walmer, Sandown, Camber—"built elsewhere along the coast."[32] The town's decline is registered in contemporary accounts, as when John Leland notes the "Decay of the Haven" in the 1540s.[33] Three decades later, William Lambarde writes that because of "the abundance of the light sand (wherewith the Sea hath of latter yeeres glut ted the haven) it is declined to great decay."[34] This decay, says William Camden, is chiefly due to the haven now not being "deepe enough to beare any tall vessels."[35]

In the succeeding 450 years, the process of silting was completed (the town is now stranded some two miles from the sea) and Sandwich has retreated into relative obscurity. But in the sixteenth century, such decline was not seen as inevitable. Town leaders were taking calculated measures to arrest and even reverse the process, ranging from dredging to building breakwaters to removing shipwrecks to proposing comprehensive schemes for a new harbor.[36] For the latter, the town appealed to central government for both expertise and monetary aid. Beginning in 1484, the citizens made separate appeals to Richard III, Henry VII, Henry VIII, and Elizabeth I.[37] In 1560 the mayor traveled all the way to London to petition Queen Elizabeth in person. Although nothing concrete had emerged from these efforts—other than a 1548 engineer's drawing for cutting an artificial channel from the Haven to the sea— the town might have been encouraged by the fact that Dover (another of the Cinque Ports) had acquired royal support for its ongoing harbor refurbishment project.[38] Starting in 1561, it also invited "strangers" (religious refugees from the Low Countries) to settle in Sandwich and practice their weaving trades. The initial group contained eighty-one individuals, but this number grew to several hundred over the next two decades, helping to bolster the town's population and revive its moribund economy.[39] Yet Sandwich was still a far cry from what it had been earlier in the century, when Henry VIII had assembled a war fleet bound for France and Venetian galleys had unloaded on its quays. Much of its former prestige and importance had slipped away even within the living memory of its older citizens. In the meantime, the harbor continued to silt up.

For all of these reasons, the citizens of Sandwich were likely buoyed by the news that the Queen was coming on progress to Kent in 1573 and that Sandwich would be part of her itinerary. Here was a golden opportunity to show Elizabeth firsthand the state of the harbor and make a personal appeal for royal aid. What did Sandwich do with this opportunity? The major primary source for answering this question is an eighty-eight-line prose narrative in the town Year Book.[40] From this relatively short account, we have a pretty good outline of the main events of the Queen's three-night visit. She arrived from Dover on the evening of Monday, August 31, entering via Sandwich's eastern gate, and processing through the town until she arrived at her lodging on Strand Street. The next day, Tuesday, she watched a mock battle that was staged on the riverbank opposite Sandwich. On Wednesday, she attended a banquet at the schoolhouse with the wives of leading citizens. On Thursday morning, she departed via the northern gate in the direction of Canterbury. The Year Book records that as she passed out of town, "Master Maior exhibited vnto her highnes a supplicacion for the Havon which she tooke and promised herself to Reade" (*K2*, 859:13–15). This last item is hardly surprising, given what we know about the desperate state of the town in the 1570s. Sandwich is unusual, however, in that its leaders waited until the very end of the visit to petition the Queen; typically towns made such appeals during the initial welcome ceremony.[41] For instance, at the Queen's entry into Worcester in 1575, the welcome speech drew dramatic attention to the city's depressed textile industry—"the wealth wasted and decayed, the bewty faded, the buyldynges ruyned . . . [and] allmost nothyng lefte but a ruynous Citie"—before asking for Elizabeth's help in reviving the city.[42] Sandwich was more subtle. Even though the state of the harbor was its most pressing concern and it enjoyed the ear of the reigning monarch for three days, there is no mention of the Haven (at least in the formal records) prior to this parting supplication. The Queen did not tour the port facilities (as she would at Bristol), nor did she hear speeches or witness pageants that gave voice to the town's anxiety about the Haven's decay. Instead, the subject was only broached in the final minutes of Elizabeth's visit.

Sandwich's approach—while much less overt than most—allowed it to pursue an alternate strategy: it downplayed its decline, and, instead, projected an image of wealth, strength, and stability. Throughout the Queen's visit, town leaders went out of their way to exhibit the town's defensive structures, stately buildings, orderly layout, and commercial activities. Viewed in this light, everything the Queen saw and did over her three-day visit helped lay the groundwork for the crucial moment of the mayor's Haven appeal. The cumulative message was that Sandwich was *still* an important military and commercial port and that it could continue to be so with a little help from the Queen.

Indeed, the surviving records focus almost exclusively on how the town fabric was prepared, where Elizabeth went, and what she saw during her visit. It is true that the town Year Book does not tell the full story of the Queen's visit—like all royal progress records it is a subjective account that "economizes," "distills," and is no doubt shaped to serve the dominant hierarchy.[43] But it surely does so in ways that reflect how the town wanted to remember the event and what meaning it attached to it. The Year Book provides minimal speech and performance details; instead it emphasizes topography, buildings, and processional routes. This textual emphasis, I believe, says something about the town's strategy. In the pages that follow, I will show how Sandwich fashioned its message of strength and vitality primarily by mediating the ways in which Elizabeth experienced the town during her three-day visit. In this sense, the entire visit was a spatial and topographical performance in which the town itself took center stage. In order to re-create and understand how the town presented itself to the Queen, we must carefully consider the physical and topographical features of Sandwich in the 1570s.[44] We can then assess how the Queen might have encountered and experienced these elements, and how the town used them to create a coordinated image of strength and vitality. As we shall see, the town's message did resonate with the monarch and was successful in getting her to take a closer look at the state of the Haven.

Defensive Structures

One of the first impressions that Sandwich hoped to convey was that it still played a vital role in the defense of the realm. Even before the Queen's actual arrival in the town, the Year Book records that the town sent one hundred soldiers to "watche upon her highnes" (K2, 856:37–38) during her weeklong stay at nearby Dover Castle. Although requested by William Cobham, the Lord Warden of the Cinque Ports, this attendance was largely ceremonial and a bit superfluous, as Dover Castle was a well equipped royal stronghold. By attending her at Dover, Sandwich was underscoring—and reminding the Queen of—its shared identity as a fellow Cinque Port. Since civic representatives typically first met the monarch at the edge of the town's liberties, Sandwich was also suggesting for itself a much larger sphere of influence. At the end of the Queen's stay at the castle, these same one hundred men, armed with "Calyvers murryons rapers & daggers" (K2, 856:41) then escorted the Queen and her retinue the nine miles back to Sandwich. Such a heavily armed guard was largely ceremonial, but it no doubt strengthened the association between the town and military preparedness.

This association was only heightened by the Queen's entrance into the town itself. The Year Book specifies that she entered Sandwich via Sandown Gate. Thus, as she approached from the east, her view would have been dominated by Millwall, the most imposing of the three earthen ramparts that enclosed the town. It featured "an uninterrupted, steep slope running from the top of the rampart to the bottom" of a wet moat that encircled the town.[45] Millwall was pierced by Sandown Gate, an impressive brick-and-stone structure comprised of "a central passageway . . . flanked by round-fronted towers that project[ed] forward into the moat."[46] Sandown Gate was among the most formidable of Sandwich's four land gates, and likely the only one that had a drawbridge over the moat.[47]

Once the Queen was inside Sandown Gate, the Year Book indicates that she was then led down Upper Strand Street to the end of High Street. Her route would have taken her past another defensive structure—the Bulwark—immediately on her right. As Clarke explains, the Bulwark was "an artillery fortification made predominantly of earth and timber" that formerly enclosed the northeastern corner of the town.[48] It had mounted guns that overlooked (and safeguarded) the approach to Sandwich along the River Stour. It also contained a structure for storing small arms, shields, and armor. In following Sandown and Knightrider Streets (the most direct approach to Upper Strand Street), the Queen would have followed along the southern edge of the fort and passed right by the brick entrance at its southwest corner. There, she would have seen displayed a huge piece of artillery known colloquially as the "murderer." After turning onto Upper Strand Street and heading for the center of town, the Queen would doubtlessly have glimpsed other defensive structures to her right. These were about fifty meters to her north, where the northwestern corner of the Bulwark dovetailed with a stretch of the town wall that ran along the quay and terminated at a fifteenth-century water gate known as "the Barbican." Occupying a strategic position where High Street met the river, the gate featured two large, round guard towers that were fitted with gun loops through which trestle-mounted guns could be fired. Its defensive capabilities notwithstanding, the Barbican was also something of a showpiece; the town spent lavishly on its checkerwork stone exterior, and it was intended to be "a symbol of urban pride."

Thus, by the time she reached the heart of the town, the Queen had passed through and by a series of formidable defensive structures, including Sandwich's largest earthen rampart, two of its most formidable gates, and its heavily artilleried riverside fort.[49] This itinerary was no accident; as Janette Dillon has pointed out, "the topography of the processional route" mattered deeply and so it was frequently chosen to highlight "special locations" within the city.[50] Most of these defensive structures had been built (or were modified significantly) in response to French threats in the second half of the fifteenth century, but they had also all been maintained and repaired—most as recently as the 1560s.[51] It is also clear that these structures had been carefully refurbished for the Queen's visit in 1573. The town's preparations for Sandown

Gate included the placing of the royal "Lyon and a dragon all gilt set vp vppon ij postes at the bridge ende and [Elizabeth's] armes was hanged vp vppon the gate" (K2, 857:40–858:1). The council also ordered that certain parts of the ramparts be "buylded" up and that the town walls be cleaned, weeded, and repaired (K2, 854:17). The town then made sure that Elizabeth passed right by these very features so that they could be shown off to best advantage. The most direct route from Dover would have brought Elizabeth in through New Gate and provided a more linear path to High Street. However, this route through town was much less fortified and more residential. Alternatively, after coming in through Sandown Gate, the royal retinue might have cut through St. Clement's churchyard to arrive at High Street sooner, but this course would have missed views of the western side of the Bulwark and the defensive structures to the north of Upper Strand Street. Given these options, it seems clear that the town was intent on highlighting its defensive features, a conclusion that is reinforced by the firing of guns near some of these sites during the Queen's arrival and departure. This dramatic display certainly heightened the association between these imposing physical structures and the actual military firepower they represented.

Although military displays were not unusual in the civic pageantry of the time, Sandwich's seems particularly calculated to speak to the Queen. As we have seen, Elizabeth was deeply concerned about the threat of foreign invasion from parties as diverse as the Spanish, the French, and the Papacy. Though Sandwich had lost much of its national military importance, the town was attempting to demonstrate that it was still a viable link in the coastal defense chain, and that it was therefore worth her continued investment. Whereas Bristol used the manpower of its militia to make a similar point, Sandwich concentrated on its defensive structures. Most of these were really just remnants of the previous century, but they allowed Sandwich to give the impression that it was much more strategically important than it really was.

Houses

Sandwich also took pains to magnify its remaining wealth and prosperity. When the mayor and town council first heard in early July that the Queen might be headed for Sandwich, the first arrangement they made was that "a Cupp of . . . gold [worth £100] havinge the arms and name of Sandwich ingraven shalbe made" (K2, 854:1–2). On July 30, two of the jurats were sent to London to commission this cup, which was then formally presented to the Queen on August 31, the day she rode into town. It was typical for Elizabeth's hosts to present her with gifts, and a gold (or silver) cup "was the customary gift."[52] As Heal has shown, such gift-giving functioned to express loyalty, strengthen social bonds, and invite reciprocity.[53] What is striking about Sandwich's cup is its £100 value. A typical gift value was more in the range of £15 to £50, depending on the size and wealth of the town.[54] Only larger and more prosperous cities like Bristol and Coventry ever gave Elizabeth such a lavish gift.[55] In fact, the £100 price tag of Sandwich's gift topped the *total expenditure* of many other cities that hosted the Queen on progress.[56] The cup thus helped create the impression of much greater prosperity than Sandwich actually possessed. By engraving both the town's name and arms on the cup, town leaders ensured that the connection between town and wealth was (literally) writ large.

During the rest of the Queen's visit, the town played up its prosperity by emphasizing one of its most characteristic features (then and now): its abundance of timber-framed merchants' houses.[57] Since many of these homes had been constructed in earlier, more prosperous times, the town council decreed a month prior to the Queen's arrival that those in "the most ffrequented and vsuall streates" were to be "Emended and repayred" (*K2*, 854:18–21). This order was followed by another a week later that "all maner of persons shall presently for bewtefyeng of the Towne against her maiesties cominge adorne dresse and paynt their houses black and whyte" (*K2*, 855:4–6). Finally, the town leaders went to great pains to detail who was responsible for painting (landlord or tenant) and what fees were to paid by those who neglected their duty. No doubt, these collective attentions to the fabric and appearance of its timber-framed houses would make them stand out as the Queen moved through Sandwich's narrow streets.

The procession through town was also orchestrated so that the Queen would linger in front of some of the most prominent houses. Once she had passed by the Bulwark and turned left onto Upper Strand Street, the Year Book specifies that "she rode forth till she came directly over against mistres Cripps howses" (*K2*, 858:7–8).[58] A little further on, she turned left onto High Street and continued, "almost as far as the pellicane [Pelican House] where stood a fyne howse newly buylt and vaulted over wheron her armes was sett and hanked with tapestrye" (*K2*, 858:8–10). It was here, with this impressively vaulted house as a backdrop, that Elizabeth heard a welcome speech and was presented with the golden cup. Afterward, she "rode vntill she came vnto Mistres Manwood's howse wherein she Lodged" (K2, 858:21–22). Clearly, individual houses figured prominently in the Queen's experience of the town. In fact, the Year Book uses these houses as narrative reference points in charting the Queen's movement through the town (suggesting that these very houses may even have been the basis for selecting the route).[59] Finally, the fact that the procession was frequently made to *pause* before these houses further invests them as "special locations" within the topography of the city.[60]

The last house mentioned above is the most important, for it was here that Elizabeth would lodge for all three nights of her visit. Manwood House was located along the River Stour on Strand Street, where the town's biggest and best houses had been built. The particular house that she stayed in has long since been demolished, though an inventory from around 1590 gives us an idea of its large size and elaborate furnishings. One room is actually referred to as the "Queen's Chamber," and its inventoried contents include featherbeds, carpets, blue and yellow window hangings, "a walnuttree chaire," "a lookinge glasse," and "a greate cypres chest."[61] But there are other, more intangible features that may explain why this house was chosen to host the Queen. First, it was owned by Roger Manwood (1525–1592), the most prominent citizen of the town. A lawyer by training, Manwood became a serjeant-at-law in 1567 and had just been appointed a justice of the Court of Common Pleas in 1572. He was also a familiar figure at court and by this time had well-established ties to the likes of William Cecil, Matthew Parker, Robert Dudley, Christopher Hatton, Thomas Gresham, Francis Walsingham, and the Queen herself (in 1578, she would name him Lord Chief Baron of the Exchequer).[62] Given this pre-existing rapport, Manwood was a natural choice to host the Queen. Hosting was, of course, a personal honor for him, but it also benefitted the town by showing that it was important enough to have so prominent a resident.

Manwood also had a "keen local attachment" to Sandwich: he was born in the town, still maintained a residence there, and also had two brothers who played prominent roles in town government.[63] Most importantly, his legal career had made him "a specialist in the complicated legalities . . . and the privileges of the Cinque Ports," and by the 1570s he "[held] a virtual monopoly in that specialized field."[64] He had begun doing legal work for the town in 1553, was made recorder in 1555, and represented Sandwich in all five Parliaments between 1558 and 1572. One of his main concerns was to defend the liberties, privileges, and exemptions of Sandwich and the other Cinque Ports, which were "always eyed jealously by London and other ports."[65] During the same years, Manwood began to accrue the national offices and courtly contacts mentioned above, which allowed him to have one foot in London and one foot in Kent, and therefore made him "increasingly valuable to Sandwich."[66] Not surprisingly, Manwood took a keen interest in the state of the Haven. On October 26, 1566, he coauthored a "Letter from Roger Manwood, Henry Cobham, and others concerning their efforts to obtain the repair of all their havens by Act of Parliament."[67] This appeal was unsuccessful, but, given Manwood's vested interest in Sandwich's continued influence and status as a Cinque Port, he probably worked closely with the town corporation during the Queen's visit to pursue this aim.

No doubt Sandwich—like all early modern towns—contained within it a variety of competing interests, but differences were typically put aside during a royal visit.[68] This tendency was probably especially true in Sandwich, as the Haven's decline was a universal problem that affected everyone. It is clear from the records that a large number of individuals met regularly in the six weeks prior to the Queen's visit and that they did so "for the benefyt and utilletie of this Towne" (K2, 853:37–38). John Gilbert, John Tyssar, Henry Boteler, Matthew Menes, Thomas Parker, Alexander Cobb, George Rowe, Edward Wood, John Wood, Richard Porredge, John Lee, Robert Bonham, Edward Peake, "dyvers of the Common Counsell," and the "whole Cominaltie of ffreemen of the Towne and porte of Sandwich" were all involved in the preparations, and many of their names also recur in the account of the royal visit itself (K2, 853:37; 854:38). On the whole, an impressive variety of Sandwich interests—mayor, jurats, soldiers, clergy, townspeople, Manwood, jurats' wives, children—all contributed to the central theme of the entertainments.[69]

The second reason Manwood House was an ideal lodging is that it was the same house that had hosted the last monarch to visit Sandwich: Henry VIII. Elizabeth's father had visited the town several times, beginning in 1512 when he assembled a war fleet in the harbor for his French campaigns. He also passed through the town in 1532 (in route to Dover) and in 1539 had lodged in this very house on Strand Street—then owned by Sir Edward Ringley—for two nights.[70] These historical associations had not faded by the 1570s, as the house was still popularly known as "the King's Lodging."[71] In recording Elizabeth's visit, the town Year Book actually describes her lodging as "a howse wherin Kinge Henry the viij[th] had been Lodged" (K2, 858:22–23)—suggesting that this fact may have been an important consideration in its selection. The house was a concrete tie to Sandwich's former glories, and having Elizabeth stay here was a way of reminding her that no less a person than the former king and her own father had recognized Sandwich's importance and held it in high regard. For Elizabeth, who deeply revered her father's memory, such an endorsement was not insignificant.[72]

The Haven

The final appeal of the "King's Lodging" was topographical: it was ideally situated along the river and in clear view of Sandwich's bustling harbor. From this site in the northwest corner of the town, the royal visitor could look downriver and enjoy a relatively unimpeded view of the entire riverfront portion of the town.[73] In 1573, this view would have included a line of wealthy merchant houses fronting the river, most with their own private quays for loading and unloading goods. There were also public wharfs, including the town quay, which housed the two-story town crane.[74] Elsewhere could be viewed a chaotic medley of other harbor facilities, including a customs house, docks, weigh beams, assorted storage buildings, and possibly a boom tower.[75] Despite Sandwich's general economic decline, it still enjoyed the administrative status of "headport" for the collection of customs in the southeast.[76] As a result, anyone looking out over the sixteenth-century harbor would have been struck by the teeming variety of watercraft arriving, departing, and unloading along the busy waterfront. Sandwich's large merchant ships may have been replaced by regional commercial craft, but toll and wharf records verify the continued frequency of coasters, ketches, plats, haynes, crayers, hoys, pinks, argosies, and colliers.[77] A variety of fishing vessels (herring boats, mackerel boats, oyster boats, busses, and picards) also plied the waters.[78] There was even a regular ferry that ran from beside the town quay across the river to Stonar, the southernmost point of the Isle of Thanet. Further to the east, Elizabeth may have been able to glimpse the well-fortified northern (river) side of the defensive Bulwark that overlooked and protected the approach to the quayside.

Thus, the position of the Queen's lodging on the western end of Strand Street was perfect for viewing the vessels, goods, activities, and physical structures that formed the commercial center of the town. According to the Year Book, once the Queen was ensconced in her lodging on Monday night, she only made two excursions into other parts of the town (the mock battle on Tuesday and the feast on Wednesday) before her departure on Thursday. Such relatively limited movements might imply that she did not get to see and experience much of the town, but as we have seen, both the location and vista afforded by Manwood's riverside house would have kept the heart of Sandwich continually before her eyes. She may not have been witnessing a formal pageant of the sort that she saw from her chamber window at Kenilworth or Norwich, but this view still had the power to speak to her. The busy harbor scene that unfolded outside her windows would have allowed the Queen to see that Sandwich was indeed still vibrant while also underscoring for her how closely the livelihood of the town was tied to the continuing functioning of the harbor.[79]

It is also clear that the town leaders emphasized the harbor through the "performance" of movement during other parts of the royal visit.[80] For, when the Queen did leave her lodgings, she was always kept in close proximity to the waterfront. On Tuesday, she was entertained with a mock battle, "the Towne havinge buylded a forte at Stoner on thother syde of the Havon" (K2, 858:26–27). Thus, the Queen would have been positioned somewhere on the Sandwich riverfront (perhaps the town quay) and would have looked out across the Haven at the martial shows. On Wednesday, she attended a banquet at the grammar school, which was located further down Strand Street, about two hundred meters to the west of the Queen's lodging. When the Queen departed on Thursday, she went back down Strand Street in the same direction before exiting the town out of Canterbury Gate. When all of the Queen's movements within the town are plotted on a map of sixteenth-century Sandwich, it is remarkable how little of the town she actually saw. From her arrival on Monday night until her departure on Thursday morning, she was always near the water and almost always along the same stretch of Strand Street. In contrast, other host cities—like Bristol and Norwich—provided a much more extensive tour of their civic spaces. I would argue that Elizabeth's carefully circumscribed experience of Sandwich was intentional on the part of the town leaders, who had planned the Queen's movements and organized her entertainments. It is not simply that other parts of the town were omitted because they had little to offer. In 1573 Sandwich boasted a court hall that had recently "undergone considerable repairs and improvements," including a new council chamber.[81] It also had three ancient parish churches (St. Clement's, St. Peter's, and St. Mary's), three almshouses (St. Thomas's, St. Bartholomew's, and St. John's), and at least two flourishing markets (Cornmarket and Fishmarket). Finally, flowing right through the center of Sandwich was the Delf Stream, a man-made channel and "considerable feat of engineering" that brought fresh water into the town.[82] Despite the relative proximity of all these landmarks to the visiting Queen, there is no record that she was shown any of them.[83] Instead, the town wanted Elizabeth's focus to be squarely on the significance of the Haven by keeping it continually before her.

The Queen's physical proximity to the harbor was supplemented by pageant devices that commented on its importance. For instance, the mock battle on Tuesday was intended to emphasize the Haven's past and future roles in military action. The Queen watched as soldiers from the town—seemingly the same ones who had attended her at Dover—first attacked and then captured a fort that had been set up across the water at Stonar. But the placement of the fort seems a little odd. Since the actual battle was on the dry land of Stonar and the soldiers had to be ferried across the Haven, it would have been more convenient to use the flat tracts of land (Castle Field) just over the town ramparts, which also had the advantage of providing a lofty viewing platform. Instead, the town went out of its way to use the Haven as the foreground for these martial exploits. Why? It may simply be, as Margaret Shewring asserts in *Waterborne Pageants and Festivities of the Renaissance,* that water is a natural stage with inherent "performance possibilities."[84] Yet, as we have seen, featuring the Haven was also a way of emphasizing its importance to the town. This strategy may well have paralleled that of Renaissance Venice, which embraced waterborne pageantry for the very reason that water was such a crucial part of its self-definition.[85] The mock battle also allowed the Haven to be mythologized. If the Queen had been experiencing the day-to-day commercial vitality of the Haven from her window, she now encountered it as the setting of dramatic and glorious events. J. R. Mulryne has described how the River Thames was similarly transformed during royal entries from a place of "daily activity and busyness" to a "secular sacred space."[86] Such a metamorphosis relies on the blending of history and myth to create a mode in which—to adapt David Bergeron—the participants were gazing at the real Haven (which was much "decayed"), but they were seeing a symbolic idea of the Haven.[87] At Sandwich, the mock battle was both a dramatic gesture to the brave exploits that had originated here in the past and also an imaginative assertion that they were now (via the pageant) continuing to occur in the present. Although the latter would seem to belong more to the realm of myth-making, it is worth noting that the pageant prominently features what had been Sandwich's main military role in the past: the transporting of troops. Instead of beginning the pageant with the troops already at Stonar, the organizers ensured that the audience actually viewed—as a part of the show—

"the capitanes aforesaid [lead] over their men" across the water to the fort (K2, 858:27–28). Stonar may not have been "the vasty fields of France," but with a little help, the pageant implies, the Haven was still viable for military transport.

Another pageant device served as a reminder of the Haven's commercial importance to Sandwich. The town's preparations included the erection of stages on Strand Street "and vppon them at euery xx foote distaunce one Chyld of thage of Eight yeares or ix or x yeres old spyninge bay yarne vppon wheles and also the scaffoldes covered with whyte and black bayes" (K2, 855:36–38).[88] By the 1570s, one of the main sources of Sandwich wealth was the weaving of light draperies, especially the bays and says that the newly arrived strangers specialized in.[89] The "scaffoldes"—which specifically featured "bay yarne" being woven and also as a finished product—are thus a celebration of Sandwich's recent commercial resurgence. Yet this resurgence could only continue if the silting up of the harbor was arrested. In other words, the future livelihood of the town was at stake, a point that is dramatically illustrated by the use of local *children* in the pageant device.[90] The placement of these scaffolds in Strand Street is also strategic. Since Strand Street was the principal waterfront street and the point of departure for textile exports, it is a reminder that these weaving activities are closely tied to the continued viability of Sandwich's harbor.

The Grammar School

The final episode to discuss involved the Queen's visit to the local grammar school. On Wednesday, the principal women of the town "made the Quenes Maiestie a [banquet] of Clx disshes on a table of xxviij foote long in the scole howse . . . Wheare she was very merrye and did eate of dyvers disshes" (K2, 858:37–859:3).[91] On the surface, such a pleasant feast would seem to be wholly unconnected to the status of Sandwich Haven. Although the school was still on Strand Street, it did not have a view of the harbor nor does the feast seem related to the themes of commerce and militarism emphasized elsewhere. Yet I would argue that the schoolhouse was a carefully chosen destination, that it was indeed relevant to the Haven, and that it formed a crucial part of the final build-up toward the formal appeal made by the mayor on Thursday morning.

The school was certainly a handsome building that would have—if nothing else—furthered the theme of Sandwich's prosperity. It had been built only ten years earlier, was finished in local yellow bricks, and featured fashionable stepped Dutch gables. This latter detail made it one of the most cosmopolitan-looking buildings in town, and may well have furthered the hoped-for impression that Sandwich was an international port. It was also spacious enough to accommodate a feast whose size (one hundred fifty dishes; twenty-eight-foot-long table) was clearly designed to impress. The main schoolroom was 48 by 22 feet, making it considerably larger than any of the halls the Queen could have visited in a private house.[92] In fact, it was probably the largest secular room in Sandwich at the time.[93]

The most important factor recommending this building was that it was a school. When it was founded in 1563, only six other towns in Kent could boast grammar schools.[94] Ten years later—at the time of the Queen's visit—many other prominent towns in Kent still lacked one, including Rochester, Dover, Folkestone, Sittingbourne, Faversham, Hythe, and New Romney.[95] Thus, the very existence of this school was an argument for the town's prominence—one thinks of Robert Tittler's claim that buildings can "represent such intangible concepts as power, authority, and legitimacy"—and so it is only natural that the town would want to highlight it.[96] The school also showed that the town was progressive and that it valued education—much like the reigning monarch, who had herself received a humanist education and been active in the establishment of grammar schools throughout the realm.[97] In fact, the Queen had approved the founding of this very school in 1563. Giving her a banquet in the schoolroom that she had helped make possible would have therefore been a nice gesture of both gratitude and flattery. Similarly, visiting the school was also a way of aggrandizing the Queen's host, Sir Roger Manwood, since he was the single individual most closely associated with the founding of the school, having donated the land whose revenue was to be used to maintain the school and pay the salary of the master.[98]

Yet the grammar school was hardly the achievement of Manwood and the Queen alone. In fact, the town itself was involved in the school's founding to an unusual degree. When the chantry school attached to St. Peter's Church was finally dissolved in 1547 (one of the final local effects of the Reformation), "there were immediate complaints in the town."[99] Nevertheless, Sandwich found itself without a school until 1563, when the mayor proposed the founding of a free school within the town and made an appeal for financial contributions. This appeal raised some £286 for the building of the new school. In practice, the mayor, ten jurats, and thirty-four common councilors contributed around £203, while 181 other residents gave £83 total—with others promising to supply building materials for the school.[100] One historian aptly characterizes the founding of Sandwich's grammar school as a "community-wide effort," and another asserts that "the real founders of the school were the people of Sandwich."[101]

The latter is probably an overstatement. The town did play a key role in proposing the idea and raising the money for the building of the school, but other contributors were needed as well. The town's impulse to build a school would have been short-lived without the endowment provided by a leading citizen like Manwood. Twelve miles away in Canterbury, Archbishop Matthew Parker "became interested in the project" and persuaded the Dean and Chapter of Canterbury to donate land that they owned in Sandwich for the school to be built on.[102] Parker also wrote to William Cecil "to use his influence in procuring from the Queen her license for the endowment and founding of the school."[103] The founding of the school at Sandwich was thus a fruitful combination of the efforts of the town government, common citizens, a wealthy benefactor, church officials, courtiers, and, ultimately, the Queen. In the succeeding years, it had continued to be a shared responsibility, with the mayor, jurats, Manwood, and townspeople involved in the day-to-day operations.[104]

The grammar school was thus an emblem of the sort of collaboration that the town hoped to forge in addressing the problem of the Haven. Some of the same individuals who had been active in founding the school—including the Queen, Cecil, Manwood, and town council—were now gathered together for the festivities at Sandwich. In addition, the town used the occasion to solicit help from other courtiers in attendance; the Year Book records that "my Lord Admyrall [Edward Clinton, Earl of Lincoln] my Lord Chamberleyn [Thomas Radcliffe, Earl of Sussex] and my Lord Leycester were made pryvie to the suyt for the Havon" (K2, 859:16–17). Though it was appealing to a variety of central government figures for assistance, Sandwich was not passively awaiting a solution. It could point to a long list of harbor modifications that it had already been pursuing for the past one hundred years.[105] The grammar school setting of Wednesday's feast helped underscore the fact that Sandwich was proposing a partnership rather than a bailout. As with the school's foundation, the town itself had initiated the process and was already investing considerable resources in repairing its harbor. As with the school's operation, Sandwich would ably maintain the new harbor once it had been established. It just needed some help with the heavy lifting. In 1563, a broad coalition had combined forces to address a local need, and it had worked beautifully, as Elizabeth could see from the stylish building, spacious schoolroom, and eager young scholars. By having

Elizabeth visit the school, the town was providing a vivid reminder of the fruitfulness of this earlier partnership and suggesting that future collaboration could be equally effective. As town officials processed through the streets with their royal visitors, they no doubt hoped they were enacting the basic assumption of the processional mode: that "a literal moving together conveyed the message that all participants shared a commitment to the same goal."[106]

The next morning, when mayor John Gilbert handed the Queen "a supplicacion for the Havon" at the gate leading out of town and toward Canterbury, this document was merely the final step of a carefully orchestrated appeal that had been three days in the making.[107] Evelyn Korsch has written that the aim of festivals and pageants "is to render the abstract character of a message visible and comprehensible by material means."[108] By Thursday morning, Sandwich had relied on its topography and buildings to do just that. The Queen's entry from the east, her route through town, the house in which she lodged, the locations and themes of the mock battle and weaving devices, and the feast at the grammar school all helped craft an image of the town and a message to the Queen. Sandwich was not a declining backwater that desperately needed the Queen's intervention. Rather, it was an important port—still militarily and commercially vibrant—that could continue to be so with a little help from the Queen.

Epilogue

Sandwich's appeal appears to have made a favorable impression. Though the actual "supplicacion" handed to the Queen on the morning of her departure has not survived, there is a document in a batch of Manwood's papers entitled, "The Proporcion of Sandwich Haven 1574."[109] It is a copy of what seems to be the town's response to a commission's inquiries regarding the Haven's decline and "how it maie be remedied." It would therefore appear that after her visit to Sandwich, the Queen appointed a commission to look into the state of the Haven. Whereas the town's reception sought to dramatically illustrate that Sandwich was important and worth helping, this document is a pragmatic discussion of exactly what form that help might take. "The Proporcion" is organized around a series of practical questions, including, "What is the principall cause of the decay of the haven," "how it maie be remedied," "what wilbe the charges by estimacion," and "how the charges may best be borne." Most questions involve the specifics of actually repairing the Haven, so there is a whole page of detailed measurements reporting the length, breadth, and depth of the Haven as well as estimates for "two cuttes to be made at the mouth of the haven" and a fourteen-foot wall to enclose them. Simple diagrams showing these measurements are included. The document is signed by two people, including Roger Manwood, and is dated September 30, 1574. One year later, in 1575, the Queen was consulting with Italian and Dutch engineers about the same sort of cut mentioned in "The Proporcion"—one that would have allowed the Stour to connect directly with the sea and bypass the silted-up areas. According to Clarke, "the engineer Andrian Andrison laid out the scheme in impressive detail, but its estimated cost of £13,000 meant that it was doomed to failure."[110]

Nevertheless, this evidence suggests that Sandwich's 1573 reception of the Queen was successful in convincing her to take more than a perfunctory look at the state of the Haven. She appointed a commission, gathered further details from the town itself, and turned the project over to engineers for analysis and proposals. In the end, as Clarke suggests, the project proved to be cost-prohibitive. Of course, Elizabeth's parsimoniousness is legendary, but it is also true that Sandwich (despite the theme of its entertainments) no longer possessed the strategic importance that it had once enjoyed—especially once Calais had been lost and the Queen had invested in nearby Dover, where the harbor was right on the coast and guarded by a large, royal castle on the cliffs above. If so, the continuing decline of Sandwich may tell us something about the limits of the "ceremonial dialogues" that were afforded by royal progresses. Even if the Queen was responsive to the aid appeals of her subjects, those requests might ultimately need to also fall within the scope of the Crown's interests in order to be acted upon. Given this limitation, it is a credit to Sandwich's carefully orchestrated entertainments that its appeal gained as much traction as it did.

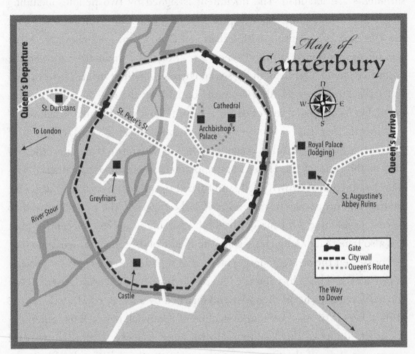

Map reproduced by Coni Porter. Reproduced from William Somner, *The Antiquities of* Canterbury, (London: R. Knaplock, 1703). Sourced from the Kent Archive and Local History Collections.

CHAPTER THREE
CANTERBURY, 1573

O n the evening after leaving Sandwich, Elizabeth arrived in Canterbury. She would spend two full weeks there, making it the longest single stop on the 1573 progress. Her official host was not the town corporation, but Matthew Parker, who had been Archbishop of Canterbury for the entirety of Elizabeth's fifteen-year reign. According to the records, the Queen arrived around 3:00 p.m. on Thursday, September 3, and remained until the afternoon of Wednesday, September 16. She stayed in her own royal palace, which had been converted from the remains of St. Augustine's Abbey in the 1530s. During her visit to Canterbury, the Queen attended evensong on the night she arrived, and returned to the cathedral both Sundays for worship. On Monday, September 7, she celebrated her fortieth birthday at a lavish feast at the Archbishop's Palace. In the meantime, she oversaw routine government business in the form of a Privy Council meeting on September 5, and negotiations with French ambassadors who were also visiting Canterbury.

Three main accounts of her visit survive. On August 17, Parker wrote a letter to William Cecil in which he detailed the many preparations he was making. A year and a half after the visit, on March 17, 1575, Parker wrote a letter to Edmund Grindal, the archbishop of York, in which he described some of the festivities. Finally, there is an even fuller description of the Canterbury entertainments in Parker's autobiography, *Matthaeus*. Since all three accounts are authored by Parker himself, it is therefore possible to infer quite a bit about his motives and intentions in hosting the Queen.

Her visit came at a pivotal moment for Parker and the English church. The 1560s had seen the rise of a disaffected group within the English church known as the Puritans, and their criticisms of the Elizabethan church had culminated in the Admonition Controversy of 1572 with textual attacks on the episcopacy. Meanwhile, the Queen and Privy Council had been slow to respond to nonconformity and were not as publicly supportive of the established church as they might have been. It is because of this, I will argue, that Parker used the opportunity of the Queen's visit to assert the authority, continuity, dignity, and effectiveness of the ecclesiastical hierarchy. The main way that he did this was through lavish hospitality and displays of clerical magnificence—one of the very things the Puritans were critical of. But far from mere ostentation, Parker's approach was intended to show that clerical magnificence was itself an effective tool that could serve social, religious, and political ends. Among other things, it could be used to shape public opinion, partner with local leaders, interpret and appropriate Scripture, ensure obedience and uniformity, aid in diplomacy, cultivate learning, and defend the monarchy. Parker makes these points through traditional forms of hospitality (open house, birthday feast, gift-giving), but also through his careful deployment of books and places. As we shall see, he relied heavily on religious and antiquarian texts and on the rich associations of Canterbury places—the Cathedral, the Archbishop's Palace, and the ruins of St. Augustine's Abbey—to underscore these messages. Without broaching the subject directly, he used the Queen's two-week visit to defend clerical wealth and rehabilitate clerical magnificence in an attempt to inspire greater public support from both Crown and Council.

Clerical Magnificence and its Critics

Felicity Heal describes ecclesiastical hospitality as an ethos that arose in the Middle Ages from the notion that the clergy, as custodians of their communities, should keep open house and provide hospitality to both visitors and those in need.[1] In doing so, they were fulfilling the biblical injunctions to dispense charity and entertain strangers.[2] Such displays of largesse also helped assert the power and dignity of the church. By the fourteenth and fifteenth centuries, bishops were expected to live in large and appropriately furnished dwellings, maintain large households with ample servants, and fill tables with food and wine from their vast estates. At the Reformation, Henry VIII reaffirmed the importance of ecclesiastical hospitality: "So long as the prelates continued to dispense hospitality he would not, he asserted, allow them to be despoiled by laymen who had already dispersed the wealth of the monasteries."[3] Ecclesiastical wealth was thus justified, at least in part, by the hospitality that the clergy dispensed. One of the main reasons for this quasi-protection was "Henry's . . . awareness that the bishops needed wealth if they were to command the respect and allegiance necessary for them to do their jobs."[4] Thus, when many cathedrals were refounded in the early 1540s, the provision of hospitality was a major feature of the statutes.[5] In practice, Thomas Cranmer (Archbishop of Canterbury, 1533–1555)—"a great housekeeper in the tradition of earlier primates"—led the way.[6]

Keeping state and dispensing hospitality were beneficial to the English church in a number of ways. In a general sense, it helped the church project an image of wealth, power, and authority so that it could command the respect it needed to enforce discipline and secure unity. Hospitality was particularly useful in forging social bonds between the clergy and the rulers of local society, which further facilitated local cooperation and good discipline.[7] Indeed, one of the advantages of bishops maintaining multiple residences was that it gave them a visible presence in different parts of their diocese.[8] Overall, such conspicuous housekeeping helped ensure local cooperation so that the new church could take root. Finally, hospitality could also buttress the church's international standing, as bishops (and especially archbishops) were sometimes called on "to receive foreign guests and men of national influence as part of their work of nurturing the English Church."[9] Thus, despite later charges of greed and worldliness by Puritan critics, "It was political necessity, not personal vanity, which dictated that [Elizabethan bishops'] housekeeping should . . . be consistent with the life style of magnates."[10]

Archbishop Parker was certainly invested in this ideal. In a 1563 letter to Cecil, he writes that "the world looketh for port agreeable" among the clergy and warns that without the maintenance of hospitality their "function should be brought to contempt."[11] Parker himself maintained a large household of around 140 people, including family, ecclesiastical officers and secretaries, household servants, and even liveried yeomen—prompting Patrick Collinson's quip that "Archbishop Parker . . . had not been told that the Middle Ages had come to an end."[12] Parker's household moved with him, and was generally to be found either at Lambeth Palace in London or the Archbishop's Palace in Canterbury. Within these spaces, Parker presided over a well-ordered and hierarchical household where twice-daily chapel services were required and both well-born and humble youths were instructed.[13] Hospitality was dispensed daily in the form of both relief to the poor and the gracious reception of Parker's more formal visitors. In the hall, tables were carefully arranged and "the sitting was such that rank was duly observed."[14] Occasionally, Parker hosted lavish entertainments for special occasions and visiting dignitaries. All of this hospitality was expensive: the single largest budgetary expenditure for the archbishop was food for his household, usually in the neighborhood of £1,300–1,400 per annum.[15] Like his predecessors, Parker saw hospitality as a crucial way to build goodwill and maintain reputation, and he used it partly to establish the dignity of his office.

Despite such continuity, the Reformation had fundamentally changed the status and ability of the bishops. First, the royal supremacy had eroded episcopal authority. Though Elizabethan bishops tried to see the monarch's involvement with the church as an alliance of strength that would help ensure the success of the Reformation, there was no getting around the fact that the Crown could now exercise "rights of government, of direction and of initiation" independent of the bishops.[16] The "institutional structures of the pre-Reformation church had effectively become the religious arm of the Queen's government"; or, as Margaret Bowker puts it more baldly, post-Reformation bishops were effectively "civil servants . . . strengthened in their office [by the monarch's power] and impotent without it."[17] The prelates' reliance on the monarchy also made them more subject to lay influence; many "bishops and higher clergy were now normally dependent upon the recommendation of a lay patron for their advancement."[18]

At the same time, the post-Reformation church's financial position had also been diminished. Even though most cathedral chapters had been preserved in the 1530s, the church still lost land and wealth, particularly in the form of manors surrendered to the Crown, whose revenues the bishops had previously used to finance activities in their dioceses. As Felicity Heal explains in *Of Prelates and Princes,* these losses continued into Elizabeth's reign, with specific policies designed to exploit ecclesiastical wealth. In 1559, some of the diocesan lands of the recently deprived Marian bishops were alienated for Crown usage. In the 1560s, the Crown began commissioning private individuals to search out "concealed lands" possibly overlooked at the Dissolution that the crown might have claim to. Such searching had become a "substantial business" by the 1570s.[19] Throughout Elizabeth's reign, prelates were also subject to paying "first-fruits" to the Crown when they took possession of a new bishopric—a practice the Crown could make even more lucrative by moving bishops around.[20] Bishops were also required to lease church estates to leading courtiers at below-market value and were subject to heavy tax burdens that sometimes included subsidies and levies for wars and defense.[21] Other financial impediments arose from social changes. In the post-Reformation church, many bishops came from humbler backgrounds than their predecessors, so they did not have personal fortunes to draw from.[22] In addition, many clergymen now had wives and families to support, but had received no extra source of income for their maintenance.[23] Because of these factors, Heal claims that the bishops had effectively undergone a change in social status: before the Reformation, bishops are often described as "spiritual noblemen," but by the Elizabethan era, bishops were "more closely comparable with the country gentry among whom they worked."[24] Ironically, the episcopacy needed to project magnificence more than ever to assert their claim to authority, and they were still expected by the Crown and secular society to keep state and dispense hospitality, but they were actually in a weaker position to do so. In fact, those bishops who were perceived as not providing suitable entertainment were often charged with avarice.[25]

At the same time, nascent Puritans wanted to further reduce the status of the bishops. From the 1560s, they began to publicly criticize the prelacy for keeping state. Puritans viewed lavish hospitality not only as a distraction from one's clerical calling, but as a sign of greed and worldly corruption. They thus "challenged the assumption that it was the duty of the godly bishop to concern himself with the rich and mighty," and instead argued that the clergy should tend their local flocks and emphasize poor relief over "secular rituals of hospitality."[26] At issue were two contrasting visions of what a leader of the English church should look like: a humble servant focused on the particular flock under his care, or a stately prelate who reflected the wealth and power of the church. In many ways, this competing vision was at the root of the Vestiarian controversy of 1565–1566, which flared up over the seemingly minor point of whether or not the Elizabethan clergy should wear surplices. Yet the larger question at stake was: To what extent should Protestant clergy be visibly set apart from the laity?

This philosophical divide intensified in the Admonition Controversy, which began when John Field and Thomas Wilcox's *Admonition to the Parliament* (1572) proposed to abolish the episcopal hierarchy and replace it with a Presbyterian model of church governance. Field and Wilcox took their cue from Thomas Cartwright's lectures at Cambridge in 1570, which maintained that "the English Church differed in a number of fundamental respects from the Church of the New Testament."[27] As eventually articulated by Field, Wilcox, and Cartwright himself, these accretions in the English church ranged from the office of bishop to the presence of "popish relics" in the liturgy. The

Admonition was quickly followed up by Cartwright with the *Second Admonition* (1572), which laid out the proposed Presbyterian church government in more detail. Meanwhile, the established church responded with John Whitgift's *An Answere to a certen Libell* (1572), and—after Cartwright's *Replye to an answere* (1573)—Whitgift's *Defense of the Aunswere* (1574).[28] In other words, the early 1570s witnessed an extremely public debate in print about the future of the English church.

For our purposes, it is notable that many of the *Admonition*'s complaints center on the worldliness and pomp of the episcopacy. "I cannot see how they can be more glorious," fumes Cartwright in the *Replye,* "unless the palace were turned into a court and their chair into a throne."[29] Instead, the *Admonition* recommends, "Take away the Lordship, the loyteryng, the pompe, the idlenes, and livinges of Bishops, but yet employ them to such ends as they were in the olde churche apointed for."[30] Better yet would be to do away with all "swelling and lofty titles" of distinction and instead "make equalitie of ministers."[31] The overall thrust of such passages is that the prelates' lavish lifestyles, high offices, and involvement in secular affairs are antithetical to the activities of the true church. These same Puritan texts instead argue for a more decentralized structure of pastors, deacons, and elders with their focus firmly on ministering to the needs of their local flocks. In response, Whitgift draws a distinction "betwixt 'the pomp and outward show' of a prince and the state of an ecclesiastical person both in titles and other majesty . . . Yet may the ecclesiastical person shew forth the countenance of his degree whereunto he is called of God, by his prince, and by the laws of that realm wherein he is subject."[32] Besides, those palace-dwelling prelates that Cartwright complains of, "I think verily take more pains and care in and for the church of God, profit their country more in one month, than you and all your company do in a whole year . . . Their pomp and their palaces are by lawful authority committed unto them; and true martyrs of God have occupied the same or like before them, and yet martyrs too."[33] In other words, not only is clerical magnificence not incompatible with genuine Christianity, it is also a positive force that helps the church do its work in the world.

At any rate, Parker's philosophy of clerical magnificence and hospitality—not to mention the episcopacy that he headed—was under fire in the 1570s by a competing vision of the church. While Presbyterianism was always in the minority, it did spread rapidly beyond London and Cambridge in the 1560s and 1570s, in part because of its ability to attract powerful lay patrons like

Robert Dudley and William Cecil—both of whom accompanied the Queen
to Canterbury in 1573. Dudley had long held reformist Protestant sympathies,
and during the Vestiarian Controversy of the mid-1560s, he gained the reputation as "the privy councilor most sympathetic to, and protective of, protestant
nonconformity."[34] Cecil was more moderate, insofar as he wanted reforms
within existing structures, but he did hope to fundamentally refashion the
episcopacy. As Usher puts it: "Rather than great princes of the church, Cecil
envisaged 'superintendents' shorn of much of their traditional temporal power
and wealth."[35] Both Dudley and Cecil not only held philosophically different
positions from the established church, they also supported and defended ministers with Presbyterian sympathies from bishops who tried to reign them in.[36]

Queen Elizabeth's religious temperament was more conservative than
Dudley, Cecil, and even Parker, but she was still slow to react against Protestant
nonconformity. The main reason for this was political; early in her reign, she
was eager to accommodate as broad a swath of her subjects within the via
media as possible. Caroline Litzenberger has shown that by the end of the
1560s, Elizabeth was exhibiting a growing impatience with nonconformity
and a subsequent desire to tighten the discipline of the church; however, such
strictures were not consistently applied.[37] This inconsistency was a source of
frustration for Parker throughout his arch-episcopate. According to V. J. K.
Brook's biography of Parker, the Queen was adept at pressuring the bishops
to "carry out business which she wanted done without herself incurring any
odium for it." She would urge—and even threaten—them "to carry out her
policies by their own authority," but offer little support and then "[blame]
them if there was failure." In this way, the Queen could initiate controversial
policies but also protect herself from the fallout. She could insist on greater
uniformity and conformity in the provinces, but then criticize Parker for the
"overgreat severity" of his visitation.[38]

The Vestiarian Controversy is a good example of the Queen's lukewarm
support. In January 1565 she wrote to Parker, ordering him to enforce the
wearing of vestments among the clergy. Parker first clarified the church's
expectations with Advertisements, and then began to enforce them among
the heretofore nonconforming ministers of London. The latter measure led
to the examination, suspension, and deprivation of London clergy who would
not conform. Throughout this campaign, "Parker hoped for the backing of
the secular authorities, but was left dangerously exposed by the reluctance of
the government to associate itself with a divisive ecclesiastical policy."[39] The

Queen would not even give her formal assent to the Advertisements, so the enforcing prelates only had ecclesiastical authority rather than the full weight of the Crown. Even though Parker eventually prevailed in bringing most of the nonconforming ministers to heel, it was a "pyrrhic victory": many moderate Puritans had been alienated from the church, pamphlet warfare broke out in London, and Parker's reputation had suffered.[40] This lack of official support was particularly galling to Parker, who wrote to Cecil during the Vestiarian Controversy asking: "Can it be thought that I alone, having sun and moon against me, can compass this difficulty? If you of her Majesty's council provide no otherwise for this matter than as it appeareth openly, what the sequel will be *horresco vel reminiscendo cogitare* [I shudder to think or remember]."[41]

As with the Advertisements above, the Queen frequently withheld official royal approval of the documents that Parker and the bishops created to maintain order and discipline in the church. The Resolutions of 1561, Eleven Articles of 1561, Articles of 1565, new statutes for cathedral churches in 1570, and Disciplinary Canons of 1571 were all proscriptive documents designed to establish church policies and expectations for its ministers and churchgoers. Even though all were sent to the Queen and many had her tacit approval, she withheld giving formal royal confirmation of any of them.[42] While this strategy protected the Queen from any backlash, it made the task of Parker and his fellow bishops much more difficult. Because their policies lacked royal authority, they were more difficult to enforce—particularly when opposed by powerful lay patrons. Indeed, without royal endorsement, the legal standing of many of these articles and injunctions was uncertain.

Such ambiguity also meant that Parker and the bishops received the brunt of contemporary criticism for the church's "sudden" emphasis on uniformity. They were seen as hectoring, misguided, and overly precise in their insistence on conformity, with "many [suspecting] that they were acting mainly out of self-interest in repressing their critics."[43] Indeed, Parker's correspondence reveals a growing sensitivity to being publicly attacked and discredited. Writing about some of the forces arrayed against him in June of 1573, Parker complains: "They say in jest that I am pope of Lambeth . . . and that I am out of all credit and of no reputation, and that they will sue to some great man of the council . . . to outface me, and to beard my authority."[44]

As this letter suggests, the situation seemed particularly dire in the months immediately prior to the Queen's 1573 visit to Canterbury. The Admonition Controversy had begun in June of the previous year and was still playing out a year later. As usual, "government support for the embattled bishops had been slow to materialize."[45] Parker had secured a largely ineffective royal proclamation to suppress Presbyterian writings in June 1573, but it was not until November—after the royal progress—that the Queen and Privy Council finally got behind the bishops in their attempt to crack down on offending ministers. Before this change, Parker's letter of March 12 to Cecil expresses the concern that the Puritans might actually win out: "The comfort that these puritans have, and their continuance, is marvellous; and therefore if her Highness with her council . . . step not to it, I see the likelihood of a pitiful commonwealth to follow."[46] Two months later, Parker's tone is even more anxious: "If it be not earnestly labored on your parties which be supreme judges, long ago called on, I fear ye shall feel Muncer's commonwealth attempted shortly."[47] Even if Parker may be exaggerating the likelihood of a Puritan commonwealth, the abolition of the episcopacy was a real possibility in these years. After all, as the Puritans were all too aware, the reformed English church had retained more traditional structures of church government than any other church that had broken from Rome, and there was no reason to assume that it should be seen as indispensable to the fledgling Church of England.[48] Litzenberger and others have retroactively seen the 1570s as a key decade in defining the "institutional identity" of the church, bringing the crown and church hierarchy into an alliance, and "finally demonstrated that the episcopate would survive in its traditional form."[49] Yet if so, this process was gradual and not inevitable, and one that certainly wasn't completed by 1573. In this light, Parker's exasperated statement to Cecil—"I refer . . . to your own considerations, whether her Majesty and you will have any archbishops or bishops, or how you will have them ordered"—is both a little petulant but also sincere.[50]

When the Queen visited Canterbury in September 1573, these issues were still at the forefront of Parker's mind, and they shaped his response to the opportunity before him. As stated previously, Parker's main goal was to reassert the authority, continuity, dignity, and effectiveness of the church—and particularly of the offices of bishop and archbishop. His main approach was to use lavish hospitality and clerical magnificence not only to aggrandize the episcopacy, but to show how such magnificence could have practical religious, political, and social functions. In doing so, Parker asserts that such a church is worth preserving and publicly supporting. This message was intended primarily for the Queen, but also for those Privy Councilors in her entourage. After all, the Privy Council played a significant role in ecclesiastical affairs despite the fact that no clerics sat on the council.[51] Indeed, some of its members (like Dudley and Cecil) had either actively frustrated or been slow to respond to Parker's attempts to impose conformity. At the same time, Parker's deployment of magnificence might also make a powerful impression on much larger groups of people—courtiers, foreign ambassadors, city corporation, local gentry, general populace, and so forth—who participated in or merely observed the activities of the two-week visit.

Parker's Preparations

One of the most intriguing ways in which Parker prepared for the Queen's visit was by sending certain texts and manuscripts to William Cecil prior to the progress. On May 9, Parker sent Cecil a twelfth-century treatise on the Exchequer written by Gervase of Tilbury, a copy of William Lambarde's unpublished *A Perambulation of Kent,* and his own *De Antiquitate Britannicae Ecclesiae.* On July 15, he followed these up with "A Discourse of Dover."[52] Why? For one thing, he knew of Cecil's keen interest in antiquities. But these texts were also meant to assist Cecil in the coming progress. According to Parker's seventeenth-century biographer John Strype, "The Queen, who would be inquisitive concerning the Places where she journeyed, might have the more Satisfaction given her by her said Treasurer, who was near her Person, and whom she looked upon as a Man of special Learning and Knowledge of the History and Antiquities of her Kingdom, and so would be most apt to put her Questions to him."[53] In this sense, Parker's textual offerings were intended to do the Lord Treasurer a favor by providing him with local knowledge that he could draw from as he played tour guide for the Queen. But this, I would argue, is only part of the explanation.

Throughout his previous fourteen years as archbishop, Parker had shown himself to be savvy in using texts to mold public opinion. As Vivienne Sanders has detailed, Parker (and his assistants) collected and then published medieval manuscripts relevant to the pre-Reformation church in England. His main objective was to "provide a comprehensive historical justification of the Elizabethan Church, to prove the antiquity of its tenets and to support its opposition to Roman Catholicism by the recounting of papal iniquities perpetrated on medieval England."[54] Parker had also used the publication of contemporary texts—such as John Jewel's *Apologia Ecclesiae Anglicanae* (1562), a second *Book of Homilies* (1563–1564), and the *Bishop's Bible* (1568)—to nurture the fledgling Church of England. Someone as savvy as Parker in the deployment of the written word would no doubt have been deliberate in choosing the texts he sent to Cecil in advance of the Queen's visit. Indeed, as we shall see, some of these texts pursue the very same goals of aggrandizing the established church and establishing its ancient dignities. In sending them to Cecil, Parker may well have been trying to influence and reshape his view of the archbishopric and its historical role in Kent. Of course, he was probably also hoping that something of this view might also make its way to the Queen, either by her perusal of the texts in Cecil's possession or by his conversational allusions to their contents.

A closer examination of the individual texts and why they may have been chosen is revealing. The first work mentioned was a Latin treatise known as a "Dialogue of the Observations of the Exchequer." It is believed to have been written by Gervase of Tilbury, "sometime treasurer of the exchequer" in the days of Henry II.[55] It would have been of particular interest to Cecil because his official responsibilities had recently shifted from Lord Secretary to Lord Treasurer in 1572. As Parker notes in the accompanying letter, "I thought it not unmeet for your office to cause it to be copied, and sent to your honour."[56]

If this text was something of a personal offering to Cecil, the "Discourse on Dover" may well have been calculated to appeal to the Queen's interests. Although its precise identification is not certain, it would seem to be a circa 1565–1570 work by one William Darell, a "Prebendary of Canterbury."[57] This antiquarian work is chiefly concerned with the history, improvements, and governorship of Dover Castle. As we have seen, Dover was one of the main destinations of the 1573 progress, and the Queen ended up spending a week there prior to visiting Sandwich and Canterbury. The town was a strategically important stronghold on the coast, had a fine royal castle, and Elizabeth was providing financial support to help reverse the silting up of its harbor.

The other two texts relate more to Parker's goal of aggrandizing the established church. The *Perambulation of Kent* was completed by William Lambarde in 1570, though it would not be published until 1576. Generally regarded as the first English county history, the *Perambulation* provides a walking tour of Kent that is organized by place. Each entry recounts the historical events and other antiquities associated with a particular town. It is not, therefore, ostensibly a work about the church, yet the places discussed are organized by ecclesiastical jurisdiction. The work is actually comprised of two perambulations: one around the diocese of Canterbury and one around the diocese of Rochester. Thus, the former section starts with the Isle of Thanet and moves in a clockwise motion around the diocese, taking in Sandwich, Dover, Appledore, Maidstone, Faversham, and Canterbury. The Rochester section starts with Gillingham and then includes entries on Rochester, Tunbridge, Greenwich, and Gravesend. Such a narrative methodology is unique for an English chorographical work. Since the genre has been associated with projecting order onto the landscape, such an approach implies that the church is a key force in establishing and maintaining local order.[58]

The content of the place entries also supports this idea. Lambarde begins the Canterbury perambulation with an eighteen-page history of the see and diocese as well as a chronological list of all of the archbishops, starting with Augustine in 599 AD. Similar descriptive categories preface the Rochester section. The particular place entries that follow these introductions frequently recount the role of the church in Kentish history. Archbishops and other clergymen founded religious houses in Newenden and Dover, established schools in Maidstone and Wye, and instituted a market fair in Ashford.[59] Lambarde also describes their role in the larger sphere, as when Archbishop Robert of Winchelsey falls out with Edward I or when Abbot Geffray asserts Battle Abbey's wreck of the sea privileges against king Henry I's officers.[60] Even though Lambarde does not always praise such clerical willfulness and openly disapproves of the abuses of the pre-Reformation church, the picture he paints of the clergy is that of an ever-present authority, arbiter, and actor in the history of Kent. By sending this text to Cecil, Parker may well be trying to underscore the established church's traditional—and ongoing—role in local governance, education, and economics. Moreover, Parker's endorsement of such a work also makes the point that he, too, is knowledgeable about and invested in the particular places within his diocese. This is an especially important point to make, given that Puritan critics often upbraided the worldly bishops with neglecting their local spheres.

The fourth and final text that Parker sent to Cecil was his very own *De Antiquitate Britannicae Ecclesiae*. This work had been completed in 1572, but it was printed privately and only in small quantities.[61] If the *Perambulation* emphasizes the established church's activities in the local sphere, *De Antiquitate* more directly glorifies the power, privileges, and continuity of the prelacy. Its introduction sets forth "the primacy and rights of the see of Canterbury," and particularly "the prime historic importance of the Archbishop's position and of his continuing rights."[62] The main body of the work is a history of the church in England, but it is a history that is told through the lives and actions of its archbishops—as if the two are closely aligned. Each archbishop is given a separate entry that ranges from one to several pages. Nor is there a dramatic break with Cranmer at the Reformation. Instead, the text presents a long, continuous, and unbroken line stretching from Augustine up to Parker himself. At a time when many people were calling for the abolition of the episcopacy, it is a striking and potentially controversial text. No wonder Parker writes to Cecil that "I am not minded to suffer [the *De Antiquitate*] abroad in this quarrelous and envious world."[63] Parker's book asserts that the English episcopacy is of great age and duration—each entry is numbered to underscore the point that there have been seventy of them. In this view, the Elizabethan Church is not a fifteen-year-old church that therefore might easily be changed for a different model. It is much older, and therefore its opponents are much more radical than they present themselves to be.

In fact, the work devotes special attention to the Elizabethan church. After the general introduction and before the arch-episcopal biographies, Parker includes pages devoted specifically to contemporary bishops. Two pages are filled with carefully drawn shields containing the coats of arms associated with each bishopric and bishop. The inclusion of such heraldry is both significant and controversial. While many of the pre-Reformation bishops had derived from the gentry and aristocracy, most of the post-Reformation bishops were drawn from more humble, middle class backgrounds.[64] The latter did not really have a claim to this social sphere aside from their clerical appointments. Clearly, Parker is trying to lend weight and dignity to the office of bishop. A third page features a chart that records basic information about each bishop, including his name, diocese, and age. Other categories give special attention to each bishop's credentials—educational institution attended, degree type, and date of consecration and confirmation. Together, these pages place the Elizabethan prelates in the same tradition as their pre-Reformation forbears. They, too, have a high social status that commands respect, and they, too, are highly educated clergymen who are qualified and worthy to hold their positions.

While the *De Antiquitate* makes a textual argument for this claim, it also provides a tangible display of the church's magnificence. Surviving copies of the book tend to be large and weighty. Like the *Bishop's Bible* of 1568, this work invests in oversized elements and lavish illustrations to convey the weight and authority of the established church. It features an elaborate title page with allegorical embodiments of various fields of learning and knowledge. Tables and charts (like those mentioned above) convey a sense of thoroughness and orderly arrangement. All of these elements help convey the idea that the *De Antiquitate* is systematic and authoritative. It is also beautiful. There are numerous embellishments throughout, like intricate page borders and geometric designs. Each biographical entry typically begins with a large "illuminated" letter and a reproduction of the personal shield of the archbishop. In some additions, these features have been vibrantly colored. Many of these flourishes were no doubt overseen by Parker himself, for as he tells Cecil: "I have within my house in wages, drawers and cutters, painters, limners, writers, and bookbinders."[65]

Parker was aware that some people might view such an elaborate production as both proud and presumptuous. It is one thing to set forth the glory of God in the *Bishop's Bible,* but to do so in a book about the lives of the "popish" archbishops might smack of the self-importance and addiction to worldly vanity that Puritan critics complained of. Parker's letter to Cecil registers his sensitivity to such possible criticism: "You may note many vanities in my doings, but I thought it not against my profession to express my times, and give some testimony of my fellow-brothers . . . and though ye may rightly blame an ambitious fantasy for setting out our church's arms in colours, yet ye may relinquish the leaf and cast it into the fire, as I have joined it but loose in the book for that purpose, if you so think it meet, and as ye may, if it so please you (without great grief to me) cast the whole book the same way."[66] Such nonchalance seems to belie the careful attention that Parker lavished on this beautiful book.

But if the *De Antiquitate* may not have been intended, as Parker put it, "to be gazed on of many folk," it was also not intended to be wholly private.[67] Parker did deliberately send a copy of the book to Cecil prior to the progress, and he eventually presented the Queen herself with one. I would argue that he did so, at least in part, to influence the way in which the Queen and the Lord Treasurer perceived the established church. As we have seen, Cecil had fundamental doubts about the episcopacy; the Queen, while more supportive in principal, had weakened the church's financial position, infringed on its prerogatives, and eroded its dignity. The *De Antiquitate* is thus a conscious attempt to rehabilitate the episcopacy and to paint it in full splendor. The presentation copy given to Queen Elizabeth is particularly magnificent.[68] It is bound in green silk and embroidered with plants and animals. The title page is hand-colored with vivid blues, pinks, oranges, yellows, and greens. The coats of arms of the bishops are also vibrantly colored and finished in gold leaf. Finally, the embellishments are particularly lavish throughout; even the index of archbishops has bright red shading for each letter. The effect of all of this visual richness and display is to emphasize the dignified state and magnificence of the leaders of the church.

As the Queen's visit drew near, Parker's practical preparations suggested an attempt to translate such splendor into lavish hospitality. In a letter to Cecil dated August 17, 1573, Parker says that he will model his reception of the Queen on "what service my predecessors have been wont to do."[69] The current archbishop was particularly knowledgeable in this regard, as one of his antiquarian interests was collecting and editing accounts of the entertainments of past archbishops, including those of George Neville (of York) and William Warham (of Canterbury).[70] Warham, for instance, famously feasted with both Henry VIII and the Emperor Charles V at Canterbury in 1510. That Parker used such prelates as guides for his own entertainment reveals that he was seeking a similar standard of magnificence. In this same letter, Parker details the preparations that he is making, ranging from where the visitors might lodge to how they might enter the cathedral to what might be served at the palace feast. In earlier letters, Parker reports, "I am now . . . preparing to go thither [to Canterbury], to make my house ready against her majesty's coming," and that "my wine, beer, and other provision be appointed and sent thither."[71] It is clear from Parker's correspondence that hospitality was a big concern and that he planned carefully and made deliberate choices. Parker's autobiography, *Matthaeus,* provides a thorough description of exactly how these hospitable plans were put into practice.[72] "For the whole time the Queen remained at Canterbury," writes Parker, "the house of the Archbishop most generously lay open to guests both from the court and from the county, and to other visitors who flocked there. And in the great chamber, three benches for diners were made ready at each meal, for lords, councillors, and distinguished guests . . . At lunches, dinners, and even breakfasts, the smaller hall was filled each day by attendants and other lesser figures among the Queen's staff, in great crowds. The tableware for these banquets, and the variety of foods are described separately in the rolls" (*JN2,* 80). Parker's account draws attention to his own "generosity" in keeping open house for the full two weeks, and he carefully describes the food, tableware, seating, and attendants required for this level of hospitality. Indeed, Parker reportedly spent a staggering £2,000 on the Queen's visit.[73]

In a subsequent letter to Edmund Grindal, Archbishop of York, Parker included yet another description of the Queen's visit with many of the same details. Grindal's response is revealing: "Your grace's large description off the enterteynment att Canterbury did so lyvelye sett furth the matter, that in readynge theroff I almoste thowghte my selfe to be one off your guests ther, and as it wer beholdynge the whole order off all thynges done ther: sir I thynke it shalle be harde for anye off our Coate to doo the lyke, for one hundreth yeares, and how longe after, godde knoweth."[74] Grindal was clearly impressed by the "whole order" and the magnificence of the entertainment, both of which will be difficult to surpass. His reaction registers that, at least for Grindal, splendor was the dominant effect. This reaction probably comes close to the effect that Parker was after. His lavish hospitality may have been motivated by the desire to be officious and accommodating to his monarch, but he was also using hospitality to make a point about the status and function of the prelacy. As Strype would write a century later, "the Archbishop's chief care was to give an Entertainment to her Majesty . . . that might answer his own figure."[75]

St. Augustine's Abbey

Parker invested in conventional markers of hospitality—food, wine, plate—in creating a sense of clerical splendor and largesse, but he also made full use of the unique features of the venue in which he was hosting the Queen. Canterbury had been the epicenter of the English church since Augustine arrived in 597 AD, so it contained many buildings and historical associations that bespoke the past and ongoing importance of the episcopacy in local and national society. Indeed, much of the city fabric had been built or financed by powerful prelates. For example, the city walls were rebuilt in stone and the formidable Westgate was added by Archbishop Simon Sudbury in the 1370s. In addition, the cathedral, Christchurch Gate, Archbishop's Palace, Dean's bridge, and various other churches, schools, and hospitals all owed their origin to clergymen associated with Canterbury. Many of their contributions are mentioned in both the biographical sketches in De Antiquitate and in the Canterbury place entry in the Perambulation of Kent. For example, Lambarde's discussion of Canterbury Cathedral emphasizes "three or foure especiall mainteiners of the building" and details the particular features that archbishops Stephen Langton, William Courtney, Thomas Arundell, and Henry Chicheley were responsible for.[76] In their visit to Canterbury, Cecil and the Queen would not only have come face to face with many of these structures, they also would have had advance notice— through the texts that Parker sent beforehand—of their connections to specific prelates. Thus, the city of Canterbury might well be seen as an emblem of the way in which ecclesiastical wealth might be used for the public good. But Parker was also interested in the possibilities of particular Canterbury sites like St. Augustine's Abbey, the cathedral, and his own Archbishop's Palace.

One of the oldest sites in Canterbury is the ruined St. Augustine's Abbey. The abbey was founded circa 598 by Augustine, who had been sent by Pope Gregory to reintroduce Christianity to southern England. The thirty-acre site is located outside and just to the east of the city walls. From the beginning, the monastery was an important religious, administrative, and educational center in the southeast. It also possessed special significance as a burial site for both the kings of Kent and first ten archbishops of Canterbury (including Augustine himself). The abbey flourished throughout the Anglo-Saxon period and was rebuilt and enlarged by the Normans. It did not, however, survive the Dissolution, and in July 1538 it was surrendered to the king. The northwestern sector of the site—comprising a gatehouse, hall, chapel, lodgings, and other domestic buildings—was converted into a royal palace. The rest of the site—including the massive church, cloister, chapter house, refectory, and infirmary—was plundered for its building materials and gradually reduced to ruin. This demolition was a slow process that lasted well into the seventeenth century.[77] In the 1570s, there would have been substantial remains of arches, towers, and walls alongside the new royal palace.

As Parker made preparations for hosting the Queen, it seems likely that he wanted her to be lodged in the palace.[78] In an August 1573 letter to Cecil, Parker describes two different lodging possibilities. He first offers his own palace to the Queen and says that he could "place for a progress-time" the accompanying Cecil, Sussex, Leicester, and Hatton there as well. Then he adds a caveat: "They say mine house is of an evil air, hanging upon the church, and having no prospect to look on the people, but yet I trust the convenience of the building would serve." He seems more enthusiastic about the second option: "If her Highness be minded to keep in her own palace at St Austin's, then might your lordships be otherwise placed in the houses of the dean and certain prebendaries." He goes on to describe the comfortable, personalized accommodations this would allow for, adding that for Cecil: "Mr. Pierson would as gladly have your lordship in his fine house, most fit for your lordship, if you think so good."[79] Not surprisingly, it is this second option that was adopted. Mary Hill Cole classifies Parker as a "reluctant host" who uses a tactful strategy to "persuade the Queen to look elsewhere for good accommodation."[80] If so, Parker's reluctance would

not seem to be motivated by the typical concerns of cost and inconvenience—
especially since he so cheerfully exceeds the mark in almost all other facets of
his hospitality. I would argue that Parker's evasion is not an avoidance of hosting
so much as an attempt to lodge the Queen at St. Augustine's Abbey.

Why? The main reason is that it would be difficult to pick another site that
so well conveyed the age and grandeur of the English church. Despite its conversion to a royal palace, the site was still very much associated with its pre-
Reformation history and its thousand-year-old founder. Parker himself refers to
it as the "palace at St. Austin's," and on John Speed's early seventeenth-century
map of Canterbury, the still-walled site is labeled "Austins Ruynes" and is
embellished with four large, jagged-looking stone "ruynes." As Speed's artistry
suggests, these historical associations endured because the site was still very
much dominated by the physical remnants of the abbey. Alongside his generic
ruins, Speed also depicts surviving features like the main abbey gate, the cemetery gate, and Ethelbert's Tower (the massive northwest tower of the church).
An earlier (circa 1570) hand-drawn map of the area has even greater detail,
including walls, gates, Ethelbert's Tower, the Abbott's hall, and the ruined north
side of the nave of the church.[81] Other visual evidence for surviving monastic
structures comes from several seventeenth-century drawings of the site, made
in part because of the picturesque appeal of the crumbling buildings.[82]

Moreover, these ruins still had the power to make quite an impression on
contemporaries. William Camden wrote that even though "the greatest part" is
in ruins, "yet it sheweth manifestly to the beholders how great a thing it was."[83]
William Somner said of Ethelbert's Tower in the 1630s that its "beauty though
much defaced and overworn, will witness to succeeding Ages the magnificence of the whole, when all stood compleat in their glory together."[84] Parker
no doubt hoped that the Queen would be similarly impressed, and see in the
stately and extensive ruins the former glory of the English church stretching
all the way back to Augustine. The Queen would have seen and experienced
the site from a variety of perspectives. The road from Sandwich would have
brought her into Canterbury along the long southern border of the monastic
site and would have paralleled the length of the massive, ruined church. She
would have then turned right at the site's southwest corner—at the abbey's old
crenellated cemetery gate—and skirted its western edge. Finally, she would
have entered the royal palace through Fyndon Gate, which had also been the
main entrance to the abbey. It was in this newly converted section of the abbey
that the Queen would spend most of her time over the next two weeks.

The royal palace was itself primarily medieval and thus bespoke the wealth and power of the pre-Reformation church. Fyndon Gate, for instance, had been built around 1300 to 1309 by Abbot Fyndon; it is "exceptionally fine and massive and capped with turrets and crenellations . . . [reflecting] the grandeur of the abbot who built it."[85] Above the gate's entrance passage is the chamber in which the Queen lodged. It is a "spacious and finely proportioned room, measuring nearly 30 ft by 20."[86] This chamber has a fireplace as well as five windows, two of which boast fine medieval tracery. An internal staircase connects the chamber to another fourteenth-century building, the former guest hall of the monastery—"a fine chamber of 53 ft by 27"—which had been converted to the principal room of the royal palace. Just beyond the hall was the guest chapel, which featured a "curious open porch below and . . . three Early English lancets above."

From the royal palace sector of the site, many other surviving ecclesiastical buildings were visible, including the Abbot's Hall, Ethelbert's Tower, the refitted great stone kitchen of the abbey, and the western edge of the cloister. The Queen's chamber itself had a window in the eastern wall that provided "fine views" over other parts of site.[87] Had the Queen climbed the staircase from her room into the northwest turret of the gate, she would have encountered even more commanding views. To the east could be seen some surviving monastic buildings in the immediate foreground as well as the more extensive ruins of the church, chapter house, refectory, and infirmary, and beyond them the seventh-century Chapel of St. Pancras (where Augustine reputedly said his first mass in Canterbury). It may even have been possible to catch a glimpse of St. Martin's Church (the oldest church in England, founded circa 580, even before Augustine's arrival) to the southeast. To the west, the view would have taken in the city walls, and rising above them the spires of Canterbury Cathedral and its massive Bell Harry Tower (completed in 1498). In other words, the view from Fyndon Gate was probably one of the grandest ecclesiastical views in all of England. Not only does it provide rich, visual evidence of the church's physical presence across the centuries, it also has what R. J. E. Boggis calls "hallowing associations."[88]

As the site of England's oldest church and the place where Augustine lived, worked, and is buried, St. Augustine's might justly be called the cradle of English Christianity. Its medley of surviving buildings—gatehouses, towers, halls, chapels—emblematize how that fledgling church flourished in the centuries that followed as a center of worship, learning, hospitality, and community. Its pillars, arches, towers, vaulting, and tracery bear silent witness to the beauty, wealth, and power of that church. Of course, the site's decline also attests to the recent struggles of that church, and its partial conversion to a royal palace is a perfect emblem of the monarchy's new powers of supreme governorship. Given the monarchy's role in bringing about the Reformation, such a change would not be seen as wholly negative by Parker. Yet the subsequent weakening of the episcopacy had (as the site also suggests) partially interrupted and impaired the church's function. Nonetheless, the abbey site conveys a clear sense of the longevity, wealth, and grandeur of the English church. It is a palpable reminder of what the English church has been and what it still might be. It is no wonder that Parker preferred the Queen to lodge here.

The Archbishop's Palace

Though Parker used St. Augustine's Abbey to evoke the church's past grandeur, he was also keen to assert the continuing dignity and magnificence of his church. For that he turned to another Canterbury landmark: the Archbishop's Palace. Built circa 1080 by Archbishop Lanfranc, the palace was located to the northwest of the cathedral. It was really more of a precinct than a palace, as it comprised a large number of structures—gatehouse, hall, private apartments, ecclesiastical courts, chapel, kitchens, stables, bakehouse, brewhouse, and so forth—centered around a large outer court. Even though Lambeth Palace was becoming more prominent in the second half of the sixteenth century, Parker's Canterbury residence was still "the most important of all the Primate's palaces" and was, as Tim Tatton-Brown says, "one of the greatest residences in England."[89] The medieval palace had been seriously damaged by fire in December 1543, and it was Parker who lovingly rebuilt and restored it in the early 1560s—at a personal cost of some £1,400.[90] Parker was motivated in part by his need for a suitable venue in which to entertain various groups.[91] In 1565, Parker hosted the Judges of the Assizes and other county elites for a grand feast in the newly restored palace. The next year, he further "reinforce[d] the bonds of local affinity" at a Whitsun feast by hosting "the leading citizens of Canterbury, their mayor, the leading gentry of Kent, the Dean and clergy of the cathedral."[92] In 1570, he used the palace to hold a grand ecclesiastical feast to celebrate the consecration of Edmund Grindal as Archbishop of York. These occasions not only allowed Parker to cultivate relationships that were crucial for the church to function effectively, they were "also a celebration of the revived power of the church, visibly displayed in the reconstructed palace."[93] One way that Parker made this association clear was by putting his own heraldic arms around the newly restored palace: on a new brick stair tower in the center of the complex, in the spandrel of a fireplace on the ground floor, and (most visibly) on a large south-facing gable (along with the year "1565") immediately adjacent to the west front of the cathedral.[94]

Even if he did not want to lodge the Queen here, Parker's correspondence reveals that he intended all along to entertain his royal visitors in the palace. On Monday, September 7, it hosted a lavish feast for the Queen's fortieth birthday. Parker also maintained an open house at the palace throughout the two-week visit for "guests both from the court and from the county" (JN2, 80). One night he even hosted a special supper for "certain of the [Privy] council, and divers of the court."[95]

The Tudor palace had many features that would have impressed Parker's guests. Foremost among these was the palace's Great Hall, which had been completed by Archbishop Stephen Langton in 1220. With dimensions of 168 by 69 feet, it was the second largest hall in Britain (behind only Westminster Hall) at the time of its completion.[96] Internally, the hall was divided into eight twenty-foot bays by elegant Purbeck marble shafts that rose majestically upward to a large-beamed scissor-braced roof. The central space was flanked by north and south aisles whose walls were pierced by huge double-transomed, quatrefoil windows. The gabled end walls likely contained oculus windows, and against the eastern wall sat a dais surmounted by an elaborate stone canopy. Overall, the hall was "a splendid and majestic structure, spacious and full of light."[97] Moreover, it was twice the size of the Queen's hall at St. Augustine's!

The building was just as impressive externally. It took up the whole south side of the palace's outer court, so it dominated the view of visitors who entered (as the Queen did) through the main gate on St. Alphege's Street. Including the solar at the eastern end of the building, the entire structure ran for nearly 200 feet. Its massive walls were broken up by magnificent buttressed transverse gables that mirrored the internal bays, and its fine entry porch at the northwest end provided access to the hall. All in all, the hall produced a "delicate, yet monumental effect," and it is no wonder that it was at the center of Parker's lavish receptions throughout the 1560s and when the Queen visited in 1573.[98]

If the hall evoked the medieval grandeur of Parker's predecessors, the north/south range catered more to contemporary standards of luxury. During the repair work of the 1560s, Parker updated and added to this suite of apartments. His additions included a long gallery eighty feet in length, a large dining room, and a brick stair tower; he also modified privy chambers, rebuilt kitchens, and planted gardens.[99] While there are no specific records of how the Canterbury palace was furnished, it was probably comparable to Lambeth Palace, where—according to a 1575 inventory—the principal rooms were hung with tapestries and richly furnished with plate, furniture, books, maps, paintings, a clock, and musical instruments.[100] It is not clear which rooms the Queen and her courtiers might have seen in addition to the hall, though Parker does report in the *Matthaeus* that on the night of the birthday feast the Queen "by a private way, . . . went up to the Archbishop's gallery" to hold a conversation with the French ambassador who was in attendance (*JN2*, 78).

What is clear from the accounts is that the Queen's entertainment at the palace was even more extravagant than Parker's previous entertainments. The *Matthaeus* reports that "in this most lavish banquet, with which the Archbishop celebrated the very day and hour on which the Queen reached the fortieth year of her life, the following arrangements were observed. Noblemen alone attended on the Queen, and as soon as she had washed her hands, she went up to a table spread out traversely in the highest part of the Archbishop's palace. She sat at the middle of this table, on a certain ancient throne of marble, decorated with cloths interwoven with gold, beneath a precious royal canopy, gleaming with gold . . . Two rows of dishes, piled with the most exquisite meat and fish, were set before them, in addition to a third, which comprised the choicest cakes" (*JN2*, 76–78). After dinner, there was music and dancing. The variety and richness of this entertainment obviously glorified the Queen, but it also served to aggrandize the host who made it possible. It was, after all, his hall, his gold cloth, and his "exquisite" food. According to Tatton-Brown, the "ancient throne of marble" was none other than St. Augustine's Chair, "the thirteenth-century Purbeck marble archiepiscopal throne apparently taken from the cathedral to the great hall for the queen to sit on."[101] In other words, Parker's own magnificence was on display. In giving what he characterizes as a "splendid and sumptuous banquet" for the Queen and her councilors, Parker was trying to impress them with the state and grandeur of the church (*JN2*, 79). In the banquet preparations, Parker even invited the Queen to "come in through my gallery, and see the disposition of the hall in dinner-time, at a window opening thereunto."[102] Parker's desire for her to have a bird's-eye view of the size, quality, and orderly arrangement of the feast he had prepared lends credence to Brook's characterization of the event as a bit of "extravagant pageantry" designed to make an impression.[103]

However, given the climate of the 1570s, Parker was not merely trying to demonstrate his own magnificence; he was also trying to justify the concept of clerical magnificence and show that it was crucial to the functioning of the Elizabethan church. He did this primarily by using the Queen's birthday feast to demonstrate the efficacy of magnificence. As we have seen, a key function of the English arch-episcopate was to "receive foreign guests . . . as a part of their work in nurturing the English Church."[104] Parker clearly embraced this function. His 1572–1573 correspondence reveals his largesse toward two Irish bishops, an Italian intellectual, and French clerics fleeing the St. Bartholomew's Day Massacre.[105] Other foreign dignitaries were sent to Parker by the Crown. When the new French ambassador was en route to a treaty signing in 1564, the Queen asked Parker to receive him, in part "to impress [him] . . . with the dignity still attaching to the Church in England and to dispel any idea that it had been reduced to the status it held in some of the non-catholic countries."[106] As it turned out, the Queen's 1573 visit was also a diplomatic occasion. Not only were English nobles and courtiers present at the birthday feast, but also the comte de Retz, Marshal of France, and Lord La Mothe, the French ambassador to England. They were newly arrived in England as part of a "special diplomatic mission" to discuss the projected match between the Queen and the duc d'Alençon.[107] Since the Queen was on progress, they met her in Canterbury and thus Parker's festivities became the backdrop against which they pursued their diplomatic aims. At the birthday banquet, Parker recorded that they were seated "on the Queen's right hand, at the end of the table," and that "their faces were turned towards the Queen, and their backs to the hall, so that they could engage in conversation with her more conveniently and more companionably" (JN2, 77). Clearly, Parker was sensitive to their presence and made deliberate arrangements to facilitate their discussions with the Queen. After dinner, diplomatic talks continued: "The Queen held a private conversation with de Retz . . . and Lord La Mothe . . . at that long table, while to musical accompaniment, the nobles engaged in dancing" (JN2, 78). Later, after ascending into Parker's gallery, "she continued her conversation with the same extraordinary Ambassador almost until nightfall" (JN2, 78).

It is worth noting that Parker had relatively little personal contact with the Queen, even though he was hosting her birthday feast in his own hall. He did not sit next to her nor did he apparently have any substantial conversation with her during the evening. Instead, he oversaw the feast but otherwise withdrew so that important (and prolonged) diplomatic conversations could occur.

Brook implicitly criticizes the Queen by saying that she displayed an "aloof dignity" by sitting apart with the French ambassadors, but I would argue that Parker, sensitive to the diplomatic opportunity afforded by the feast, voluntarily withdrew so that the Queen could make the most of the occasion. This is perhaps why, at the end of the evening "she summoned the Archbishop, and told him how much pleasure and honour she had felt at that day's banquet . . . [and gave] him the greatest thanks" (*JN2*, 78–79). Regardless of the precise cause of the Queen's gratitude, other members of the court in attendance— including those who were not sympathetic to prelatical pomp—could see that the archbishop's lavish and carefully executed hospitality had helped facilitate an important diplomatic moment.

Parker also used the occasion to demonstrate the church's ability to forge local consensus. Some of the same local constituents that he had entertained in 1565 and 1566 were also invited to the Queen's birthday feast in 1573. In addition to the Queen, French ambassadors, councilors, noblemen, and "distinguished ladies," there were also tables for "the Mayor of Canterbury, with the leading men of that city, and the noblemen and women of the county of Kent" (*JN2*, 78). Parker presumably wanted to include civic elites and local gentry in order to honor and further good relations with them, as social bonds between clergy and local leaders were crucial in fostering cooperation and good discipline, but their presence was also intended for the Queen and her court. The feast was an opportunity for Parker to underscore his own good local relations and the broad-based consensus that he had been able to build in his diocese. In doing so, he may have even been trying to counter contemporary Puritan complaints that the prelates prioritized worldly concerns at the expense of their local "flocks."[108] Parker's use of the banquet also showed that the episcopacy's much-maligned hospitality was a way of bringing all levels of society into the fold. The Queen's birthday feast physically assembled all ranks of ruling society in a visual display of order and inclusiveness.

We can see Parker laying the groundwork for this effect earlier during the Queen's progress through Kent. On August 25, nine days before the Queen arrived in Canterbury, Parker had journeyed east and "met her Highness as she was coming to Dover upon Folkestone Down, the which I rather did, with all my men, to shew my duty to her, and mine affection to the shire, who likewise there met her."[109] Parker's presence aided the gentry—the "300 knights and nobles of Kent gathered there" (*JN2*, 73)—in providing a grand, formal welcome to the county. "Shew[ing] . . . mine affection" thus takes the form of supporting their efforts and swelling their numbers. At the same time, Parker was also showing his affection for the gentry *to the Queen and court.* In other words, his presence also highlighted the congenial local relations that both primate and local gentry shared. For both the Dover welcome and the palace feast, it is clear that Parker is using the royal progress to enrich and display local relationships. Ecclesiastical magnificence is ultimately valuable because it can be deployed to benefit the larger goals of the Elizabethan church.

Canterbury Cathedral

If Parker's goals at times include diplomacy and local interactions, they are most focused on spiritual edification. Thus, Parker's final site—Canterbury Cathedral—underscores the effectiveness of the church's religious function. The records reveal that Parker made the cathedral a focal point of the royal visit. The Queen worshipped at the cathedral no fewer than three times during her stay in Canterbury. She attended evensong on the night of her arrival, September 3, and then attended the Sunday service on September 6 and September 13. One of Parker's goals in featuring the cathedral so prominently may well have been to emphasize its splendor and magnificence. In the letter to Cecil, Parker's plans call for the Queen to enter through the massive west door, process down the nave into "the midst of the church," then "through the quire, up to the traverse next to the communion-table."[110] She thus moved through the entire length of the church, passing by and through the main sections of the nave, crossing, transepts, choir, presbytery, and high altar. In doing so, she took in the full beauty and grandeur of the cathedral. She probably entered the cathedral close via the colorful and exquisitely carved Christchurch Gate. She would then have been greeted by a dramatic view of the length of the church, topped by the huge Bell Harry Tower. William Camden registers the cathedral's impressiveness, saying that it has "so great a majestie and statelinesse, that it striketh a sensible impression of religion into their mindes that behold it a farre off."[111] Once inside the west door (or finely carved south entrance porch), the viewer was looking down the length of a sublime perpendicular nave. After reaching the crossing and looking two hundred feet up into the fan vaulting of the central tower, the visitor would then pass through the massive carved stone screen (circa 1400) into one of largest choirs in England. Even if much of the moveable wealth of the cathedral had been despoiled in the 1530s—including the gem-encrusted shrine of St.

Thomas à Beckett—this was still a magnificent space. William Somner wrote in the 1630s of the "spacious and stately Fabrick" of the interior, the fine tapestries hanging on the stone choir screens, the beauty of the high altar, the quality of the stained glass, and the profusion of monumental tombs.[112] Canterbury Cathedral was and is one of the most beautiful churches in England, and we must remember that this was the first time the Queen had laid eyes on it. It had the potential to make a powerful impression.

Aside from its sheer splendor, the cathedral helped Parker aggrandize the role of archbishops in the church. Historically, the archbishops had played a key role in building and maintaining the church; we have already seen how Lambarde's discussion of Canterbury Cathedral—in one of those texts sent to Cecil in advance of the progress—singles out the past contributions of particular archbishops to the physical fabric of the church. But the tomb monuments of the cathedral provide even more powerful evidence for the connections between the archbishops and this sacred space. After the first ten archbishops were interred at St. Augustine's Abbey, forty-seven of the subsequent fifty-nine were entombed in the cathedral. As Camden wrote, the cathedral "may justly vaunt of many famous mens tombs and monuments."[113] In 1573, twenty-two archbishops still had visible monuments in the church—including Reginald Pole, who, having died in 1558, was the most recently deceased archbishop. Their monuments, tomb chests, effigies, brasses, and plaques could therefore be found throughout the cathedral: Simon Islip and William Whittlesey in the nave, William Warham in the north transept, Stephen Langton off the south transept, William Courteney in the Trinity Chapel, Reginald Pole in the Lady Chapel, and John Morton down in the crypt. In her journey from the western door to the high altar, Queen Elizabeth would have passed by some twenty monuments, which together provided a rich, visible record of the age and continuity of the ecclesiastical hierarchy. The Queen spent much of her time in a "traverse" (a sort of temporary, enclosed chair) near the high altar, surrounded by some of the most prestigious and splendid prelatical monuments. In the presbytery were interred archbishops John Stratford, John Kempe, and Henry Chichele; just up the stairs and flanking the high altar were the monuments of Simon Sudbury and Thomas Bourchier. Chichele's monument is particularly fine: an ornate and brightly colored canopy with niches for carved saints, angels, and biblical figures.

The historical power and status of the archbishops were also embodied in two thrones that occupied this portion of the cathedral. Just to the east of the southern choir stalls sat the archbishop's throne, a carved wooden chair with a canopy that the archbishop sat in during cathedral services. Up the stairs and beyond the high altar was St. Augustine's Chair, which was typically used for the consecration of new archbishops. As its name suggests, it was believed to date from Augustine himself and was thus a potent symbol of the ancient authority of the primate. Its position in the center of the highest part of the cathedral made it especially prominent. In fact, when one walks down the nave, the chair is framed perfectly in the center of the screen's keyhole doorway looking into the choir. If this was, as Tatton-Brown suggests, the "ancient throne of marble" that the Queen sat on during her birthday feast at the palace, she would have gotten a particularly close-up look at this venerable chair.

Canterbury Cathedral's final arch-episcopal association is also its most famous: its site as the martyrdom of Archbishop Thomas à Beckett, and the subsequent establishment of a shrine that became the focal point of pilgrimage throughout England and Western Europe. Of course, the shrine that occupied the Trinity Chapel beyond the high altar had been taken down decades earlier. The area was now simply referred to as "the monuments" and saw limited use.[114] Nor did the Tudor site of the martyrdom in the northwest transept contain any special marker or visible reminder of the day in 1170 when Beckett was struck down.[115] Yet the event itself still resonated powerfully and was an inescapable part of the lore of the cathedral and the city of Canterbury. After all, centuries of pilgrimage had contributed much to its wealth, development, and importance.

This event also embodied—and perhaps continued to embody—the tensions between the English monarchy and the leaders of the English church. Camden's post-Reformation take on Beckett's death is revealing: "Thomas Becket the Archbishop: who being slaine in this Church by Courtiers, for that in maintaining of the Ecclesiastical liberties, he had stubbornly opposed himselfe against the king."[116] Camden reduces the conflict to a question of authority between leaders of church and state, yet even if Beckett was punished for his stubbornness in the short term, history shows that Henry II's actions only strengthened the church and its claims in the long term. I am not suggesting that the tensions between the Queen and Parker were anything like this; the legal status of the royal supremacy and the weakened status of the church had altered the dynamic. Indeed, Parker was much more interested in gaining the Queen's public support, and he never publicly defied her in the way that Grindal would a few years later. But if Camden is any judge, Beckett was an uncomfortable figure for the Tudors. He was a reminder that, at the very least, you had to be careful how you treated the established church, even if you had the upper hand. Parker did nothing to emphasize the cathedral's associations with Beckett, though he did propose that on one Sunday the Queen hear a sermon delivered in the chapter house, located just off the cloisters on the north side of the cathedral complex. As the most direct route would have been through the northwest transept, the Queen may well have passed right by the spot where Beckett had been murdered some four hundred years previously.

For the most part, the monuments, thrones, and historical associations of the cathedral would have aided Parker's attempt to emphasize the dignity and magnificence of his office, and they help account for his attempts to have the Queen frequently visit the cathedral. But she was not only there as a first-time visitor; she was also there to worship. The surviving accounts reveal that Parker was particularly concerned about both the form and content of the services. In the letter to Cecil, he made detailed suggestions regarding both the evensong and the Sunday services that were then, for the most part, carried out. The letter to Grindal reports that after the Queen's entry at the west door, "We then kneeled down, and said the Psalm *Deus misereatur,* in English, with certain other collects briefly; and that in our chimmers and rochets. The choir, with the dean and prebendaries, &c. stood on either side of the church, and brought her Majesty up with a square song, she going under a canopy, borne by four of her temporal knights, to her traverse placed by the communion board."[117] This was clearly a very deliberate and carefully choreo-graphed religious moment that emphasized the formal liturgy of the church. The *Deus misereatur* (Psalm 67) and collect were both stipulated by the *Book of Common Prayer* for that day and service.[118] Meanwhile, Parker's references to the "rochets" and "chimeras" reveal that the attending bishops wore vestments.

These formal elements are just the sort of thing that newly emergent Puritans—"committed to purging the Established Church of its popish 'superstitions'"—might take issue with.[119] As we have seen, the Vestiarian Controversy of the mid-1560s had concerned the very issue of whether or not the clergy should wear the surplice. Even the "square song" played during the processional was contentious, as it was the sort of sophisticated musical composition that the godly did not like—they preferred metrical psalms sung by the entire congregation rather than the "curious singing" of choirs.[120] These differing philosophies of worship were not just theoretical; there was a good bit of variation in parishes across England. According to Brook, "Services and prayers . . . were said by some in the chancel, by others in the body of the church, or from the pulpit. The order of the Prayer Book was kept precisely by some, others inserted metrical psalms. Some wore a surplice, others did not. The table was variously set in the body of the church or in the chancel, altar-wise, either a yard from the wall or in the midst of the chancel."[121] This was, of course, the specific variation that Parker was endeavoring to bring into con-formity. Thus he used this moment to model—for all in attendance—what orthodox practice should look like. The intent was not merely instructional; Parker's investment in such formal elements was an attempt to display the full order and dignity of the English church.

Parker no doubt also hoped that the Queen's participation might encour-age conformity. This seems to have been Parker's main motive in wanting her to take communion during her visit to Canterbury. As he made preparations for the progress visit, Parker wrote to Cecil, "It would much rejoice and sta-blish the people here in this religion, to see her Highness that Sunday (being the first Sunday of the month when others also customably may receive), as a godly devout prince, in her chief and metropolitical church openly to receive the communion, which by her favour I would minister unto her. *Plurima sunt magnifica et utilia, sed hoc unum est necessarium* ['There are many things that are great and useful, but this one thing is indispensable']."[122] The communion service was particularly given to "great variation"; according to Brook, "Some ministers wore surplice and cope; some surplice only; some neither. A chalice might be used, or a special communion cup, or a common cup. Some used leavened bread, others wafers. Some received kneeling, others standing, oth-ers seated."[123] So if Parker could get the Queen to take communion in the chief church of the realm, then the way in which she took it would set a clear stan-dard and thereby "stablish the people here in this religion." One would expect the Queen to be a willing collaborator. Indeed, Cole identifies the fostering of religious uniformity as one of the Queen's main goals on the 1573 progress.[124] But the Queen had repeatedly withheld her public support by declining to give the royal assent to any number of advertisements, canons, articles, and resolutions promulgated by the bishops between 1561 and 1571. As a result, the prelacy's ability to enforce obedience had been hindered and now—with the eruption of the Admonition Controversy—severely handicapped.

For Parker, the idea of administering communion to the Queen must have seemed like a tantalizing prospect. If he could not receive her formal assent, getting her public participation was the next best thing. In deliberately specifying that "I would minister unto her," Parker could ensure that all of the particulars would conform to officially sanctioned church practices. The Queen's participation would thus be tantamount to her tacit endorsement. This is why he wrote the Latin phrase "There are many things that are great and useful, but this one thing is indispensable." I would argue that Parker is not referring to the centrality of communion in worship, but to the necessity of getting what would amount to the Queen's endorsement. This reading is perhaps supported by the fact that there is no record of whether or not the Queen took communion at Canterbury.[125] Surely if she had, Parker would have reported it either in his private correspondence to Grindal or in the account he gives in *Matthaeus*. The Queen, too, it would seem, realized what was at stake in her participation, and chose to continue her strategy of withholding.

Even if the Queen may not have publicly taken communion, Parker could nevertheless highlight the many functions of the cathedral itself. After the Reformation, not only the wealth, but also the role and function of cathedrals was diminished. "What," asks Patrick Collinson, "could a cathedral contribute to the service of God after the Protestant Reformation had undermined the value of good works, attributing salvation to faith alone? And when the transcendence and otherness of God had replaced the medieval notion that the holy could be localized, even possessed?"[126] Of course, most cathedrals were re-founded in the 1530s and 1540s as secular foundations and did play an important part in sixteenth-century religious life—in the provision of hospitality, as communities of learning and scholarship, as supporters of grammar schools, relievers of poverty, and stimulants to local urban economies.[127] But like so many other aspects of the established church, cathedrals were under increasing attack by the 1570s. Puritans like John Field complained that they were "the dens . . . of loitering lubbers" where deans, vice-deans, canons, treasurers, singing men, organ players, pensioners, readers, and vergers all "live in great idleness, and have their abiding . . . The church of God never knew them; neither doth any reformed church in the world know them."[128] Others acknowledged that they did house learned and able men, but that they unadvisedly concentrated talented divines together rather than spreading them more equally throughout the realm.[129] Still others thought that cathedrals were superfluous, and by the 1580s there were even proposals for dissolving cathedral foundations and using their endowments to fund the wars in the Netherlands.[130]

Against this antagonistic backdrop, Parker was keen to justify cathedrals and their roles, and he used the Queen's visit to do so. One approach was to highlight the beautiful and orderly settings created by cathedrals and to emphasize the worship, reverence, and due conformity that they inspired. We have already noted Parker's careful combination of space, formal liturgy, and music at the Queen's first entry into the cathedral. During this same evensong service, the French ambassador was recorded as having been so moved by the music that he said, "Ye Gods, I believe no prince in the whole of Europe, no, not even the most holy father, ever heard the like."[131] Certainly, the high quality of their music was one of the things that separated cathedrals from other churches. Stanford Lehmberg points out that "throughout the Tudor period, musicians made up a majority of the persons serving in all of the English cathedrals, and musical standards remained high"; however, the Puritans "disagreed vehemently with this sense of priorities" and wanted to "[shift] the emphasis from singing to preaching, even to the point of disbanding the musical establishments entirely."[132] Parker's investment in music is thus all the more striking, and it suggests that he was keen to demonstrate the transcendent effect that cathedral music could have.

Parker did not only defend the cathedral along the lines of traditional worship; he also highlighted the ways in which cathedrals might be repurposed for post-Reformation needs. In a letter written to Cecil before the royal visit, Parker proposes that after taking communion, the Queen might hear the dean preach in the "the common chapter, being the place of sermons."[133] At Canterbury, the chapter house had been converted from a daily meeting place for monks to a preaching hall, no doubt owing to its relatively large size and excellent acoustics. The chapter had even built a wooden balcony to accommodate more people. By inviting the Queen and other courtiers to leave the cathedral presbytery and hear a sermon in the chapter house, Parker was drawing attention to the ways in which the cathedral had been adapted to the Protestant emphasis on preaching.

Finally, Parker used the Queen's visit to highlight the functions of the cathedral's prebendaries. The prebends were highly educated canons who helped with the administration of the cathedral, preached a specified number of times per year, and were in turn allotted stipends. At Canterbury there were twelve prebends, and each was allotted a house in the cathedral precinct. Like other "odious" features of cathedrals, by the 1570s prebends were under attack by Puritans, who grouped them among the "loitering lubbers" who were little better than modern-day monks. Even earlier, Cranmer had complained that "commonly a prebendary is neither a learner, nor teacher, but a good viander";

Elizabethan bishops routinely complained during their visitations about the pride, whoredom, and ignorance of some prebends.[134] Popular resentment toward prebends was increased by the fact that some of them collected their stipends but maintained minimal residence at their cathedrals—and even rented out their houses. At Canterbury, Parker took measures during two visitations of the cathedral (in 1570, and again in 1573) to increase the residency of prebends; one of his main reasons seems to have been that otherwise their absences would "seriously hinder the hospitality due from the Chapter to important travelers."[135]

During the Queen's visit in 1573, Parker highlighted the prebends' role as hosts. In the letter in which he encouraged the Queen to stay at St. Augustine's, he recommended that Cecil and the other "lordships be otherwise placed in the houses of the dean, and certain prebendaries."[136] Among the latter, he specifically mentions Thomas Lawse, John Bungey, and Andrew Peerson. In referring to Bungey, he also specifies that his house is "where the Frenche Cardinall laye"—a reference to the hospitality that the Huguenot refugee Odet de Coligny enjoyed in Canterbury for several months before his death in 1571. By offering these houses and referring to past episodes of hospitality, Parker is underscoring the vital role that Canterbury's prebends played in the functioning of their cathedral. Canterbury's prebends were learned and active scholars, a point that Parker made by including "The Discourse of Dover"—likely composed by the prebend William Darell—among the texts that he sent to Cecil in advance of the progress. In all of these areas—setting, music, chapter house, prebends— Parker uses the opportunity of the Queen's visit to show the wider importance and functions of cathedrals to those who might need convincing.

Gift-Giving

The final way in which Parker appealed to the Queen and her retinue was through gift-giving. At the end of the *Matthaeus* entry on the Queen's visit, Parker carefully records a series of gifts that he gave to the royal visitors. To the Queen, he gave a splendid golden salt cellar and an "outstanding" horse. To Cecil and a few other lords, he also "bestowed horses of this kind." To other courtiers and counsellors, he gave a book of anti-Catholic polemic, *De Visibili Rom'anarchia*. He proffered two books—a commentary on Ecclesiastes and a small Bible—to the ladies and noblewomen. Finally, "among the attendants and servants of the royal household, he distributed more than 500 gold pieces"

(*JN*2, 80). The description reveals Parker's eagerness to extend his largesse beyond the Queen to the full range of visitors in attendance. It also shows that he conceived of these guests hierarchically (according to both social status and gender), and that he put a great deal of thought into selecting gifts that were appropriate to each group. In her recent book, *The Power of Gifts*, Felicity Heal has written extensively on the various purposes and meanings of gift-giving in early modern culture.[137] Some of the main ways that gifts functioned for the giver were to express authority, secure loyalty, and display magnificence. Parker's progress gifts partake of all these functions, though again they are deployed particularly to display the status and function of the established church.

The *Matthaeus* devotes the most space to describing the salt cellar that Parker gave to the Queen:

> Besides this splendid and sumptuous banquet, the Archbishop bestowed certain distinguished gifts upon the Queen, namely a salt cellar made of gold, into the cover of which was inset a jewel, an agate, containing St George killing the dragon, along with verses in French upon the customary royal insignia; in the curved section or hollow of this was enclosed another agate, incised into which was a true likeness of the Queen on white agate. On the top of its cover, a small golden boat held a rectangular diamond. The Archbishop gave the Queen this salt cellar as a gift, with six Portugese gold pieces enclosed within it, each of which was worth three pounds and ten English shillings, and its value was reckoned at more than 200 English marks. (*JN*2, 79)

Heal characterizes a salt cellar as a gift of "great value and ostentation" and notes that it was the sort of gift that was typically given by nobles and their wives to the monarch.[138] Thus, Parker's choice of such an ornate object can be seen as an assertion of the high social status of the episcopacy, a status that (as we have seen) had actually been eroded considerably. The *Matthaeus*'s description clearly emphasizes the monetary value of the gift. It is made of gold, encrusted with jewels, filled with currency, and worth 200 marks—or around £133.[139] At the same time, the salt cellar is also a work of great intricacy and artistry. It features carefully mounted jewels that are incised with both a scene (St. George killing the dragon) and a portrait (of Elizabeth). French verses are inscribed into the vessel, and a golden boat floats on top of its cover. The salt cellar's distinctiveness and ingenuity would have made it just the sort of gift that Elizabeth would have liked.[140] Moreover, this salt cellar's hybrid status as both plate and jewel made it a more intimate gift than the more generic plate (gold and silver cups and bowls) that most private hosts gave to the Queen on progress. Parker even took pains to customize the monetary portion of his gift. Gifts of cash were much more common and acceptable as "tokens of goodwill" than they are in modern times; even so, they might seem a bit impersonal unless they "could also be differentiated from daily exchange by [their] physical appearance as well as the circumstances of presentation."[141] Parker does just that. He puts his monetary gift of £21 into the form of gold (rather than silver, the customary metal of currency), gives it an exotic Portuguese mint, and encloses it within an elaborate salt cellar. He thus renders his monetary gift both unique and original.

Parker's other gift to the Queen also partakes of this same combination of magnificence and intimacy. According to the *Matthaeus:* "Moreover the Archbishop gave her as a gift an outstanding horse, which she had seen and noticed among the other horses of his cavalcade, when (as we said) she passed by the Archbishop's retinue on Folkestone Hill" (*JN* 2, 79). As with the salt cellar, the nature of the gift itself is significant. According to Heal, horses were the gift of choice from the English Crown "to foreign monarchs and often from them in return."[142] Again, Parker's choice of gift seems an attempt to assert the status of himself and his bishops, who had previously been seen as the pre-Reformation "princes" of the Church. At the same time, Parker was also keen to show his knowledge and understanding of the Queen. Seneca's much-heeded advice on gift-giving was that one should seek to please and delight the recipient. In this sense, the rarity or thoughtfulness of a gift might be even more important than its cost—particularly if it bespeaks "an awareness of the nature of the recipient." In this case, Parker observed the Queen's reaction to a particular horse some nine days before, and then presented her with the very animal that she had "seen and noticed."Whereas the salt cellar had clearly been many months in the planning, the horse is presented as a form of spontaneous largesse, a bit of gallantry designed to surprise and delight the Queen. One of the disadvantages of a horse gift, according to Heal, is that "they were not clearly demarcated as unique"—as horses tend to look alike.This is perhaps why Parker goes out of his way to distinguish this horse as being "outstanding" and noteworthy; certainly, the Queen noted its distinctiveness from other horses in the "cavalcade," and recognized it when the Archbishop presented it to her.

The *Matthaeus* notes that Parker "also bestowed horses of this kind upon certain noblemen then accompanying the Queen" (*JN2, 79*). These recipients likely included William Cecil, Thomas Radcliffe, Robert Dudley, and Christopher Hatton, since these were the men for whom Parker had taken special pains with regards to lodging arrangements. These four men were both important and influential: Cecil, Dudley, and Radcliffe were among the seven to ten core privy councilors, and Hatton would soon join them. The first two had Puritan leanings, while the latter were more conservative and even Catholic-leaning. Parker's equine gifts thus allowed him to gratify, honor, and display clerical magnificence to men of different religious leanings. Moreover, since "many royal ministers and nobles gave and received horses internationally," Parker's gift could be read as a claim of social equality.[143] We do know from an August 17 letter to Cecil that Parker had been planning this gift for some time and that he had already broached it with Cecil: "I am in preparing for three or four of my good lords some geldings, and if I knew whether would like you best, either one for your own saddle, or a fine little white gelding for your foot-cloth, or one for one of your gentlemen or yeomen, I would so appoint you."[144] Parker's attempt to tailor his gift to please Cecil can also be extended to Dudley, who, as Master of the Queen's Horse and a renowned horsemen himself, would derive particular pleasure from such a gift.

Books were the final type of gift that Parker bestowed on his guests. As Heal notes, books were a special kind of gift that could combine "personal, ideological, and aesthetic qualities."[145] They could also be used to offer advice and encode messages to a recipient—particularly in matters of state and religion.[146] During his ecclesiastical career, "Matthew Parker," says Heal, "elevated the giving of the book to an art form," and he used it for purposes ranging from "direct propaganda" to "a more subtle tool of persuasion."[147] Indeed, we have already seen the ulterior motives that likely animated Parker's reasons for sending the four pre-progress texts to Cecil. In this section, the *Matthaeus* records that "to certain noble individuals and councillors in the hall, he gave a book recently published in Latin, *De Visibili Rom'anarchia,* written against the *Monarchia* of N. Sanders" (*JN2, 79*). Nicholas Sanders was a Catholic whose *De visibili Ecclesiae Monarchia* had been published abroad in 1571. Not only did it attack the Reformation and the English Church, it also "concerned the honour and state of the realm, the dignity and legitimation of the Prince" and had even cast aspersions on Lord Burghley.[148] Parker had promptly commissioned several clergymen to write public responses to different sections of the book, including George Acworth, whose *De Visibili Rom'anarchia* attacked the preface of Sanders's work.[149] In distributing Acworth's contribution to the fray, Parker was underscoring the capacity of his church to enter the international arena and defend the cause of true religion as well as the monarchy with which it was so closely aligned.

The other two gift books are also religious in scope. According to the *Matthaeus*, "To the ladies and noblewomen, the Archbishop gave a Commentary on Ecclesiastes, translated into English, and a smaller English Bible, bound with great skill and decoration" (*JN2*, 79). The former was written by Martin Luther and had been rendered into English in 1573 by an unknown translator.[150] The edition is in octavo format: perfect for holding in the hand and slipping into one's pocket. The "smaller English Bible" was likely a quarto edition of the much larger *Bishop's Bible* that had been published in 1568.[151] Both texts are apt representatives of the established church's activities in making the holy scriptures more available and understandable to a lay audience. Both the Bible and the Commentary on Ecclesiastes were rendered into vernacular English and were in relatively small, usable forms; these were practical gifts the ladies could use on a daily basis.

At the same time, both texts make claims about the church's continuing authority as scriptural arbiter. For instance, the Argument to the Commentary establishes that "this booke [Ecclesiastes] is one of the most difficulte books of the whole Scripture" (*ES*, 6 verso)—and is thus in special need of careful analysis and interpretation. It then goes out of its way to assert that the church and the church alone has this responsibility. The prefatory material claims that the book's "tytle of Ecclesiastes, or Preacher" does not refer to Solomon but to the text itself: "For where he was a kyng, it was not his dutie or office to preach but the Priestes, and Levites" (*ES*, 10 recto). According to the anonymous translator, much of the book was indeed spoken by Solomon, but these things were uttered in the presence of others and "afterward, some of the rulers of the Cominaltie, or clergie noted them and gathered them in this order" (*ES*, 10 verso). The clergy, then, are the actual authors of this biblical book. The book is called Ecclesiastes "not [because] Salomon was any Preacher, but [because] the booke maketh as it were a publicke Sermon" (*ES*, 10 verso). This would seem to be an elaborate treatment of a relatively minor point of authorship—especially since Solomon, reputedly the wisest person to ever live, might be given the benefit of the doubt. But the preface uses the question of authorship to carefully differentiate the authority of political leaders and clergymen, and to make the point that it is the latter who are more properly the arbiters and interpreters of scripture. This is certainly a point that would resonate in Elizabethan England, where the precise nature of the Queen's supreme governorship of the church was far from clearly defined. In fact, the point about clerical authority is made three times over: in the claim that the clergy authored this biblical book, in the fact that Luther authorized the detailed commentary on Ecclesiastes that follows, and in the fact that the text was now being distributed by Archbishop Parker.

The *Bishop's Bible* reflects some of these same episcopal claims. It was colloquially known as the *Bishop's Bible* because it was produced by the prelacy—Parker and individual bishops actually did the work of translation—and also because it attempted to revise the overt Calvinism of the popular Geneva Bible of 1560. Its name may as well refer to the level of mediation provided by the bishops. The 1568 version contains some forty-seven pages of preliminary material, including a five-page preface, a six-page prologue by Cranmer, and detailed tables of "Proper lessons to be read" on Sundays, "Proper psalmes [for] certayne dayes," and "The order howe the rest of holy Scripture . . . is appoynted to be read."[152] These recommendations are then integrated into an eighteen-page calendar specifying what to read on each day of each month. In the Scriptures themselves, marginal notes appear frequently to label, summarize, and provide commentary. Clearly, the established church has much to say about how the Scriptures should be ordered, approached, and interpreted. It is the bishops who mediate between the individual believer and the mass of scripture and provide scaffolding so that the latter can be approached most fruitfully. The 1569 quarto edition distributed by Parker at Canterbury had most of these same paratextual features.[153] Like the Ecclesiastes volume, it made a strong claim about the scriptural authority of the established church.

All three gift books are also aesthetic objects that seek to visually delight their recipients. The quarto Bible features an elaborate title page and engravings of dramatic biblical scenes. *De Visibili* has ornate, illuminated-style letters and geometric patterning at the beginnings and ends of its books. The Commentary on Ecclesiastes features multiple fonts that cleanly distinguish the biblical passages from their adjoining commentary. All three books were handsomely bound at the London press of John Day. Parker himself draws attention to the Bible being "bound with great skill and decoration" (*JN2*, 80), and the Ecclesiastes Commentary is encased in clean, white vellum.[154] Such attention to aesthetic detail reflects positively on Parker and the church that he represents. Like the *De Antiquitate*, these texts function as a tangible display of the church's magnificence and sophistication. In this sense, the gift books are consistent with—and perhaps permanent reminders of—the other forms of magnificence that Parker had displayed throughout the visit.

Taken as a whole, Parker's deployment of magnificence during the Queen's 1573 visit was multi-functional. His investment in hospitality (and particularly his use of key texts and places) allowed him to emphasize the wealth, grandeur, authority, and continuity of the episcopacy. At the same time, these strategies allowed him to emphasize the diverse functions of the established church, including its ability to forge local consensus, facilitate diplomacy, inspire devotion, enforce conformity, engage in international polemic, defend the monarchy, and make the Scriptures accessible while also mediating their interpretation. Overall, Parker sought to create an image of the importance and vitality of the established church. In doing so, he defended that church against its detractors and appealed to the Queen and her councilors for public support.

Epilogue

Were Parker's efforts effective? In the short term, the Crown did take actions to support the bishops in the wake of the Queen's visit to Canterbury. Back in London on October 20, the Queen issued what has become known as the Proclamation of 1573. This document empowered the bishops to more strictly enforce the Act of Uniformity and more thoroughly suppress Presbyterianism—though it also blamed the current disorders on the laxity and negligence of the bishops themselves.[155] On November 8, the Privy Council got behind these efforts by directing the bishops to proceed with an "episcopal inquisition" of non-conforming ministers, which resulted in many suspensions and deprivations.[156] However, this crackdown may even had "intensif[ied] the schismatic tendencies of the Presbyterian movement" in the short term, and it was not exactly the sort of support that Parker craved.[157] The bishops were not only publicly castigated, they alone had to carry out the difficult work of enforcement and absorb the ire it generated. Yet from Parker's perspective, at least it was a step in the right direction.

But perhaps Parker's efforts were more successful in the long term. If the 1570s was the key decade for bringing the crown and church hierarchy into an alliance, and "finally demonstrated that the episcopate would survive in its traditional form," Parker's efforts were surely a part of that process.[158] Parker would be dead by 1575, but just around the corner was a "new era of harmony between Elizabeth and her bishops, as crown and episcopate came to share the common purpose of eradicating political Puritanism and grass-roots Presbyterianism."[159] It may be that this form of episcopal government naturally appealed to the Queen's religious temperament, and Parker did not change her mind.[160] However, he did at least give that temperament its fullest display at Canterbury in 1573 and demonstrate the potential fruitfulness of such a partnership.

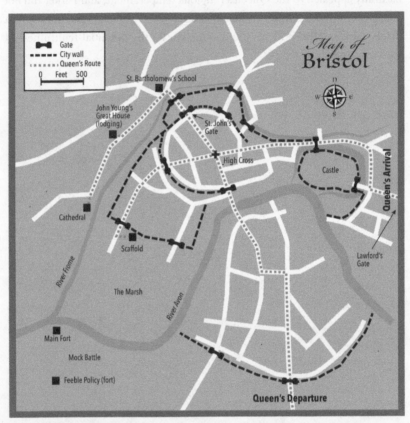

Map reproduced by Coni Porter. Reproduced from Nigel James's "Bristol, 1574," in John Nichols's "The Progresses and Public Processions of Queen Elizabeth I: A New Edition of the Early Modern Sources," ed. Elizabeth Goldring, Faith Eales, Elizabeth Clarke, and Jayne Elisabeth Archer, vol. II, 1572–1578 (Oxford: Oxford University Press, 2014). © in the editorial matter and arrangement Elizabeth Goldring, Faith Eales, Elizabeth Clarke, and Jayne Elisabeth Archer 2014. Reproduced with permission of the Licensor through PLSclear.

CHAPTER FOUR
BRISTOL, 1574

In 1574, the Queen left the relative safety of Kent to embark on travels much farther afield. In mid-July, the court departed on a ten-week progress to the western parts of the realm that included stops in Hampshire, Wiltshire, Somerset, and Gloucestershire. About halfway through the progress, they arrived at Bristol, a destination that turned out to be the furthest west the Queen would ever penetrate on any of her progresses.[1] That she felt comfortable enough to journey 120 miles west of London was, in some ways, a sign that the alarms of 1568 to 1572 had been quieted. Yet in other ways, the instability of those years may well have been the impetus behind this western progress. Now that the rebellion of 1569 had been crushed, Elizabeth may have wanted to go out among her people in order to inspire confidence, cultivate loyalty, and take the pulse of the provinces. In particular, she may have wanted to make sure that distant cities like Bristol were both loyal to her and prepared to maintain order on her behalf.

The Queen arrived in Bristol on August 14 and remained for a full week. It is a visit that continues to resonate in the modern city of Bristol. For instance, the twenty-pence visitor's guide to St. Mary Redcliffe is headlined by a quote attributed to Queen Elizabeth declaring it to be "the fairest, goodliest and most famous parish church in England." The Hall of the Society of Merchant Venturers (now used more for wedding receptions than overseas commerce) proudly displays the saddle that the Queen sat on as she processed through the early modern town. Even the lobby of the NatWest Bank on Corn Street is given over to a key episode from the Queen's visit wherein the "loyal wives of Bristol" were granted the right to dry their laundry on nearby Brandon Hill. A marble relief carving of the Queen, the wives, and their laundry is accompanied by a lengthy plaque explaining the event. Today, nearly 450 years after the fact, the Queen's visit continues to be a point of pride in the city's colorful history. But what did her visit mean in 1574?

Fortunately, the city corporation has preserved a detailed record of the Queen's stay in the city.[2] She arrived from the east on Saturday, August 14, and was met at the city gate by the mayor and city council. Together, this delegation processed through the streets of Bristol, stopping at the High Cross, St. John's Gate, and the grammar school for orations and pageant devices. The Queen was then escorted to the home of local dignitary John Young, where she would be lodged for the week. The next day, Elizabeth attended Sunday worship at the cathedral. During the remainder of the week, she engaged in a number of activities: a tour of the port facilities at the mouth of the Avon, visits to several parish churches, a stop at the city jail (where she pardoned nine condemned prisoners), and attendance at various entertainments that had been devised for her visit.

Given Bristol's size and importance, it is not surprising that the Queen visited the city and stayed for a full week. In the sixteenth century, Bristol was home to 11,000 people, making it the third most populous city in England.[3] It was also the third wealthiest city; its position near the mouth of the Avon, opening out onto the Severn Estuary, had made it an important port and a center of both regional and international trade.[4] In both population and wealth, it ranked far behind London but only just behind Norwich; it was easily the most important city on the western coast of England. As C. E. McGee notes, Bristol was therefore an "obvious [destination] for a monarch intent on using progresses to consolidate her power."[5] From McGee's perspective, the visit afforded the Queen an opportunity to physically occupy and project her authority over an important provincial town that was far removed from London. But the royal visit was also an opportunity for Bristol. With the Queen's attention firmly on the city, Bristol could actively fashion and project a particular image of itself to the reigning monarch.

It is clear that in 1574, Bristol recognized the gravity of the Queen's visit and spent accordingly. The records of the city corporation indicate that the then-enormous sum of almost £1,000 was expended in hosting the Queen.[6] These expenses ranged from painting and gilding the city gates and High Cross to leveling the principal streets with fifty-three loads of sand to installing the Queen's arms and the town's arms on the wall of the Guildhall. The city also took pains to entertain the Queen, most particularly in hiring Thomas Churchyard—a widely known literary figure who was well on his way to becoming the most prolific publisher of Elizabeth's reign—to write and direct the pageants.[7] As one might expect, the themes of these pageants flattered Elizabeth's person, praised the wisdom of her reign, and professed the city's undying loyalty to her. Such elements have led commentators like historian David Harris Sacks to describe the pageants in submissive terms: "The pageants emphasize the city's place in the larger organization of the state and their own subordination to the monarchy . . . the underlying theme was the city's place in the royal chain of command."[8] Although there are plenty of obsequious passages that encourage such a reading of the Bristol pageants, a closer examination of the city records and pageant texts reveals that Bristol did not *only* flatter the visiting monarch. Instead, the city was trying to project a particular image of itself to respond to the exigencies of a specific historical moment.[9]

As it turned out, August 1574 was the only occasion on which Bristol hosted the Queen during her forty-five-year reign. What did it do with this opportunity? What image of itself did Bristol fashion? The short answer is a thoroughly *militaristic* one. In preparation for the Queen's visit, the city corporation purchased two tons of gunpowder, collected 130 pieces of cannon, and enrolled 400 infantry and clothed them in the city uniform. When the Queen arrived, she was saluted by deafening peals of cannon and musketry. According to William Adams's *Chronicle of Bristol,* "300 small shot was discharged on the key, & 100 peces of ordinance, & then 2 volleys more of small shot."[10] The 400 city soldiers then escorted the Queen to her lodging, and, for the rest of the week, either stood guard outside the building or accompanied her wherever she went. Finally, the main entertainment for the week was an elaborate mock battle that lasted several hours a day for three days. These battles included hundreds of uniformed soldiers, exploding gunpowder, a mock fort being razed to the ground, and a naval engagement on the nearby river Avon.

Such a martial show was somewhat surprising for a city whose prosperity and reputation was founded on trade. It was also a departure from other cities that hosted the Queen, many of which tended to emphasize their own local distinctiveness. Sandwich in 1573 included a pageant device that celebrated the city's ties to the weaving industry. At Norwich in 1578, Elizabeth was met at the city gate by King Gurgunt, the town's mythical founder. Bristol had similar distinctions that it could have exploited in its pageants: it, too, boasted a legendary founder—the Trojan prince Brennius—and it was also renowned for its trading activities and status as the key western port of the realm. Yet the city corporation chose to emphasize the city's martial prowess. A careful examination of the historical context reveals why. I argue that Bristol's entertainments were intended to function as a calculated argument meant to affirm the authority of the civic corporation against other local, regional, and national authorities.

Bristol in 1574

The citizens of Bristol had a long tradition of self-government. In 1373, Bristol became the first town outside of London to be granted county status; this meant that it had its own mayor, council, sheriff, and county courts. Another charter, granted in 1499, confirmed and expanded the county's privileges.[11] In 1542, Henry VIII created the diocese of Bristol, and since Bristol now had a cathedral, it was elevated to city status. By the time of Elizabeth's visit in 1574, Bristol had a mayor, six aldermen, a common council of forty-three men, two sheriffs, a chamberlain, and a recorder. The city also returned two members to Parliament. But even as the Bristol elite were consolidating their powers in the early modern period, the city corporation was not without its rivals. At various times, the church, neighboring counties, the Council of the Marches, the local landed gentry, and the Court of Admiralty all attempted to impinge on the jurisdiction of the corporation. According to Patrick Carter, "Even armed with its royal charters, the corporation needed to be ever vigilant in asserting its privileges in the face of challenges from other authorities."[12]

One of the city's main rivals was outside ecclesiastical influence. Historically, the strongest local threat to the city corporation was the Catholic Church. For instance, in the 1490s the clergy of the wealthy St. Augustine's Abbey clashed repeatedly with city officials over issues ranging from the abbot's right to hold a manorial court to perceived abuses of sanctuary. These disputes culminated in a full-scale riot in 1496.[13] This threat to civic authority was dramatically removed with the Reformation and Dissolution in the 1530s, when the city actually added former monastic property to its own land holdings. And even though the creation of Bristol diocese in 1542 (St. Augustine's became the new cathedral) created a new clerical elite, it was an elite that the city corporation soon came to dominate.[14]

But the new diocese was itself vulnerable to outside influence. When Henry VIII was creating a number of new dioceses in the 1540s, Bristol was originally made a rural deanery of the diocese of Gloucester; however, last-minute dealings had made Bristol its own independent diocese. Yet the new diocese was poor and, according to Martha Skeeters, under constant threat of being reorganized or even re-absorbed into a more established diocese.[15]

In 1562, the vacant bishopric of Bristol was given in commendam to Richard Cheyney, the Bishop of Gloucester (which meant that he exercised authority over both dioceses, even though he was already entrenched in Gloucester). Apparently, Cheyney was covetous of annexing Bristol territory. Skeeters explains: "He was not able to retrieve any of Bristol's territory, but the possibility that Bristol would lose a Gloucestershire portion or be subsumed in the diocese of Gloucester remained a threat to the integrity and even existence of the diocese, particularly as long as the bishop of Gloucester held Bristol in commendam."[16] This is perhaps why Bristol went on the offensive and complained to the Privy Council about Bishop Cheyney in 1568. Even though the substance of the complaint is doctrinal—the bishop is accused of holding anti-Calvinist positions—it may well have been a pretense for discrediting the bishop. Cheyney himself believed that "unless he was deceived, 'their chief mark that they shoot at is not freewill or such like,' but rather his own defeat . . . the issue was one of authority rather than doctrine."[17]

Bristol's rivalry with its neighboring county figured into other disputes as well. With its attainment of county status in 1373, Bristol had stopped being part of Gloucestershire; yet it still had to report to its larger and more populous neighbor in military affairs. Most notably, Bristol had to send militia troops to the general muster in Gloucester (which occurred sometimes as frequently as twice a year). This was not only an extra expense for the city, but it also meant that Bristol could be subject to the interference of county commissioners. In 1561, "distaste for cooperating with the county induced the city to send its chamberlain all the way to London to plead for separate musters."[18] The petition—helped along by the gift of a butt of sack to the High Steward of London[19]—was successful, and Bristol was finally free to have its own militia and its own muster.

But perhaps the biggest threat to the city's authority was the Council of the Marches. So that they might impose order on distant parts of the realm that had long been subject to border raids and local rebellions, the Tudors created two special councils: the Council of the North and the Council of the Marches. The latter was centered in Ludlow and exercised authority over all of Wales as well as the English border shires of Shropshire, Hereford, Worcester, Gloucester, and Bristol. Even though the council was often composed of local gentry from western shires, it was basically an arm of the central government intent on maintaining order in a difficult and distant region. The council's powers included hearing and judging criminal and civil offenses, enforcing religious uniformity, and maintaining public order. It also had the ability to intrude into local government. Not surprisingly, the city corporation of Bristol resented the council and clashed with it repeatedly in the 1540s and 1550s. Penry Williams tells us that "finally, in 1562, the mayor and some of his aldermen went to London with a protest, and, after considerable expenditure, secured permanent exemption for the city from the jurisdiction of the Council."[20] Even so, this exemption proved to be tenuous and Bristol's dealings with the council were far from over—especially as the 1570s saw fresh disorders just across the border in Wales.[21] Thus, in the very years leading up to Queen Elizabeth's 1574 visit, the city corporation was working to safeguard and expand its authority on multiple fronts. Having recently freed its militia from neighboring interference, it was currently fighting to extricate itself from the outside influences of the Bishop of Gloucester and the Council of the Marches.

These struggles for local autonomy were intensified by the Northern Rebellion of 1569, which played out some two hundred miles to the north. In November 1569, Thomas Percy, 7th Earl of Northumberland, and Charles Neville, 6th Earl of Westmorland, amassed an army of local followers who were sympathetic to the old religion. After holding mass at Durham Cathedral, the army took Barnard Castle and threatened to lay siege to the city of York. One of their objectives seems to have been to replace Queen Elizabeth with the Catholic Mary, Queen of Scots. However, once the royal army of 14,000 troops finally arrived in the north, the earls fled to Scotland and their followers dispersed. Even though the rebellion was far from succeeding, it was a full-scale crisis that shook the Elizabethan regime. In his recent book *The Northern Rebellion of 1569,* K. J. Kesselring describes the crisis as a landmark event in Elizabeth's reign.[22] The thirty-five-year-old Queen was personally shaken by the revolt, in part because she saw it not just as the actions of two disenchanted earls, but as a popular rebellion that could occur elsewhere. This is why the rebels were punished so unmercifully, and why within months the Crown had issued the *Homily against Disobedience and Wilful Rebellion,* which would be read regularly from every pulpit in the realm. According to Kesselring, the years following the rebellion were marked by a heightened concern with order and "a hardening of attitudes and stiffening of policy" on the part of the Crown.[23] The delayed response to the rebellion had also exposed deficiencies in the Elizabethan militia system. The equipment was outdated, the men were poorly trained, and it had taken almost a month to assemble a viable fighting force. After the Northern Rebellion, the Crown set about revitalizing the militia, which meant raising standards and putting pressure on the county commissioners who were tasked with mustering, equipping, and training the men in each county.[24] The commissioners' task was not an easy one, and there was much grumbling, evasion, and foot-dragging, particularly among the gentry.[25]

Yet the Crown was intent on improving military preparedness; not only was England faced with the specter of internal rebellion, it also had to worry about foreign invasion. Relations with Spain had soured throughout the 1560s and England was now casting a wary eye across the Channel, where, by 1569, the Duke of Alba and his army were entrenched in the Low Countries. Meanwhile, Mary Stuart's imprisonment in England (beginning in 1568) was beginning to foment foreign interference (and talk of invasion) not only on the part of the Spanish, but also the French and the Papacy. Significantly, these foreign threats crystallized in the very years of the earls' rebellion, leading Kesselring to identify the Northern Rebellion as the "central element of a crisis that stretched from 1568 to 1572."[26]

The Northern Rebellion and its immediate context thus impacted the Crown in two important ways as far as my argument is concerned: it created a heightened concern with order and rebellion, and it lead to a preoccupation with the effectiveness of the militia. Of course, the citizens of Bristol had not rebelled against their monarch. But they might well worry about what these developments would mean for their city—which was, after all, a city located far from London and near the Welsh frontier. It was, according to Jonathan Barry, "the military key to the region."[27] Would the Crown decide that Bristol needed help maintaining order and defending itself? Would other authorities—like the Council of the Marches—move in under the pretense of stabilizing a vulnerable region? Would the city corporation's hard-won gains in religious, military, and political power be negated?

During these crucial years, Bristol sought to maintain its authority by securing urban patrons who would back the city in its disputes with potential challengers. One of its main patrons in the 1560s was William Herbert, 1st Earl of Pembroke, who had been honored with the office of Lord High Steward of Bristol. As a Privy Councilor and Lord Lieutenant of two counties, Pembroke was an excellent friend to have at court. But Pembroke's death in 1570 meant that Bristol needed to seek a powerful patron to replace him. The three main candidates for High Steward seem to have been William's eldest son Henry, the newly minted 2nd Earl of Pembroke; Edmund Brydges, Lord Chandos; and Robert Dudley, Earl of Leicester. Leicester was given the honor, probably because of the greater influence that he could wield at court. However,

Leicester's attention was diverted in many other directions, so he proved an expensive patron to cultivate. In 1571 the city sent him "eight hogsheads of wine . . . at a cost of 30 pounds," following up in 1572 with a gift of "two hogsheads of sack." Nevertheless, Bristol used Leicester's influence to seek commercial benefits from the Crown and to continue to appeal for the appointing of a separate Bishop of Bristol.[28]

Not wanting to burn bridges unnecessarily, the city also sought to maintain good relations with Pembroke and Chandos. They sought to mollify Pembroke by sending city officers to pay him a personal visit in London; meanwhile, Chandos "was consoled with the gift of a butt of sack."[29] Even though Pembroke was "piqued" at being passed over for the High Stewardship, he remained a patron of the city.[30] He served as Lord Lieutenant of Bristol and Somerset, which meant that he oversaw the trained bands that Bristol had fought so hard for in the 1560s.[31] As such, Pembroke would have had a vested interest in maintaining the autonomy and effectiveness of Bristol's citizen militia. In the long run, Pembroke proved an important patron to cultivate: in the 1580s he would become Lord President of the Council of Marches and Lord Lieutenant of Wales. Lord Chandos, however, likely proved to be more of a rival than a patron. As Lord Lieutenant of Gloucestershire, Chandos oversaw the county militia from which Bristol had striven so hard to extricate itself.[32]

During the royal progress of 1574, Bristol would have sought to honor its existing patrons and cultivate new ones.[33] City leaders would have been particularly keen to target any other Privy Council members who were in attendance. For one thing, the Council was deeply involved with military affairs on the county level: it "[exercised] authority over the national musters," and each of its members was expected to serve as a Lord Lieutenant on the county level.[34] The Privy Council also dealt with issues of borough privileges as well as the management of sedition and disorder—both of which were relevant to Bristol's situation in 1574.[35]

Surviving records do not give a full list of exactly which nobles and Privy Councilors accompanied the Queen to Bristol. However, we do know that Leicester; William Cecil, Lord Burghley; Francis Walsingham; and Edward Clinton, Earl of Lincoln were in attendance.[36] The presence of Lincoln, would have been especially significant for Bristolians. He had been Lord High Admiral (or head of the navy) for the entirety of Elizabeth's sixteen-year reign. Since England had no standing army, this effectively made him the chief military officer of the realm.[37] If Bristol intended to demonstrate that it had a strong militia and that it could maintain order in the west, Lincoln would be a vital person to convince. Not surprisingly, the corporation took special pains to accommodate the admiral. According to the mayor's audit book, the city's progress preparations included "mending the way in Magdalen lane where the Erle of Lyncoln lay" (RB, 87: 4–5).

Martial Shows

With the Queen and potential patrons in attendance, the city needed to create suitable entertainments to speak to its audience. Given this historical backdrop, it is not surprising that the city officials would create distinctively martial pageants in order to highlight the military prowess of Bristol's citizen militia and to underscore the city's ability to prevent rebellion in the west. I would now like to look more closely at how the actual entertainments convey that message. The first way that they do so is in the corporation's hiring of Thomas Churchyard to compose the orations and entertainments that would be performed for the Queen. The choice of Churchyard is particularly revealing, for he was not just a poet, he was also a career soldier who had participated in military engagements in Scotland, Ireland, France, and the Low Countries.[38] Four years previously, Churchyard had published *A Discourse of Rebellion,* which pointedly criticizes the Northern Rebellion. It would be difficult to think of a writer who was more qualified to be a mouthpiece for the themes of military strength and political order that the corporation was so interested in conveying.

The pageants themselves were, not surprisingly, thoroughly militaristic. I have already drawn attention to martial elements like the firing of cannons, the use of uniformed soldiers, and the extended mock battle. These are the very same aspects recorded so enthusiastically by contemporaries. Robert Ricart makes much of the "[400] soldiers in one sute of Apparell, where of [300] weare harquebussiers, & [100] pikemen in Corselettes," and of the mock battle, calling it a "martiall experiment beinge verie costlie and chargeable (especially in gonnepowder)."[39] Adams gushes about the "great charges, especially of gunpowder, whereof was no spare made to give content, which shewes delighted & pleased our queene and nobillitie well."[40] Both accounts play up the quantity— and cost—of gunpowder used in the pageants, which was indeed unusual for the period.[41] The suggestion is that the city was willing to invest considerable resources in its attempt to create a particularly martial effect.[42]

In her book *The Elizabethan Militia,* Lindsay Boynton refers to the Britsol entertainments as a "muster"—which she elsewhere defines as "a formal, public inspection of all the county forces followed, as a rule, by some form of concerted military exercise."[43] In this reading, the four hundred soldiers presented to the Queen upon her arrival would function as the inspection while the mock battle later in week would be the military exercise. If so, the entire pageant can be seen as a military maneuver designed to illustrate that Bristol's militia was up-to-date and effective.[44] Given the Queen's post-1569 preoccupation with militia preparedness and the resistance that some counties were showing to her measures, this would have been a powerful and timely message. By foregrounding the city's martial strength, Bristol was affirming the effectiveness of its newly independent militia, differentiating itself from the evasions of other counties, and asserting its ability to defend itself and to maintain order in the west on behalf of the Queen.

Though the military action thus spoke volumes, understanding was not left to chance. Churchyard created a number of speeches that establish these military themes and reflect on the nature of dissension and rebellion.[45] For the first day, Churchyard crafted a series of speeches delivered by various allegorical figures to welcome the Queen to the city. After processing to the High Cross at the center of the city, the Queen was greeted by an "excelent boy" atop a scaffold in the person of Fame. One of Fame's tasks is to introduce the coming entertainments, which he refers to as "warlike pastimes" and "sights and shoes of war." In this very first speech, then, the pageant proclaims its own military bent. At the next stop in the procession—St. John's Gate—the figures of Salutation, Gratulation, and Obedient Goodwill provide more detail about these military shows. After declaring that the Queen is "most welcom to this Western coest," Salutation asks for the monarch's help as a pretense for introducing the mock battle plot. According to Salutation, Dissension has bred a brawl between Peace and War. As a result, Peace has built a fort (which stands on law and order) that War (representing the wicked world) will attack. Since the fort represents Peace and "takes thy part O Queen," it is hoped that she will prove a "noble Judge" and help "decied the matter throw." Even though the mock battle would not begin for another two days, the speeches of Fame and Salutation clearly establish the battle as the central event of the week. Moreover, Salutation's attempt to clarify the allegorical meaning of the battle suggests that it will not simply be a military spectacle; its symbolic meaning is of the utmost importance. Even from Salutation's short gloss, the inference is that Bristol also loves peace, that it too stands on law and order, and that it is loyal to the Queen.

The next speaker, Gratulation, makes this inference more explicit. He begins by further characterizing Dissension—not as an obvious vice, but as a "sottell Snaek" that creeps into the breasts of men "with sopple sugred words." It first draws its victims away from their daily pursuits, then feeds their humors and breeds mischief, and finally culminates in "wicked warrs, and wilfull brawls." This characterization explains how Dissension has recently contrived to gain such a foothold in the realm. But Gratulation immediately declares that the people of Bristol are ever-vigilant against such an insinuating foe:

> not [one] within this soyll:
> But reddy aer with loss of lief,
> To give thy foes a foyll.
> For proof the feble youth,
> And baebs of tender aeg:
> Daer draw their swords, in this attempt,
> To corb disorders raeg. (RB, 97: 2–8)

Not only does the city oppose Dissension, but it fights actively and sacrificially— "reddy . . . with loss of lief"—against it. Furthermore, this stance is not limited to the leaders of the city, but encompasses "all within this soyll." The defensive abilities of tender babes and feeble youth notwithstanding, these words must have resonated deeply for a Queen who was particularly preoccupied with issues of order. Churchyard also adds a dramatic confirmation to these ideas. His stage directions specify that at the moment Gratulation speaks the words "Daer draw their swords, in this attempt, / To corb disorders raeg," all three allegorical figures drew their actual swords.[46] This action thus provides a dramatic, visual gesture that underscores Bristol's loyalty to the Queen and its willingness and ability to maintain order on her behalf.[47]

Immediately after this speech, Elizabeth was escorted to the "Great House" of John Young, her lodging for the week. But even this coda was a further demonstration of what she had just seen and heard. According to Churchyard's account, "[three] hondreth Soldiors well appointed, wayted on her highnes to her lodgyng, and thear she being setled, they shot of thear peeces in passing good order, at which warnyng the great Artillery went of, a hundred and xxx cast peecis, and so the watche charged, and a hundreth shot apoynted for her Gard" (RB, 97: 24–29). If the drawing of the three swords was meant to be symbolic, these gestures were surely meant to be a more substantive demonstration. By offering the services of—but also displaying—its soldiers, guns, artillery, and armed guard, the city was showing that it possessed the actual manpower and resources to back up its professions of loyalty.

The next day being Sunday, the Queen worshipped at Bristol Cathedral, a few streets over from her lodging. There, Churchyard had arranged a special speech and a song to welcome the Queen to "the Colledg." The speech begins by flattering the Queen and stating how proud (though unworthy) the cathedral is to host her. The descriptions of the church are very self-effacing—"poer Colledg," its "naked buildyngs baer," "so small a [cell]" for "poer Preests" (RB, 98: 25, 26, 29, 34). Such humility is no doubt a rhetorical device, but it also seems a frank acknowledgement that Bristol was one of the more poorly endowed dioceses in the realm.[48] Churchyard's song then returns to the previous day's theme of order and dissension, but it does so in a pointedly religious way. After comparing the Queen to a sun that shines on the cathedral, the song warns:

> Away you bosom Snaeks,
> That sowes dissenshon heer:
> Go make you neasts, whear Serpents breed,
> This soyll and coest is clear. (RB, 99: 4–7)

Given the location of its utterance, "heer" would seem to be the religious establishment in general and Bristol Cathedral in particular. Thus, the dissension referred to is not the political disorder of the previous day, but what the song later calls the "Hidras hed" of religious controversy. As the Elizabethan Settlement of 1559 had done little to actually establish religious uniformity, the ongoing efforts of both Catholics and Puritans to reshape the state church was a constant source of instability, even when it did not lead to open rebellion, as it had in 1569. The end of the song refers to this "troblous time," which may well be a direct reference to the Northern Rebellion and its fallout. In any event, it may be surprising to find such a frank acknowledgement of religious conflict, given the popular perception that progresses tended to celebrate the monarch and affirm the status quo. However, the song invokes dissension here precisely so that Bristol might be more clearly differentiated from it. The assertion that "this soyll and coest is clear" functions to assure Elizabeth that Bristol diocese did not contain the same religious dissension that other parts of the realm were breeding. It might have been a relatively new diocese and its church fabric might have left something to be desired, but it was religiously stable and unified. Given the diocese's fear of reabsorption and concern with outside ecclesiastical influence, the song thus functioned to affirm its diocesan authority against its rivals.[49]

The most elaborate discussion of the theme of rebellion occurs in the speeches associated with the mock battles held on Monday, Tuesday, and Wednesday. In the printed account of the pageant, Churchyard alerts the reader to the importance of the text that accompanies the action: "For the better understanding of the devised triumphe . . . you must heer the speeches or els shal you be ignorant of the hoel matter" (RB, 99: 23–25). It is the same assertion that Salutation made two days earlier: the battle is no mere spectacle, but holds important meanings.

Indeed, the battle begins with a dialogue between Dissension and the main Fort, called Peace (though later associated with the City itself).[50] Dissension criticizes the stagnant contentment of Peace and its adherents, saying that they "sleep and snort, in sweet, perfumed sheets" and "caer not what, great glory elders won." In contrast, Dissension associates itself with laudable qualities like bravery, fame, and the desire for heroic action. This is a much subtler— and seemingly more positive—characterization than the "Hidras hed" of religious dissension. Failing to make any headway with Peace, Dissension then addresses itself to "the warrs." Dissension repeats the notion that Peace is only sustained by people who want to enjoy their wealth and that "peace is bent, / to trus up soldiors all" (RB, 101: 9–10). That is, Peace does not acknowledge the bravery and mettle of the military profession:

> Peace calls you roges, and swashing dicks,
>> that stand apon you braues:
> A swarm of wasps, a flok of wolus,
>> a neast of theeus and knaues
> That livs by spoyll and morthers viell,
>> and triumps still in bloed. (RB, 101: 29–34)

Dissension is here indicting one of the things that defines Bristol: its trade and wealth. The suggestion is that strong military values are incompatible with a peaceful, trading city like Bristol. Its populace has difficulty recognizing— much less practicing—such values. Such an objection is not illogical and is just the sort of claim that rival authorities—like the Council of the Marches— might make to siphon away some of Bristol's autonomy in the tumultuous years following the Northern Rebellion.

In fact, Dissension's claim about Bristol's antipathy toward soldiers might reflect an actual perception of the city in the 1570s. According to John Latimer, "During the Irish rebellions of this period, the city suffered severely from the frequent presence of large bodies of soldiers, sent down from London for embarkation, but often detained for weeks by contrary winds. The troops, impressed from the lowest classes, spent their time in debauchery and rioting, setting the civic authorities . . . at defiance."[51] This volatile situation led to a number of conflicts between the city corporation and unruly soldiers—including the "setting up a gibbet in High Street, to terrify the rage of the soldiers" later on in the decade.[52] On top of these hardships, the Crown also required the city to provide rations, pay, and even conduct money for the soldiers. Bristol could (and did) appeal for recuperation of these expenses, but "the Chamberlin had to ride up to Court, and . . . it was never an easy matter to wring money from the penurious Queen."[53] In any event, the city's contentious relationship with these bands of soldiers could well have given the impression—not only to the soldiers but also to the central government—that Bristol was less than supportive of the country's war efforts in Ireland. As the full mock battle would soon make clear, this was a false perception. But on the first day, War is sufficiently inspired by Dissension's words to march its armies forward, attack a smaller fort called Feeble Policy, and raze it to the ground. War then begins to lay siege to the main fort, Peace.

The second day of the mock battle centered around a naval engagement on the river Avon. After some preliminary skirmishes on land, a ship attempting to bring "vittayls" to the fort was pursued by three "brave Galleys" up the Avon. These boats then engaged in a "shoe of fight . . . till the very night approtched" (RB, 103: 30). This episode, though doubtlessly entertaining, also served to display the city's martial prowess on the water. The same ships and galleys that were the foundation of Bristol's seaborne trade could be appropriated for military maneuvers. At the conclusion of the mock battle on the following day, the Queen would gain firsthand experience of these vessels by boarding a galley and sailing down the river to inspect Bristol's port facilities at Kingsroad.

By the third day, both Peace and War (and perhaps the royal visitors) were weary of all this fighting. The day thus began with a parley and the introduction of a new figure, Persuasion. According to Churchyard, his function is to "unfold what follies and conflicts rises on Civil broils, and what quietnesse comes by mutual love and agreement" (RB, 103: 38–40). At first, Persuasion seems like yet another expression of the pageant's pacifist themes, but Churchyard uses this figure to examine a couple of crucial but yet-unanswered questions: Given the value of peace, how is it best maintained? And is a city such as Bristol really the most effective agent for stamping out dissension and disorder? Persuasion addresses its speech to the Fort, which represents not only Peace, but, Churchyard now tells us, the City itself. After duly denouncing war, Persuasion then notes some of the positive uses of war:

> Yet Warres is suer, a needfull thing,
>   for mans offence, A scorge:
> A Salue to heale the sinfull soule,
>   and for the staet A porge. (*RB*, 104: 8–11)

And if God can use war for His purposes, so, too, can civil authorities:

> The sword that takes away the life,
>   makes peace whear it is worn . . .
> So warrs whear they aer vsed well,
>   keeps world in fear and awe. (*RB*, 104: 34–35, 40–41)

In other words, force—or the threat of force—is an important tool for maintaining peace; "quietnesse" is just as much a product of strength as it is peace. Such a conception goes a long way toward refuting Dissension's earlier claim that a peaceful, trading city is incompatible with strong military values. As Persuasion explains, Bristol can be devoted to peace and also ready and willing to exercise force in order to maintain it.

The City itself responds to Persuasion and expands on this idea in what is the longest single speech (eighty lines) of the entire pageant. The City asserts its preference for Peace over War in this dispute, primarily because Peace best serves its own civic values:

> Our traed doth stand on Sivill lief,
>   and thear our glory lies.
> And not on strief the ruen of staets,
>   a storm that all destroys. (*RB*, 105: 39–42)

In other words, an atmosphere of tranquility is much more conducive to the commercial activities that Bristolians typically pursue. But, the City points out, such activities do not only serve Bristol, they also enrich the rest of the realm and allow Bristol to serve as a "stoer howse" when times are lean—thus helping to ensure a broader order in the kingdom. Nevertheless, the City also acknowledges Persuasion's point that peace cannot be achieved simply by avoiding conflict. Rather, peace must be pursued deliberately and maintained with force. In Bristol's case, a combination of order, law, and due correction is used to "Reform the rued, rebuek the bold, / and tame the contrey wyeld" (*RB*, 106: 13–14). Such lawful coercion is much different than the arbitrary "uproer" and "brawls" championed by Dissension.

Although Churchyard welcomes this distinction, he is perhaps also concerned that it perpetuates the perceived gap between a peaceful trading city and true military values. After all, the sword of law is different from the sword of war. Thus, Churchyard goes out of his way to assert that the City's reliance on civil order does not mean that Bristol cannot *fight* when it has to. "And thoghe our joy, be moest in peace," says the City,

> Yet haue we soldyars as you see
> that [stirs] but whan we pleas
> And [serves] our torns in howshold things,
> and sits in shop at eas.
> And yet daer blaed [it] with the best,
> when cawse of contrey coms
> And cals out courage to the fight,
> by sound of warlike Droms. (*RB*, 106: 27–34)

The city militia is more than capable of holding its own in armed conflict. The citizens of Bristol may sit in their shops under normal circumstances, but they can instantly transform into courageous soldiers who can "blade it" with the best that anyone else has to offer. The "as you see" of the opening line indicates these very soldiers have been on display for the past four days precisely to prove the point that Bristol's bands are brave, well trained, and highly disciplined. Whether they are needed to put down rebellions or defend the country from foreign invasion, they will be up to the task.

Despite Dissension's earlier claim, this passage demonstrates that pacifism and military values are indeed compatible. In fact, Churchyard next affirms that such a combination is actually preferable to mere militarism. He does this by having the City exalt a different type of soldier than the glory-seeking model previously offered by Dissension. Two days previously, Bristol had been accused of not properly valuing the soldier's profession ("peace is bent, / to trus up soldiors all")—perhaps because of its recent troubles with those heading to the Irish wars. The City responds here by claiming that "A Souldiour shalbe liked well, / if his dezarts be sutch" (*RB*, 106: 39–40) and distinguishing between those with "noble mind[s]" and those that "glory all in warres, / and peace disdains in deed" (*RB*, 107: 1–2). The latter are likely to be bloodthirsty, reckless, and dangerous to the commonwealth—perhaps because they have no stake in the community. Bristol's merchant soldiers are a much better bet to maintain order precisely because their military values are guided by the goal of peace. Bristol's militia has the martial skill, but it is its commitment to trade and civil life that ensures it will use force to create stability and not disorder.

Ceremonial Supports

Churchyard's speeches are clearly the culminating treatment of Bristol's military themes. In explaining the meaning of the martial shows, they provide an extended intellectual engagement with the complexities of war and peace, but they were not the only level on which Bristol appealed to its royal visitors. Without the mock battle, the speeches would have merely been a dry abstraction. As we have seen, one of the city's main goals was to *demonstrate* its military prowess. It did so through the four hundred infantry who met and accompanied the Queen, through the cannons and muskets that were shot off at regular intervals during the week, and through the three-day mock battle itself. The latter required the careful synchronization of large groups of men pursuing simulated military objectives on both land and water. As such, it was a demonstration not only of the skills of its soldiers, but also of its civic leaders' abilities to assemble, organize, and deploy large groups of people in a harmonious and effective way.[54] The effect seems to have approximated Margit Thøfner's "aesthetic of processions," which she principally locates in a "beautifully coordinated" and "well-disciplined militia."[55]

Aside from the formal entertainment of the mock battle, the city also made use of less obvious ceremonial practices to underscore military themes and forge subtle meanings.[56] For example, the city leaders exhibited a careful attention to space. When Bristol's trained bands held their first autonomous muster in 1562, they did so on a marshy strip of land outside the southwestern wall of the city.[57] By the 1570s, this open area had become the designated training area for the militia.[58] The land must have been functional, but it was probably less than ideal. It is repeatedly referred to as "the marsh" in local records, and its watery soil must have accounted for its lack of development at a time when suburbs were forming outside of the city walls in all other directions. When the Queen's impending visit was announced, one of the city's main preparations was to improve this space. According to the Mayor's Audits, the city paid for the sanding and levelling of the marsh (RB, 86: 36–37). There was also a separate payment to John Field "for his payns in dressing the marsh" (RB, 87: 36). City leaders no doubt realized that if Bristol was going to effectively stage a muster that would validate the city militia, it needed an impressive—or at least serviceable—military plain on which to conduct exercises. It might be a marsh, but they could not afford for it to look like one.

The city also seems to have realized that the marsh could play a positive role in the festivities. One of its merits was that it was a large, empty space just outside the city walls. It could therefore be appropriated to different uses. It would continue to serve as a military space during the Queen's visit, but urban leaders worked to more closely integrate it with the rest of the city. They did this primarily by bringing the city out into the marsh. The Mayor's Audits record a payment for "setting vp a gallery in the marsh for the Quenes Maiestie to se the tryvmphes" (RB, 86: 40–41). This must have been a platform for viewing the three-day mock battle, which took place just beyond the marsh and across the River Avon. The viewing gallery's practical function was to bring both Queen and court closer to the action, but it also served to extend the city beyond its own walls. By locating spectators, festivities, and temporary architecture in the marsh, the corporation effectively made the city's designated military space a more integrated part of the city. The forts that were constructed at the far end of the marsh (and across the river) further enclosed the marsh and made it seem more like an urban space. In doing so, Bristol effectively made its military values seem like an intrinsic part of the city.

In addition, Bristol created an appropriate soundscape to underscore the militaristic themes of its pageants. We have already noted the firing of cannons and discharging of musketry that occurred throughout the week. These reverberating noises served not only to display Bristol's firepower, but also to engage the auditory senses of the visitors. They would have punctuated the events with deafening explosions that would have conveyed the city's military might in an almost visceral way. Other military sounds would have been more musical. Like other large cities, Bristol possessed a city waits—a group of professional musicians who were employed by the corporation to play at civic ceremonies. This four-person ensemble would certainly have been included in the progress festivities of 1574.[59] We also know that the waits had recently diversified its musical offerings. In 1561, shortly after Bristol had secured separate musters for its city militia, "two drums were purchased to give a martial tone to the music of the city waits."[60] During the Queen's visit, the waits would have been well equipped to provide a bellicose soundtrack for the parading soldiers and military skirmishes. Finally, the churchwarden's accounts record a number of payments to bell-ringers at churches in the center of the city. For example, at St. James, there were payments for nine "Ringers for Ringinge when the Queens maiestie Came in . . . And all the while she was here till her departing." In other cities, church bells might be rung during the royal entry (as at Coventry in 1566), but at Bristol they resounded throughout the week. Daily ringing must have involved considerable time on the part of the participants, since at St. Mary le Port they were even "payde for ther vytalles for ryngyng whyle the queen was here" (RB, 93: 20–21). Why were the citizens so willing to invest in extended bell-ringing? On one level, it could simply be that bells create loud, reverberating noises that could be added to the peals of cannons and muskets. But bell-ringing is physically demanding and was considered a form of exercise in Elizabethan England, thus, sustained bell-ringing could have been a way of displaying the agility and physical fitness of Bristol's citizens. Further, playing complicated songs using different bells requires careful coordination and flawless execution. The nine ringers at St. James, for instance, would have needed to be coordinated and precise. In this sense, bell-ringing is similar to the military maneuvers and themes displayed elsewhere.

Bristol also made use of a particularly resonant piece of civic regalia: its processional sword. This sword had been created in 1373 as a part of Bristol's elevation to county status—the very status that gave the mayor the right to have a sword borne before him.[61] The sword was thus an important symbolic object that conveyed the autonomy of the city in decidedly military overtones. The city leaders planned all along to feature the sword prominently, as one of their preparations for the progress was to replace the original two-hundred-year-old scabbard with a new one. The mayor's audits record a payment for "newe making and dressing the Scabbard with pearles" (RB, 87: 14–15). It is this upgrade that caused the sword itself to become known as the Pearl Sword.[62] The scabbard—which survives to this day—is covered in velvet and lavishly embroidered with seed pearls.[63] Pearls were particularly favored by and associated with Elizabeth, so their inclusion on the scabbard was likely a way to honor her majesty. Aside from adding pearls, the "newe making" involved affixing three decorative metal bands to the scabbard. The outer two—at the tip and mouth—are engraved with elaborate scrollwork and foliation. The golden central locket is larger and more detailed; it depicts a phoenix with wings outspread standing on a jumble of broken columns. It is a striking image that is also designed to compliment the Queen. By the 1570s, the phoenix—"a mythical bird symbolizing rebirth and chastity"— had become associated with Elizabeth "as an emblem of virginity, uniqueness and as reassurance that she would be able to regenerate the dynasty."[64] The sword is thus a military object, but one that overtly blends loyalty to the Queen with martial prowess. Not surprisingly, the sword featured prominently in the festivities. During the entry it was carried before the mayor as the city officers processed through town with the royal visitors.[65] Indeed, the mayor's audits record a special payment made to a "mr Dowting master Swordberer" (RB, 87: 16). The effect would have been to make the processing mayor appear as a quasi-military figure. As we have seen, swords also figured prominently at St. John's Gate, when Salutation, Gratulation, and Obedient Goodwill dramatically unsheathed their swords at the climactic end of Gratulation's speech. It is tantalizing to imagine that the Pearl Sword might have been used here, but even if it was not, this moment helped confirm swords as a key emblem of Bristol's military theme. It is a particularly apt emblem because it embodies several recurring ideas, including civic autonomy, military preparedness, loyalty to the Queen, and maintaining peace via the threat of force.

Finally, Bristol's entertainments were enhanced by the careful selection of clothing. In the decade before the Queen's visit, the council had passed a number of ordinances stipulating what mayors, sheriffs, and councilmen were to wear on formal occasions and festival days, suggesting that it was especially cognizant of the power of ceremonial attire.[66] It is therefore not surprising that Bristol took special pains with the appearance of the four hundred soldiers who greeted the Queen and escorted her throughout the week. We know from Ricart that they were all clothed "in one sute of Apparell" (RB, 91: 1). This seems to have included specially made doublets and caps, both of which are mentioned in the mayor's audits. The soldiers were probably wearing an embellished version of the city uniform. According to Latimer, the city had in 1561 commissioned new uniforms in the city colors (red, blue, and yellow), enhanced with "two buttons of gold, and tassells to hang at the top." A few years later, they had also decided to upgrade the city seal so that it would appear more impressive when it adorned

the flags and ensigns that were used at the militia muster. In 1569, they successfully applied to the Herald's College for a crest and supporters to go along with
the ancient shield of the city.[67] The result was a distinctive (if busy) design that
included a ship and castle on the shield, unicorn supporters, and a crest with two
hands issuing from the clouds, one hand holding a scale and the other a serpent.
This new coat of arms would have doubtlessly appeared in close association with
the uniformed soldiers as they accompanied the Queen around the city and participated in the mock battle. As such, the city colors and arms would have been
a powerful and ever-present visual throughout the week. These markers would
have clearly identified the soldiers as Bristol's own and underscored the point
that their military prowess was a reflection of the city as a whole.

Together, these elements of space, sound, regalia, and clothing would have
worked together to strengthen and enrich the martial ideas that were offered in
the pageant speeches. Even though the mock battles were the ostensible focus of
the week's entertainment, the city corporation could look on with the knowledge that their royal visitors were not just seeing an empty or generic spectacle.
Instead, they could be confident that the martial action—in concert with the
speeches and the other processional modes I have discussed—underscored a
number of important messages that were meant to speak to the tumultuous
political climate of the 1570s. First and foremost, that Bristol was loyal to the
Queen. Second, that it was a peace-loving city that opposed religious and political rebellion of all sorts. And third, that Bristol possessed a strong, capable militia
that qualified it—and not some other authority—to maintain order in the west.

Epilogue

Were Bristol's efforts successful in safeguarding its civic authority? In the years
that followed the Queen's visit, the corporation aggressively pursued many of
these same objectives. In 1575, the mayor, aldermen, sheriffs, and other common councilors submitted a "suyte . . . to the Quenes Highnes for the obteyn-
ing of a perpetuall exemcion of this citie of Bristowe from the jurisdiction of
the Councell of the Marches."[68] Even though the city had been granted such an
exemption in 1562, Bristol wanted to ensure that this measure was both permanent and formalized—which is why the suit specifies that "the same . . . be
had under the Great Seale of Englond." The corporation was also active on other
fronts. In 1576, we find it attempting to block Gloucester's petition to establish
its own customs house so that it would no longer be a "creek" of Bristol; not

surprisingly, Bristol represented such a development as "highly injurious to [its own] local commerce."[69] Throughout the 1570s and 1580s, Bristol continued to make "repeated appeals" for the appointment of a separate bishop so that the diocese would no longer be held in commendam by the bishop of Gloucester.[70] Closer to home, the corporation took action to maintain its privileges and diminish the influence of rival local authorities. The ordinances of the Common Council include a 1576 dictate that "suits between Bristol burgesses [are] not to be taken to courts outside [the] city's jurisdiction," as this negatively affects "the maintenance of the franchises and libertyes of this citie." That same year, the council stipulated that "no burgess of this citie shall weare the livery of any lorde gentleman" since such a show of divided loyalty would be "contrarye to the oulde [oath] of a burgess allreadye agreed upon."[71]

Bristol's efforts at preserving its civic authority were largely successful. Even though Gloucester did secure its own customs house in 1580, Bristol was able to keep its city militia (and muster) separate from that of its county rival. Moreover, the Diocese of Bristol was eventually freed from the Diocese of Gloucester. When Bishop Cheyney died in 1579, his successor John Bullingham also held Bristol in commendam. However, in 1589, Richard Fletcher became the sole bishop of Bristol.[72] The city was also able to maintain its independence from the Council of the Marches. Even though its 1575 petition for perpetual exemption went unconfirmed, Bristol remained largely clear of the council's interference.[73] Indeed, the 1580s saw the "first faint signs" of regional opposition to the council's power and "by the 1590s a more considerable movement had begun with the object of exempting all four English shires from the Council's authority."[74] By this time, there was very little chance that an already exempt city like Bristol would have its status revoked.

It is plausible to suggest that the 1574 pageants helped lay the groundwork for these successes. By foregrounding the loyalty and military preparedness of Bristolians, these entertainments dramatically asserted that the city could be counted on to maintain order in a volatile region. In the succeeding decades, the Crown did nothing to suggest that it thought otherwise. Bristol must have deemed its reception a success because it repeated many of these same messages in the 1613 visit of Queen Anne. The city entertained James I's consort with another highly militaristic spectacle that included a mock sea battle (on the river Avon) as well as occasions to demonstrate "the prowess of the city's Trained Bands."[75] As in 1574, Bristol may have thought that a reminder of its loyalty and vigilance was particularly well timed. Just as Elizabeth's visit had come in the aftermath of the Northern Rebellion, so Queen Anne's visit came on the heels of the 1605 gunpowder plot—an event that was still "painfully etched in Stuart memory."[76] In this context, it was again worth demonstrating that Bristol was a force for order in the face of domestic disturbances.

The patronage connections cultivated during the 1574 visit also featured decisively in Bristol's subsequent expansion of civic autonomy. Leicester continued to serve as High Steward until his death in 1588, and the city solicited his assistance for both commercial and religious suits.[77] When Bristol gained a new charter in 1581, it relied on help from two other men who had been at the 1574 entertainments: Francis Walsingham and John Popham.[78] Popham was a Somerset lawyer who had served as a Bristol MP in the early 1570s and as the city recorder throughout the decade. In fact, it was in his capacity as recorder that Popham delivered the city's welcome speech during the royal entry. Popham soon ascended to national office, becoming solicitor general in 1579 and attorney general in 1581—the very year that Bristol attained its new patent. During the proceedings, Popham was instrumental in the final ratification of the new charter. In honoring Popham early in his career, Bristol had created an urban patron who would maintain an interest in his old city.

Besides pageants and patrons, other factors doubtlessly contributed to Bristol's growing independence. In the decades following the Queen's visit, worries of internal rebellion faded or were at least replaced by fears of foreign invasion.[79] The Welsh Marches also gradually became less contested and more peaceful, so that by 1689 the Council of the Marches was disbanded. But the most important factor was the emergence of Bristol itself. As the seventeenth century dawned, Bristol was well on its way to becoming a "great regional entrepot" and a "major overseas trading centre"—with commercial networks extending to "the Mediterranean, the African coast, the offshore Atlantic islands and the shores of North America."[80] As Bristol became wealthier and more populous— growing from 12,000 to 21,000 residents over the course of the seventeenth century—its city government naturally came to supersede the claims of other local authorities.[81] The story of Bristol's seventeenth-century development risks making the corporation's triumph seem inevitable, but in 1574, its primacy was not a foregone conclusion. Bristol had only enjoyed city and diocesan status for thirty-two years, while its independent militia and exemption from the Council of the Marches had only been effected in the previous decade. In the year of the Queen's visit, Bristol knew that its autonomy was far from assured, so it responded with these well-crafted and dynamic "sights and shoes of war."

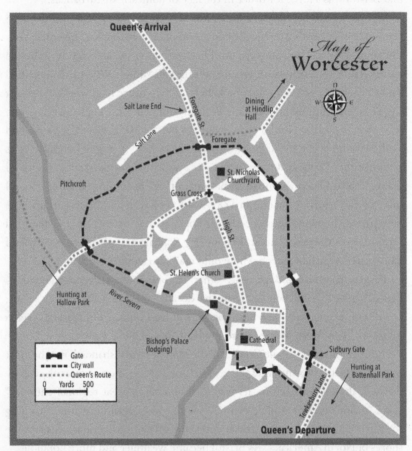

Map reproduced by Coni Porter. Map reproduced by Coni Porter. Map reproduced by Coni Porter. Reproduced from Nigel James's "Worcester, 1575," in *John Nichols's "The Progresses and Public Processions of Queen Elizabeth I: A New Edition of the Early Modern Sources,"* ed. Elizabeth Goldring, Faith Eales, Elizabeth Clarke, and Jayne Elisabeth Archer, vol. II, 1572–1578 (Oxford: Oxford University Press, 2014). © in the editorial matter and arrangement Elizabeth Goldring, Faith Eales, Elizabeth Clarke, and Jayne Elisabeth Archer 2014. Reproduced with permission of the Licensor through PLSclear.

CHAPTER FIVE
WORCESTER, 1575

The 1575 progress is in many ways the climax of the "long, elaborate, memorable progresses of the 1570s."[1] It stands out for both its length and its itinerary. At 139 days, it was the longest single progress of Elizabeth's reign; no other progress lasted longer than 75 days. The Queen and her court departed London in late May and traversed some ten counties—Hertfordshire, Bedfordshire, Buckinghamshire, Northamptonshire, Warwickshire, Stafford-shire, Worcestershire, Gloucestershire, Oxfordshire, and Berkshire—before returning to London in early October. The 1575 progress was also far-reaching: it was one of only four progresses in which the Queen ventured further than 110 miles from London.[2] In early August, the Queen spent two weeks in Staffordshire, which (along with a 1566 visit to Lincolnshire) was the farthest north that she ever traveled.[3]

On August 13, she arrived in Worcester and spent a full week in the city. The Queen was fêted in grand style. She heard orations, viewed pageant devices, received elaborate gifts, visited the cathedral, and hunted deer in the countryside. Worcester spent lavishly to entertain the Queen. In fact, its total expenditure of £173 was double the city's annual budget and a much higher total than was spent by other regional centers that hosted the Queen.[4] This figure is all the more striking because the Queen lodged in the bishop's palace throughout the week and visited the estates of country gentlemen during three of the days; thus, the city corporation would have been freed from some of the more onerous costs associated with hosting. Why, then, did Worcester spend so much money, and where did it go?

As we have seen, Sandwich spent lavishly in order to appear more prosperous than it actually was. Worcester, on the other hand, acknowledged in its welcome speech that it was "wasted and decayed" from its former glory. As we shall see, it spent generously for a different reason: to express a particular kind of hospitality that it hoped would secure patrons who could safeguard the health of its flourishing but fragile cloth industry. Since the eighteenth century, Worcester has been associated in the public mind with economic activities like glove-making, horse-racing, Lea and Perrins sauce, and (more recently) charity shops. But in the sixteenth century, it was one of the most important cloth-making centers in England.

Worcester in 1575

Worcester became a center of cloth production as early as the thirteenth century, and by the early modern period it was "a fully fledged textile town."[5] In the 1540s, John Leland wrote that "noe towne of England at this present tyme makethe so many clothes yerely as worcestar"—and contemporary scholarship seems to confirm this claim.[6] Worcester was best known for making a high quality broadcloth that was "famous far and wide" until at least the late seventeenth century.[7] Although the entire region participated in the manufacture of these tightly woven wool broadcloths, Worcester's were generally regarded as the best. Its citizens started with the finest raw wool in England—the "Leominster ore" produced in nearby Herefordshire and Shropshire—which was then sorted, carded, spun, and woven to produce the cloth. Although most broadcloths were then sent to a fulling mill for finishing, Worcester's were actually fulled by foot to create an even more high quality fabric.[8] The result was, as local antiquarian Thomas Habington describes it, a cloth "so exceedinge fine as all that eaver weare before or synce coulde neaver yet showe the lyke."[9] Nor was Habington guilty of county bias; throughout the sixteenth century, Worcester broadcloths were in high demand on the Continent, and the "top quality ones were probably the best of their kind on earth."[10]

Worcester was not only notable for the quality of its cloth, but also for the unusually high proportion of residents who were involved in its production. In a typical early modern English town, it was rare for more than 25 percent of the populace to be engaged in a single industry.[11] The percentage might be slightly higher in textile towns like Norwich, Colchester, Reading, and Coventry, where some 30 percent of the residents were involved in the production of cloth.[12] In Worcester, this figure was above 40 percent and probably closer to 50 percent in the second half of the sixteenth century.[13] Because making broadcloth was a laborious and multi-step process, the cloth industry provided work for trades as diverse as carders, spinners, weavers, fullers, shearmen, dyers, carriers, and clothiers. And in Worcester, spinning (of wool into yarn to prepare it for weaving) "provided a source of extra income for many a Worcester household otherwise unconnected with cloth-making."[14] So pervasive was the wool industry in sixteenth-century Worcester that G. D. Ramsay has called it "perhaps the closest English approximation to a continental clothmaking town after the fashion of Florence or Ypres."[15] At a time when other English textile towns like Lincoln and Coventry were declining, Worcester was a "remarkable" exception.[16]

One reason for Worcester's success was the extent to which the city had been able to control the conditions of local production. In 1534, the city had gotten Parliament to pass an act that effectively stifled rural cloth-making in the surrounding countryside. This was followed by a 1558 city ordinance that prevented citizens from using weavers who lived outside of—but within twelve miles of—the city.[17] As Worcester's cloth industry became more "self-contained and independent," it could then be more easily regulated to ensure quality.[18] This task was made easier by the fact that clothiers dominated the city government, generally accounting for one-half of the ruling council of the Twenty-Four.[19] Furthermore, rather than allowing the individual guilds to set and enforce industry standards, the city corporation directly controlled the cloth industry. Worcester's 1555 charter of incorporation, for example, gave the city increased regulatory control over enforcing full apprenticeship and inspecting cloth for quality control.[20] Such measures were crucial because the production process involved so many independent steps, and because it was the fineness of Worcester broadcloth that distinguished it from its competitors.

Regardless of the local control that Worcester clothiers had achieved, many market factors were beyond their scope. For one thing, the cloth trade itself was particularly subject to the vicissitudes of the market and was thus "notorious for its liability to boom and slump."[21] The last major national slump had occurred in the 1550s, in the midst of which Worcester reported 200 idle looms and more than 1,000 people out of work.[22] Although the market did rebound, it continued to fluctuate from the early 1560s to the early 1580s.[23] Given Worcester's unusual dependence on a single industry, such instabilities would have a heightened effect on the local economy.

Further complicating things for Worcester was the fact that almost all of its broadcloths were made for export to the European market. This meant that the sale (and prices) of Worcester broadcloths could be influenced by distant factors like piracy, war, foreign competition, and the economic policies of other nations. Throughout much of the sixteenth century, Antwerp was the center of the European cloth market. Each year, English cloth exports were taken up the River Scheldt to be sold and redistributed at this international entrepot, but the Antwerp market began to be threatened in the 1560s by the emerging conflict between Spain and the Low Countries. English access to Antwerp was interrupted in 1564, and then ruptured more permanently in 1569 when the Duke of Alba arrested a group of English merchants.[24] With the decline of the Antwerp market and the danger (from both the Spanish and Protestants) of trading on the Scheldt, English merchants had to search out new markets in places like Emden and Hamburg (both located in modern-day Germany).[25] Thus, at the time of the Queen's visit in 1575, there would have been much uncertainty—and probably some anxiety—about the health of the international cloth market.

Other commercial worries could be found a bit closer to home, in London. For if most high quality broadcloths ended up in Antwerp, they almost all went through the English capital. Over the course of the sixteenth century, London's share of the export cloth trade had risen from 61 percent (in 1510) to 84 percent (in 1534) to 93 percent (in 1569).[26] In some ways this was only natural and convenient, since London could—as it did in so many other industries—consolidate labor and facilities. The London cloth market was located in Blackwell Hall, a cluster of buildings near the Guildhall that featured specialized salesrooms for different kinds of cloth. Here, country clothiers (or their agents) would sell to cloth dealers, who were merchants who typically belonged to the Merchant Adventurers. The cloth was then transferred to warehouses to be stored (and sometimes finished) until its removal to seagoing vessels bound for the Continent.[27] Earlier in the century, some Worcester merchants were still dealing directly with Continental buyers, but by the second half of the sixteenth century, "Worcester cloth was marketed almost solely in London" and no Worcester clothiers participated directly in the export trade.[28] London's dominance of cloth exports was further formalized in 1564 when the Queen granted the Merchant Adventurers a near monopoly on cloth exports.[29]

The ascendency of London was not necessarily harmful to Worcester; after all, it consolidated and simplified the market greatly so that the clothier's main job (aside from "[organizing] the market for the [local] manual laborer") became "the delivery of the cloth to the London market and finding a purchaser there."[30] Yet the London merchants were animated by a very different set of interests. In 1523 and again in 1552, they sought to limit the rights of foreign merchants at Blackwell Hall—whereas the country clothiers welcomed foreign competition for their broadcloths. London merchants were also keen to standardize weights and dimensions of cloth and to enforce quality standards; an "elaborate codifying act" of 1552 saw to the former, while the latter was addressed in 1560 with the introduction of a "new and efficient team of cloth-searchers" at Blackwell Hall who could reject inferior cloth and even impose fines. Not surprisingly, cloth manufacturers—including those at Worcester—resented and even challenged some of these developments.

The final macro player who influenced the cloth export market was the English monarch. As G. D. Ramsey has written, "At all times the fortunes of the woolen industry were related to the favour of the English Crown. Its foreign policy might help or hinder the merchants in their quest for access to foreign markets, while on its domestic authority there hinged the law and order essential to the smooth production of cloth."[31] Yet the Crown exerted more than just a general foreign and domestic impact; it was also directly involved in the regulation of the wool industry. Wool did, after all, account for some 75 percent of all English exports, making it "the single most important commercial enterprise in England."[32] The Crown thus set customs rates, sold export licenses, stipulated how many cloths could be exported each year, and entered into international negotiations (e.g. at Bruges in 1565 and Bristol in 1574) to safeguard English wool interests. Since wool customs duties were also "a major . . . source of revenue for the Crown," central government had many inducements to ensure the health of the cloth industry.[33] But by what policies and according to whose interests? The English wool industry was comprised of very different—and sometimes competing—interests, including the Crown, Parliament, city, country, individual trades, merchants, and even foreign governments. Not surprisingly, the cloth industry was therefore "more liable than most to political manoeuvre."[34] In 1566, for example, the cloth finishers of London were able to push through parliamentary legislation that required one in every ten exported cloths to be dyed—a statute that benefitted their particular trade but caused much time, expense, and acrimony amongst the city merchants.[35] If Worcester was going to safeguard its particular interests on the national and international level, it needed strong advocates.

Historically, Worcester had tried to influence national policy primarily through its parliamentary representation. Unlike many cities that allotted one of their seats to a member of the local county gentry, Worcester was "quite unusual" in electing only its own citizens for "virtually the whole of that vital century between 1540 and 1640."[36] One of its main motives seems to have been a desire to defend the city's cloth interests—a task that it felt its own citizens could do best. Indeed, Worcester's parliamentary representatives played a key role in securing a new charter for the city in 1555 that gave the corporation increased regulatory powers. In 1551, representatives had helped redress a parliamentary act that had set Worcester broadcloth quality standards so high as to make their prices uncompetitive.[37]

A corresponding reason for electing citizens may well have been the desire to avoid local gentry influence. Alan Dyer has noted Worcester's relative "backward[ness] in acquiring its fair share of independent self-government." Even though the city had been self-governing since the twelfth century, Worcester had not become formally incorporated until 1555. Even then, it lacked the county status that many other cities of its size had attained. As a result, the city was in "a state of continual friction with the shire authorities over a variety of issues, stemming from the political weakness of the city beset by a county administration manned by its social superiors, the local gentry." These tensions covered a variety of issues, ranging from the jurisdiction of county courts to the powers of the sheriff to the city's contributions to the county militia. Even privileges that the city had ostensibly gained in the 1555 charter had to be "claimed and defended repeatedly during the ensuring decades."[38] It is not surprising then that the city did not want to invite undue influence from local gentry. Instead, Worcester preferred to keep its distance from the great landed families of the county. Thus, "it is very difficult to find many traces of the city either being influenced by great families or trying to win their friendship."[39] Unlike many other cities of the period, Worcester did not appoint a High Steward. It did fill the office of city recorder, but its choices are revealing. In most cities, this office was filled by a lawyer from a distinguished local family insofar as it was treated as an opportunity for a city to forge patronage with and invite influence from a prominent gentry family. But in Worcester, the trend from the middle of the sixteenth century was to "choose younger sons and less powerful county families" for its recordership—seemingly "to avoid involving itself with an over-influential, and so demanding, patron."[40]

Such cautious measures helped Worcester to safeguard its own fragile privileges and interests, including the local control that it had achieved of its clothing industry. But such insularity also came at a cost. In choosing not to cultivate the influence of its own county families, Worcester lacked the national advocates that cities like Leicester and Warwick enjoyed.[41] This was an especially troubling state, since, as we have seen, the wool industry was particularly subject to national and foreign policies. Worcester needed to impact the center, for "without some kind of influential contact at Court it was very difficult for any town to make its opinions felt."[42] This is why the Queen's visit in 1575 was such a crucial opportunity for the city. It provided a chance to bypass local magnates and appeal directly to both the Queen and the influential courtiers who accompanied her.

Bell's Oration

When the Queen and her entourage arrived at the northern edge of Worcester on Saturday, August 13, the city's welcome oration immediately broached its chief economic concern. After a short preamble on the "first foundacion" of the city, the speaker, William Bell, the deputy recorder of the city, asserted the centrality of the cloth industry to Worcester, claiming that it dated back nine hundred years and that it had always been "the onelie relief & meyntenance of this Citie."[43] In fact, said Bell, the "trade of clothynge" had almost single-handedly made Worcester a flourishing, wealthy, populous, able, and beautiful city. Then Bell's speech changes abruptly: "But why . . . do we shewe your maiestie of thinges that late were & now ar not . . . synce at this day your maiestie shall see and fynde the wealthe wasted and decayed, the bewty faded, the buyldynges ruynou[s] . . . So that of all that was ther is allmost no thyng lefte but a ruynous Citie or decaied, Antiquities" (*JN2*, 353). According to Bell, the local economy had declined dramatically so that Worcester was now but a "ruynous" shell of its former self. The wool industry was subject to depression in the 1550s and fluctuations thereafter, but it was relatively healthy by 1575. Dyer has documented that most areas of the Worcester economy were stable in the 1570s, including food, wages, prices, and the city budget.[44] In fact, the city's population was actually increasing and—far from featuring decayed and ruinous buildings—Worcester was enjoying something of a building boom in this decade.[45] Even allowing for the fact that there was a local downturn (or even the perception of one), this dire state of affairs would seem to be an exaggeration on Bell's part.[46] Yet if so, it was also a useful exaggeration. Bell was able to make the point that the city's economy was vulnerable and subject to fluctuations (as indeed it was). His description of waste, decay, and ruin also created a sense of crisis that the Queen might feel compelled to respond to.

    To that end, Bell next explains the perceived causes of Worcester's plight: "Nether bewayle we our losses to come by any other meanes then by casu ally of vnlooked for trobles," explains Bell, "as the breache of faytheles merchauntes, and restraynt of trafyque . . . [and] one especiall apparaunt Impedyment by the nomeber of pyrates apon the seas" (*JN2*, 353). In Bell's eyes, it was merchants, restrained commercial traffic, and pirates that were the greatest threats to the local economy. The merchants most likely refer to the London merchants at Blackwell Hall who bought Worcester broadcloths for resale abroad. The nature of their particular "breach of faith" is unclear, though Bell might have in mind the activities of the Blackwell cloth-searchers who had controversial powers of inspecting, fining, and even rejecting what they deemed to be inferior cloth. The second factor, "restraynt of trafyque," is another ambiguous but understandable complaint, as country cloth manufacturers generally benefitted from free trade and open markets so that their cloth could command the highest prices. Bell could be making a plea for the Merchant Adventurers to have less and/or foreign merchants to have more access to the London cloth market. He is more likely referring to the Spanish/Dutch conflict, which had severely ruptured trade and wrecked the Antwerp market. This reading is strengthened by Bell's follow-up phrase: "which trafyque beyng now restored by your maiesties pryncely providence, breedyth in vs an assured hope shortelie to see the restitucion of our former florisshyng estate" (*JN2*, 353). This would seem to refer to the 1574 Treaty of Bristol, which had repaired commercial relations between England and Spain in the Low Countries, and included the provisions that merchants would be compensated for losses and that "neither prince might shelter rebels against the other nor freebooters at sea."[47] Apparently, this latter item was still a big problem, since the third impediment to trade that Bell identifies is the great "nomeber of pyrates apon the seas." Piracy was particularly rife in the English Channel and North Sea in the 1560s and 1570s. In addition to "normal" piracy, the French religious wars and the Spanish/Dutch conflict led to privateering on both Protestant and Catholic sides. As a result, "the waters of western Europe became unprecedentedly dangerous for peaceful traders" and had substantial effects on both markets and consumers.[48] Nevertheless, Bell facilely suggests that the Queen might simply deploy the royal navy to rectify this state of affairs: "So may your highnes when so euer it shall seeme good to the same very easly daunte & represse thos Robbers that your subiectes may with safetye sayle & vse their trafyque" (*JN2*, 353).

What all three of these impediments—merchants, war, and pirates—have in common is that none of them are local and all of them are effectively outside of the city's control. Bell's characterization of them as "vnlooked for trobles" suggests that they were unexpected, but also perhaps that they were outside the scope of things the city might prepare for or hope to address. But they are, as Bell also suggests, factors that the Queen might address on the city's behalf through diplomacy ("restraynt of trafyque") and direct action (pirates). Even though Bell may have in mind specific policies, his appeal is also broad enough to stand for general future interests.

The oration then shifts again. After asserting the city's decay and identifying its various causes, Bell next imagines the rejuvenation of the city. He claims that the Queen's arrival already "pronosticate[s] vnto vs the confusion of all our Aduerse fortune in to a more happy & prosperous estate" (*JN2*, 353). As a sign, Bell points to the "populus concourse of the multitude" and "the howses & habitacions Lately Ryson from their rufull ruyn to a more lyvely and freshe furnyture" (*JN2*, 354). Although this revitalization of people and buildings is clearly associated with the Queen's physical arrival, it also seems to be emblematic of the beneficial effects that her future policies might have. Moreover, this depiction of Worcester's resurgence also suggests that its decline need not be permanent—that it can recover and is still worth helping. So Bell has it both ways: he creates a sense of crisis that speaks to Worcester's dire need for royal assistance, but he also asserts Worcester's continuing vitality.

The location of this speech is a key part of its effect. The Chamber Order Book of Worcester specifies that it was delivered at the northern edge of the town liberties "at Salte lane ende in the foreyate streete" (*JN2*, 339). This would have been outside of the city walls in the suburbs north of the Foregate. In the 1570s, this area had cheaper housing and was mainly occupied by poorer laborers and small-crafts men, making Bell's exaggerated claims of urban decay seem more accurate.[49] However, once the Queen and her entourage heard the speech and entered the city proper, they would have found themselves in a tidy, well-built urban space of timber-framed houses, graceful churches, and an impressive guildhall. The main thoroughfare they processed down was High Street, "a very fayre and longe walke answearable to the magnificence of the city."[50] In this way, the physical movement from the suburbs into the city enacted the speech's shift from decline to vibrancy.

Overall, this formal welcome speech is very important. Like all welcome orations, it constitutes the city's initial contact with the visiting monarch and sets the tone for her visit. But it is also unusually frank about the city's most pressing economic concern. It establishes Worcester's reliance on cloth manufacture, asserts the decline of this industry due to factors outside the city's control, and dramatizes the role that the Queen might play in promoting its recovery. This is indeed the theme of the Worcester pageants in a nutshell.

It is clear that city leaders put special care into the delivery and content of this speech. One month before the Queen's arrival, the city asked William Bell—rather than the city's recorder, Sir John Throckmorton—to deliver the welcome oration. Bell had attended Oxford, and, as his son later wrote, "For his eloquence he was esteemed, and was known as another Cicero."[51] Bell was also from the nearby village of Hanbury, so he probably had a firm understanding of the local economy and the city's anxieties. Nonetheless, the preparations record that he was "spoken with touchyng the oracion"—presumably so that the city might help shape the actual content of the speech (*JN2, 339*). Afterward, the city seems to have been pleased, for Bell was compensated generously with £20 for "his Iorneys . . . and his paynes" (*JN2, 356*) in preparing and delivering the speech. Even though Bell delivered the welcome oration, it is clear that he spoke on behalf of the city in addressing this crucial issue. It is also clear that Worcester wanted the speech to endure beyond the moment of its utterance. During the visit itself, copies of the speech were made and distributed to "dyuers honorable" guests and possibly the Queen herself (*JN2, 343*). In this way, the oration was given a textual life that would hopefully resonate long after the event, thus increasing the chances that Worcester's appeal would be remembered and acted upon. That a copy of the speech was also preserved in the city records (along with the general narrative of the Queen's visit) says something about its centrality in recording what the Queen's visit meant to the city.

Perhaps somewhat curiously, the wool industry is not mentioned much in the subsequent description of the Queen's visit. Even though some pageant descriptions and speeches have been lost, broadcloth does not seem to be a recurring theme among those that remain. But it is not, I will argue, that this subject has been broached and then moved to the back burner. Instead, Worcester uses the rest of the Queen's visit to create a basis for why the Queen might respond positively to the city's appeal for central support. In order to do so, Worcester turns to a particular deployment of hospitality.

Hospitality

Hospitality was, of course, something that all cities (and private individuals) proffered the Queen when she visited them while on progress. After all, she was the guest and they were the hosts. This is why Elizabeth was always formally received into the community at the outset of her visit, and then—like any guest—was lodged, fed, and entertained for its duration. As Felicity Heal has shown, most early modern cities had ample experience in dispensing this sort of hospitality, as they regularly extended it to other dignitaries who visited town, including magnates, bishops, and county gentlemen. On these occasions, urban hospitality might take the form of "elaborate welcomes," gift-giving, "ceremonial organization and display," lodging accommodation, feasting, and even formal entertainments. In fact, such hospitality was frequently a "major [item] of expenditure" in the annual civic budget. Why were cities so willing to invest in the reception of prominent outsiders? Urban hospitality—like all forms of hospitality and "good housekeeping" in the early modern period—was underpinned by a variety of religious (charity, golden rule), political (display of power), and social (neighborliness) motives. One of its most important benefits was the honor and prestige that it conferred on the town, thereby enhancing its reputation to outsiders. As Heal argues, "These activities were as necessary an aspect of the behavior of urban oligarchies as was a display of good lordship for the great nobleman. Since the status of the town was less secure than that of the landed magnate it may even be that reputation-enhancing gestures were even more mandatory in a civic context than in the countryside." More practically, urban hospitality might also help create an expectation of reciprocity between the host city and the visiting dignitary. Such reciprocity was not primarily monetary, but rather an ethic of neighborliness that took the form of bonds of political and social patronage.[52]

Even before the Queen's visit, Worcester was already heavily invested in this sort of hospitality. Dyer indicates that in the second half of the sixteenth century hospitality was the third-biggest line in the city budget. Even though Worcester was wary of local challenges to its power, the city still publicly received "bishops, assize judges, county magistrates, members of the Council of the Marches, important nobles and anyone with access to influence, especially with the central government." In the sixteen years prior to the Queen's visit, Worcester had hosted the entire Council of the Marches no fewer than four times.[53] Thus, the city had a history of using hospitality to pursue local interests and forge amity with other local power brokers. Of course, a visit from the reigning monarch was a much bigger endeavor and there was much more at stake. If Worcester were to secure the patronage of the Queen, it would need to make quite an impression. More so than any other city that the Queen visited, Worcester invested in hospitality with the twin aims of enhancing its reputation and inviting reciprocity.

A close reading of the Queen's 1575 visit bears this out. One of the more curious features of Worcester's reception of the Queen is the extent to which the city leaders inserted themselves into various episodes throughout the week. Their involvement has a fairly conventional beginning with their welcoming of the royal party at Salt Lane End. Like most other cities, Worcester sent a delegation of civic offers to meet the Queen at the edge of its legal boundaries. These six individuals were Christopher Dighton and Richard Spark (bailiffs), Thomas Heywood and John Coombs (aldermen), George Warberton (high chamberlain), and the aforementioned William Bell (in place of the recorder, John Throckmorton).[54] After ceremonially yielding their maces to the Queen (who then ceremonially "redelyuered the same"), Bell gave the oration, the Queen was presented with a silver cup, and the city officers rode before the Queen and escorted her through town. As Mary Hill Cole reports, such behavior on the part of civic officers was typical at the Queen's entry into a town.[55] What is unusual about Worcester is that these same six city leaders continued this function of greeting and formally escorting the Queen throughout the week. For example, the very next morning (Sunday), the Queen went to Worcester Cathedral "to here seruice & sermon" (*JN2, 345*). Since she had spent the night at the Bishop's Palace, this involved exiting the walled compound of the palace, turning right onto Bishop's Street, proceeding about fifty yards to the junction with High Street, and then turning right into the cathedral close. In other words, she was beginning and ending on cathedral chapter property and would only be in the city's jurisdiction for about 150 feet. Yet, Dighton, Spark, Heywood, Coombs, Warberton, and Bell all accompanied her on horseback, and twelve other city leaders (who had previously served as bailiffs) were positioned in "scarlett gownes at the ende of the highe streete turnyng in to the churchyard" (*JN2, 345*).

Such behavior would seem to be overkill, but I would argue that the city leaders were proactively responding to a potential problem. This problem was that it was not precisely clear that it was the city of Worcester that was hosting the Queen. During her weeklong stay, Elizabeth was lodged in the Bishop's Palace, and thus might be said to technically be the guest of Nicholas Bullingham, the current Bishop of Worcester.[56] During the days, the Queen spent a lot of time visiting the local gentry, journeying to John Habington's

Hindlip Hall and Hallow Park on Tuesday and Thursday, and Anthony Bourne's Battenhall Park on Friday. Thus, other than the Queen's formal entrance into and departure from Worcester, she really only traveled through the city while on her way to other places. Obviously, Worcester was a big part of why the Queen was visiting this particular part of her realm and why she was staying a full week, but, strictly speaking, the city had minimal involvement in both the Queen's lodging and entertainment. If Worcester were to base its economic appeal on the claims of hospitality, it had to establish that it was actually hosting (or at least co-hosting) the monarch. This is perhaps why city leaders took such an active role in asserting themselves in situations that did not really require their presence. When the Queen arrived at the Bishop's Palace on her first night, we are told that "after she came in to the grett chamber Master Baylyffes Master aldermen the said orator & highe Chamberlayne kneelyng as she came by them did putt downe their maces And she bowyng her hedd towardes them thanked them for her myrthe And offered her hande vnto them to kysse, which doone they departed" (*JN2*, 345). While the Queen was settling into her suite at the Bishop's Palace, it is the city officials who position themselves even in her private chamber and relinquish their maces. This was probably due to the indulgence of Bishop Nicholas Bullingham, a native of Worcester who had close connections to its leaders and was unusually sympathetic to its economic concerns.[57]

On Tuesday, when the Queen left the Bishop's Palace to visit John Habington at Hindlip, these same six men escorted her to the northeastern edge of the city liberties and then "at her maiesties commyng homewardes towardes the Citie The said Baylyfes aldermen orator & high chamberlayne mett her maiestie as before without the citie abowt viij of the clock in yevenyng And so did beare their maces before her maiestie vnto the Palace gate" (*JN2*, 346). As we can see from these two examples, Worcester city leaders worked hard to make themselves a part of both the Queen's lodging and her daily excursions. Nor was this mere officiousness. That they always prominently carried their maces—the symbols of their civic authority—made it clear that they were interacting with the Queen as official representatives of the entire civic corporation.[58] In doing so, they sought to drive home Worcester's role as both host and dispenser of hospitality.

A primary feature of Worcester's hospitality was its attempt to enhance the city's reputation. One of the ways the city pursued this aim was by investing heavily in the Queen's entry into the city—especially since, as Heal points out, ceremonial organization and display was closely tied to the "collective reputation" of the city.[59] While all progress cities sent delegations to meet the arriving Queen at the city boundary, Worcester was unusual in its emphasis on (and recording of) the ceremonial display. The Chamber Order Book devotes a lot of space to describing the Queen's first sight of the city. It is clear that the particulars—who was in attendance, what they were wearing, and how they were arranged—was very important to the city. The plan called for the bailiffs, aldermen, and high chamberlain to meet her at Salt Lane End and "beare their maces on horseback before her maiestie" (JN2, 339). The twelve members of the Twenty-Four that had previously served as bailiffs would be present in. "scarlett gownes faced with blak satten with doublettes of satten" (JN2, 339). The remainder of the Twenty-Four will be accoutered "in murrey in grayne And the [members of the council of the Forty-Eight] in their lyuerey gownes of violett in grayne faier & comelye with the rest of the freemen and euery occu-pacion by hym self in their gownes & other decent apparell on a rowe on the easte syde of [Foregate Street] And before euery occupacion their streamers to be holden" (JN2, 339). On the whole, this was a very large, formal group. It comprised the city's chief officers, both of its ruling councils, and all of its guilds and associated freemen. In total, it probably amounted to no fewer than 250 to 300 people.[60] The description reveals that the city leaders were not only interested in sheer numbers, but also in the display of "faier and comelye" costumes. One item in the preparations even specifies that "the lyuery gownes of euery company . . . [are] to be viewed by Master Baylyffes & their breethern" to ensure that they were "comelye & decent" (JN2, 340). Moreover, these "gownes" are to be of varied and vibrant colors, including scarlet, black, mur-rey (mulberry), violet, and turkey (red). The "streamers"—or banners—held by each guild would have provided a further source of color and visual inter-est.[61] Worcester was clearly trying to convey a sense of formal pageantry. They may well have taken inspiration from their own annual Corpus Christi processions, which prominently featured the city's guilds.[62] Whereas those shows served to ratify the oligarchy to the rest of Worcester, this ceremonial arrangement was aimed at a different, external audience.

The arrangement and positioning of these brightly colored groups was designed for maximum dramatic effect. They were positioned where Salt Lane ran into Foregate Street, right where the road from the northeast came around a bend and provided a dramatic view of the city. As Elizabeth rounded the bend, she would have been struck with the sudden sight of the city and its assembled dignitaries. The size of the latter would have been magnified further by the fact that they were all standing in a row on the east side of Foregate Street, "stretchyng vp verry neere to the foregate" (*JN2*, 342). Thus, the 250 to 300 people would have occupied some 800 linear feet of ground and appeared to stretch into the distance. In this way, city leaders adopted the established processional convention of using a vast number of participants "to display an image of civic bourgeois wealth and power" to the royal visitors.[63] That this large group was strategically positioned where the city came dramatically into view would have furthered the impression that Worcester was a large, vibrant, and well-organized urban space.

Other features in the account suggest that enhancing the reputation of the city was a continuing goal. The Chamber Order Book not only reports on the hospitable events that Elizabeth partook of—that she heard a welcome oration, processed through the streets, observed pageant devices, and visited the cathedral—it also takes special care to record the Queen's *reaction* to each of these events. She affirmed that "hit was verry well" upon first receiving the city's ceremonial mace, and she responded to the gift of the silver cup with "good likyng" and hearty thanks (*JN2*, 342–43). She was attentive and receptive to the Latin oration at cathedral. Not only does the account note what she said, but also how she said it—frequently using adjectives like "cheerful," "loving," "hearty," and "merry." The account also registers the Queen's non-verbal reactions of movement and gesture, such as when she bows, kneels, offers a hand to kiss, stands up in her coach, and turns to face the crowd. Finally, it also takes a particular interest in reading the Queen's countenance at various moments—be it "attentive," "cheerful," "smiling," "merry," or "diligent"—to gauge her response to the unfolding events. It is clear that the Worcester account takes great pains to record the *effects* of these events on the Queen, particularly as they reflected how she thought about Worcester and its people.

The account also frequently registers the reactions of the large group of privy councilors and courtiers that had accompanied the Queen to Worcester. When the narrative describes a major episode of the visit, it often includes a phrase such as "wherunto her Highnes & the rest did geue verry Attentyve eare" or "att whiche place her maiestie & the rest of the honorable with as good likyng as before" (*JN2*, 343–44). Later, the account even records individual comments made by Lord Burghley and the earls of Leicester, Warwick, and Sussex professing their esteem for the city and its people. The account's emphasis on such reactions makes it obvious that one of Worcester's chief goals was to enhance the city's reputation in the eyes of these outside visitors, and that it should be perceived as being generous and honorable.[64] The account reveals that Worcester believed this goal had largely been achieved. After the Queen's departure on Saturday, August 20, the city leaders "departed home to their howses with grett Ioye, that her maiestie with the rest of the nobles, the trayne with the officers of the howse & her men had geven the citie so good reporte of good likyng of this citie And of their Interteynement by the citesyns" (*JN2*, 349). That the Queen and all of the other visitors had been impressed with the city is clearly the source of their satisfaction.

Reciprocity

Though citizens no doubt took pride in the enhanced honor and reputation of the city for its own sake, the account also indicates that they were hoping to parlay this good will into reciprocity. In his book *Hospitable Performances,* Daryl Palmer explains that one of the key features of early modern hospitality was that its exercise created a "code of exchange" between host and guest.[65] For the host, hospitality not only created "access" to the guest, but also "agency."[66] In Worcester's case, it now had the opportunity to do something for the Queen—in dispensing hospitality—that it would not otherwise have had. In turn, the Queen's "consumption of [this] hospitality created what Blau calls a 'diffuse future obligation' to reciprocate."[67] Even though this "debt" was really more of a neighborly than a monetary obligation, "welcoming and entertaining gave hosts an opportunity to sketch the form" that the future benefit might take.[68] For Worcester, the ideal form of reciprocity would have been helping to safeguard its wool interests on the national and international stage.

From the outset of the Queen's visit, Worcester took steps to draw attention to and intensify this dynamic of reciprocity. Sprinkled throughout Bell's welcome oration are assertions of ways that the city has supported and benefitted the Queen. For instance, they have been "alweys a frontier and Bulwarke of bolde & obedient seruiceable subiects agenst the sundry invasions & vndue attemptes of the welshe men" (*JN2*, 351). At the Queen's coronation seventeen years earlier, the city's joy had taken the form of "theffuse expence of their wealthe as the like is neuer remembred to be doon" (*JN2*, 353–54). So loyal and supportive of the Queen were Worcester citizens that "if all iuste lawes had not cast apon your maiestie the Inheritaunce & rightful succession in this Kingdom we myght my Lords in merite most iustlie haue elected her maiestie therevnto" (*JN2*, 354). Though Cole is correct in identifying this statement as unintentionally dangerous in sentiment (that an English monarch might be elected rather than put in position by God), it nonetheless illustrates Worcester's striving to make a virtue of its loyalty.[69] Together, these statements illustrate Worcester's longstanding support of the Queen. Even though the Queen had enjoyed these benefits prior to her visit, it was her physical arrival that gave Worcester the opportunity to articulate and claim them in the context of the hospitality that it was currently dispensing—hopefully increasing the Queen's "future obligation."

At the same time, the welcome oration also registers the Queen's benevolence to the city. Since her coronation, she had confirmed the city's charters, helped re-found the local grammar school, and "enlarged augmented and confirmed" a local charitable foundation for the "meyntenaunce of certen poore people for euer to be relieved amongst vs" (JN2, 352). Bell no doubt mentions these benefices to express the city's gratitude, but he is also suggesting that Worcester and the Queen *already* enjoy a mutually beneficial relationship of reciprocity. Worcester had given political and financial support to the Queen in the past, and she had reciprocated with specific civic, educational, and charitable benefits. Near the end of the speech, Worcester pledges to continue its heartfelt support of the Queen: "We ioyfully caste our cares vowying for our partes with vnfayned hartes the willyng expence of our goodes and lyves at your maiesties commaundement" (JN2, 354). What the speech does not overtly state, but seems to imply, is that the Queen might therefore make a reciprocal pledge for Worcester's benefit.

If this oration attempts to assert a dynamic of reciprocity based on past actions and future pledges, then other parts of Worcester's reception seek to cultivate personal bonds between Queen and people in order to strengthen the bonds of reciprocity. Although all civic visits depend on a public audience, Worcester was unusual in the prominence and involvement of its citizens. The account notes the presence of a large group of residents at almost every episode with phrases like "the people beyng Innumerable in the streetes & Churchyard" and "the streetes beyng replenyshed with people" (JN2, 345, 348). Moreover, the people are characterized as active participants rather than mere sideline observers. They shouted and cheered, offered prayers for their monarch, and even provided lighting—"every howse in the streetes havyng . . . torches & candles burnyng on euery syde"—on two occasions when the Queen passed through the city in the dusk (JN2, 343, 346). Thus, the account gives the impression that the whole city (and not just a handful of civic leaders) was engaged in hosting the Queen—something that Cole says was "crucial" for paving the way for a "successful [ceremonial] dialogue between Elizabeth and the town."[70]

The account also depicts the gradual development of an actual dialogue between Queen and people. After the welcome oration and at several subsequent points, the people cried, "God save your grace," and the Queen thanked them cheerfully. As the visit progressed, these interactions became more natural and less formulaic. While returning from Hindlip on Tuesday, the Queen rode through the crowd on horseback and made "commfortable speeches to her subiects" (*JN2*, 346). At her departure on Saturday, we again find her "chierfully & comfortably spekyng to the people" (*JN2*, 348). These off-the-cuff moments were no doubt a public relations tool for Elizabeth, but the Worcester account depicts them as evidence of the city's growing rapport with the Queen. In fact, when the Queen decided to extend her stay in Worcester for three additional days, the account chalks this up to "the good likyng that hir maiestie had of this Citie/ of the people & of her place" (*JN2*, 348). It was a manifest sign that the city's hospitality was working and that these personal interactions with the people were a contributing factor.

Worcester's most direct attempt to build an expectation of reciprocity was through gift-giving, a common feature of civic hospitality that often took the form of gifts of food or wine. During a royal progress, almost every village, town, or city that the Queen visited would give her something, most commonly a gold or silver cup.[71] Worcester did the same. After the welcome oration, Bell presented her with a "syluer cupp with his cover dooble gylte worthe ten poundes . . . the fairest that mought be fownd in London And in the same cup [40] poundes in half soueraigne of her owne quoyne & stampe" (*JN2*, 343). At £50, this was a generous gift that exceeded those of other comparable cities like Northampton (£26), Canterbury (£30), Southampton (£40), and Lichfield (£40).[72] In addition to the Queen, the city also gave liberally to others in her retinue, including individual courtiers and servants of the royal household, such as "the Queenes musicions," the "messyngers of the Queenes chamber," "the makers of wayes," "the Clerk of the markett of the Queenes howshold," and "the Quenes maiesties bakers" (*JN2*, 355). Of the estimated £173 that Worcester spent on the Queen's visit, more than half of this total (about £89) was dispensed as gifts. Such largesse may suggest a general attempt to enhance the city's reputation. It is likely that Worcester was able to devote comparably more of its hosting budget to gift-giving because most of the lodging, feeding, and entertainment expenditures were being shouldered by the Bishop of Worcester and the local gentry the Queen visited.

Nevertheless, Worcester's generosity was not a case of spontaneous largesse, but a conscious strategy. The city's preparations for the Queen's visit go into great detail on how much money was to be collected (£212), the different sources it would be taken from (treasury, council chamber, citizens), and who would collect it (generally four individuals per ward) (JN2, 340–41). These arrangements suggest that from the beginning, monetary expenditure was a key mode of the hospitality that Worcester sought to dispense. The preparations also contain details about gifts, most notably the silver cup for the Queen and a gilt tankard for Sir James Croft, Comptroller of the Queen's Household. The events narrative maintains this focus on gift-giving by carefully noting each time a gift is presented to a visitor. The Queen received her cup (filled with coins) on Saturday, Croft was presented with his tankard on Monday, and later in the week Burghley, Leicester, Warwick, and Sussex were all given gifts of hippocras, a spiced wine. The presentation of monetary gifts for the Queen's servants is not mentioned in the narrative, but such gifts are referred to as a key item in the preparations and are carefully tallied up at the end. Together, such textual details make it clear that Worcester consciously invested in gift-giving.

The reason for this is that gift-giving was the form of hospitality that was most associated with reciprocity. In early modern culture, where "personal bonds of patronage, affinity, and deference were central to political identity," gifts were seen as crucial to maintaining social bonds.[73] The basic principle of Seneca's highly influential De beneficiis is that "doing good turns and reciprocating them was the way in which the true community of men was maintained."[74] By giving or receiving a gift, one entered into a "circulation of benefits" that perpetuated itself in future reciprocal actions.[75] The modern mind might cynically view Worcester's behavior as trying to "buy" favor from the Queen, yet in the early modern practice of hospitality, gift-giving was no mere financial transaction, but "an intimacy that brought donor and recipient into a direct relationship."[76] Palmer thus distinguishes a gift from a commodity because the latter is a one-time profit that is then used up, whereas the former engenders a "feeling bond" that continually increases.[77] In this reading, Worcester's gifts were a concrete demonstration of the genuine esteem in which it held the Queen, and that is what it hoped the Queen would reciprocate. And if so, Worcester also seemed to be suggesting a particularly concrete way that she might respond: by looking out for its wool interests. Perhaps, then, Jayne Archer and Sarah Knight's characterization of gift-giving as a way to "entangle the Queen within a relationship of mutual obligations" is more accurate.[78] There is no doubt that this strategy had served Worcester well in the recent past, since gifts and cash had played an important role in the city obtaining a new charter in 1555.[79] It is therefore not surprising that the city would reinvest in this strategy twenty years later.

In 1575, Worcester relied heavily on gifts to cultivate the patronage of influential men who served on the Privy Council. Given Worcester's economic concerns, these councilors would have been a natural audience to appeal to. First, Privy Councilors were active in international affairs and diplomacy, which gave them a crucial role in the formulation of foreign policy. As such, they could be potential allies in shaping foreign markets and stabilizing England's relations with other countries. Second, Privy Councilors were active in suppressing piracy, both in formulating and enforcing policies against "lawlessness at sea" in all its forms. Hence, they would have been a key secondary audience for Bell's request that the Queen "daunte & represse thos Robbers" who were plaguing maritime trade. Finally, the Privy Council was actively engaged in regulating commercial activities throughout the realm, including the wool trade and textile exports.[80] Their approach to economic issues, however, was piecemeal at best. As Michael Barraclough Pulman observes, "All in all, the council's motives for interfering in the national economic life were mixed and arose out of the particular situation in which it found itself involved at any given moment. It appears to have had no overall plan other than to further a national interest that varied according to circumstances and to have made no attempt to integrate the various business efforts of individuals or cooperating groups of Englishmen into a coherent, coordinated whole."[81] If such a situational approach made the council's actions toward the wool industry hard to predict, it also meant they might well be susceptible to outside influence from one of the interested parties.

This helps account for personal visits that the civic officers paid to members of the Privy Council during the week of the Queen's visit. On Tuesday, they welcomed Sir James Croft, on Wednesday they called on Leicester, and on Thursday they made separate visits to Warwick, Sussex, and Burghley. That the city sent the same six-person delegation (bailiffs, aldermen, high chamberlain, and orator) shows that these were formal and even ceremonial excursions rather than casual visits. Moreover, the account almost always specifies the guest's office alongside his name. Thus, Croft is described as "Countroller of her maiesties howshold & one of her maiesties pryvye councell," Leicester is "master of the Queenes maiesties horses," Sussex is "Lord Chamberlayne," and Burghley is "Lord Threasurer." These designations suggest the realm of influence of each man, and thus seem to help explain why the delegation is calling on him in the first place. Finally, all of these visiting courtiers are presented with gifts, suggesting both the city's esteem and also its hope for reciprocity.

The most important guest from Worcester's perspective may well have been Sir James Croft. He was the first courtier visited by the city delegation, and his gift was the only one (besides the Queen's cup) that the city made special preparations for. He was singled out, the records indicate, "for his councell & fryndshipp shewed to this Citie" (*JN2*, 340). Croft was the head of a powerful family in Herefordshire, the county that bordered Worcestershire to the west. From 1563 until his death in 1590, Croft represented that county in every Parliament and "was the dominant figure in Elizabethan Herefordshire."[82] Owing partially to his connections with the Earl of Leicester, Croft was appointed comptroller of the Queen's household in 1570 and soon thereafter became a member of the Privy Council.[83] Despite Croft's growing national influence, his main "fryndshipp" to the city of Worcester would seem to be the fact that he owned some property in the Worcester area and that in the 1572 Parliament he had supported an unsuccessful bill to make a cut of water from the Severn into Worcester.[84] Even if Croft's previous support was being exaggerated, he was just the sort of person whose patronage Worcester would like to cultivate. By 1575, he was well connected nationally both formally (Queen's household, Privy Council, Parliament) and informally (he was on good terms with the likes of Burghley, Leicester, and the Queen). At the same time, he had strong ties to the west Midlands; he was at the center of an intricate network of relationships, and he well understood that region's main economic focus of raising sheep and making cloth. He also had particular ties to Worcester, since he owned property there and had served alongside its chief civic officer (Christopher Dighton) in the 1572 Parliament, where his support of the water bill indicated that he understood and was responsive to the city's needs. Perhaps most importantly, he was local, but not *too* local. Croft's sphere of local influence was primarily in Herefordshire, where he held numerous local offices.[85] Because he did not hold any offices or wield much influence in Worcestershire, the city would not have to give up any of its jealously guarded independence in cultivating Croft's support.[86]

On the Monday that the city delegation visited Croft, he was, according to the records, being lodged in a certain Mr. Steyn's house, most likely in Friar Street. Thus, the city was actually, and not just theoretically, hosting Croft. Croft's response to their arrival was warm, as he "honorably enterteyned them And toke them all by thandes" (*JN2*, 345). Such familiarity would seem to suggest the same sort of neighborly dialogue that the records try to depict else-where between the citizens and their Queen. When Croft was presented with the tankard—which was a substantial gift for a courtier on a royal progress[87]—the orator Bell "besought his honor to accepte the same as a sklender token of their grett good will & thankefulnes for his honorable favor" (JN2, 345–46). The gift of plate—a common "material display of largesse"[88]—is thus described as the city's response to past favors that Croft had bestowed. As with the Queen, this language suggests that Croft and the city were *already* in a relationship of reciprocity. Croft's response to the gift is also carefully recorded. Not only did he accept the tankard, he also "promesed to love them as his good neighbours And feynd them in any thynge that he cowlde do them good in that they hereaf-ter shalbe bold with hym" (JN2, 346). Far from this gift cancelling the debt that Worcester owed Croft, it cements the bond they already share and opens new horizons of mutually beneficial actions. In pledging his good will and future help, Croft models the idea of "diffuse future obligations" that are so central to the practice of early modern hospitality. Such a response was no doubt music to Worcester's ears. They probably would not even have minded the ambiguous nature of Croft's pledge—"any thynge that he cowlde do them good in"—since the city was not angling for action on a specific policy so much as advocacy for future scenarios that might arise. As Lorraine Attreed points out, urban patron-age "purchased influence and a devoted relationship as often as direct action."[89] Nonetheless, by singling Croft out from the rest of the Queen's retinue and honoring him with this gift, Worcester believed it was both acknowledging his past behavior as well as strengthening the bond between them moving forward.

The city delegation's visits to other Privy Councilors follow a similar pat-tern and are presented as being similarly successful. During Wednesday's visit to Robert Dudley, the Earl of Leicester, housed in the home of one of the cathedral's prebends, the city officers proffered a "[humble] wellcome" and the gift of "[two] gallons of Ipocras Beseechyng you to beare your honorable favor towardes this Citie" (JN2, 346). Here, the desired reciprocity is stated directly rather than implied. The earl's understanding of this expectation is registered clearly in his response: He "tooke them all by the handes And thanked them hartelie And said as folowyth. I Assuer you, tis a citie That I Love with all my harte And if I may any wey do it good you shall fynde me willyng and reddy'" (JN2, 346–47). The record of Thursday's encounter with Robert's brother Ambrose Dudley, the Earl of Warwick, is abbreviated for efficiency's sake—they "wellcome[d] his honor with the like present to whom the orator spake in effecte as before to the yerle of Leycestor"—but Warwick's response is noted carefully: "This is a proper citie, hit is pytty it shuld decay & become poore And for my parte I will devise some way to do it good" (*JN2*, 347). Both men invoke the favorable reputation of the city, declare their affection for it, and pledge to act on its behalf. Warwick even alludes to the economic issues that are, as we have seen, most pressing from the city's perspective. Together, Croft, Leicester, and Warwick model the sort of response that Worcester hoped its gift-giving would garner. Regardless of their intentions, these men at least register their understanding that Worcester's hospitality is predicated on and motivated by the desire for reciprocity.

Afterward, the city delegation called separately on Sussex and Burghley and made similar gifts of hippocras.[90] They were unable to meet with Sussex, "beyng in his bedd & somewhat disseased," though he sent them "verry hartie thankes by his secretary" (*JN2*, 347). The delegation was able to get an audience with Burghley, though his response extended no further than "tak[ing] them all by the handes And thank[ing] them all for their gentle curtesie" (*JN2*, 347). These visits were therefore less effective, though they nonetheless illustrate Worcester's casting of as wide a net as possible in the search for potential patronage. Near the end of the city's account is included a careful list of all the most prominent people who accompanied the Queen on her visit to Worcester. There are separate sections for noblemen (Burghley, Sussex, Warwick, Leicester, Knollys, Croft, Thomas Smith, Walsingham, Sutton, Howard, Seymour, Strange, Sackville), Bishops (Worcester, Hereford, Gloucester, Lichfield and Coventry, Rochester), and Ladies of Honor (wives/widows of Northampton, Sussex, Warwick, Leicester, Hunsdon, Cobham, Stafford, Paget, and sisters of Oxford, Bath) (*JN2*, 349–51). I would argue that this was no mere record-keeping exercise, but a conscious intent to create (at least in textual form) a cadre of influential people whom it had hosted and who might be sympathetic to the city in the future.

A Royal Relationship

Queen Elizabeth herself was the city's greatest hope, as she had the most direct hand in regulating the wool industry and in determining English access to markets abroad. We have already seen how Bell's welcome oration attempts to create a dynamic of reciprocity between city and Queen by enumerating the ways in which each had benefitted the other over the prior seventeen years. Worcester also asserts a much longer history of mutualism between itself and previous English monarchs. The very beginning of the welcome oration refers to "your maiesties noble progenitors to whom this poore citie hath byn especially bounde" (*JN2,* 351). Bell begins with the seventh-century Saxon king Wulfhere, who is credited with granting the charter that "made worcester a Citie" (*JN2,* 351). He then rattles off seven other monarchs—Offa, Edgar, Henry II, Richard I, Edward II, Richard II, Edward IV—who "endewed this citie with sundry charters liberties & pryvileges" (*JN2,* 352). In turn, the people of Worcester served these monarchs as a "bulwarke of bolde & obedient seruiceable subiects agenst the sundry invasions & vndue attemptes of the welshe men" (*JN2,* 351). In other words, previous kings have made special allowances for Worcester, and the city has rewarded that faith by loyally stabilizing a potentially volatile region. Bell then asserts that this reciprocal relationship has also flourished under the Queen's "nearest & dearest progenytors . . . whos grett & kyngly favor [h]as this citie happelie fealte" (*JN2,* 352). He specifically mentions each of the previous Tudor monarchs—Henry VII, Henry VIII, Edward VI, and Mary—taking care to state their familial relationship to the Queen: "your maiesties grantfather," "your highnes father," "your maiesties brother," and "your highnes dearest sister." In other words, everyone else in Queen Elizabeth's family has enjoyed this special relationship with Worcester, and, by implication, so should she. Finally, Bell invokes Worcester's most recent royal visit—that of Henry VII in 1486: "[It so pleased] that second Salamon your highnes grantfather in his kynglie person to gether with the Queene his wyff, the Countes of Rychemonde his mother And prynce Arthur your maiesties derest vncle, to visite this citie. wheer duryng the tyme of his abode hit pleased his highnes so thankfully to Accepte of the poore good will and Loyall affeccion of the Citesyns as at this day ther remayne in Regyster of Recorde . . . sondry comfortable speeches witnessyng the same" (*JN2,* 352). As this earlier progress illustrates, there is not only a precedent of reciprocity between previous monarchs and Worcester, there is also a precedent of hospitality that serves to ratify this bond. Presented in this way, the Queen's 1575 visit is not so much an attempt to "entangle the Queen within a relationship of mutual obligation" as it is a way of maintaining an existing and historically documented—"in Regyster of Recorde"—relationship between Worcester and the monarchy.

Beyond the welcome oration, Worcester sought to highlight this already-existing relationship throughout the Queen's visit. The city's preparations specify that it paid to have the Queen's arms painted on both the inside and outside of four of the city gates, which the Queen would have seen at her entry, departure, and on various excursions as she passed in and out of Foregate, Sidbury Gate, and Bridge Gate. The city also "set out very comely with colors the front of the Geld Hall, with gelding of the Queen's arms," which Elizabeth would have passed by at least five times during her stay.[91] Finally, arrangements were made for an existing statue of a king in Sidbury Gate to be freshly painted. This last detail seems to be a particularly apt emblem for Worcester's larger strategy of drawing attention to and reinvigorating what they saw as a pre-existing royal relationship.

Worcester's most obvious asset in forging a connection between itself and the monarchy was its cathedral. For here were interred the bodies of both King John (1166–1216) and Elizabeth's uncle, Arthur Tudor (1486–1502). Although the latter was never actually king, he would have succeeded his father, Henry VII, had he not died unexpectedly of the "sweating sickness," at age fifteen. In life, both John and Arthur possessed close ties to the city of Worcester. During the seventeen years of John's reign, he visited Worcester no fewer than nine times.[92] He was attracted by the fine hunting in the area, particularly the royal forests of Kinver and Feckenham. Worcester's proximity to Wales also made it an ideal base "for meetings with the Welsh princes to broker peace and establish territory."[93] Finally, John was drawn to Worcester for religious reasons. Its cathedral housed the "magnificent reliquary shrines" of two saints: Oswald (961–992) and Wulfstan (1062–1095). The latter had only been canonized in 1203, and from that time John had developed a "particular reverence for this saint."[94] He regularly visited Worcester to pray at Wulfstan's shrine on major holy days like Christmas and Easter. At his death in 1216, John was buried in Worcester Cathedral in accordance with the terms of his will.

Prince Arthur's connections to Worcester were not quite as strong. He had been baptized by the Bishop of Worcester (albeit in Winchester) in 1486, and his marriage by proxy to Catherine of Aragon had taken place in 1499 at Tickenhill Manor, some fifteen miles from the city. He had indeed visited Worcester in person with his parents and grandmother—as the welcome oration is keen to point out—but this had been in 1486 when Arthur was only a few months old. More than anything, it was the circumstances of his death that would bind the Prince to Worcester. After his marriage to Catherine in November 1501, the newlyweds traveled to Ludlow Castle, Shropshire, to set up court (as Arthur was now Prince of Wales). However, the Prince grew ill in March, was dead within a month, and his body was taken to nearby Worcester for interment.

Both men's tombs feature prominently in Worcester Cathedral. John is buried in the center of the eastern end of the choir, right in front of the high altar. His ornate tomb chest is topped with a life-sized effigy that "portrays the king in full regalia with crown, sword and scepter and with a lion at his feet." Hovering on his shoulders and swinging tiny censers are carvings of saints Oswald and Wulfstan. Prince Arthur's tomb is positioned to the right of the high altar. His tomb chest is enclosed within "a magnificent chantry chapel . . . which takes up the whole south side of the crossing."[95]

The account of Queen Elizabeth's visit suggests that seeing these royal tombs was a priority for her. On the very evening that she arrived, she visited the cathedral. After a brief welcome ceremony and prayers at the north door, she processed into the church "and so vp in to the chauncell wher she Diligently viewed the Tombe of kyng Iohn to gether with the chappell & tombe of her deere vncle late prynce Arthur all rychelye & Bewtyfully Adorned" (*JN2*, 344). The tombs of John and Arthur seem to have been the main focus of the cathedral visit, and the Queen is depicted as giving them a thorough inspection. Why was she so drawn to these tombs? Certainly, royal burials outside of Westminster Abbey and Windsor Castle were rare. Of all the cities that Elizabeth visited on progress, only three—Winchester (with William II), Gloucester (Edward II), and Canterbury (Henry IV)—could boast royal burials. Worcester had the good fortune to possess two. Of course, the Queen was no mere tourist. She was viewing the graves of—and perhaps paying homage to—her royal predecessors. King John has never been considered a shining embodiment of princely wisdom, but he was not quite the negative figure for the Tudors that he is from the view of the twenty-first century. In 1529, Henry VIII had refurbished John's tomb as "part of a Tudor rehabilitation campaign of John . . . because he had resisted Pope Innocent III, a precedent which suited Henry VIII very well."[96] Later, both William Shakespeare and John Speed depict King John primarily in terms of his defiance of the Pope. Arthur had had a much more limited scope of action in his short life, but he was Queen Elizabeth's close kin. Calling him Elizabeth's "deere vncle" was probably a stretch—he died thirty-one years before her birth—but Arthur was nonetheless a close relation for a monarch whose parents and siblings were all long dead by 1575. It is perhaps only natural that the Queen would be particularly drawn to these tombs.

The next day, the Queen spent additional time in the cathedral attending Sunday services. After processing again through the nave, she entered the choir and was seated "in the vpper ende of the chauncell next to Prince Arthurs chappell" (*JN2*, 345). She was therefore once again in the same area of the church that she had visited the previous evening. As we shall see, this area not only housed the mortal remains of two royal figures, it was also a richly symbolic royal space. Ute Engel explains that after John's death in 1216, his predecessor Henry III "was necessarily concerned that the place where his father was laid to rest should be furnished in a manner worthy of him." Henry III therefore initiated and funded a renovation of the entire east end of the cathedral. This included the installation of a large sculptural programme in the choir, the existence of which "in the interior of an English church is unique." The space contains stone carvings of a "series of English royal saints and forebears of King John" that are "directly related to its function as the burial place of King John."[97] From her seat to the right of the high altar, Queen Elizabeth would have been able to look up on the north wall of the choir (just above the pulpit she was facing) and see statues of kings and queens that included King David, Edward the Confessor, Henry III and Eleanor, John and Isabella, as well as a generic carving of a good (English) king and a bad (pagan) king.

Arthur's chantry chapel is also laden with royal imagery. When it was built in 1504, its grid-like exterior was covered with carvings of royal badges, shields, and coats of arms. Many of these heraldic devices celebrate the Tudor union of Lancaster and York (white roses, red roses, Tudor roses), the Prince of Wales (garters, ostrich feathers), and Arthur's marriage to Catherine (pomegranates, sheaves of arrows). The chapel exterior also features some eighty-eight carved individual figures, including angels, saints, apostles, and kings. In the latter category are representations of biblical kings (David, Solomon, Jechonias, Jesse, Ozias), Saxon kings (St. Edmund, Walstan, St. Kenelm, Edward the Confessor, Edward of the West Saxons, St. Ethelbert, Ethelred), and more recent English kings (Edward II, Edward IV, Edward V, and Henry VI).[98] Inside, through the open tracery of the chantry chapel, is Arthur's tomb chest, plus more carvings, including what is purportedly the figure of Henry VII.[99] According to Phillip Lindley, the overall effect of such iconography "stress[es] [Arthur's] royal lineage and marriage" and "emphasizes that the chantry chapel is that of a royal prince."[100] Elizabeth's "diligent" viewing of the tomb on Saturday night would no doubt have given her ample time to view and appreciate these details. And on Sunday, she was seated just north of the chapel, only inches away from the eye-level figures of the five biblical kings and King Ethelred.

During these two visits to the cathedral, the Queen was thus immersed in a richly decorated royal space of tombs, effigies, sculptures, and heraldic devices. The entire chancel was effectively a "royal burial site."[101] That such a royal space existed in Worcester gave credence to its claim in the welcome oration that previous monarchs had placed a high value on the city and that the city had rewarded this well-placed trust. What better proof than that two of Elizabeth's royal progenitors were being permanently hosted by the city? And now, Queen Elizabeth was also being hosted in this space. In recognition of this latest royal visitor, the plaster on the eastern wall of Arthur's chantry chapel had been painted with the royal arms of both Queen Elizabeth and Prince Arthur.[102] Even though the Queen's physical stay in the cathedral would be brief, she, too, was now a part of its royal iconography and the special relationship that it represented.

As we have seen, Worcester's response to the opportunity of the Queen's visit was both deliberate and coherent. It used its welcome oration to assert the city's chief economic anxiety: the vicissitudes of the cloth market and the city's inability to control the national and international factors that were affecting it in the 1570s. Worcester then used the rest of the week to solicit help from both the Queen and the Privy Councilors who accompanied her. The city based its appeal on the claims of early modern hospitality, which could create both access and agency for the host. Worcester used ceremonial display, attentiveness to its guests, and other reputation-enhancing gestures to show that it was vibrant, generous, honorable—and worth helping. In turn, the royal visitors' consumption of this hospitality created a social bond that theoretically entailed an obligation of future reciprocity. To strengthen this claim of reciprocity, Worcester highlighted its past support of the Queen, cultivated a neighborly dynamism between Queen and people, and engaged in lavish gift-giving. Finally, Worcester used the welcome oration and especially its cathedral to depict a pre-existing and mutually beneficial relationship between the city and the Crown. The implied logic was that since Worcester had long been and would continue to be hospitable to the Crown, the Queen should respond reciprocally by safeguarding its broadcloth industry—the form of the future benefit that it had already "sketched" out.

Epilogue

Was this elaborate appeal working? It is difficult to determine the Queen's perceptions of this message and still harder to establish what her response might have been. The account records her numerous expressions of pleasure and gratitude—"good liking," "thanks most heartily," "pryncely and loving speeches"—but positive language could also be disingenuous; as Heal reminds us, it could even be a substitute for meaningful action.[103] Still, we can look at how the Worcester account characterizes the Queen's response and what it emphasizes. If nothing else, it does reveal much about what the city's priorities were and what it at least hoped it was accomplishing as host. We have already taken this approach in establishing the city's focus on the enhancement of its reputation (in reporting visitor responses) and the cultivation of neighborliness (in describing frequent interactions between people and Queen). We have also looked closely at the words proffered by Croft, Leicester, and Warwick when they received their gifts—words carefully recorded because they perfectly encapsulate the sort of reciprocity that Worcester sought from these councilors. But how did the Queen respond to Worcester's appeal for reciprocity? A couple of moments near the end of the week yield some useful insights.

On Thursday, the Queen went hunting at Hallow Park. This deer park was leased to John Habington and was located some two miles northwest of Worcester. To reach it, the Queen once again processed through the city, crossed over the Severn on a stone bridge, and began to ascend Henwick Hill. As she did so, she was afforded a view of the open field of Pitchcroft on the other side of the Severn. After marveling at the large number of horses grazing on it, she was told "that it was a common grounde & kepte seuerall [of] her maiesties horses & of her retynewe & trayne, for the which she gaue the citie grett thankes" (*JN2*, 347). The account then asserts supplementary information: "Duryng which tyme of her maiesties abode here ther were pastured/ by credible reporte above xv hundred horses & geldynges, without [paying] any thyng therefore savyng small rewardes to watchemen who kepte them day & nyght . . . And thankes be to god, Amongst the said grett nomeber of horses and geldynges not one horse or geldyng was either stolen strayd away, or peryshed" (*JN2*, 347). Clearly, this horse-tending service was a point of great pride to the city, and in a lot of ways it emblematizes the sort of hospitality that Worcester was attempting to extend. It involved the common lands of the entire city, it was offered to not only the Queen but to her "retynewe & trayne," it was graciously and unobtrusively performed, and it was done with a high degree of success (not a single horse lost!). When the Queen found out, she was suitably grateful.

Afterward, she continued to Hallow Park, where she hunted and killed two deer. She then instructed John Habington: "Lett one of the buckes be brought to the one baylyffes howse And the other buck to the other baylyffes howse . . . Which buckes were brought [to] the baylyffes howses Accordynglye" (*JN2*, 348). In this way, Worcester's city officers became the beneficiaries of a generous gift of venison. The account implies that the gift is a direct response to the horse-tending at Pitchcroft the Queen had just witnessed (as the former immediately follows the latter), though it may be more of a general response to Worcester's gift-giving and hospitality over the previous five days. Regardless, that the Queen proffered a gift of *venison* is significant. According to Heal, venison "had a particularly rich role in the repertoire of exchange."[104] Since only the elite had access to deer parks, a gift of venison "was marked by its prestige and its ability to confer a measure of honor on the recipient . . . [As] a reward for dependents, [it was] an especially powerful gesture in the cycle of local reciprocity."[105] Indeed, gifts of deer marked the royal progress visits to Coventry in 1566 and Warwick in 1572, when the earls of Leicester and Warwick (respectively) closed the visits by proffering venison to the cities that they served as patrons. But at Worcester, the Queen herself was the benefactor. From Worcester's perspective, this gesture may well have been taken as a sign that the city's strategy of reciprocity was working and that the Queen understood and embraced this dynamic. Finally, this episode embodies the city's hope that even when the Queen is away from the city (whether in Hallow Park or London), she will still be mindful of Worcester and act on its behalf.

A final anecdote records an attempt to ensure that such reciprocity might not stop at venison, but be extended to the clothing industry. Two days after departing the city, the Queen and her retinue reached the Gloucestershire border and prepared to depart from the Worcestershire delegation that had been accompanying them. At this moment, the Queen pulled Bishop Bullingham aside for a private conference, during which she said: "My Lord I pray you commend me hartelie to the Baylyffes of worcettor & to their breethern and to the whole citie, And I thanke them hartely for my good interteynment, and for the good chere they made my men" (*JN*2, 349). Bullingham shrewdly used the occasion to try to channel the Queen's good will and gratitude into something more concrete: "Hit may please your maiestie. So it is their trade is not so good as it hathe ben for the meyntenance of their lyvyng/ but their poore good wills & hartes your maiestie hathe" (*JN*2, 349). The Queen's response was sympathetic but also ambiguous: "I perceave that verry well And I like as well of them/ as I haue liked of any people in all my progresse/ ye in all my lyff" (*JN*2, 349). On the one hand, the Queen's words could be read as evasive; that is, she was only responding to Bullingham's last phrase about her having the people's "good wills & hartes" and was paying them a nice compliment in return. On the other hand, she could have been responding to Bullingham's entire comment. That is, she "perceave[d] . . . verry well" the connection between the hospitality she had just thanked them for and the economic request that the Bishop was conveying. Read this way, she might have been saying that of all the people who have hosted her while on progress, those in Worcester have the most claim on her.

The Queen's responses were not taken as empty words back in Worcester. On the contrary, these "comfortable commendacions & sayenges of hir maiestie towardes this citie" were carefully noted by the Bishop, and when he returned to Worcester he gathered together the city leaders and "vttered vnto them the said pryncely & lovyng speeches of her maiestie, prayng them to vtter the same to the residue" (*JN2, 349*). The account thus reveals that the Queen's parting words were seen as comforting and loving and that they were treasured, repeated, and carefully written down. Even though her words do not make any overt commitments, they effusively validate both the people of Worcester and the quality of their hospitality—which were, after all, the basis of Worcester's approach and the foundation of its economic appeal. Whether or not the Queen took any immediate action on their behalf, the citizens of Worcester could rest assured in the knowledge that they had enhanced the city's reputation and strengthened the bonds of patronage and reciprocity. If, as Palmer says, the benefits of hospitality do not "[cease] in the practicing," but continue to "ripple" and resonate, then Worcester had won for itself both the Queen's good will and the promise of future consideration.[106]

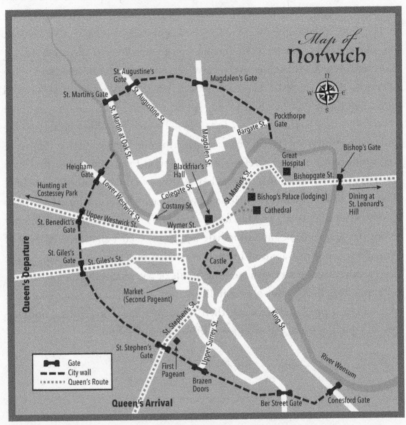

Map reproduced by Coni Porter. Reproduced from Norwich 1540–1642, ed. David Galloway, REED (Toronto, 1984), xcvi. Courtesy of the Records of Early English Drama.

CHAPTER SIX
NORWICH, 1578

The Queen followed the epic progress of 1575 with two less ambitious years. She stayed much closer to home on the 1576 progress and did not go on progress at all in 1577[1]. However, in 1578 she embarked upon a ten-and-a-half-week progress to East Anglia. Previous progresses had targeted particular regions to the north (1566, 1575), west (1574), and south (1569), but Elizabeth had never ventured very far into East Anglia.[2] The 1578 progress would rectify that, as the Queen traveled extensively in Suffolk and Norfolk and spent time at the estates and in the towns of her subjects in East Anglia. One of her main destinations was Norwich, the largest provincial city outside of London. The Queen and her retinue arrived on August 16 and spent a week in its environs. Like other cities, Norwich welcomed the Queen warmly and proffered a variety of entertainments throughout the week. However, my emphasis in this chapter will be less on the ways in which the city spoke to the Queen and more on how the city corporation used the occasion to speak to its own citizens and improve its own internal dynamics.

In the sixteenth century, Norwich was the second city of the realm in both wealth and population.[3] In 1404, it had been granted county status by Henry IV and had developed a robust tradition of local government. It boasted a mayor, two sheriffs, twenty-four aldermen, and sixty councilmen; the city even had its own militia that held separate musters from the county of Norfolk. The physical fabric of the city was also impressive. Norwich's city walls enclosed an area some six miles in circumference.[4] These walls averaged twenty feet high and were surmounted by forty watchtowers and pierced by twelve gates. All in all, Norwich possessed the "longest circuit of urban defences in Britain."[5] Within the walls, the city skyline was dominated by a formidable Norman castle and a splendid cathedral with the second-highest spire in England. Other prominent buildings included some fifty-six parish churches, a large fifteenth-century guildhall, a Great Hospital, a grammar school, a workhouse, and the riverside palace of the Duke of Norfolk. The latter was adjacent to the River Wensum, which wound through the northern sector of the city, providing drinking water and water for trade and industry. South of the city, the Wensum merges with the River Yare and flows eastward to Great Yarmouth—giving the Norwich trading access to the North Sea. Within the city itself, Norwich boasted one of the largest markets in England, embellished by an ornate, pavilioned market cross that had been erected in 1518. As Penelope Corfield suggests, Norwich's importance is perhaps best characterized by its multiple roles: "At once the county capital, a cathedral city for a diocese that stretched over Norfolk and Suffolk, a grand forum for agricultural exchange, a major shopping mart, a cultural meeting place, the communications headquarters for central/east Norfolk and a major textile town."[6] Along with Bristol, Exeter, York, and Newcastle, Norwich was one of only five English provincial cities that "could claim to be significant regional cities with extensive trading connections and elaborate civic privileges."[7]

Like these other cities, Norwich trailed London significantly in both wealth and population. Norwich's population was around 16,000 in 1578, whereas London's was around 150,000. Yet Norwich was much less reliant on London than were most provincial cities. The inland waterways and harbors of East Anglia and Norwich's proximity to the coast meant that it was well positioned to trade with the Continent.[8] In contrast, the roads to London were poor and hindered by the low-lying Fens. Norwich was actually closer to Amsterdam than London, and the former could be much more easily reached by water. As a result, the city developed "a strong sense of both civic identity and regional autonomy."[9] Norwich was, in the sixteenth century, very much "a world in itself . . . [T]he city was capable of handling its own affairs, and communications to and from either Westminster or Whitehall were infrequent."[10]

An example of such self-sufficiency can be seen in the wool market. Unlike Worcester and other cities, Norwich merchants cut out the London cloth halls and exported directly to the continent via Great Yarmouth. Despite attempts to the contrary, "London interests had made little headway in [their] efforts to control the marketing of Norwich cloths."[11] From the late Middle Ages, the manufacture of wool was the single most important economic activity in the city. In fact, Norwich owed its unprecedented fourteenth- and fifteenth-century growth and prosperity to its thriving wool industry. Its main textile product was worsted, a dense woolen cloth that was woven and then exported to the Continent.

The Strangers

By the middle of the sixteenth century, the main source of the city's prosperity was under threat as worsted began to be replaced by new, lighter Dutch hybrids known as "the new draperies." Worsted belonged to traditional English wool manufactures, and tended to be "heavy, durable, high-quality, relatively expensive cloths."[12] In contrast, the new draperies were lower quality and less durable, but also lighter, cheaper, and able to be produced in a variety of exotic patterns—thus expanding the market to poorer consumers, the fashion-conscious, and those who lived in warmer Mediterranean climates.[13] Because of the emergence of the new draperies, the worsted market was shrinking and there was a significant dip in Norwich exports by the middle of the sixteenth century.[14] In 1565, a severe winter and a disastrous harvest had compounded economic anxieties. According to city records, the situation in Norwich was dire: "The comodities of woorsted makynge is greatelye decayed . . . wherebye people became poore, manye lefte ther howses and dwelte in the countrye, that howses decayed for lacke of fearmes, and that they were letten at small prises, and the cityte lyke to decaye yf prudente polici did not assyste the same."[15] With the economy at its nadir, mayor Thomas Sotherton made the momentous decision to seek outside assistance. His plan was to invite religious refugees from the Low Countries—men who specialized in the weaving of the new draperies—to settle in Norwich, practice their crafts, and help revive the local textile economy. With the help of Thomas Howard, the 4th Duke of Norfolk, the city successfully petitioned the Queen for royal permission to invite the Dutch artisans. Her letters patent, issued on November 5, allowed for some three hundred immigrants (thirty master weavers with households no larger than ten each) to settle in Norwich and practice their crafts: "The faculties of making bays, arras, says, tapstrey, mockadoes, staments, carsay, and such other outlandish commodities as hath not bene used to be made within this our Realme of England."[16] The expectation was that not only would the immigrants manufacture new types of cloth for export, they would also teach native craftsmen the art of weaving the new draperies.[17]

Norwich was not the only English city to absorb Continental refugees in the sixteenth century. With the Spanish bearing down on the Low Countries and the intensification of the French religious wars, a flood of Protestant refugees left their home countries. Between 1567 and 1590, some 100,000 Dutch Protestants fled the Netherlands, and thousands more left France, particularly after the 1572 St. Bartholomew's Day Massacre.[18] Many crossed the channel and came to England. Not surprisingly, London absorbed the most refugees. Some 50,000 passed through London from the mid-1550s to the mid-1580s, with about 10,000 living in London circa 1585.[19] While some returned to the Continent, others settled in English provincial cities, including Sandwich, Southampton, Colchester, Maidstone, Rye, Winchelsea, Halstead, Great Yarmouth, King's Lynn, Harwich, Dover, Boston, Ipswich, and Norwich.[20] One of the earliest immigrant communities was established at Sandwich in 1561, and it was from this colony that Norwich's 300 immigrants came in 1565. The Protestant refugees who settled in these cities and towns comprised a mixture of ethnic and cultural extractions (Dutch, Flemish, Walloon) and spoke a variety of languages (Dutch and French) and dialects.[21] Most native Englishmen simply referred to them as "aliens" or "Strangers." In most cases, their arrival and settlement was carefully facilitated by the Crown. Typically, cities made requests to the Queen (as was the case in Norwich), though in some cases (as at Canterbury), the Privy Council enjoined cities "to accept immigrants in government-coordinated removal and dispersal schemes."[22] Despite logistical issues, the central government was generally eager to accommodate and settle arriving refugees. In part, this was out of religious solidarity. With England emerging as a leading Protestant nation and Elizabeth touted as Defender of the Faith, it could hardly turn a blind eye to its Protestant neighbors in distress. But Elizabeth and her government also embraced the incomers because of the unique economic opportunity that they presented. Since so many of the refugees were skilled artisans in cloth-making and other trades, here was a chance to generate new commodities, enhance technological skills, increase trade, and reduce dependence on foreign goods.[23] William Cecil was especially attuned to these potential benefits, and he actively defended the Crown's asylum policy against its detractors.[24]

Thus, in many ways the arrival of Protestant refugees in Norwich in 1565 can be seen as part of a larger national pattern that played out in many other prominent towns in southeastern England. Yet Norwich's experience was also atypical, simply because of the large numbers of immigrants that it took in. The initial 300 immigrants that had been invited in 1565 blossomed to 2,866 in 1568, and 3,993 in 1571.[25] By 1578, the Strangers accounted for some 6,000 people out of a total population of 16,000. Norwich was thus second only to London in its total number of resident aliens, and—since Strangers accounted for over one-third of its population—Norwich absorbed the largest percentage of any city in England.[26] Ultimately, this influx of skilled artisans did revive Norwich's economy, allow it to reclaim its position in the export market, and pave the way for the city's unprecedented growth and prosperity in the seventeenth century. But these benefits did not accrue immediately, and, in the short term, the large number of Strangers and the rapidity with which they arrived created palpable tensions in the 1560s and 1570s.

In these early decades, the Strangers experienced a relatively hostile reception from Norwich natives. Despite being invited by the mayor and supported by the central government, the Strangers found that "most of the inhabitants disliked them as foreigners and feared them as business rivals."[27] Throughout the populace they were "regarded with the utmost suspicion," which resulted in "an acutely xenophobic atmosphere."[28] Such a dynamic was typical of other English cities, where "the aliens usually endured an ugly rite of passage before natives more or less grudgingly accepted them as members of the community."[29] Integration proved more difficult in Norwich than in other cities like Canterbury or Colchester and was probably exacerbated by the Strangers' rapidly swelling numbers in the first decade of their arrival.[30] As a result, there were two early attempts to expel the Strangers from the city. In 1567, mayor Thomas Whalle failed to convince a majority of the city council to consent to such a plan, so he complained to the Privy Council that "the Strangers were constantly at loggerheads with the local citizens" and that he was "of the opinion that the Strangers had done more hurte than ever they did goode and that they did but sucke the lyvinge away from the English."[31] The Privy Council decreed that no additional Strangers would be allowed to settle in Norwich, though such a regulation was clearly not enforced.[32] Then, in 1570, a Catholic plot (Throgmorton's Conspiracy) opposing the imprisonment of the Duke of Norfolk sought to involve the local populace by promising to eject the Strangers from the city. Although the plot failed to gain popular support, it nevertheless demonstrates "that a significant level of anti-alien sentiment must have existed for the conspirators to have depended on its expression to ensure the success of their enterprise."[33] That there were two attempts in three years to expel the Strangers suggests that their position in Norwich was indeed tenuous.

Of course, the Strangers did have active supporters. The city leaders who had originally invited them to settle in Norwich no doubt did so because they took a broader view of the potential economic benefits of an alien settlement. In *Strangers Settled Here Amongst Us,* Laura Hunt Yungblut draws a distinction between the typical attitudes of national and local officeholders and the people that they governed. She argues that the former were quicker to grasp the long-term economic benefits of the Strangers whereas the latter were more likely to see them as economic competitors.[34] Thus, local officials often defended and protected refugees while native artisans were more inclined to react with hostility. As ecclesiastical historian John Strype was to later write: "The better sort of the queen's subjects were very kind unto these poor protestants; and glad to see them retired unto more safety in this country. But another sort (divers of the common people and rabble, too many of them) behaved themselves otherwise towards these afflicted Strangers, men and women, who grudged at their coming hither, and would call them by no other denomination than *French dogs*."[35] While this dichotomy is useful in characterizing native reactions to the Strangers, it is also (as Yungblut herself points out) overly simplistic: "distrust of foreigners was not restricted to the lower classes."[36] No less a national leader than Sir Nicholas Bacon called for the expulsion from England of all French immigrants in 1576. And on the local level, the Privy Council had to issue continual orders "demanding better treatment of alien residents in the various towns" because "local authorities were not always disposed to follow strictly the directives of central government."[37]

In Norwich, there is also evidence of a lack of official support for the Strangers. When mayor Sotherton initially invited the Strangers in 1565, he had failed to gain the full support of the city council and had to use his own mayoral seal to overcome the opposition.[38] From that time on, "there was always a party in the Corporation of Norwich opposed to the Strangers"—if for no other reason than that popular resentment could be exploited for power.[39] This dynamic was manifested most dramatically in the two attempts to oust the Strangers, but it was a continual problem throughout the second half of the sixteenth century, wherein "the commoners and some of the chief citizens raised many clamours against them."[40]

Still, the majority of the city council were supportive of the Strangers and were certainly more sympathetic than the townspeople. One reason may have been the composition of the city government. John T. Evans points out that, "In Elizabethan Norwich, a greater variety of trades were represented in the magistracy than in most other cities."[41] Since all of these trades were feeling the larger decline of the city, there was probably the general feeling that everyone could benefit from the rising tide of a revived economy. The city council was also not dominated by a single economic interest. Even though Norwich was a textile town, its government was not dominated by weavers or clothiers (as in Worcester). In fact, textile workers were actually under-represented on the council because so few of them were freemen.[42] Instead, the merchant and distributive trades dominated the city offices. Grocers and mercers were among the richest and most influential in Elizabethan Norwich.[43] Since these trades exported cloth and imported luxury goods from the Continent, they had much to gain by the revival of the export economy. Whereas native worsted weavers might fear the new draperies, mercers could just as easily export the new textiles as the old. Thus in Norwich, the weavers were in direct economic competition with the Strangers, but they were under-represented on the council. One exception was Thomas Whalle, the mayor who tried to oust the Strangers in 1567. That he was by profession a weaver of russell (a worsted-based cloth that had been produced for decades by native weavers) is instructive and may well account for his vehement reaction against the Strangers. More typically, in Norwich, those economic groups that had the most to gain by the Strangers were in the ascendancy, and thus tended to be supportive of the new immigrants.

This support, however, was always carefully qualified. In practice, the city leaders sought to carefully regulate and control the activities of the Strangers. As Barbara Green and Rachel Young put it, "The authorities issued a mass of regulations designed to encourage the Strangers to produce new types of cloth and sell them wholesale to Norwich merchants, and to discourage them from doing anything else."[44] In this way, they hoped to extract the value of the Strangers' economic participation while preventing them from adversely affecting other trades. Some restrictions had been spelled out in the 1566 Articles that governed the Strangers' arrival—they were not to participate in the retail trade ("not to buy or sell goods not made by them") nor "to sell in open shop any commodity other than in gross."[45] However, these regulations proved to be ambiguous and had actually fueled some of the tensions in the late 1560s.[46] Thus, in 1571 the city issued the much more comprehensive Book of Orders. This lengthy document regulated many aspects of the Strangers' lives; for example, it imposed a curfew (8:00 p.m. by the bell of St. Peter Mancroft) and set forth the conditions under which the Strangers could remain in the city (a certificate of good behavior from their congregational minister, subject to mayoral approval).[47] The Orders were particularly thorough with regard to trade restrictions. The Strangers could only sell their cloth in specified sale halls, and even then only between the hours of 1:00 and 5:00 p.m.[48] These goods were also subject to special tariffs and customs rates.[49] Although the

Strangers could sell their goods in London and other large towns—though not in villages or market towns—their parcels had to be packed up and sealed in the presence of local "searchers."[50] Those Strangers who were not involved in the manufacture of cloth had additional restrictions. For instance, tailors, butchers, shoemakers, and cobblers had to cover their shop windows with lattice and could only sell to fellow Strangers; those who sold to English customers were subject to fines for each offense.[51] As consumers, Strangers were prohibited from buying sheep or other skins, and they could not purchase wool before midday.[52] Later, they were subject to corn-buying restrictions and prevented from baking white bread and selling aqua vitae in the streets.[53]

Despite such restrictions, the Book of Orders did not have a wholly negative effect on the immigrant community. For one thing, it helped ensure the Strangers had a political and judicial voice. Both the Dutch and Walloon populations were to choose representatives (eight Dutch, four Walloon) to serve as their *hommes politiques*. These men were empowered to settle disputes among the Strangers and to represent the community in its dealings with the English.[54] In addition, the Orders gave the Strangers recourse for any disputes they had with the native population by setting up the mayor and his court as arbiters. Finally, the restrictions found within the Book of Orders were similar to those found in other cities (like Canterbury) and did not actually prevent the Strangers as a group from flourishing economically.[55] Nevertheless, the Book of Orders did formally codify the differences between natives and Strangers and effectively fixed the latter as second-class citizens.

Formal regulations were not the only barriers working against the integration of the Strangers into their adopted city. As mentioned above, many natives exhibited open hostility. Their reaction can partially be understood as the manifestation of that famous English xenophobia. While it is possible to exaggerate its scope and intensity, as Yungblut has shown, it is rooted in "repeated historical examples . . . of a continual anti-alien sentiment."[56] That the immigrants are referred to repeatedly in the Norwich records as "Strangers" helps underscore the fact that they were primarily perceived in terms of their foreignness. Such a perception was no doubt magnified by the cultural and especially linguistic differences that set the Dutch and Walloons apart from the native townspeople. But the Strangers were also "othered" because they were perceived as economic competitors that might be a threat to English livelihoods. Some of these fears were rooted in reality. For example, English weavers and Strangers were in competition for the same supply of raw wool; this is the reason for the aforementioned regulation that prevented Strangers from purchasing wool before midday.[57] It is also true that the influx of immigrants put pressure on the local housing market and drove up rental prices. While this was good news for landlords, it caused resentment among the native poor.[58] Other economic anxieties were more speculative: the fear that the Strangers would duplicate existing trades, that they were secretly exporting goods, or that they would impinge on the retail trade.[59] Meanwhile, these fears were exacerbated and seemingly confirmed by the fact that the Norwich economy did not turn around immediately. In 1570—five years after the Strangers' initial arrival—"the native industry had not yet begun to benefit from the introduction of the 'new draperies.'"[60] This gave the impression that the Strangers were flourishing at the natives' expense and led to further resentment. Such a perception was heightened by the seeming lack of cooperation between the two groups. Contrary to expectation, the Strangers "were reluctant to teach their [weaving] techniques and the Norwich weavers slow to learn them, so that most of the 'new draperies' were produced by aliens until after 1600."[61]

In addition to economic barriers, there were also religious differences. To some extent, there was common ground between English Protestants and Continental refugees who were being persecuted because of their reformed religious beliefs. However, there were also native fears that the newcomers might be "too" Protestant or that they might have dangerous sectarian opinions that tended towards Anabaptism. The Crown itself was wary of this threat: Henry VIII had burned four Dutch Anabaptists, while in Elizabeth's reign a Dutch minister with Anabaptist leanings had been banished in 1560.[62] At Norwich, the rapidly increasing number of immigrants in the late 1560s, "so far above those licensed, caused some alarm, a cry having arisen that many Anabaptists were amongst them."[63] Even if the vast majority of Strangers were not Anabaptists, they still represented a more reformed version of Protestantism that "constituted potential danger for the Church of England."[64] This fear gained traction in light of the rise of English Puritanism in the late 1560s and early 1570s, since Puritans consciously invoked Continental models in their attempts to reform the established church. One might then expect that the more Puritan-minded natives of Norwich would find common ground with the Strangers. Yet according to Bernard Cottret, "similarities" did not translate into "complete identification": there were key differences between English Puritanism and Continental Calvinism, not to mention barriers of language, insularity, and prejudice.[65] There is in fact little evidence of religious solidarity between the two groups or that "the Strangers contributed very much to the Protestant cause" in Norwich.[66] In fact, natives may even have resented that foreign congregations were not subject to the same restrictions they faced themselves.[67] Whereas the 1570s saw increased emphasis on conformity in English churches, the Strangers were allowed to have their own churches and worship in their accustomed ways.

Others feared that the Strangers were still loyal to the homelands they had left. With the possibility of invasion from both the Spanish and the French in the 1570s and 1580s, some people feared that the immigrants might side with the invading armies. Or worse, that the Strangers were actively working as spies or agents of foreign countries and that they had entered England only under the guise of religious asylum.[68] Refugees were suspected on these grounds even in the highest levels of government, particularly after the discovery of the 1571 Ridolfi Plot, "a proposed operation which had as its primary component a foreign invasion of England coordinated with an internal rebellion."[69]

Whether or not English men and women believed such conspiracy theories, their distrust of the Strangers was probably heightened by the insularity of these immigrant communities. "The primary characteristic of this relatively massive immigration," writes Cottret, "is that it retained the character of a self-contained community, grafted onto English society."[70] Wherever they emigrated, the Strangers tended to cluster together and maintain their cultural identity and institutions. In London, they "tended to congregate in relatively few wards" in the eastern end of the city.[71] In Norwich, the Strangers settled primarily in five northern wards—West Wymer, Mid Wymer, Coslany, Colegate, and Ryebridge—in close proximity to the River Wensum.[72] In these same areas, they also had their own churches: the Dutch Strangers were granted Blackfriars Hall (part of the old Dominican friary that had been adapted to civic use in the 1530s) as a house of worship while the Walloons were allowed to use the Bishop's Chapel in the cathedral close. As noted above, the Norwich Strangers had their own separate cloth hall (in the former church of St. Mary the Less) and they elected their own political leaders. The Stranger community also maintained its own police force and was responsible for the poor relief of its members.[73] Finally, some Strangers wore visibly different attire—"Dutch" cloaks, hats, and hoods—than their native counterparts, so that they would have looked recognizably different as they moved through the streets of Norwich.[74]

Many of these separate arrangements no doubt resulted from the language barrier. The newly arrived refugees typically did not speak English nor did they learn it right away. According to William Moens, even "in the first half of the seventeenth century as much Dutch and French was spoken in Norwich as English."[75] Dutch was more common since the majority of the Norwich immigrants were from the Low Countries. In 1571, the ratio of Dutch to Walloon immigrants was around 3 to 1 (3,000 to 1,000).[76] The Dutch language was given added vitality by the printer Anthony de Solempne, who emigrated from Brabant to Norwich in 1567 and set up the city's first printing press. The majority of works that Solempne printed were in Dutch, including an edition of the Psalms and a translation of the New Testament (both in 1568).[77] He also printed historical works like *Chronye Historie der Nederlantscher Oorlogen,* or "a record of the troubles in the Netherlands to the year 1580."[78] Such works were clearly aimed at a local Dutch audience and helped give the Dutch language a formal presence in the Strangers' adopted country.

Besides printing, other skilled trades flourished in the Stranger community in Norwich. Though many Strangers were involved in the making of the new draperies (as wool combers, spinners, weavers, and dyers), others were recorded as masons, carpenters, joiners, smiths, merchants, hatters, shoemakers, hosiers, tailors, basketmakers, locksmiths, goldsmiths, and gardeners.[79] The Dutch also had their own doctors, ministers, and schoolmasters. Legal services were provided by the aforementioned hommes politiques, who were empowered to "[advise] their brethren on various business and family matters, acting as notaries and preparing testaments and nuncupative wills."[80] Such diversity of trades and services allowed the immigrant community to be even more self-contained and self-sufficient.

Finally, in these years, the Strangers were still very much connected to their home countries. Many of the Continental cities that the Strangers had emigrated from were only about 100 to 150 sea miles away. That many of the Strangers made occasional visits back to their native cities can be deduced from a 1575 regulation requiring that "those going from Norwich without passports 'over into their own countrye' should be fined 6s. 8d. for each offence."[81] As Peter Clark writes, "These migrants and their descendants remained for many years in contact with their homelands."[82] Letters from these decades give a strong impression that the Strangers still had one foot on the Continent, with the immigrants writing "instructions even for the due education of their young brothers," and family members back home promising to help them return and get re-established "if they found they could not get on in their new country."[83] With the fluidity of events in France and the Low Countries, many Strangers undoubtedly hoped that their exiles were merely temporary rather than permanent. In the meantime, the Strangers' experience might be characterized as being "fraught with conflicting feelings: the relief of refuge, the shock and isolation of displacement, uncertainty about the possibility of return, and concern for those left behind."[84] Such a mindset would seem to work against seamless integration into a new community, so it is not surprising that Stranger communities have been characterized as "clannish" and inward-looking.[85] This is in fact one of the things that contemporary Englishmen noticed and even complained about. A 1571 petition against the London Strangers asserts that they comprise "a common wealth within themselves . . . [and] though they be denized or born here amongst us, yet they keep themselves severed from us in church, in government, in trade, in language and marriage."[86] This complaint seems to parallel the situation in Norwich, where the self-contained nature of the immigrant community both worked against real assimilation and also fed native perceptions and distrust.

The soaring numbers of refugees entering Norwich in the 1570s also contributed to difficulties between the native and immigrant communities. In 1570, Strangers accounted for about 3,000 of a total population of 12,000; by 1578, this number had climbed to 6,000 out of 16,000. Thus, in the eight years prior to Queen Elizabeth's visit, Norwich's population had grown by some 33 percent and the vast majority of these newcomers were Strangers.[87] Given the rapid increase and large proportion of immigrants, it is no wonder that the civic community experienced some turbulence. The resulting tensions in this decade are most clearly registered in the records of the Norwich Mayor's Court, one of the most powerful instruments of civic government. It was composed of the current mayor (who served as chief justice) and those aldermen who had previously served as mayor (these associate justices usually numbered around eight men).[88] These men were highly experienced in the inner workings of city government and thus capable of executing the court's varied duties: enforcing the law, safeguarding public morality, administering poor relief, controlling trade and industry, maintaining public health, and fostering education.[89] In 1571, the Book of Orders had also established the Mayor's Court as the main adjudicator of disputes between the natives and Strangers. Throughout the 1570s and 1580s, these disputes most commonly involved market issues and economic disagreements. One of most frequent complaints arose from natives trying to prevent or limit the Strangers' participation in specific trades. In the years 1568 to 1573, the dyers, shearers, butchers, smiths, cordwainers, and joiners all petitioned the court to place restrictions on the Strangers.[90] The Court's response varied. The alien joiners were forced to close their own shops and work with Englishmen, while the Strangers were allowed "one dyer of their community to dye their commodities."[91]

As was the case in other English cities, exact economic arrangements between natives and immigrants were not clearly set forth in the official regulations and had to be worked out in practice.[92] Sometimes, the Norwich records have the feel of natives picking fights with Strangers and trying to maneuver for maximum advantage. In 1568, for example, the glovers complained that the Strangers were buying up all of the sheepskin from the butchers, so the Strangers were commanded not to "bye nor bargayne with any bocher eyther for shepe skyns, lambe skynnes nor calve skynnes at ther perilles and in payne of fforfyture of the same."[93] One month later, these same glovers had the audacity to complain that they had visited the house of Stranger Peter Byllet, who had refused to share his specialized "manner and waye of pullyng the shepskynnes."[94] In these and other cases, natives were often appeased by the local authorities. Yet there was also a recognition that some natives were just stirring up trouble. As the Book of Orders was being established in 1571, the Dutch leaders asked for Mayor John Aldrich's assistance "agaynst them that take the benefyte of the statues ageynst the pore straungers without cause."[95]

Sometimes the court does seem to be genuinely trying to address problems that the aliens created or were perceived to create. In 1578, the drapers complained that the Strangers were buying inferior wool that was woven outside of the city; while this practice no doubt arose from the wool-buying restrictions within the city that the Strangers were already subject to, such a practice could affect the quality (and reputation) of Norwich exports. In the same year, the Mayor's Court heard complaints against bay-making Strangers for washing and scouring their cloth in the River Wentsum and harming the water quality.[96]

Indeed, on some occasions the newly arrived Strangers all but invited such conflict. After all, they had emigrated not only for religious reasons, but also for economic opportunity.[97] They were naturally eager to pursue their own economic interests and chafed at the regulations that were imposed on them. Some of the incoming Strangers were not only skilled weavers, but masters of their trade who had been men of wealth and influence in their home countries; yet here in Norwich their activities were being micromanaged by men who (in their eyes) were only local drapers.[98] It is also probable that many of the restrictions placed on the Strangers were not discussed prior to their arrival in

Norwich.[99] As a result, "many of the Elizabethan immigrants did indeed push the limits" of the statues governing their activities.[100] In Norwich, the records suggest that—contrary to the regulations—some Strangers did engage in the retail trades.[101] In 1578, the master of the sale hall, William Littlewood, complained that the Strangers "did not observe the hours for sealing their commodities . . . neither did they pay the hallage."[102] It is hard to evaluate the substance of this complaint or, if it is accurate, the motives of the Strangers. The latter could range from a lack of understanding to active circumvention to economic necessity.[103]

Nor were the Strangers quietly subversive or non-compliant. The immigrant community sometimes complained to the authorities about what they perceived to be unfair treatment. In 1571, the Strangers wrote to the Privy Council to protest attempts to make them sell their commodities only to the freemen of the city. More often, they petitioned the Mayor's Court—as, for example, in 1577, when they objected to the aforementioned corn-buying restrictions that they were subject to.[104] They also took steps to safeguard their own commercial interests. In 1578, the Stranger russell weavers "were afraid that their goods were being made by natives" so they came to court "to complain and claim their privileges."[105] Indeed, "the Strangers kept a good look out on the goods made by the English, fearing lest Norwich should lose its good name for the quality of its manufactures."[106] In other words, the 1570s saw repeated conflicts in the Mayor's Court between the natives and the Strangers, and these clashes did not always conform to the simple dynamic of persecutor vs victim. Thus, the years leading up to the Queen's visit were characterized by continuing friction between the two groups.

Yet there are also signs that relations were gradually improving. For one thing, disagreements were at least being addressed by a formal institution of the city following a known protocol. Unlike the early years, there were no further attempts to expel the Strangers from the city. There is also no record of violence or rioting. One factor may have been that the Strangers and natives were increasingly likely to be found living and worshipping side by side. Even though the Stranger community was concentrated in the aforementioned five city wards, there were populations of Strangers to be found in all thirteen wards. Even Ber Street, the ward having the smallest proportion of Strangers in 1571, still had a population of 207 Strangers out of a total ward population of 1,012.[107] Strangers and natives were also becoming more likely to worship in the same parish church. Many newcomers worshipped with the Dutch and

French congregations in Blackfriars Hall and the Bishop's Chapel, respectively; however, there would have been no way that the full Stranger population of 6,000 (in 1578) could fit into these two buildings. Indeed, the larger pattern of Huguenot emigration prepares us to expect that "within the lifetime of the first generation of refugees and certainly within that of the second that most [Huguenots] joined Anglican . . . congregations."[108] Parish records reveal that as early as 1569 to 1571, some Strangers were getting married and baptizing children in the church of St. Laurence.[109] There is also an entry for a Dutch man (Joisus de Frese) marrying a Norwich-born woman (Mary Maynard) in the church of St. George Tombland in 1569.[110] A few Strangers were already choosing to be buried in their local (Anglican) parish churches.[111] The 1579 tomb monument of the wealthy doctor Martin Vankurnbecke and his wife, Johanna—"the earliest surviving monument in the city to members of . . . [the] stranger community"—can still be seen in St. Mary Coslany.[112] In other words, despite the ongoing formal economic tensions between natives and Strangers, members of both communities were seemingly being drawn closer together through the experience of daily living.

There are also signs that the city leaders were increasing their support of the Strangers. According to Yungblut, the language of the 1571 Book of Orders "indicates that at least the mayor, the sheriff, and all the aldermen were still ambivalent about the presence of the immigrants."[113] If so, many of these same city leaders seem to be more outwardly supportive of the Strangers by 1578. By this point, the Norwich economy was beginning to turn around and the positive economic impact of the Strangers was more visible. In 1575, Mayor William Farrour praised the Strangers for their role in economic revitalization: "They brought a grete commoditie thether . . . which were not made there before, whereby they . . . set on worke our owne people within the cittie . . . we think our cittie happie to enjoy them."[114] City records indicate that by the middle of the decade, native boys were beginning to be apprenticed to Stranger masters in a variety of trades.[115] These developments seem to reflect what Ursula Priestley has called a "softening" of attitudes toward the newcomers by the late 1570s.[116]

One event that was most indicative of this process is the city's shielding of the Strangers from Tipper's Grant in 1578. As Cottret explains, "The freemen [of London] wanted to revive an ancient law, according to which every foreign merchant had to reside with an English host, who had to keep an eye on his guest."[117] This practice, known as "hostage," was a way to regulate and keep tabs on the activities of foreign merchants and alien residents. In 1576, hostage was indeed revived, and the office of "hostager or host" was granted to one William Tipper, a London grocer who was actually acting as a proxy of Christopher Hatton. The office was potentially lucrative because hosts received payment from the guests who "resided" with them as well as "a percentage on their purchases and sales."[118] Theoretically, Tipper's office entitled him to collect such fees directly from immigrants or sell the privilege to local hosts. The revival of hostage met with "immediate opposition" both domestically and internationally and does not seem to have been enforced very successfully.[119] But it initially caused great alarm in Stranger communities throughout England. When Tipper attempted to exercise his office in Norwich in March 1578, "many [Strangers] left the city and others prepared to do so."[120] At this point, some members of the city corporation stepped in and purchased the right of hostage from Tipper for the sum of £70 13 shillings and 4 pence—though they did so purely to protect the Strangers and without any intention of exercising this right.[121] They then sent letters to the foreign church congregations explaining their actions: "For your better quyete, and for thexperience we have had of your godly disposicion, and good behavyour amongs us; we have also satisfied the seyde Wylliam Typper, and receyved his authoritie (by deputacion) into our hands, to that ende, that none of you shoulde be molested or trowblyd, but to procede in your lawefull exercises, as you befor have done withoute anye feare or greyfe."[122] This letter was signed by "Yr Lovinge ffrends": mayor Thomas Cullie, John Aldrich, Robert Wood, Robert Suckling, and Thomas Peck.

All five of these men were grocers and mercers who had been mayors of Norwich in the 1570s.[123] This meant that they were all members of the Mayor's Court, and were thus part of the inner circle of city government. In fact, only four other men would have also been on the Mayor's Court in 1578: Thomas Sotherton, Thomas Greene, Thomas Layer, and Christopher Some.[124] Sotherton was the mayor who had invited the Strangers in 1565, so he was probably also sympathetic to the Strangers' plight. It is not clear why the other three men did not sign the letter to the foreign church congregations, but it is possible that they were less supportive of the Strangers. As mayor in 1571, Greene had "signed and delivered a protest against the settlement of Dutch and Walloons in the city."[125] Christopher Some's profession is recorded as a "dornix weaver," a traditional woolen cloth that would have been in competition with the new draperies woven by the Strangers.[126] At any rate, the possibility that Greene, Some, and Layer were less supportive of the Strangers would fit with Moens's assertion that "there was always a party in the Corporation of Norwich opposed to the Strangers."[127]

Regardless, the response of Cullie, Aldrich, Wood, Suckling, and Peck to the threat of Tipper's Grant is noteworthy. In purchasing the right of hostage from Tipper (and then declining to act on it), they showed that the majority of the Mayor's Court was firmly behind the Strangers. Though they had adjudicated complaints about the Strangers for a decade and had themselves imposed restrictions on the incomers,[128] the Mayor's Court had come to understand the importance of keeping the Strangers in Norwich, and they were willing to absorb a considerable financial burdern (£70) and personally assuage the Strangers' anxieties in order to do so.

Preparations

The Mayor's Court would play a primary role in determining the form and content of the civic pageants associated with Queen Elizabeth's 1578 visit to Norwich. The response to Tipper's Grant was in March 1578. On May 1, one of the men who signed the letter, Robert Wood, was elected mayor of Norwich, and he would have taken office in June—just in time to preside over the initial planning meeting for the Queen's upcoming visit. As mayor, Wood would have been the person who was most responsible for determining the details of Norwich's reception of the Queen.[129] City records show that Wood worked closely with the entire council and that he made use of other city officers (like the "Chamberlyne and his fower Councellors") in coordinating the preparation efforts.[130] These preparations ranged from cleaning and repairing the fabric of the city to purchasing gifts for the Queen's entourage. But Wood also understood the importance of what the Norwich Assembly Proceedings Book refers to as the "setting forth of Shewes at the Quenes maiesties coming."[131] For these preparations, Wood seems to have relied more on his inner circle. One of the scaffolds used during the Queen's entry on August 16 was set up "ouer against Maister Peckes dore"—suggesting former mayor Thomas Peck's active involvement in the pageants.[132] As we shall see, the seemingly disparate venues and speakers featured throughout the week can almost all be linked back to the various prerogatives of the Mayor's Court. Wood also sought external assistance by hiring the poets Thomas Churchyard, Bernard Garter, and William Goldingham to devise entertainments on behalf of the city. Yet Wood's desire to put this important aspect of preparation in the hands of professionals did not mean that the mayor and his court gave up creative control. Churchyard records that he "came to Norwiche aboute that businesse, and remained there three long weekes before the Courte came tyther, deuising and studying the best I coulde for the Citie."[133] As outsiders, Churchyard and his fellow poets would need to work closely with their patrons to determine the form and content of the pageants.

Just what would these pageants attempt to accomplish? As I have shown, by 1578 Wood and the other city officers were generally supportive of the Strangers, but they were also painfully aware of continuing internal frictions and of the lack of integration between the native and immigrant communities. They also knew that hosting the reigning monarch was a momentous occasion in the life of their city. Not only was it an opportunity to enhance its prestige and reputation to a national and courtly audience, it was a chance to transform the internal dynamics of the city. I argue that even as the Norwich pageants aggrandize the Queen and profess the city's loyalty to her, they are also at least partially devoted to addressing this other, much more local problem. As Felicity Heal and others have demonstrated, early modern city oligarchies well understood how civic ritual could be used to forge urban identity.[134] Norwich in particular had a long tradition of processional performances that may well have contributed to its historically strong sense of civic identity.[135] The city used the occasion of the Queen's visit to attempt to dramatically unify its divided population. By their nature, royal visits encouraged local factions to temporarily put aside their differences, and could help "sharpen" provincial identities.[136] But the Norwich leaders took a much more deliberate approach: They used some aspects of the pageants to help educate the Strangers in the audience about the history and traditions of their adopted city. In doing so, they attempt to more thoroughly acculturate the incomers. At the same time, many of the pageant themes subtly appeal to native inhabitants to be more understanding of and sympathetic toward vulnerable outsiders.[137]

In many ways, I follow Scott Oldenburg's assertion that in times of xenophobia against immigrants, literature can be used to imagine possibilities of inclusivity and shared community.[138] Pageants—with their creative blend of rhetoric, symbols, and costumes—function in much this same way. They are performative spaces that might be conducive to imagining shared ground, a common story, and a shared identity. In Norwich, the Queen's visit afforded a unique opportunity to construct community in a particularly dramatic way.

This is not to say that the city leaders used the Queen's visit as a mere pretense for working out local kinks. The Norwich pageants do take the Queen as their main theme and do reflect the standard pageant conventions of the day. They praise the Queen's person, extol her governance, and assert the city's undying loyalty and devotion to her. Like most cities, Norwich was desperate to make a good impression on the reigning monarch. Yet even as they pursue these aims, the entertainments present the Queen in a way that is serviceable to addressing the internal dynamics that city officials were so preoccupied with in the 1570s. They depict the Queen as someone who values unity and who works to promote its benefits throughout her realm. They also present the Queen as a locus around which fragmented identities might cohere. The pageants suggest that by drawing near to the Queen, both native and Stranger populations will also effectively move closer toward one another. Thus, the Norwich pageants, though ostensibly focused on the Queen, nonetheless speak to and try to improve the internal dynamic of the city.[139]

This approach to the Norwich pageants is in contrast to the critical tradition. As with most royal progresses, the tendency has been to view the Queen's visit through a monarchical lens. In other words, why did Elizabeth journey to East Anglia in 1578 and how did she use the progress to work toward these goals? Her motives are typically ascribed to a desire for increased religious conformity—since Norwich's Bishop Edmund Freak was "known to be more lenient to local recusant families than he was to the Puritan gentry."[140] Other national issues of great moment that get discussed in relation to the 1578 progress are the Queen's ongoing marriage negotiations and the debate about whether or not to commit military aid against Spain in the Low Countries.[141] Those scholars who do consider the pageants devised by the city tend to be dismissive. For example, James Day characterizes the Norwich entertainments as "grovelling speeches," "platitudinous welcomes," and "foolery ad nauseam . . . discharged at point blank range" and laments that "there was no escape for the Queen."[142] Such approaches also assume that the Queen was the only intended audience. C. E. McGee suggests that among all of the civic pageants devised for Elizabethan progresses, the "local concerns of Norwich fade out most fully from [their] civic shows," and indeed that "the city pursued no particular local causes" and that "court culture took over Norwich's entertainment of the Queen."[143] Zillah Dovey's lengthy account of the Norwich pageants does not even mention the Norwich Strangers or their prominent role in the pageants.[144] As I have already taken great pains to point out, the large influx of

Strangers was a crucial part of Norwich history in these years and a central focus of the 1578 pageants. Thus I intend to look closely at these pageants from the city's perspective in order to discover how—given that internal tensions were the key local issues—the city leaders used the opportunity of the Queen's visit to address them.

The Royal Entry

There are two main accounts of the Norwich pageants: Bernard Garter's *The Ioyful Receyuing of the Queenes most excellent Maiestie into hir Highnesse Citie of Norwich* and Thomas Churchyard's *A Discourse of the Queenes Maiesties entertaine-ment in Suffolk and Norffolk.*[145] Both were published within a month of the Queen's visit to Norwich. As both Garter and Churchyard devised entertainments for the Queen's visit, so both authors had an insider perspective. However, neither work offers a comprehensive account. Even though Garter published first, he consciously omits Churchyard's "shewe[s], which I leaue to himselfe to vtter: bycause my hope is, he will manifest that amongst the reste shortely" (*JN2*, 817).[146] As a result, there is very little overlap between the two accounts, with each author describing the particular entertainments that he devised.

My focus will be on Garter's *Ioyful Receyuing,* as he seems to have worked more closely with the city leaders. As we shall see, Garter's entertainments fea-ture topical references and general themes of unity that resonate more directly with the local situation in Norwich in the 1570s. In contrast, Churchyard's par-ticipation in the pageants is more closely tied to the royal court. Zillah Dovey characterizes him as "a kind of professional impresario to the Court, [who] was sent to Norwich to organize some of the entertainments."[147] During the Queen's 1578 progress to East Anglia, Churchyard was present at Norwich but also traveled with the court throughout East Anglia—as his more expansive publica-tion title suggests. In contrast to Garter, the pageants that Churchyard devised for Norwich tend to be highly allegorical and mythological.[148] Churchyard did work with the local officials, but there are suggestions that he worked more closely with the Queen's officials during the visit.[149] For example, Churchyard's *Discourse* reports that on Thursday morning "my Lorde Chamberlaine [Thomas Radcliffe] gave me warning the Queenes highnesse woulde ride abroade in the after noone, and he commaunded me to be ready, dutifully to presente hir with some Shewe" (*JN2*, 737). Garter's *Ioyful Receyuing* provides an account that seems more in tune with the city's perspective. Not only does it contain the particular entertainments that Garter devised, it also includes orations by the mayor, schoolmaster, and Dutch minister, who all have clear ties to the Mayor's Court, suggesting that Garter's devices were part of that same guiding hand. In addition, all of these elements work together to advance a particular program for addressing Norwich's internal tensions.

On the afternoon of Saturday, August 16, as the Queen approached Norwich from the southwest, the city sent a special delegation to meet her at Harford Bridge some two miles from the city proper. In many ways, Norwich was adhering to standard conventions in welcoming the monarch. Like other cities in the 1560s and 1570s, Norwich's delegation was comprised of the mayor and other chief officers, it met the Queen at the edge of the city liberties, and it engaged in the ceremonial surrender (and then reacquisition) of the city mace. As was also typical, Norwich's mayor, Robert Wood, delivered a welcome oration and presented the Queen with a silver cup on behalf of the city. Garter's account faithfully records these expected details, but it also suggests that Norwich placed a special emphasis on the civic procession to and from Harford Bridge. Long before the Queen arrived, the welcome party lined up to depart the city. The procession was led by sixty of the most "comelie" bachelors of the city, mounted on horseback and "appareled all in blacke sattyn doublets, blacke hose, blacke taffata hattes and yellowe bandes, and their universall liverie was a mandylion of purple taffata, layde aboute with silver lace; and so apparelled, marched forwards, two and two in ranke" (*JN2*, 787). Behind them, someone representing King Gurgunt, the legendary founder of the city, was attired in green and white silk and a feathered black hat and mounted on a "brave courser." Gurgunt was attended by "three henchmen in white and greene: one of them did beare his helmet, the seconde his tergat, the third his staffe" (*JN2*, 787). Next came "a noble companie of Gentlemen and wealthie Citizens, in velvet coates and other costly furniture, bravely mounted." After this group came the city officers and sword bearer, "with the sworde and hatte of maintaynaunce" (*JN2*, 787). Then came the mayor, twenty-four aldermen, city recorder—all in "scarlette gownes"— followed by the former mayors (now all members of the Mayor's Court) in "scarlet cloakes" (*JN2*, 787). At the end of the procession walked all of those who had served as sheriffs, attired "in violet gownes and satten tippets" (*JN2*, 787). As these details indicate, the descriptive emphasis is on the careful organization, vibrant colors, expensive fabrics, and symbolic props that characterize the procession. It is clear that the procession was intended to convey great pomp and ceremony, in which the wealth, hierarchy, duties, and privileges of the city leaders are given dramatic and visible expression.

The intended audience was not just the Queen, but also the local populace. After all, the participants departed the city in this order rather than getting into formation once they arrived at Harford Bridge. "Thus euery thing in due and comely order, they al . . . marched forwardes" for the two-mile walk to the bridge (JN2, 787).[150] That the local populace was on hand is suggested by the precaution: "Then followed diuers other, to keepe the people from disturbing the array aforesaide" (JN2, 787). "The people" also seem to have accompanied the procession all the way to Harford Bridge, because Garter records that at the Queen's appearance there, "the acclamations and cries of the people . . . ratled so loude, as hardly for a great time coulde any thing be hearde" (JN2, 787). The populace's prolonged exposure to this impressive delegation (they also had to wait an hour at the bridge before the Queen would actually arrive) may well have been intended to remind them of the power, authority, and wealth of the city corporation that ruled over them—and perhaps even express that corporation's authority to construct communal identity. At the same time, the active participation of the populace—both natives and Strangers—in these events united them and made them a part of the enactment of civic identity that was occurring.

When the Queen finally did arrive, the mayor's formal speech of welcome furthered many of these ideas. In making the simple point that he speaks on behalf of everyone, Wood says, "Truely on mine owne part, which by your Highnesse authoritie and clemencie . . . do governe this famous Citie, and on the parte of these my brethren, and all these people, which by your authoritie we rule" (JN2, 789). In acknowledging the royal source of his authority, Wood also reminds the assembled population (of both natives and Strangers) of that authority, and perhaps of their identity as one city and one people ("all these people"). Later in this short speech, Wood also mentions Norwich's status and privileges, "whiche we received of the most mighty Prince Henry the Fourth, in the fift yere of his raigne, then to us granted in the name of Mayor, Aldermen, and Sheriffs, whereas before tyme out of minde or mention, we were governed by Bayliffes . . . which ever since have bene both established and encreased with continuall priviledges of Kinges" (JN2, 789). This passage is a clear assertion of the discrete political identity that Norwich had possessed for almost two hundred years. For some of the assembled citizens, this would have been a well-known point of pride; for more recent arrivals, it would have been a way of educating them and engrafting them as participants in a very long civic tradition.

After the mayor's oration, the royal party, civic delegation, and everyone else processed the two miles back to Norwich. When they arrived outside of the city walls at St. Stephen's Gate, the aforementioned King Gurgunt was positioned to deliver a forty-four-line poetic address.[151] Among other things, Gurgunt's speech talks about his role in founding the city of Norwich in the fourth century and building the (actually Norman) castle visible from this spot.[152] Though ostensibly for the benefit of the Queen, this speech (like the mayor's oration) also dramatically reminds the assembled populace about the age and mythical history of their native / adopted city. Scott Oldenburg observes that states often build nationalism by appealing to a common origin myth.[153] Gurgunt's person and speech seem similarly serviceable for constructing a common civic identity. Other parts of the speech praise the Queen by drawing parallels between Gurgunt's ancient accomplishments and Elizabeth's more recent achievements. The "Foure speciall poyntes . . . concurring in us both" include these monarchs' ability to unite their people (Gurgunt's grandfather united the warring British princes, while Elizabeth's grandfather "did conclude the broyles" of York and Lancaster), strike at Roman corruption (Gurgunt's father is credited with sacking Rome, while Elizabeth's father broke with the Catholic church and symbolically "spoile[d] hir neare of all hir glittering tire"), and facilitate educational growth (Gurgunt allegedly founded some Cambridge schools that Elizabeth has helped make famous throughout the world) (*JN2*, 791).

The fourth parallel has a decidedly local application. Gurgunt asserts that "I thirtie wandring ships of banish men relieved" (*JN2*, 791)—a reference to his "encounter[ing] thirty ships of people banished from Spain when returning from Denmark, and subsequently grant[ing] the refugees land in Ireland in which to settle."[154] The contemporary parallel is Elizabeth's decision to grant asylum to Protestant religious refugees: "The throngs of banisht soules that in this Citie dwell, / Do weepe for joy, and pray for thee with teares untold" (*JN2*, 791). These lines clearly reference the Stranger community in Norwich. Gurgunt not only draws attention to their many hardships (wandering, banishment), he also suggests that the relief they have been given is an act of charity and compassion. By putting contemporary Strangers in the context of these earlier Spanish refugees, they too are mythically celebrated as a part of the storied history of the city. Their arrival is made a little less foreign insofar as they are not an aberration but a pattern in the city's history. By crediting not just the town but the Queen with their relief—after all, she issued the letters patent in 1565—Gurgunt is also reminding the native inhabitants that succoring the

Strangers is sanctioned and approved by the Queen herself. Finally, the speech begins to sound the note of unity that will be of crucial importance later in the pageants. The same Queen that invited the Strangers has already been identified as a Queen of unity. In the first parallel, it is the Tudor dynasty that ended the Wars of the Roses and "first uniting all did weare the crowne" (*JN2*, 791). The next part of the welcome procession furthers this idea of unity.

Leaving the site of Gurgunt's speech, the procession then entered the city proper through St. Stephen's Gate. In preparation for this moment, the gate had been "gallauntly and strongly repayred" (*JN2*, 792). It had been given a new portcullis, and both its outward and inward sides had been "enriched and beautified" (*JN2*, 792). On the outside had been painted a variety of heraldic emblems, including the Queen's arms and badge, the city arms, and the scutcheon of St. George. "God and the Queen we serue" was written beneath. On the inside of the gate was placed a red rose, a white rose, and "in the middest was the whyte & red Rose vnited, expressing the Union" (*JN2*, 792). In case this image needed interpretation, the following quatrain appeared underneath:

> DIVISION kindled stryfe,
> Blist VNION quenchte the flame:
> Thence sprang our noble PHAENIX deare,
> The pearlesse Prince of FAME. (*JN2*, 792)

In a straightforward way, these verses endorse unity by contrasting the strife of division with the blessings of union. Though ostensibly a comment on Henry VII's uniting of Lancaster and York some ninety-three years previously, their message of descrying division was perhaps even more topically relevant to the fractured population of contemporary Norwich. It is worth noting that this paean to unity was placed on the *inside* of the city gate, an especially prominent place for city inhabitants to see it both before and during the Queen's arrival— whereas the Queen herself may not have even seen it unless she turned around as she passed within the gate. Moreover, the message was not just textual but also visual: the separate and then united roses were a simple, powerful image that even non-English speakers could readily comprehend. At the same time, the inner gate was a genuine celebration of the unity that the Queen represented. Both dynastically and personally, she served as a model of unity and a locus around which unity might cohere.

As the royal procession passed through St. Stephen's Gate, it entered the heart of the city. Even today, one is still struck by the dramatic views of the square castle keep planted atop its earthen mound and of the cathedral's soaring spire just beyond. The Norman castle had been a royal fortress until the 1340s, when it was transferred to the city and became the county gaol. It was thus a formidable symbol of civic authority in 1578. The cathedral had been re-founded in 1538 and so was outside the city's jurisdiction, but its spire was a visible reminder of Norwich's ecclesiastical importance to the rest of the region. Either here just inside the gate or further along St. Stephen's Street, a stage of 8 feet by 40 feet had been set up.[155] Even though the Queen had already been ceremonially welcomed at Harford Bridge and heard an oration from King Gurgunt, Garter identifies this as the "first pageant." Remarkably, the city officials placed members of the Stranger community on this stage and gave them a dramatic voice in the proceedings.[156] Although this pageant could be read merely as a celebration of local textile production, I argue that it chiefly functions to both idealize the activities of the Stranger community and praise their contributions to Norwich.

Garter records that high above the back of the stage were written the following phrases:

THE CAUSES OF THIS COMMON WEALTH ARE,
God truely preached.

Iustice duely executed.————The people obedient.

Idlenesse expelled.————Labour cherished.

Vniuersall concorde preserued. (*JN*2, 793)

These short phrases align the Stranger participants with conventional values of piety, justice, obedience, and hard work. The text asserts that they share the values of the local population; they are not dubious foreigners looking to take advantage of the natives and thrive at their expense. At the same time, these words may also have been intended to assuage native concerns by asserting that the Strangers would in fact be held to these standards—for it was the city authorities who had the power to execute justice, expel idleness, and ensure that dangerous religious opinions were not tolerated. The last phrase—"Vniuersall concorde preserued"—seems especially significant, as it serves as a reminder to both groups that concord is a key value and that the city authorities would work to preserve it.

On the same stage, "from the standing place downward," were painted representations of the chief economic activity of the Strangers: weaving. Seven different kinds of looms were depicted, with each one labelled to identify the kind of textile it produced: worsted, russels, dornick, tuft mockado, lace, caffa, and fringe. Such variety was surely intended to celebrate the ways in which the Strangers had diversified Norwich's textile production. Indeed, the astute observer may already have noted this variety in the clothing worn by the city's welcome delegation: "All of these wonderful materials—the velvets, the satins, the taffetas, and laces—were all made completely in Norwich by the Strangers, at this early date."[157] But if the first pageant displays the Strangers economic contributions, it also suggests that they have worked side by side with—rather than replaced—native weavers. As Nancy Ives points out, the first three looms in the pageant depict traditional English-Norwich products, whereas the last four are newer fabrics brought by the Strangers. Nor were the two groups necessarily in competition, since the Strangers actually required worsted yarn as a basis in the manufacture of some of the new draperies.[158] Together, these images illustrated the variety, interdependence, and labor that went into the Norwich textile industry. That such mundane economic activities would be emblematized and "beautified with painters worke artificially" helps elevate them to the realm of art.

Painted alongside these looms was a "portrature of a Matrone, and two or three children" with the caption: "Good nurture chaungeth qualities" (*JN*2, 793). The portrayal of the human participants would serve as a reminder that not just Dutch and Walloon men, but women and children participate in and benefit from the textile economy; thus, it may be something of an appeal for native empathy. The somewhat ambiguous caption is also worth noting. "Good nurture chaungeth qualities" could refer to weaving, since it is careful labor that transforms raw wool into finished cloth, but it also seems relevant to the matron and her children, providing assurance that the second generation of Strangers will gradually become acculturated in Norwich. It may also be a reminder to native townspeople that if they want the Strangers to change their "qualities," they need to nurture and accommodate the immigrants so as to facilitate their integration.

Garter records that the pageant featured not just painted "portratures" of weavers and textiles, but the entities themselves: eight "small women children" on each side of the stage spinning and knitting worsted yarn, men in the center of the stage engaged in manufacturing the different kinds of textiles, and "before euerye man the worke in deede" (*JN*2, 793). If the aforementioned paintings of looms and people helped elevate and aestheticize the Strangers' economic activities, the inclusion of actual Strangers surely helped humanize and present them as vital members of the commonwealth. That the pageant also shows the production of cloth at different stages—spinning, weaving, finishing—serves to further emphasize the painstaking labor involved in its production. This further aligns the Strangers with the value of labor, one of the six chief "causes of this common wealth." At the same time, the inclusion of an actual specimen of each type of finished cloth emphasized the beautiful, colorful product that resulted.

On this same stage, observed Garter, was "a pretie boy richly apparelled, which represented the Commonwelth of the Citie." At a certain point, this boy stepped forward and delivered a twenty-four-line speech to the assembled crowd. Parts of this speech merely interpret these visual aides by explaining the finer points of the weaving process. But the speaker also goes out of his way to closely identify these activities with the livelihood of the Stranger community in Norwich:

> In this small shewe our whole estate is seene;
> The welth we have, we finde proceede from thence.
> The idle hande hath here no place to feede,
> The painfull wight hath stil to serve his neede. (JN2, 794)

These last two lines again emphasize the labor expended by the weaving community, and very clearly link back to the printed values of "Labour cherished" and "Idleness expelled." A little later in the speech, Commonwealth adds: "And all to drive dame Neede into hir cave, / Our heades and hands togither labourde have" (JN2, 794). Again, the emphasis is on the Strangers' hard work and basic economic motivations. Many locals in the 1560s and 1570s saw the immigrants as economic rivals who did not work very hard and who grew rich at their expense. These lines seek to correct this misconception by presenting the Strangers as hardworking, driven by economic necessity, and as living just a step above subsistence.

This speech also tackles the Strangers' difficult reception:

> Againe, our seate denyes our traffique heere,
> The sea too neare decides us from the rest,
> So weake we were within this dozen yeare,
> As care did quench the courage of the best:
> But good advise hath taught these little handes
> To rende in twayne the force of pining bandes. (JN2, 794)

Here the speaker gives the lie to the assumption that the Strangers have had an easy time in Norwich. He draws attention to the sense of isolation, the economic restrictions, and the second-class status that have plagued the Strangers. At the same time, the last two lines assert (perhaps over-optimistically) that things have been getting better of late. In fact, the speech ends on an upswing: "Thus through thy helpe and ayde of power divine, / Doth Norwich live, whose harts and goods are thine." The speaker moves from discussing the Stranger community in isolation to integrating them into a larger conception of "Norwich" that would seem to include both Strangers and natives. The suggestion of the speaker—who is, after all, identified as "the Commonwelth of the Citie"—is that the Strangers are now an integral part of Norwich.

Although ostensibly delivered to the Queen, this speech also seems to be directed toward the native townspeople, who would have been thronging the processional route. By allowing the Strangers to participate—and be featured—in the first pageant, the city officials were going out of their way to validate this beleaguered group as a vital part of the civic community. The Strangers are also given a voice, which they use to characterize themselves, refute misconceptions, and plead their case for acceptance. The narrative that emerges is that they are hardworking, motivated by economic necessity, and have struggled mightily in their new home. At the same time, they have contributed significantly to Norwich's prosperity and well-being, and are now becoming part of their adopted city.

If the first pageant invites empathy for and understanding of the Strangers, the second (and final) pageant of the entry seeks to integrate Strangers and natives alike into a more cohesive vision of the city. After leaving the first pageant, the royal procession continued along St. Stephen's Street before bearing left onto White Lion Street and emerging into the midst of the city's large outdoor market space.[159] There, the Queen was presented with a triumphal arch, comprised of a central entryway and two side gates, the whole structure painted to look like jasper and marble. On top of the gates was an eight-foot-wide stage, on which stood "fiue personages appareled like women" (JN2, 795) who represented the City of Norwich, Deborah, Judith, Esther, and Martia (an ancient English Queen). The substance of the pageant was each woman delivering a twenty- to thirty-line speech in succession. The City of Norwich spoke first, offering the Queen a welcome, profuse compliments, a prayer for God's blessing, and a request to look indulgently on the city's "slender shewes" (JN2, 796). Though these are pretty conventional professions of loyalty, what is striking is that they are delivered in language that pre-supposes a stable and homogenous civic identity:

. . . thou art my ioy next God, I haue none other,

My Princesse and my peerlesse Queene, my louing nurse and mother.

My goods and lands, my hands and hart, my limbes and life are thine,

What is mine own in right or thought, to thee I do resigne. (*JN2, 796*)

Significantly, the City of Norwich claims to speak on behalf of everyone and in language that reflects not only shared purposes and feelings, but shared goods, lands, limbs, and lives. Thus, Norwich's 10,000 natives and 6,000 Strangers are here reduced to a single entity with a single viewpoint.

This imaginative leap was furthered by the specific location in which it was being made. The second pageant was purposefully set in the city's marketplace. With dimensions of around 650 feet by 300 feet, Norwich's market was one of England's largest, and thus conducive to giving the Queen and her subjects unobstructed views of one another.[160] The market was also the symbolic center of Norwich for its own inhabitants. It was the main public space— "represent[ing] voluntary exchange" and "notionally belong[ing] to all"—where inhabitants came together for everything from commerce to recreation to civic ceremonies.[161] Not surprisingly, it also featured some of the city's finest buildings. The market was bounded to the west by the soaring perpendicular architecture of the "city church," St. Peter Mancroft.[162] On the eastern edge of the market was the ornate Guildhall, the largest and most impressive building of its kind outside of London.[163] The market's center was dominated by the early sixteenth-century Market Cross, "a graceful structure reaching 60 to 70 ft. and standing on a 30 ft. wide plinth."[164] These impressive structures were potent symbols of civic authority, but they also represented the potentially unifying forces of commerce, religion, and civic life that imposed order, structure, and homogeneity on the city's inhabitants. If civic unity was possible, it would seem to be most plausible in this shared public space.

The imagined union between natives and Strangers also works because the inhabitants of Norwich are being defined in relation to something far beyond their city walls: the Queen herself. As we have seen, 1570s Norwich was riven by linguistic, cultural, and ethnic differences, but what better way to elide these differences than to subsume them into something larger. The aforementioned biblical speakers—Deborah, Judith, and Esther—suggest why such subsumption might be both possible and desirable. As their speeches make clear, each biblical woman was chosen by God to deliver her people from oppression and vulnerability. The prophetess and judge Deborah helped free the Israelites from the Canaanite King Jabin and his "cruell Captain Sisera" (*JN2, 796*). Judith cut off the head of the Assyrian General Holofernes in order to save her hometown of Bethulia. The Jewish queen Esther overcame the wily Haman and averted the genocide of her people. Each biblical speaker recounts her exploits and then draws a parallel to Queen Elizabeth, who is also (as Esther says) a "refuge" and "rocke" to her people (*JN2, 798*). All three speeches emphasize female power as well as the vulnerability of the people whose delivery is recounted. Deborah is associated with "uphold[ing] the simple, meeke, and good, [and] pull[ing] downe the proud and stoute," Judith repeatedly refers to her status as a "poore widow," and Esther and her people are threatened by the "fretting heads of furious Foes" (*JN2, 797*).

One reason that the Queen is imagined to be so sympathetic to the downtrodden is that she herself has been in their shoes. As Esther puts it:

> Thy God thou knowest most dread and soueraigne Queen,
> A world of foes of thine hath overthrowen,
> And hither nowe triumphantly doth call
> Thy noble Grace, the comforte of vs all. (*JN2, 798*)

One can see why this portrayal of Queen Elizabeth might resonate powerfully with the Strangers. She knows what it is to be vulnerable, and now that she is Queen, she uses her position (like her biblical forbears) to defend and uphold those who are threatened by the strong. At the same time, this portrayal of the Queen is also broad enough to appeal to native English men and women beset by the actual (and imagined) foreign and domestic enemies of the 1570s. As Esther promises, "So fraude, nor force, nor foraine Foe may stand / Againste the strength of thy moste puyssaunt hand" (*JN2, 798*). Thus, the second pageant does not just offer the Queen as the site around which fractured identity can cohere, it also gives clear and enticing reasons as to why she is such a fit receptacle.

Overall, then, the city officials seized the opportunity of the Queen's entry into Norwich to set in motion a number of key themes that might speak to their assembled constituents. They used opening features like the ceremonial procession and the mayor's oration to assert the city corporation's authority and its capacity to construct a common civic identity. That identity is then concretely expressed in terms of Norwich's ancient foundation, its distinctive architecture, its role in national history, its economic specialties, its social values, and in the rights and privileges that the city has accrued over the centuries. These markers of identity are a reminder and a point of pride for native inhabitants, but serve as a way of educating and acculturating newly arrived immigrants. At the same time, the Strangers are not merely subsumed into an existing identity; they are imagined as contributing to an evolving identity. Gurgunt's speech puts them in the context of previous refugees, making their arrival and succor a pattern, rather than an anomaly, in the city's history. The Strangers are also given a prominent role in the first pageant, which humanizes them, praises their work ethic, recounts their struggles, idealizes their motives, refutes misconceptions, and celebrates their contributions to the revival of the Norwich economy. There is particular emphasis on the latter point, as samples of the new draperies are both displayed on stage and worn by city officials in the ceremonial procession. As the spokesperson of the first pageant asserts: "We bought before the things that now we sel" (*JN2, 794*).

In moments like this, the Strangers are portrayed as valued—but in a sense still separate—members of their adopted city. Thus, other parts of these opening "shews" seek to integrate them more thoroughly. Along with their native counterparts, they participate in the procession to Harford Bridge, applaud the Queen's arrival, accompany her through the narrow streets, and stand in the central marketplace. In speeches by the mayor, by "Commonwealth," and by the "City of Norwich," they are verbally joined to native inhabitants by being referred to as one people and one city. However, given the longstanding friction between the two groups, more than just semantics would be needed to bring them together. Thus, the entry festivities deliberately take up the theme of unity. At St. Stephen's Gate, the populace is presented with the simple but effective image of the red and white rose uniting. As this image suggests, the Queen can serve as both a model for and a locus around which such unity might cohere. She is herself an embodiment of concord. Like Gurgunt, she is associated with bringing together warring factions. She understands that "division kindle[s] strife" while "blist Union quenchte[s] the flame" (*JN2, 792*). It is the second pageant that really sets forth her unique qualifications as a unifier. Before she came to the throne, she experienced hardships and overcame threats. As a result, she is now acutely sensitive to the needs of her people. Like Deborah, Judith, and Esther, she has a special place in her heart for the vulnerable and downtrodden—and will work to make sure that all of God's people will flourish. The implication is that all of her subjects can trust her and that as they move closer to her, they move closer to each other.

After the last of these varied and lengthy entertainments, the Queen left the marketplace and traveled through the city streets "directly to the Cathedral church, where Te Deum was song" (*JN2*, 800). After the service, she was finally allowed to settle into her lodgings in the nearby Bishop's Palace, where she would reside for the next six days. Garter records that on Sunday and Monday, "by meanes of the wether she went not abrode" (*JN2*, 800). However, many other shows and entertainments were scheduled throughout the week. On Tuesday, the Queen went hunting at Costessey Park, some three miles west of the city. The city used this occasion for Churchyard to stage "The Shew of Chastitie" as she departed the city via St. Benet's Gate; on her way back, she stopped to listen to an oration from the minister of the Dutch Church. On Wednesday, the Queen dined at Mount Surrey, Philip Howard's estate to the east of the city. On her return, another of Churchyard's devices—"Manhood and Dezarte"—was nixed because of the weather, but Stephen Limbert, the master of the local grammar school, was able to deliver an oration as the Queen passed by the Great Hospital. On Thursday, bad weather prevented the Queen from riding out in the afternoon, so Churchyard's show had to be canceled a second time. However, Henry Goldingham's mythological masque was performed before the court in the evening. Both Queen and court departed on Friday, so there was a last flurry of entertainments, including speeches, devices, and shows by Garter, Churchyard, Goldingham, Limbert, Mayor Wood, and others. These varied offerings may seem like a bit of a hodgepodge, but they were in fact better coordinated than they first appear. Many of these speakers and institutions had direct links to the Mayor's Court, suggesting that mayor Wood and his inner circle were pulling the strings. In addition, many of these entertainments serve to further develop the above-mentioned themes of unity and concord.

The Dutch Minister's Oration

One of the most important of Norwich's ceremonial moments, for my purposes, was the oration delivered by the Dutch minister on Tuesday afternoon. Along with the first pageant discussed above, this was another occasion in which the Stranger community was directly given a voice by city officials. In this case, the mouthpiece was one Hermanus Modert, a "charismatic ex-monk" who had arrived in Norwich sometime after 1568.[165] As minister of the Dutch Church, Modert was a key leader in the Stranger community. This is because "the Dutch and Walloon communities in Norwich . . . [were] centred on their Churches," which not only had spiritual authority but were also "depositories of . . . linguistic identity" and helped maintain law and order within the community.[166] As leader of the Dutch congregation, Modert would have worked closely with the city officials on a range of issues affecting the Stranger community.[167] In this instance, it is likely that mayor Wood and his inner circle both solicited Modert's participation and also worked closely with him on the content of his oration. Regardless, Modert would have been perceived as the de facto leader of the larger of the two Stranger communities, and by allowing him to speak, the city leaders were validating and legitimizing the Dutch community that he represented.

Not only the speaker, but the setting was also crucial for this oration. As mentioned above, the Queen was returning from hunting in Costessey Park. As she re-entered the city from the west (via St. Benet's Gate) and returned to her lodging (at the Bishop's Palace) in the cathedral close, she would have traveled down Upper Westwick Street and into Wymer Street. In the sixteenth century, this was the area of the city that was most closely associated with textile production, in part because of its proximity to the River Wensum. It is therefore not surprising that this area—on both the north and south sides of the river—was home to a large proportion of Norwich's Strangers. Indeed, the Dutch Church was also located here (along Wymer Street) in part of the old Blackfriars monastic complex. This handsome group of medieval flint buildings included a large preaching nave, friars' chancel, cloister, refectory, crypt, chapel, and anchorite cells. The monastic foundation was dissolved at the Reformation and the buildings passed to the Crown. In 1538, the city purchased the entire complex and repurposed it for civic usage.[168] In 1565, the old friars' chancel—which became known as Blackfriars—was given to the Dutch Strangers as a worship space.[169] That this gesture was seen as something more than a temporary measure can be inferred from the fact that the Dutch promptly began burying their deceased members in the floor of their "new" church.[170] Other buildings on the site—including St. Andrew's Hall and the cloisters—were used to store, examine, and seal cloths made by the foreign weavers.[171] It was in front of this architectural complex that the Dutch Minister delivered his oration to the Queen. It is hard to imagine a more fitting place. In many ways, this neighborhood and these buildings were the spiritual, domestic, and commercial heart of the Stranger community in Norwich.[172] Featuring this space was a reminder to the assembled populace that the Strangers did indeed have their own spaces and had become a physical part of the city.

At the same time, this space continued to have associations with the civic corporation. The old preaching nave—which became known as St. Andrew's Hall—continued to be used by the city and its guilds as an assembly and banqueting space. In addition, many civic elites (including members of the Mayor's Court) had prominent houses in close proximity to the Blackfriars complex.[173] The area in front of the Blackfriars complex was also an open civic space featuring an outdoor pulpit. Thus, the Dutch Minister's Oration was delivered in a setting that had close associations with both the Strangers and the civic corporation. As an architectural complex that had been partially appropriated for the use of the Strangers, the Blackfriars was a visible symbol of the ways in which the corporation had sought to accommodate and support the immigrant community. As Hermanus Modert spoke, this setting would have given the impression that he spoke on behalf of the Strangers but that he did so with the support and endorsement of the city corporation. The Blackfriars setting of Modert's speech is thus a prime example of Kathleen Ashley's observation that processional routes—and stops—actively defined which urban places were important and J. R. Mulryne's related claim that participation in festival can "imaginatively [reassign]" the meaning of a building.[174]

What did Modert say? He began by thanking the Queen and Mayor Wood for granting asylum to the Strangers. He is grateful that "we live under so good a tutor, being Magistrate in this thy Citie of Norwich, which thy Majestie hath of clemencie graunted unto us for a mansion-place, which were banished for Christ his religion" (*JN2*, 803). The dubious claim that Norwich has become a "mansion-place" for the refugees gains strength from the speech's setting, and Modert may well have gestured to the Blackfriars complex behind him or to the surrounding neighborhood that many Strangers called home. A little bit later, Modert exaggerates the positive reception that the Strangers have received: "That we finde the minds of the people favourable towards us . . . we give immortall thanks" (*JN2*, 803). As he characterizes the experiences of the Strangers in Norwich, Modert uses a variety of first-person plural pronouns ("we," "our," "us," and so forth), suggesting that he is indeed speaking on behalf of the Strangers. The effect may have been heightened by having the members of the Dutch congregation gathered behind Modert in the open space between the street and the Blackfriars complex.

As the line "we . . . which were banished for Christ his religion" indicates, Modert plays up the religious—rather than the economic—motives that brought the Strangers to Norwich. The rest of his oration makes an elaborate parallel between Queen Elizabeth and the Old Testament Joseph: "The good-nesse of God towards youre Majestie is lively drawne out of the historie of the innocente and most godly Josephus" (JN2, 803). Both were mistreated by their siblings. Just as Joseph was sold into slavery and taken to Egypt, so Elizabeth was wrongfully imprisoned by her sister Mary. Yet both were protected from their oppressors and ultimately "brought unto highe dignitie and royall kingdome" (JN2, 803). As rulers, neither Joseph nor Elizabeth used their position to pur-sue vengeance; instead, they displayed the higher virtues of temperance, forti-tude, and justice. It is because Elizabeth "doest followe most holily, the minde of Josephus," that Modert offers a special prayer for God to bless her reign.

At the same time, this detailed parallel invites a consideration of the simi-larities between Joseph and the Stranger community. The Dutch had also been forced to dwell in a foreign land, and they, too, had met with distrust and oppression. The first part of the oration describes the ordeal of the Strangers in precisely these terms: "godly men" who became "miserable and dispersed members of Christ [subject] to everie kinde of injurie" (JN2, 803). Later, when Modert describes Joseph's situation, it is in strikingly familiar terms: "His life . . . put in hazarde in a straunge kingdom, unto the providence of God, that he seemed to hang of no other thing than the only will of God." Indeed, Joseph's situation seems much more applicable to the Strangers, since Elizabeth herself was never "put in hazarde in a straunge kingdom" whereas the Strangers had had to endure much turbulence in England. And yet, just as Joseph was shielded by God, so, too, had the Strangers been providentially preserved from their trials and tribulations. At the end of the oration, Modert presented the Queen with a cup worth £50, which Garter reports was engraven with the following lines:

> To royal scepters, godlinesse,
>   Iosephus innocent,
> Doth take, from brothers bloudie handes,
>   and murtherers intent.
> So thee, O Queene, the Lord hath led
>   from prison and deceite
> Of thine, unto these highest toppes
>   of your princely estate. (JN2, 804)

By engraving these lines on the cup, the Strangers made the parallel with Joseph the dominant and enduring theme of the oration.[175]

Given the vulnerable state of the Strangers in Norwich, we can see why they might be eager to do so. The biblical episode of Joseph provides a way to characterize the Strangers' situation and also assuage the anxieties of both natives and foreigners. To the native observers, such a parallel suggests that the Strangers are (like Joseph) a godly and benevolent force that will behave with temperance and fortitude if given a chance. The parallel also covertly warns the natives that to continue to oppose and oppress them might be to go against the will of God. Or, in terms of the story, to play the part of Joseph's murderous and recalcitrant brothers. To the assembled members of the Dutch church, the parallel encourages them to see themselves as being favored and protected by God. At the same time, it also instructs them to be Joseph-like in patiently bearing their sufferings—meaning not to be defiant, quarrelsome, or seek to repay evil with evil. Instead, with God's help, they are to take the ill intent of others ("brothers bloudie handes") and make it into something good ("godlinesse"). But they are also to be wary. In the inner part of the cup presented to the Queen, Garter reports that "there was the figure of a Serpent enterfolding itselfe; in the middest whereof did sit a Dove, with this sentence of Christe, *Mat.* 10.16 *Wise as the Serpent, and meeke as the Dove*" (*JN2*, 804). Though ostensibly meant to affirm the personal qualities of the Queen, this combination is good, practical advice for anyone who (like the Strangers) is operating in a hostile environment.

I have been discussing Modert's focus on Joseph as if he were mainly an emblem of the Strangers. But in fact, the rhetorical success of this element is enhanced when Joseph is seen as a stand-in for *both* Queen Elizabeth and the Strangers. In praising Elizabeth for the Joseph-like way in which she has handled adversity, Modert is also setting her up as model for the Stranger community that is now in a similar situation. Not only has the Queen formally extended asylum to these refugees, she can also profoundly identify and sympathize with them. She, too, has been in their situation, and has emerged triumphantly. If part of the acculturation process is to give immigrants something or somebody on which to graft their identity, then the Queen fulfills that function. The Strangers can now truly feel as if Elizabeth is their Queen too. And in drawing closer to her, the Strangers also create common ground between themselves and native citizens, since both groups share this adulation of and loyalty to the monarch. In this way, the Queen becomes the receptacle of the unity that city leaders are trying to fashion.

Still, jointly focusing on the Queen does not magically remove the long-standing points of tension between the two groups. Just because they all love the Queen does not mean that they all love each other. The city leaders seem to realize this, as other parts of the entertainments throughout the week are used to further flesh out the theme of unity, with many of the other orations and pageant devices attempting to define what unity is (and is not) and discussing how it might be facilitated and maintained. Three key aspects emerge: empathy, diversity, and friendship.

Empathy

The first sub-theme revolves around the cultivation of empathy or pity for other people. In the Norwich pageants, this quality takes the appropriate form of sympathizing with outsiders and/or the downtrodden. Of course, this form of empathy is a biblical ideal (as in the Good Samaritan story), and we have already seen it make an appearance in both the second pageant (in the market-place) and in the Dutch Minister's Oration. In the second pageant, Deborah, Judith, and Esther are all godly leaders who deliver their downtrodden people from injustice and oppression. In glorifying these women, the pageant implies that the natives of Norwich should behave similarly in empathizing with the lowly and vulnerable in their own midst. In the Dutch Minister's Oration, Joseph himself is mistreated and "put in hazard in a strange kingdom" (*JN2*, 803). But God delights in succoring the weak, especially if they remain faithful to him. Thus, the Norwich pageants try to inculcate a sense of empathy for the lowly and oppressed that seems clearly relevant to the city leaders' goal of softening attitudes toward the Strangers.

The city leaders also try to make empathy a defining civic virtue of Norwich. This goal comes into particular focus in what Garter calls "The Oration of Stephan Limbert, publike Scholemaster" (*JN2*, 807). On Wednesday, the Queen dined with Philip Howard, son of the 4th Duke of Norfolk, at his house atop St. Leonard's Hill to the east of the city. On her return to Norwich, she re-entered via Bishop's Gate, proceeded down Holme Street and, in about 300 feet, passed alongside the Great Hospital. Here, outside "the Hospitall Dore, Maister Stephan Limbert, Maister of the Grammer Schoole in Norwich, stood readie to render hir an Oration" (*JN2*, 805). Limbert was a Cambridge graduate who had been master of the grammar school since 1569. The city had acquired the grammar school from the cathedral in 1547, and it was the Mayor's Court that had appointed Limbert to this position.[176] Because of his learned credentials and connections to city officials, Limbert was a natural choice to deliver the oration. However, the speech was not given outside the grammar school (which was in an old charnel house in the cathedral complex), but in front of the Great Hospital. It, too, was overseen by the city, and had also been re-established in 1547 in the same charter that set up the school.[177] Thus, the location and speaker both closely tie the oration to the Mayor's Court, and suggest that Limbert probably worked closely with Wood and others on the speech's content.

One of the main goals of the speech was to aggrandize the Great Hospital and highlight the city's role in its maintenance. It had been founded in 1249 as the Hospital of St. Giles to minister to the needs of the poor and aged. When the Crown granted it to the city in 1547, it was with the stipulation that it continue to be used for local poor relief. The new charter specified that it would house forty residents and included the hiring of some ten other domestic, religious, and administrative persons to maintain them.[178] Near the end of Limbert's speech, he gestures to "all these subjects of Norwich [that] desire me to say the same in their behalf" (*JN2*, 808)—suggesting that the fifty-plus residents of the Great Hospital may have been assembled behind him in a powerful visual display. The overt purpose of Limbert's speech is to praise Queen Elizabeth for her own "uncredible readinesse to relieve the neede of poore men" (*JN2*, 807). Limbert notes specifically her support for the Great Hospital, which he claims was "instituted" by her father Henry VIII, "confirmed" by her brother Edward VI, and "by your maiestie . . . of late notably encreased and amplified by the landes & possessions of Cringleforde" (*JN2*, 807–8). Limbert is referring to the aftermath of Throgmorton's Conspiracy of 1570, in which the Queen added the forfeited estates of George Redman of Cringleford to the hospital's endowment.[179]

However, the speech's content and location of utterance also serve to showcase Norwich's own highly developed poor relief system. In 1570, the city leaders commissioned a special census to quantify and categorize the extent of poverty in Norwich. They then attacked the problem with a combination of education, workhouses, restrictions against begging, and compulsory taxes for poor relief. Indeed, in the 1570s, Norwich spent some £500 per year on poor relief, "more than was spent on all other civic matters put together."[180] Norwich's approach was highly innovative: its poor census was a "landmark," and it was also the first English city to "[establish] a permanent scheme of poor relief."[181] In fact, Norwich became a model for many of the national changes for dealing with poverty that were instituted beginning in 1572.[182] Limbert's speech draws attention to and justifies the city's recent focus on poor relief. Limbert describes "releev[ing] the neede of poore men" as a great and singular benefit, "the which of many vertues none can be more acceptable unto God" (JN2, 807). He also invokes classical authorities like Plato—"There shall be no beggar in our state"—and Homer—"for all Strangers and beggars are from Zeus" (JN2, 807–8).[183]

In Norwich, the Great Hospital was both the centerpiece and symbol of this charitable mindset. According to Ellie Phillips, urban leaders transformed it into the "pre-eminent charitable establishment in the city" that was the "centerpiece of the city's poor relief scheme."[184] This is perhaps why Limbert says, "This hospitall of poore men is moste famous" (JN2, 807). When the city acquired the hospital in 1547, it modified and redirected many of the institution's pre-Reformation practices. Instead of being preoccupied with the spiritual and religious health of its residents, the new hospital devoted resources to physical and secular concerns—food, clothing, bedding, and medical care. Whereas earlier residents served as choristers whose energies were expended in commemorating the dead, residents now received an education and were then apprenticed to a suitable trade. This shift in focus reflected the humanist ideal of education as a key component of social reform.[185] The Great Hospital also came to be clearly identified as a civic institution. It was overseen and administered by city leaders, an association that was strengthened by the uniforms that some of the residents wore. Thirteen of the forty residents "wore gowns bearing the [red cross] livery of the Company of St. George."[186] This company—which had been the Guild of St. George prior to the Reformation— gave generously to the hospital and had a membership drawn mostly from the city corporation.[187] Thus, when residents left the hospital and walked through the streets of the city, they were visible reminders of the city's ongoing commitment to addressing the problem of poverty. As Phillips says, "By 1571, the [Great Hospital] was . . . a showpiece for civic policy."[188]

One of the reasons for the Great Hospital's prominence was that—like the Blackfriars—it occupied a physically impressive complex of buildings. The old Hospital of St. Giles included not only an infirmary, but a large medieval church (nave and chancel) as well as a refectory, cloister, porch, and tall bell tower. When the Queen paused on Holme Street for Limbert's oration, she would have been facing the long south front of the building complex, which included most of these buildings. Not only were they sizable edifices, they were also beautiful: most of them had been built two hundred years previously in the decorated perpendicular style and they represented "an investment in artistic patronage at the highest level."[189] Internally, these buildings had been converted in 1547 and again in 1570 to suit the post-Reformation goals of the city corporation. The medieval chancel and infirmary had been walled off to create separate men's and women's wards, which allowed the old crossing and chantry chapel to function as a separate parish church (St. Helen's).[190] Thus, the Great Hospital was the physical embodiment of the city's commitment to poor relief. Featuring the Hospital as the setting for Limbert's oration was a way of reminding not only the Queen but also the assembled crowds that empathy for the poor was an existing part of Norwich's civic identity.

Such empathy is clearly applicable to the Strangers. In the first place, many of the incoming refugees were actually poor.[191] The strictures of economic necessity are certainly played up in the first pageant in lines such as, "The painefull wight hath still to serue his neede" and "all to driue Dame neede into hir caue" (JN2, 794). But even those Strangers who were more prosperous were still seen as second-class citizens who could not fully participate in the life of the city. Like the poor, they were a vulnerable and downtrodden group. Thus, the pageant's emphasis on empathy actively encourages native citizens to see it as a civic virtue that might be extended to other groups like the Strangers.

Nevertheless, no Strangers were actually associated with Great Hospital. This is because the Stranger community was responsible for taking care of its own poor. In Norwich and other English cities, authorities worried that the immigrants would become a financial burden on their local parishes, so they were generally excluded from poor relief. Instead, the immigrant Dutch and French churches took the lead in providing assistance to members of their own congregations. Typical measures included visiting and assessing the needs of the poor, collecting funds, distributing alms and bread, caring for orphans and the infirm, and even helping unemployed Strangers to find work. In Norwich, the Strangers began implementing these measures when they arrived in 1566. In fact, Yungblut argues that many of the measures that characterize Norwich's "groundbreaking" poor relief scheme of the early 1570s derive directly from things the Stranger community was already doing.[192]

The Strangers positively impacted the Norwich poor in other ways. Even though the Strangers were already taking care of their own, they may well have been required to make contributions to the city's general poor relief fund.[193] In addition, they created employment opportunities for the native poor. One of the motives for inviting the Strangers in 1565 was the expectation that they would "sette on worke" the poor of the city by creating textile jobs so that "the poore here might be exercized in theyr spynninge and woolle worke."[194] By 1578, this goal had been measurably fulfilled. In St. Stephen's parish, for instance, "over 50 percent of the poor spinners were spinning white warp, which was introduced by the Walloons mainly, and it forms the basis of almost all of the new draperies."[195] This economic impact would seem to extend the meaning of the phrases "Labour cherished" and "Idlenesse expelled" that were written over the stage of the first pageant.[196] Not only does it refer to the fact that the Strangers themselves worked (and were not a drain on the Norwich economy), it may also mean that the Strangers' new cloth-making methods had ensured that natives were saved from idleness and given work to do.

The point is that the Norwich Strangers themselves had an impressive track record of empathizing with and assisting the downtrodden. They possessed and practiced the virtue of empathy and were not mere recipients of it. Empathy was thus imagined as a shared civic virtue that natives and Strangers had in common and that they might extend to one another. Indeed, Limbert's oration attempts to dispel the notion that cooperation is a zero-sum game where giving some people a hand up means dragging others down. He describes England under Elizabeth's social and economic policies as a Hesiodian paradise that "abounde[s] with all manner of graine, woll, cattell, and other aydes of mans life" (JN2, 808). In other words, empathy toward—and policies benefitting— the poor and other vulnerable groups can actually increase the overall health of the commonwealth.

Limbert's oration was thus a key aspect of the city leaders' attempt to facilitate unity between natives and Strangers. The speech asserts the importance of empathy, enshrines it as a civic virtue, and suggests the mutual benefits that it can lead to. Such empathy is further validated by its direct association with

Queen Elizabeth. By locating this virtue in the royal visitor (and playing up her support of the Great Hospital), Limbert makes it easier for members of these fragmented groups to adopt.

Diversity

The second way that Norwich pageants attempted to facilitate unity was by emphasizing unity through diversity. The city leaders did not use these "shews" to posit a total assimilation of the Strangers into Norwich society. As Cottret points out in *The Huguenots in England: Immigration and Settlement, c. 1550–1700*, the modern idea of assimilation "was practically unknown" in the sixteenth century and would probably have been objectionable to both groups.[197] Instead, the pageants construct a kind of unity that is not based on sameness or homogeneity but instead maintains the diversity of its component parts. Oldenburg calls this approach to early modern immigrants "provincial globalism" and describes it as having elements of both conformity and inclusiveness; it involves "a degree of assimilation, [but] not total surrender of cultural identity."[198] The Norwich pageants seem to reflect this approach by including moments that are conducive to teaching the Strangers about the heritage, history, civic traditions, and mythical foundation of their adopted city. At the same time, the pageants do not gloss over the fact that the Strangers are a separate population with their own church, language, and economic specializations. In fact, these aspects are highlighted—and even celebrated—by giving the Strangers their own stage (the first pageant) and their own spokesperson (the Dutch Minister). The latter's oration even features a cup presentation that was separate from the one given by the city, which allows the Strangers to show their own loyalty to the Queen and tailor their Joseph-themed gift to their own experience. The implied message for the Strangers is that becoming part of Norwich does not mean giving up their own cultural identity. This kind of unity might have also appealed to natives who might worry that their own culture and traditions could be weakened, co-opted, or replaced by mixing with the Strangers. Thus, the pageants posit a form of unity in which each group nevertheless gets to keep its markers of identity.

It is this type of unity around which much of the pageant imagery revolves. We find it most dramatically in the red and white roses at St. Stephen's Gate (*JN2, 792*), where the roses depicted separately and then together: "in the middest was the white and redde rose united, expressing the Union" (*JN2*, 792). It is the very nature of this union that is compelling. The separate red rose and white rose combine not to form a larger rose of either color (or a pink one that combines both), but the Tudor rose: an inner circle of white petals within an outer ring of red petals. The roses combine but keep their individual colors intact. It is an apt emblem of the hoped-for union between natives and Strangers, wherein each group retains some of its characteristic features. For the townspeople who saw the painted emblem, it functioned as a clear, simple image for how two might combine to form one.

This concept of unity through diversity occurred elsewhere throughout the week. It is present, for instance, in the intertwining of the serpent and dove on the Strangers' cup: "a Serpent enterfolding itselfe: in the middest whereof did site a Dove" (*JN2*, 804). The two are paradoxically yet harmoniously combined, but each retains its identifying characteristics: "Wise as the Serpent, and meeke as the Doue" (*JN2*, 804). It is also found in the epilogue to the second pageant: as the Queen passed under the triumphal arch and into the marketplace, the city waits played softly on their instruments while "one of them did sing this Dittie" (*JN2*, 799). Garter records the five stanzas of this song, which tells of classical goddesses striving good-naturedly for supremacy. Each goddess is associated with a particular quality or virtue: Juno, riches; Venus, love; Diana, chastity; Ceres, agricultural bounty; Pallas, prudence; and Minerva, eloquence. Jove adjudicates:

> My sweetes (quoth he) leaue of your sugred strife,
> In equall place I haue assignde you all:
> A soueraigne wight there is that beareth life,
> In whose sweete hart I have inclosde you all. (*JN2*, 799)

Of course, that sovereign wight is none other than Queen Elizabeth. The goddesses' reactions are also predictable: "They skipt for joy, and gave their franke consent." Nonetheless, this "dittie" goes beyond conventional praise of the monarch. Not only does it depict the Queen as a unifier—by bringing the striving goddesses into harmony and agreement—it depicts her as incorporating their individual virtues into her composite self. Their virtues are combined but still recognizably distinct in the person of Elizabeth. The word used by the Dutch Minister was "enterfold[ed]"; here it is "inclosde." Perhaps this is why the goddesses react with such contentment.

Again and again, the Norwich pageants offer illustrations of a type of unity that involves preserving the diversity of its component parts. This idea is even reflected in the accompanying soundscape, where the music for one of Churchyard's devices is described precisely in these terms. In preparation for the Queen's "rid[ing] abroade" on Thursday, Churchyard dug a "cave" in the ground outside of the city and filled it with twelve people dressed like water nymphs (JN2, 737).[199] These preparations called for musical accompaniment: "And in the same caue was a noble noyse of Musicke of al kind of instruments, seuerally to be sounded and played vpon, and at one time they shoulde be sounded all togither, that mighte serue for a consorte of broken Musicke" (JN2, 737–38). The effect was intended to be one of concordia discors, in which harmony arises from variety and difference. Here the source of harmony is dramatized: the instruments were first played separately and then dramatically combined "at one time" into a beautiful composition. Because of the deliberate set-up of the individual instruments, the audience was then prepped to recognize and distinguish them within the larger composition.[200] Thus, "broken Musicke" functions as another apt illustration of the particular type of unity that I have been describing.

City leaders probably did understand that if the Strangers remained in Norwich, a more thorough blending of the two groups would eventually occur. Particularly in an urban setting, intermarriage and integration were almost unavoidable. Indeed, such integration was already beginning to occur in the mid-1570s as Strangers and natives lived, worked, and worshipped side by side. In the larger pattern of Huguenot immigration, large populations did "become integrated in the end, but they did so imperceptibly—as it were, surreptitiously."[201] But in the historical moment of the Queen's visit—only thirteen years since the Strangers' arrival—it was much safer and more serviceable (for both groups) to imagine that the two groups might combine but preserve their distinctiveness.

Friendship

And yet, a final strand of the pageants does gesture toward a more thorough and intimate union of the two groups. On Friday, Master Limbert was asked to deliver a second oration to the Queen as she departed the city. This oration was not delivered because of time constraints, but it is clear from its planned timing and location that it was supposed to feature prominently and serve as a concluding or encapsulating statement.[202] This speech does imagine a sort of genuine amity or friendship between the two groups. Like many other speeches, Limbert's second oration is ostensibly focused on the Queen. It begins by asserting that those of "all ages and degrees" lament the departure of their Queen (*JN2*, 821). Limbert compares the populace to "sucking babes" who are being pulled "from the breastes and bosomes of their most loving mothers" and to "sonnes and fathers [sundered] through some miserable misfortune" (*JN2*, 822). Despite such implied trauma, Limbert professes the love, good will, obedience, and reverence of the assembled masses.

He then launches into a paean of friendship. This is a surprising rhetorical move, since friendship is typically seen as a union of equals (whereas Limbert's earlier analogies of babes to mothers and sons to fathers implies a seemingly more appropriate hierarchical relationship). But if friendship is not a great fit for talking about the Queen's relationship to her subjects, it is quite serviceable for describing the type of internal unity that the city leaders wanted to facilitate. "Great is the force of friendshippe and familiaritie," declares Limbert, "which oftentimes bringeth to passe, that they, which eyther by some kinde of fellowshippe, or by an accustomed condition of life, in tracte of time haue bin closely knitte, and so become both of one minde, and as it were growne togither, that hard and scant they may be seperated, & set in sunder" (*JN2*, 822). Limbert is explicitly glorifying friendship and describing the conditions of familiarity and time that help bring it about. It occurs, Limbert suggests, when people are brought together by "some kinde of fellowshipped or by an accustomed condition of life." This description might well apply to Strangers and natives, who had then been living in close proximity for the past thirteen years. Limbert also depicts what such friendship looks like: people become "closely knitte . . . of one minde, and as it were growne togither." In other words, they are united by a strong bond that is difficult to sever.

Limbert illustrates this dynamic state through the famed friendship of Theseus (mythical founder of Athens) and Pirithous (King of the Lapiths in Thessaly): "Hereof sprang the faithfulnesse of Theseus, commended by the mouth and monumentes of all men: and the entier friendshippe of innumerable more, whom no daungers, nor labours, eyther by sea or land, could sequester from their sweete society & comfortable company, with whom they long had liued" (*JN2*, 822). Here, Limbert treats friendship not as a commonplace relationship, but as an exalted ideal that is "commended by the mouth and monumentes of all men." By describing the state of friendship as "sweete society" and "comfortable company," he stresses the long-term benefits that accrue to those who live long together as friends.

A little bit later in the oration, Limbert provides a final illustration of friendship via the relationship between the soul and the body. He asserts, "Nature at no tyme tyed any thyng with a straighter knotte, or set seuerall things at greater agreement, than the soul and bodie" (*JN2*, 822). Typically, when this dichotomy is invoked, it is to register the tension between the two or to prioritize the soul at the expense of the body. Limbert, however, emphasizes their "agreement" and interconnectedness: "the incredible consent and concorde of them both, the mutual care and regard of succouring each other resting in them both: and the grieuous departing, at the houre of death, the one from the other remaynning in them both" (*JN2*, 822). This friendship involves not just comfortably living together, but actively caring for and succoring one another.[203] Friends are so intertwined with and involved with one another that, even when parted at death, each still retains something of the other. Having suggested that unity is desirable and that it is born of empathy, understanding, and diversity, the pageants now depict friendship as the full flowering and highest expression of unity. It is worth noting that despite their close union, the soul and body still retain their distinctiveness—so this analogy is consistent with earlier formulations of a unity that preserves its component parts.

In addressing the Queen, Limbert makes the conventional profession of love and obedience to the reigning monarch, but he also singles out the benefits that this type of friendship have produced. He points to the "peace and tranquilitie" of the twenty years of Elizabeth's reign and catalogues the "exceeding great daungers" that have been avoided—largely through wise policy rather than the use of force. Her reign has seen threats "extinguished, without any tumult at all, or very little (doubtlesse) insuing among the people" (*JN2*, 823). Though applied to the Queen's foreign and domestic policy, this state of affairs also accurately described the situation in Norwich over part of the same period. Since the Strangers' arrival in 1565, there had been some turbulence but, on the whole, tensions had been dealt with (if not quite extinguished) via policy and law rather than violence. This fruitful approach had served both England and Norwich well over the past two decades. Now, suggests Limbert, it is time to take the next step and let peace blossom into friendship: "Ought not then a singulare love and good-will to be lincked with that lawe, and necessitie of obedience?" (*JN2*, 823). To his earlier characterization of friendship as noble, strong, sweet, and intimate, Limbert now adds the tangible civic benefits of domestic order. A little bit later, he is even more insistent: "What is he for a man so savage and obstinate, whome these so singular and rare vertues may not allure to all love and allegiance?" (*JN2*, 823). Again, in all of these depictions of friendship, Limbert is ostensibly talking about the affection between the Queen and her subjects, but his glorification of friendship and concord would seem to have obvious applications to the local situation.

And yet it is not merely a case of Limbert speaking to the Queen while really addressing a secondary, more local audience. As we have seen elsewhere, the Queen is meant to demonstrate the specific virtues that the city leaders are encouraging their constituents to adopt. Because she herself embodies friendship, she can become a tangible model to emulate. At the same time, she can function as a locus around which further friendships might cohere. She is a sort of common ground: as natives and Strangers move toward her in friendship, they also move closer to one another.

Overall, the mayor and his court used the occasion of the Queen's 1578 visit to emphasize themes of unity that were serviceable to healing the divisions between the 6,000 Strangers and 10,000 natives that comprised Norwich's population. The pageants first establish the desirability of unity and then explore ways and contexts—empathy, diversity, friendship—in which it might be pursued. The entertainments rely on a number of different "media" to convey these messages, including formal orations, biblical and mythological characters, visual emblems, music, and prominent buildings. Most of these modes would have provided clear meanings that would have been accessible for those Strangers in attendance who did not yet speak English.[204] Unity is also subtly encouraged by the collective language that many of the pageant speakers employ. The mayor continually uses pronouns like "we," "us," and "our" (*JN2*, 789). Limbert claims to speak on behalf of "all these subiectes of Norwich" (*JN2*, 808)—as if they were a single people. Gurgunt similarly describes those within the city gates as "loyall subiects . . . / Whose hartes ful fast with perfect loue to thee do cleaue" (*JN2*, 792). Finally, the word "Norwich" sounds like a chime in many of the speeches. There are not one but two allegorical manifestations of the city: the "Commonwelth of the Citie" in the first pageant, and the "Cittie of Norwich" in the second pageant. The latter announces to the Queen that "My goods and lands, my hands and hart, my limbes and life are thine" (*JN2*, 796)—as if Norwich were a single entity with one heart, one life, and one will. The effect of all this collective language is to elide the normally prominent differences between the natives and the Strangers. The speakers refer to them as if they are already one unified people; they boldly construct a shared identity that did not quite exist.

But perhaps the most prominent tactic for nurturing this fledgling unity was to give it a clear focus around which it could cohere: the person of the Queen. Throughout the entertainments, Elizabeth is explicitly depicted as a unifier. Her past deeds and current policies reveal her understanding that "DIVISION kindled strife, / [But] Blist UNION quenchte the flame" (*JN2*, 792). She is also depicted as embodying the specific traits that allow unity to be constructed: empathy, diversity, and friendship. Her associations with Joseph, Deborah, Esther, and Judith suggest both that she knows what it is to be oppressed and that she is now particularly devoted to looking after the most vulnerable of her subjects. At the same time, her brand of unity (the Tudor Rose, the serpent, and the dove) is not homogeneity, but something that allows for and embraces the diversity of its component parts. Finally, Elizabeth is an embodiment of true and mutually beneficial friendship. She is thus set up as a sort of model that might encourage Norwich inhabitants to embrace similar values. Even more than that, she serves as a focus of shared identity and loyalty that might bring the two groups closer together. This is perhaps why Limbert, as he moves toward a final farewell at the end of his second oration, says, "Concerning your Maiestie, whose presence this day will shutte from our sight, we will notwithstanding in your absence behold and reuerence, we will loue youre Highnesse with all oure heartes, mindes, and endeauoures . . . your Maiesties good estate . . . we will commende to Almightie God in oure dayly Prayers" (*JN2*, 823–24). These sentiments go beyond lamenting her departure or offering well wishes. Instead, they imagine that the Queen, though physically absent, will persist as an object of love, reverence, and daily prayer. In other words, Limbert imagines that she can continue to be a unifying focus for the inhabitants of Norwich.

Epilogue

Did she? Or, at least, did the Strangers and natives become more unified as a result of the Queen's visit? It is difficult to say. The records of the Mayor's

Court suggest that there were far fewer complaints against the Strangers in the 1580s than there had been in the 1570s. In 1583, Strangers Adam Kynot and Jamys Wallwyn were brought before the court for buying "a great quantitee of corne" in the county and then selling it in the city, thus altering the price of corn citywide.[205] In 1584, some citizens complained that seven Strangers were buying commodities wholesale for retail purposes, "to the great decay of the citizens of this citty."[206] Yet these disputes revolved around general entrepreneurial behavior rather than the intractable rivalries of specific trades that we saw in the 1570s. Another thing that appears in the records is a pronounced attempt to stabilize the existing population of Norwich Strangers. In 1580, the Mayor's Court refused entry to two groups of arriving Strangers and "commaunded that they shalbe sent owte of this cytie."[207] City leaders also took pains to prevent natives from circumventing established immigrant protocols. In 1585, Henry Fond and Thomas Weavers were "specially commaunded . . . [to] not bryng any straungers or alyens into this citie but sutche as doo inhabitt and dwell therin allready."[208] The city authorities naturally wanted to control emigration, but they may also have been concerned that the fragile unity they were fostering not be continually undone by fresh arrivals from the Continent.

At the same time, the existing Stranger community took pains to safeguard the integrity of their presence in Norwich. In 1585, the "politique men" of both the Dutch and Walloon congregations submitted names of the "leawd," "wicked and ungodlye" among them that they wanted the Mayor's Court to banish from the city.[209] They then collaborated with city leaders to round up and send away these offending persons. The impression is that the existing, law-abiding Strangers did not want their growing stature and acceptance to be compromised by newcomers or loose cannons, so they worked with the city to safeguard the integrity of their population.[210]

The city leaders reciprocated by defending and supporting the existing Stranger population. In 1583, "one Nicholas Wryght, an informer, molested and troubled the Strangers, and they requested that he might be called on to answer for this."[211] The mayor and aldermen responded by writing to the Privy Council to complain about Wryght and affirm their support of the Strangers. The city and the Strangers also began to work together on issues of poor relief. In 1581, one Nicholas Beoscom—known as "the Pynner Duicheman" because of his skill in pin-making—was approached by three alderman about residing at the Great Hospital for "teaching of children his science of makyng pynnes."[212] In 1587 and 1589, both the Dutch and Walloon congregations had difficulty in meeting the needs of their poor, so the city stepped in to make up the difference.[213] This was a crucial first step toward erasing the distinctions between the native poor and the Stranger poor. Another key milestone came in 1598, when the Strangers were able to gain the freedom of the city and "allowed . . . to sell their goods on equal terms with other [native] freemen."[214] Such developments have prompted historians like John Pound to assert that "by the turn of the century, the major difficulties between the English and their alien counterparts had been overcome."[215]

Of course, it is difficult to say how much, if any, of this was a direct result of the 1578 entertainments. Certainly, some of these developments can be seen as part of the natural acculturation process that was bound to happen. The Strangers' growing acceptance was also likely helped by economic trends; as worsted production continued to decline, more and more of Norwich's workers came to participate in the production of the new draperies.[216] In addition, as Frank Meeres has shown, natives and Strangers intermarried with growing frequency in the 1580s and 1590s, and the children of these mixed couples were duly baptized in Norwich city churches.[217] Yet it is also worth noting that Norwich's integration of its Strangers was ahead of the curve nationally. A series of Parliamentary debates over the participation of foreigners in the retail trade took place in 1593.[218] This was not an isolated issue, but a manifestation of a developing "protectionist English nationalism" that was championed by none other than Walter Raleigh.[219] Centered in London, this line of thought was accompanied by "anti-alien activity" that included libels against foreigners.[220] Even though the 1593 parliamentary bill was defeated, the decade still saw "mounting xenophobia" following bad harvests in 1594 through 1598.[221] In contrast, complaints against Strangers in Norwich had all but ceased by the 1590s.

It is thus tempting to imagine that the 1578 pageant themes of unity, empathy, diversity, and friendship had found fertile ground amongst the city's inhabitants. At the very least, Queen Elizabeth seems to have understood what the city leaders were trying to accomplish. Upon her departure from Norwich, she gave £30 "towardes the relyffe of the poore straungers that ar remayning and dwelling in the Citie of Norwich."[222] In demonstrating her empathy for the poor, she would seem to have been enacting the principles of Limbert's speech before the Great Hospital. Significantly, she singled out the Strangers for beneficence, thereby indicating that they were a particularly vulnerable group. In fact, after giving money, "she especially recommended the Strangers to the Mayor and Aldermen, requesting that they should not be oppressed in any manner."[223] Despite the pageants' idealized representation of civic unity, the Queen knew that the actual dynamic between natives and Strangers was not perfect. Thus, her donation of £30 functioned as a symbolic gesture that publicly affirmed and supported the Strangers.[224] The city leaders made it into an even more ceremonial moment: They had the money conveyed to the Mayor's Court, where it was delivered in the presence of the Dutch and Walloon ministers to the respective deacons of each church.[225] This way of proceeding not only formally demonstrated the Queen's support for the Strangers, it also put the city's stamp of approval on it. The incident reflects the city's desire to model and foster a similar empathy and sympathy among the native populace. As in other parts of the entertainments, they used the Queen as both model and locus around which that response might cohere.

CONCLUSION

In the early seventeenth century, three black pears were added to the coat of arms of the city of Worcester. Traditionally, this change is associated with Queen Elizabeth I's 1575 progress visit. The story goes that as the Queen processed through the city streets, she noticed that the branches of several lovely pear trees were weighed down with ripe fruit. Elizabeth was impressed that the townspeople had refrained from surreptitiously picking and eating these plump pears. Imputing this restraint to the goodness and selflessness of Worcester's citizens, she made several favorable remarks on their behalf. What the Queen did not realize was that this particular variety of local pear was bitter to the taste and therefore undesirable to eat.[1] Naturally, the city officials did not bother to correct the Queen's misperception. Instead, they smiled knowingly and allowed her to believe that Worcesterians were indeed unusually courteous and deferential. Later, the city commemorated the native pear's role in facilitating the Queen's favor by adding it to its coat of arms. Today, the black pear continues to feature in city heraldry and has also been adopted by Worcester's cricket and rugby teams.

This story is not found in the official documents and may well be apocryphal. It is, however, a fitting emblem for the dynamic I have been describing in these six case studies. First, the anecdote nicely captures the overriding aim of urban hosts to create a positive impression that would be conducive to a good relationship between city and monarch.[2] These six cities were keen to idealize and embellish their existing characteristics so that they could be properly valued and appreciated by the center. The pear story is atypical in that it was a serendipitous occurrence rather than a carefully planned perception, and, indeed, it is this very unintentionality that makes the story so memorable. But in effect, it is not that different from Sandwich's exaggeration of its prosperity and importance, or Oxford's embellishment of its humanist culture, or

Norwich's construction of a fictional unity between its native and Stranger populations.

Moreover, all of these cities achieved their effects by manipulating local knowledge in order to control the Queen's perceptions. Everyone in Worcester knew that the black pear was not palatable, but they happily allowed the Queen to think otherwise. Other civic hosts leveraged their knowledge of the local economic, political, and religious situations to frame their requests. They actively deployed local topography, buildings, and activities to guide their visitors' perceptions in ways that that would be advantageous to their cities. The pear anecdote fits Worcester's aims perfectly because it reflects the city's particular strategy of using hospitality to facilitate reciprocity. The uneaten pears helped establish that the townspeople were generous, honorable, and selfless, and thus invited the Queen's economic intervention on their behalf. Finally, the pear's afterlife on the coat of arms illustrates the enduring significance of a royal visit. In all six of the cities chosen for this study, the Queen's visit entered the popular imagination and took on a life of its own; indeed, Elizabeth's visits are still proudly discussed and commemorated in these communities some 450 years later. Such continued commemoration reflects the hope of urban hosts that the visit would continue to resonate in the form of future consideration and future benefits.

These six chapters have provided detailed examinations of Queen Elizabeth I's visits to six English cities between 1566 and 1578. Unlike most treatments of the royal progress, mine has focused on the town's perspective and tried to describe their imaginative response to the enormous opportunity of hosting the reigning monarch. I have first of all sought to establish the precise local context of each visit by identifying the particular problems or challenges that mattered most to each town in the year of the Queen's visit. In Worcester it was the economy, in Canterbury religion, in Oxford education, in Sandwich topographical decline, in Bristol rebellion, and in Norwich immigration. In examining these historical backdrops, this book has shed light on a number of underemphasized sixteenth-century domestic issues and explored how they were negotiated on the local level. At the same time, these local issues were inevitably tied to larger, national developments that characterized the mid-Elizabethan period, including the rise of Puritanism, the challenges faced by the wool industry, the influx of religious refugees, and the growing concerns of internal rebellion and foreign invasion. With these contexts in hand, I have then provided careful analyses of the entertainments that town leaders devised to "speak to" and influence their royal visitors. Civic hosts used the occasion to subtly broach local needs and concerns, influence crown policies, and cultivate potential patrons who could give them much-needed channels of access to the center. Of the Queen's eighty-three visits to towns during her numerous progresses, records of only ten have survived in any detail. Thus, these six case studies are well positioned to add to our understanding of early modern civic pageantry and also fill in gaps about the other urban visits that we know less about. What sort of patterns do these six visits reveal?

Pageantry

Queen Elizabeth I's visits to these six English cities deepen our understanding of the most conventional aspects of civic pageantry: devices and orations. Most cities featured pageant devices that are consistent with what we find in Lord Mayor's shows of the same time period. That is, they take the form of temporary scaffolds erected in the streets that were decorated with painted images, inscribed with short captions, and mounted by costumed characters who gave speeches or participated in some sort of dramatic tableaux. Pageant devices at Worcester, Norwich, Sandwich, and Bristol featured a rich variety of characters and stories taken from the Bible, classical mythology, local history, and allegory. For example, the Norwich entry featured King Gurgunt, the "Commonwelth of the Citie," eight weavers, three biblical personages (Deborah, Esther, and Judith), and Martia, an ancient English queen. As at Norwich, most of these devices were employed during the royal entry, though Sandwich's lone device was saved for the Queen's departure. As these examples suggest, English towns had an established set of pageant conventions to draw from by the 1560s, but these same conventions could be modified and tailored to their specific purposes. It is worth noting that neither Oxford nor Canterbury featured this sort of formal pageant device. Their receptions were presided over by university officials and Archbishop Matthew Parker, respectively, rather than by civic corporations. It may be that city streets were a less appropriate venue for these hosts because they directed institutions that were geographically within but legally separate from the urban community. Both hosts did arrange highly performative equivalents—the university staged plays and held formal disputations, whereas Archbishop Parker orchestrated a highly theatrical cathedral worship service—but these events took place in venues that better suited the purview of their leaders. At any rate, this pattern suggests that pageant devices were more of a tool for corporation hosts.

As we have seen, these devices were not used to merely praise and flatter the Queen. Instead, they helped demonstrate civic values and themes that laid the groundwork for the city's appeal. Thus, Salutation, Gratulation, and Obedient Goodwill all drew their swords at Bristol to dramatically demonstrate the military vigilance the city wanted to be associated with. At Norwich, King Gurgunt provided an origin myth for acculturating recent immigrants and also articulated the city's ancient tradition of taking in persecuted refugees. Finally, at Sandwich, the weaving device served to demonstrate both the importance of the city's textile economy and its corresponding relationship to the viability of the decaying Haven.

These pageant devices were often supplemented by formal orations that helped explain or reinforce intended meanings. Many occured during the royal entry in the form of welcome speeches. For example, Bell's oration at Worcester broaches the city's main economic concerns and even proposes solutions. At Oxford, the Queen was welcomed by no fewer than seven speeches. Other orations were then made throughout the week and at the Queen's departure. In Norwich, they augmented the theme of unity by addressing its component parts of empathy, diversity, and friendship. Meanwhile, Bristol's mock battles incorporated allegorical speakers to explain that the city's love of peace was not incompatible with martial values.

These orations were delivered by a range of different speakers. City officers like the mayor or recorder were natural mouthpieces for a city's message. But less official orators also addressed the Queen, including schoolmasters, soldiers, ministers, regius professors, and children. The identity of a spokesperson could itself be a reflection of civic values: Allowing the Dutch minister to address the Queen was a powerful way for Norwich leaders to publicly validate the presence of the Strangers. Similarly, regius professors delivered some of Oxford's welcome speeches because they were apt emblems of the sort of royal patronage that the university hoped to perpetuate. Although speakers' own perspectives may have entered into their words and sentiments, both circumstantial and documentary evidence suggests that the goals of the city corporation (and university) were guiding these key rhetorical moments.

The prominence of orations in these case studies is in keeping with David Bergeron's claim that English pageants invested significantly in the written and spoken word. In fact, several cities created textual versions of their entertainments. At Worcester and Oxford, copies of welcome speeches were presented to the royal visitors. During the mock battle at Bristol, one of the soldiers swam across the Avon to give the Queen a book "which vttred the hoell substance of this deuice." At Elizabeth's departure from Sandwich, the mayor handed her a written petition for her assistance in saving the harbor. And, of course, contemporary printings of Bristol and Norwich entertainments gave those royal visits a wide circulation.

Those texts served to crystallize and reinforce pageant themes and also to ensure that civic messages would endure even after the otherwise ephemeral substance of the pageants had "melted into air." As we saw in the Introduction, such texts can not only preserve, but also idealize and add to the entertainments. Neale's *Topographica Delineato* is a good example. Since the Queen did not actually see most of the Oxford colleges, Neale's book offered a verbal and pictorial tour that took her inside the university's hallowed spaces. The *Delineato* prefaces the tour with a fictional dialogue between the Queen and Leicester that effectively models the response that Oxford wanted the actual Queen to have to her university visit. Thus, supplemental texts imaginatively reinforced the larger goals of entertainment hosts.

In between her formal entry and departure, the Queen was treated to an array of other interactions with her civic hosts, including mock battles, religious services, feasts, plays, academic exercises, and hunting excursions. Many of these activities do not fit neatly into the conventional categories of pageant devices and orations, so they are often overlooked or seen as less important parts of the royal reception. Yet these events were not meant solely to entertain the Queen and pass the time. They frequently involved activities that were either vital to the city or helped distinguish it from other urban centers. Mock battles were an assertion of the strategic importance and military preparedness of Sandwich and Bristol; debates, lectures, and plays at Oxford were meant to illustrate the depth and practical value of humanist culture; and Elizabeth's birthday feast at Canterbury served to demonstrate how clerical magnificence could function as an effective consensus-building tool. These activities were thus a key part of how civic hosts presented themselves and framed requests for aid, consideration, and patronage.

These case studies also reveal that English civic hosts were well aware of the rich possibilities of festival practice. They adroitly used processional modes like music, food, topography, movement, color, clothing, regalia, gifts, space, and architecture in order to leaven their ceremonial dialogues. For example, sound played a supplementary role in many of the entertainments. The most frequently utilized sounds were cannons, bells, and musical accompaniment. Two of the cites (Bristol and Norwich) had their own city waits that participated in processionals. These auditory elements not only added a soundscape to the royal visit, they could also underscore important pageant themes. Sound was especially important in Bristol, where cannons, city waits, and bell-ringing all contributed to the martial display. At Norwich, "broken music" served as an emblem of the particular type of harmony that the corporation was keen to endorse. Finally, at Canterbury, church music both added to Parker's display of magnificence and also helped defend the value of the cathedral in the post-Reformation English religious landscape.

Clothing also featured prominently in many of these receptions. City preparations reveal detailed plans for cleaning existing apparel and purchasing new. The robes of city officers, the livery gowns of guild members, and the uniforms of soldierly escorts and mock-battle participants draw special mention. At Norwich, the recorded sartorial details include satin doublets, taffeta hats, silver lace, and velvet coats. Not surprisingly, vibrant colors were the norm. At Worcester, the "faier and comelye" costumes of the participants were scarlet, black, mulberry, violet, and red. At Bristol, the red, blue, and yellow uniforms of the trained bands were similarly arresting. All of these details suggest that clothing was an important part of the visual pageantry and that it, too, could be used to convey meaning. At Oxford, the differing robes of the doctors, masters, bachelors, and younger scholars helped the university project an image of order, specialization, and self-contained sufficiency. At Bristol, having the militia in the city colors helped strengthen the desired connection between the city, its trained bands, and military preparedness.

These case studies also attest to the diversity of ceremonial props that were used in English entertainments. Among the most frequent was the city mace. At Worcester (and most other cities), this symbol of civic authority was featured prominently in the royal entry, where it was yielded to the Queen, redelivered to the city, and then borne before the city officers as they led the monarch through the streets. Bristol accentuated another piece of regalia: the civic sword. The corporation commissioned a new scabbard prior to the Queen's visit so that during the processional it could be borne aloft and signify both the city's martial prowess and its loyalty to the Queen. Elsewhere, other props played significant roles, including the "murderer" artillery piece at Sandwich, the throne of St. Augustine and the tombs of his successors at Canterbury, and the carved statues of Worcester cathedral.

In addition, all six cities welcomed the Queen and asserted their devotion to her through strategic gift-giving. Such largesse was already a familiar mode for cities who regularly gave gifts to honor local gentry and other patrons. The scale of this practice was naturally heightened for a royal progress. Most host cities adhered to the traditional expectation of a piece of plate (usually a silver cup) or a monetary gift. But even within this category, cities could send a tailored message. Sandwich gave the Queen an unusually valuable cup for a town of its size in a calculated attempt to suggest that it was more prosperous than it actually was. At Norwich, the Strangers used their otherwise conventional gift of a cup to draw a biblical parallel between themselves and the Queen. Other hosts proffered less conventional gifts, including a gilt tankard, a salt cellar, spiced wine, horses, and books. Each of these gifts was chosen deliberately to further a particular agenda. As we have seen, Archbishop Parker was especially thoughtful in selecting books for various audiences in the royal retinue. The most unusual offering was Oxford's gift of honorary degrees. This gesture did not cost the university anything, yet it asserted that a university education was among the most valuable gifts anyone could receive. At Worcester, in the Queen's own gift of venison to the city officers, we even see something of the code of exchange that gift-giving could initiate.

Along with these tangible forms of civic image-making, hosts also exploited the subtleties of processional movement, space, and architecture. In determining which parts of the urban fabric were seen (and not seen), processional routes could shape the Queen's experience of the city. This strategy is seen most dramatically in Sandwich, where the entry route was altered to highlight the town's defensive structures, and where for the rest of the visit the Queen was deliberately kept in the immediate vicinity of the town's bustling harbor. As the Sandwich visit reveals, towns had a good bit of agency in determining Elizabeth's movements because they selected where she lodged and what venues hosted activities during the week. While the Queen moved between these locations, city leaders could emphasize the more impressive parts of their town's fabric and feature particular buildings, landmarks, and views. Even when the Queen's itinerary was subject to circumstances outside the city's control—such as which direction the Queen would arrive from and depart to—the city corporation had advance notice so it could plan activities at the appropriate city gate. In Norwich, the corporation successfully piggy-backed on

Elizabeth's excursions to visit local gentry by "intercepting" her on her return and highlighting key buildings that lay in her path.

In all of these encounters, cities showed a penchant for deploying space in meaningful ways. Some of the urban spaces that featured in these case studies included streets, harbors, markets, suburbs, military parade grounds, fields, gardens, heaths, libraries, halls, chapels, cloisters, rivers, courtyards, and quad-rangles. Many of these spaces had pre-existing associations—commercial, reli-gious, martial—that cities could activate and emphasize in their ceremonial dialogues. As Hester Lees-Jeffries reminds us, a city is not "an empty stage or blank page," but a sort of "text" that already inscribes "historical association, communal memory, and accumulated civic pride."[3] Thus, Bristol had the Queen spend three days on a viewing platform in its military "marsh," whereas Oxford immersed its visitors in the colleges, public schools, and other academic spaces of the university. These spaces were often embellished and appropriated to serve particular ends. Bristol sanded and leveled its marsh and also constructed temporary architecture to more tightly integrate its military space with the rest of the city. Similarly, Worcester used the contrast between its suburbs and city center to dramatize the welcome oration's claims of decay and revival. Other spaces could be reshaped completely: at Oxford, the church (St. Mary's) that hosted the three days of formal disputations was dramatically transformed into an intellectual theater that glorified humanist learning. These examples suggest that early modern civic hosts had a keen understanding of how the construction and organization of space could generate meaning.

English cities further exploited the possibilities of space during royal pro-gresses in two additional ways. One of them involves what Margit Thøfner refers to as an "aesthetic of processions"; in the Low Countries, it was associ-ated with a beautifully coordinated procession of a well-disciplined militia.[4] For contemporaries, its appeal was in the "subordination of individual dress and deportment to the co-ordinated behavior of a group."[5] A similar militaristic effect was created at Sandwich and Bristol, with their carefully choreographed mock battles. But this aesthetic was also present, I would argue, in Worcester and Norwich, where the towns' receptions featured long lines of guild mem-bers standing at attention in their colorful robes. It can also be seen at Oxford and Cambridge, with their careful hierarchical groupings of bachelors, mas-ters, and doctors. As at Antwerp, the common denominator was in the large groups of people who were carefully arranged and functioning together. It is no accident that this sounds like an apt metaphor for effective civic government.

By featuring a large, diverse, and orderly assemblage of people, town leaders demonstrated their own mastery of space, which was, by extension, a way of showing their competence, authority, and political aptitude. Such demonstrations also functioned as part of the city's idealized portrayal of itself as orderly, disciplined, and worthy of the Queen's trust and support.

A second spatial possibility exploited by towns is the dynamic of situating an imaginative world within a real world. As Bergeron puts it: "The pageant stands at the intersection of fiction and reality because it occurs in real time (an actual occasion and real place) and yet evokes a fictional world through emblematic techniques and historical allusion."[6] English civic pageantry of the sixteenth century sought to create an idealized or heightened version of the city, and it did so in ways that were obviously fictional (scaffolding, costumes, allegorical figures, and so forth). Yet because this imagined world was anchored in the reality of the actual city—it took place in the actual streets and among its actual residents—this fiction seems more real, more immediate, and more attainable than it otherwise might be. For towns, this makes civic pageantry more powerful than any Westminster petition could ever be. With the latter, the town must ask the distant monarch to perceive the town's need, understand why their request is so important, and imagine how her assent might transform the town. But with the former, the town can vividly demonstrate each of these elements. Pageantry can also shrink the gap between the imagined world and the real world. A mock battle, though fictional, can dramatize the actual military prowess of Bristol's trained bands. Similarly, Norwich's pageantry exaggerates the harmony between religious refugees and city natives, but it does so in an attempt to actually bring the two groups closer together. The most dramatic example of this dynamic, however, is Sandwich's decision to use the Haven as the setting for its mock battle. By causing its visitors to gaze upon the decayed Haven while they simultaneously watched a vivid re-enactment of its former glories, Sandwich could memorably assert its potential for a revitalized role in England's coastal defenses.

Finally, these case studies reveal the profound ways in which English cities used architecture to speak to their royal visitors. Though many constructed scaffolds for pageant devices and forts for mock battles, these cities were less likely to create elaborate temporary structures than were their Continental counterparts. Whereas Rome and Vienna might erect triumphal arches, obelisks, and porticos to transform their cityscapes, English cities were keen to emphasize their existing buildings. The six entertainments studied in this volume have featured a diverse range of permanent structures, including houses, guildhalls, high crosses, walls, gates, bridges, markets, quays, parish churches, cathedrals, grammar schools, colleges, hospitals, jails, palaces, castles, fortifications, and even ruined abbeys. City records reveal that many of these buildings were carefully repaired, refurbished, and repainted in preparation for the Queen's arrival. Sometimes the subsequent reception featured old buildings, as when Parker used the medieval cathedral, bishop's palace, and abbey to underscore the longevity and ancient dignities of the episcopacy. Other receptions highlighted new buildings. At Oxford, university officials immersed the royal visitors in the newly constructed splendor of Christ Church in order to promote the new learning to a new class of people.

Cathedrals, guildhalls, and city gates were some of the structures most commonly featured in these entertainments. The Queen attended services in the cathedrals of Worcester, Bristol, Norwich, and Canterbury. Given that these religious spaces were the most grandiose and ornate buildings of each city, it is not surprising that they were part of the itinerary. And yet, each of these four cities used their cathedral to speak to the Queen in a particular way. In Worcester and Canterbury, hosts utilized the full fabric of the building, including its nave, choir, tombs, chantries, chapter house, thrones, sculptures, and carvings. As the seats of civic authority, guildhalls were natural processional stops, and they featured in Bristol, Worcester, and Norwich, three of the four cities that were hosted by corporations. In the case of the latter two, the corporation even painted the Queen's arms on the exterior of the building. This gesture would have conveyed the corporation's loyalty to the Queen while also reminding those they governed of the higher power from which they drew their authority. Finally, city walls and gates—physical demarcations of urban space as well as imposing structures in their own right—featured prominently in royal entries and departures. They were typically refurbished beforehand, embellished with decoration, and chosen as sites for speeches and pageant devices. For example, King Gurgunt delivered his oration outside St. Stephens Gate, Norwich, which was adorned with heraldic emblems, poetic verses, and a Tudor rose.

This study also suggests that the Queen's lodgings were chosen with special care. In these six cities, she stayed in two bishop's palaces (Worcester, Norwich), two private residences (Bristol, Sandwich), a college (Oxford), and in her own occasional royal palace (Canterbury). As temporary residences during her time in each city, these lodgings served as the places where the Queen ate, slept, dressed, received informal visitors, and spent the majority of her time. They also provided her a second, more intimate host within the larger hosting of the city. For all these reasons, the Queen's lodging was carefully selected and could even play a role in pageant themes. Sandwich chose Manwood House because it was a large edifice with elaborate furnishings; owned by a prominent local courtier with intimate knowledge of the Cinque Ports; and had previously been visited by Elizabeth's father, Henry VIII. Further, the house's location provided a sweeping view of the very harbor that was the object of Sandwich's appeal for royal aid. The evidence suggests that other lodgings may have been chosen based on their topographical locations or the vistas they provided. At Canterbury, Parker deliberately wanted Elizabeth to stay at her own royal palace because it provided "one of the grandest ecclesiastical views in all of England," including the ruined magnificence of St. Augustine's Abbey. At Oxford, the Queen's position on the east side of the unfinished quadrangle at Christ Church helped serve as a visible invitation for royal patronage.

Some hosts emphasized the entire cityscape rather than a particular building. As the Queen departed Coventry in 1566, upon reaching the town's outer limits, "at the request of the maior she turned her horse and Loked toward the citie wheyre she might presently viewe and behold the Scituacion thereof."[7] No doubt the mayor hoped to delight the Queen with a panoramic view, but he also wanted to convey a final impression of the town as beautiful, orderly, and advantageously sited. There are numerous similar—though less formal—moments in these case studies. For example, Worcester officers and guild-members positioned themselves to welcome the Queen at Salt Lane End, just where the road curved in from the northeast, providing a dramatic view of the city. At Norwich, the Queen's procession was made to linger just inside St. Stephen's Gate, where the weighty Norman castle and soaring cathedral spire dominated the horizon.

As these examples suggest, cities deliberately featured structures that would contribute to the image they hoped to project to royal visitors. For example, Sandwich sought to appear prosperous by refurbishing its fifteenth-century timber-framed houses and then featuring them on the processional route along High Street and Strand Street. In other cities, the monarch's attention was focused squarely on a particular building, such as the Archbishop's Palace in Canterbury or Christ Church College in Oxford. As with space, many buildings possessed existing or embedded associations that the town could use to its advantage. Sandwich was able to highlight and embellish its existing defensive structures in order to play up its strategic importance. Similarly, since Canterbury cathedral was the recognized epicenter of the English episcopacy, Parker could use this building's visual splendor, prelatical associations, and beautiful music to demonstrate the majesty of orthodox worship.

Other buildings might have less obvious existing meanings, but could be, as Frank suggests, "adapt[ed] . . . to new purposes" and even have their meanings "imaginatively reassigned" by their participation in festival.[8] At Oxford, both Christ Church hall and St. Mary's Church were deliberately transformed into Roman spaces in order to further the university's association with humanist culture. At Canterbury, the chapter house cum sermon hall became an emblem of the adaptability and relevance of the post-Reformation cathedral. In some instances, English cities used temporary architecture alongside permanent architecture to imbue the latter with new meanings. At Bristol, the temporary forts served the practical function of providing structures to be defended and besieged in the mock battle, but they also made Bristol seem more militaristic. Since these forts were sited just beyond the city's actual stone walls, they added to the hoped-for impression that Bristol was well-equipped to maintain order in the west.

At their most potent, buildings become a way to visibly symbolize city values and convey meanings. By arranging for certain orations to be delivered in front of Blackfriars Hall and the Great Hospital, Norwich leaders were able to both endorse the Strangers and foreground empathy for the downtrodden as a core civic virtue. In these six cities, buildings even provided entry points into the patronage relationships that hosts were so eager to form with their progress visitors. At Worcester, the cathedral and its two royal tombs were used to assert a pre-existing and mutually beneficial patronage relationship between the city and the crown. Oxford was especially thorough in using its existing buildings to cultivate patronage. It lauded Elizabeth's forebears for their contributions to the university's fabric, gave her a book that depicted college buildings as living legacies of their founders, and lodged her in an unfinished college that might serve as a suitable object of her largesse. Finally, buildings could even serve as emblems for the form that a patronage relationship might take. At Sandwich, the grammar school was meant to illustrate a highly collaborative and successful past approach that might now be fruitfully applied to the repair of the harbor.

Overall, these six receptions exhibit a variety of festival modes, including pageant devices, orations, sound, clothing, props, gifts, processional movement, space, and architecture. By skillfully combining these different elements, our civic hosts were able to create rhetorically complex performances with a heightened "unity of meaning."[9] Bristol's military preparedness could thus be simultaneously expressed in allegorical speeches, mock battles, sound, clothing, and civic regalia. At the same time, as Kathleen Ashley asserts, such "multi-layered performance[s]" can also "create multiple meanings" for different audiences.[10] A single pageant element might construct civic identity, flatter Elizabeth, and also invite a courtier to take a more active interest in town affairs. At Norwich, many of the episodes are ostensibly talking to and about the Queen, but they are simultaneously instructing the native and Stranger populations on the finer points of empathy, concord, and diversity.

Cities

Because civic entertainments both project an image of the city to outsiders and construct civic identity for its own residents, they can help us understand how cities were defined and perceived in Elizabethan England.[11] One clear tendency of the entertainments was to carefully define the geographical footprint of the city. Both the welcome and departure ceremonies typically occurred at the outer edges of the city liberties (which marked the corporation's jurisdictional parameters). Liberties often began more than a mile from the built-up area of the urban environment, so they were not obvious visual markers of city parameters. However, highlighting them helped cities augment their size and importance. This practice was especially notable at Oxford, where the university delegation was able to greet the Queen before the city corporation, since the liberties of the former began one mile beyond the latter. As the Queen and her retinue drew closer to the city proper, they encountered suburbs— narrow strips of houses on the main roads leading into the city—and arrived at the walls and gates. These structures both defined the main built-up area of the city and served as gateways into the urban community. Because gates were so important as thresholds, they often hosted progress welcomes. Once inside, the procession moved slowly through the main streets, passing public buildings, churches, prominent houses, market crosses, and other key structures. These locations were often featured either during the entry or later in the week, thus establishing their importance as markers of civic identity. Such a role is underscored by the tendency to repair or beautify these buildings prior to the royal visit. Overall, these six studies reveal that urban communities followed this general pattern of highlighting their liberties, walled areas, streets, public spaces, and prominent buildings as key components of the city's physical identity.

Entertainment content added important—if less tangible—components to these cities' self-definition. Welcome speeches often detailed the city's origin, privileges, importance, and form of government. Subsequent pageant devices and speeches might celebrate local history (Norwich) or underscore chief economic activities (Worcester). We even get discussions of distinctive city values, as when Bristol explains how its love of peace and commerce nonetheless gives rise to a particular type of martial valor. Other cities identify their contributions to the nation as a key part of their identity. Thus, Canterbury facilitates and defends orthodox religion, Sandwich is a key link in the chain of coastal defense, and Oxford provides well-educated and practical civil servants. All of these categories helped urban communities establish their distinctiveness and elucidate how they wanted to be seen and valued by the center.

Pageant practices also suggested that cities were seen as *human* communities that were comprised of different categories of people. Though a range of stakeholders participated in hosting the monarch, the most prominent group was typically the city corporation. As we have seen in Bristol, Sandwich, Norwich, and Worcester, the mayor, city officers, and other councilmen were chiefly responsible for preparing the city and planning its entertainments. These leaders also functioned as the face of the city during the royal reception. During the entry, they met the Queen at the outer liberties, proffered her a gift on behalf of the city, and led the procession back through town. During the week, a delegation of officers visited the Queen, escorted her on excursions, and delivered the formal farewell at her departure. The corporation's ceremonial prominence underscored its dual role as local leaders and as mediators between the urban community and the central government—supporting Robert Tittler's observation that towns were becoming more oligarchic over the course of the sixteenth century and that they often used civic ritual to validate and legitimize their authority. Of course, city corporations were never monolithic and contained within themselves a number of competing interests and factions. Such divisiveness was generally not visible during a royal reception, where, as Mary Hill Cole reminds us, local officials tended to be united by a common purpose. Nevertheless, we can detect a few fissures at Norwich, where the pro-Stranger part of the mayor's court seems intent on convincing not only the townspeople but other councilmen of the worth of the recent immigrants.

However, if the corporation was the ceremonial face of the city, it was only part of the civic body. These pageant receptions feature a number of other local citizens who did not hold elected office. At Worcester, the members of the economic guilds play a significant role in the entry. At Bristol, it is the trained bands who not only participate in the mock battle, but also serve as her majesty's personal escorts throughout the week. At Norwich, local religious and educational leaders have significant interactions with the Queen. And at Sandwich, the jurat's wives feast the Queen at the local grammar school. The participation of these groups suggests that they were perceived as a crucial part of the urban community with special roles to play. There is a similar dynamic at Canterbury and Oxford, where church and university leaders involve other key constituencies. At Oxford, the vice chancellor and the heads of colleges are the main hosts, but they solicit the help of faculty, students, alumni, and other administrators in the entertainments. At Canterbury, Archbishop Parker utilizes the prebends as lodging hosts and as exemplars of the sort of scholarship that had grown up in the fertile soils of the cathedral community.

Beyond these particular groups, civic receptions also relied on the participation of the townspeople as a whole. Artisans, craftsmen, laborers, shopkeepers, merchants, and innkeepers were all heavily involved in the preparation and execution of the royal reception. They sanded roads, painted houses, removed dung heaps, brewed beer, built scaffolds, lodged and fed members of the Queen's retinue, and (at Worcester) tended hundreds of the visitors' horses without incident. Their most important role may have been to serve as an engaged audience that filled the streets and registered the city's enthusiasm for hosting the Queen. As Cole remarks, "Without this nonofficial participation of the larger body of citizenry, the queen would have entered the town in silence and obscurity. For the ceremonial dialogue to exist, an involved observing crowd needed to fill the civic arena."[12] The crowd played an especially important role at Worcester, where its clapping, shouting, and lighting of torches not only provided a festive backdrop, it also strengthened the rapport—and bonds of reciprocity—that Worcester sought to create.

Why did the average citizen participate so willingly in hosting the Queen? It is true that, as at Sandwich, some preparatory measures were mandatory and fines were stipulated for noncompliance. But no one was forced to stand in the streets and cheer the Queen. Most townspeople probably did so because they realized that this was a momentous occasion—for themselves and their city—and they wanted to put their best foot forward. It is possible that the occasion stirred a latent sense of pride or loyalty to their native city. But as these case studies reveal, individual citizens often had a personal stake in the local issue that was being broached by the pageant entertainments. At Worcester and Sandwich, the health of the textile industry and the silting of the Haven affected almost everyone in some way. One did not have to be a member of the civic corporation to understand the value of making a good impression on the monarch. It is worth noting that the average citizen experienced the progress visit as both an audience member and as a participant. As audience members, they witnessed ceremonies that validated the corporation's authority and reinforced the hierarchical relationships that structured civic life. They were thus the recipients of a particular vision of the city that their leaders were constructing. But as active participants, the townspeople assisted in hosting the monarch and articulating the city's needs. These contributions helped validate their membership in the urban community and strengthen their partnership with other parts of the hierarchy. Finally, because they were participants in—rather than passive recipients of—the civic ideal that the pageants constructed, they may have been more likely to espouse this particular vision of what their city was and what it might be. I am not arguing that this always happened during a royal visit, but merely that it *could* be a galvanizing moment in the life of the town. Early modern hosts seemed to realize this too, which is why Norwich in particular tried to use the occasion of the Queen's visit to unify its local population.

At the same time, early modern cities were not only composed of the governed and their governors. These case studies reveal the tendency of urban communities—particularly during the royal progress—to broaden the definition of the city in order to partner with local and regional men of influence. At Sandwich, Sir Roger Manwood was an integral part of the Queen's reception. Though born in the town, Manwood's primary seat was then at Hackington (just outside Canterbury), and he had pursued a courtly career that had culminated in his appointment to national office in 1572. Nevertheless, he hosted the Queen at his old Sandwich residence and lent his considerable local legal knowledge to help make the case for royal aid. At Worcester, Sir James Croft arrived as a privy councilor and member of the Queen's entourage, but because of his status as a regional magnate, he was marked out as a special friend of the city. Such inclusiveness is typical of the progress receptions examined in this book. Yet cities were also cautious in selecting potential patrons; Bristol and Worcester were particularly wary of giving any share of influence to local gentry who might rival or complicate their authority.

City partnerships with men of influence also included clerical leaders who had local connections. At Worcester, the Queen was hosted by Bishop Nicholas Bullingham and lodged in his ecclesiastical palace. As a native Worcesterian and brother-in-law to Mayor Christopher Dighton, the bishop gave the corporation access to Elizabeth and helped facilitate its appeal for economic aid. At Canterbury, Archbishop Parker emphasized his friendship to the city by highlighting the contributions of past archbishops to the city fabric and by inviting the current corporation officers to the Queen's birthday feast. In doing so, he illustrated the fruitful ways in which church dioceses could collaborate with local authorities. This is why Bristol's corporation objected to the Diocese of Bristol being held in commendam by the Bishop of Gloucester, and why it sought a resident bishop instead.

Overall, these progress entertainments reflect a notably expansive definition of the city. Under normal circumstances, corporations tended to be restrictive, as they regulated who had the freedom of the city, when local farmers could enter to sell their produce, and which outside influencers might hold offices or represent the city in Parliament. But during the royal progress, they sought to add to the ranks of the urban community rather than exclude people from it. More than anything, city leaders wanted to build a coalition that would support the city and look after its interests. This is why their entertainments tended to treat existing patrons as "one of their own" and to welcome potential patrons with open arms. The best example is at Oxford, where honorary degrees were used both to graft recipients into the university community and to give them responsibility for safeguarding and expanding Oxford's privileges. As this model of patronage solicitation suggests, those who esteemed the city, had its interests at heart, and would support it could justly be said to be a part of that city.

Patrons

It is because of urban leaders' desire to build a coalition that civic entertainments would attempt to speak to a wide variety of target audiences. Naturally, Queen Elizabeth I was the primary audience. As the reigning monarch, she had considerable power to affect the very areas—economy, religion, military, immigration—that these cities sought assistance with. For example, she could step in and offer direct royal assistance with a silted harbor, as she had previously done at Dover. With a single document, she could create policies with the Dutch and Spanish that would materially affect Worcester's broadcloth industry. But even if she did not step in directly, the Queen was at the apex of the national patronage system and could influence others below her to address the needs of these cities. She could prod nobles or wealthy merchants to found an Oxford college. She could lean on her privy councilors as they set priorities and carried out their duties. The Queen expected people that she had elevated to be public benefactors, and she might easily suggest the form that their largesse would take.

Nevertheless, early modern cities did not put all of their eggs in Elizabeth's basket or rely on the theoretical trickle-down effect of patronage. During the royal progress, they attempted to speak to a variety of secondary audiences. Chief among these was the Privy Council. Since the business of the realm was still being conducted during summer progresses, many PCs accompanied the Queen on her travels—particularly that core group of seven to ten councilors that included Burghley, Leicester, Sussex, Lincoln, Walsingham, Knollys, and Croft. The Elizabethan Privy Council wielded considerable power in the policy areas that most affected these towns and was seen as something of a problem-solver for the localities. The council also gave formal advice to the Queen, which she often heeded. It is therefore not surprising that PC members were singled out for special gifts at Worcester and Canterbury, given honorary degrees at Oxford, and made privy to the suit for the Sandwich Haven. These case studies reveal that cities tended to target individual members instead of just making a blanket appeal to the entire council. Burghley and Leicester were natural targets for cities, since the former was Lord Treasurer and the latter was a proven patron of urban communities. It did not hurt that both men enjoyed particularly close relationships with Queen Elizabeth. Proximity to the monarch may also explain why Hatton (whose star was on the rise) was honored with attentions at Canterbury and why Knollys (the Queen's cousin-in-law) was given an honorary degree at Oxford.

Other PCs may have been appealed to because of their realm of political influence. For instance, Bristol and Sandwich both catered to Lincoln (the Lord High Admiral), while Oxford's singling out of Burghley may have been linked to his position as Master of the Court of Wards. A privy councilor's geographical power base could also be a factor. Worcester proffered gifts of hippocras to four councilors, but chose to distinguish Croft—whose power base was in the region—with the more lavish gift of a gilt tankard. At times, hosts even sought to influence PCs who might be predisposed *against* their viewpoint. Parker's show of episcopal magnificence may have been partially to influence the Puritan-leaning Burghley and Leicester. At the same time, Parker attempted to widen his position even further by giving extravagant gifts to the more Catholic-leaning Lincoln and Hatton. Like other civic hosts, Parker understood the prudence of influencing not only friends but also those who could potentially obstruct the need that was being articulated.

Besides privy councilors, many other adherents accompanied the Queen on her civic visits, including courtiers, nobles, bishops, local gentry, foreign ambassadors, household officers, musicians, heralds, and a large train of servants for feeding and clothing the itinerant court. Host cities responded by casting as wide a patronage net as possible. At Canterbury, the categories of people that Parker gave gifts to included the Queen, privy councilors, "certain noble individuals and councillors in the hall," "ladies and noblewomen," and "the attendants and servants of the Royal household" (*JN*2, 79–80). At Worcester, the corporation not only proffered gifts to the Queen and privy councilors, they also offered "rewardes" to royal servants and carefully recorded all of the noblemen, bishops, and ladies of honor who had been in attendance. In both cities, it is especially notable that noblewomen, ladies of honor, and household servants were honored, since these individuals did not formally wield political power or make policy decisions, yet cities understood that these visitors could have considerable influence on those who did. They knew that guests' impressions of host cities and their hospitality would be thoroughly discussed in privy chambers and other inner sanctums, so they went out of their way to ensure that all of the visitors were gratified. This is why Worcester was so careful to record the reactions—both verbal and non-verbal—of the "honorable" people who attended the Queen.

Civic hosts also used progress visits to strengthen their relationships with existing patrons. These attempts often took the form of publicly aggrandizing the city's allies in front of the royal visitors. At Sandwich, the town hosted a large banquet at the grammar school that Manwood had helped establish. When the Earl of Warwick accompanied the Queen to Warwick in 1572, he was presented with a fat oxen and ten sheep. By honoring Manwood and Warwick in front of the Queen, these cities assured Elizabeth that those whom she had elevated had in turn become generous patrons to others. The gesture doubtlessly sweetened the existing relationship between city and patron—and sought to inspire future benefits. The latter was probably Worcester's main goal in honoring Sir James Croft, since he had actually done very little to benefit the city up to that point. Publicly acknowledging a patronage relationship could also help shape the future form that it might take. When Oxford praised its Chancellor for a job well done, the university was not only implying that additional royal interference was unnecessary, it was also trying to assure Leicester that his current level of (relatively low) oversight was sufficient.

Civic hosts endeavored to speak to multiple audiences, and in many cases they angled for assistance with particular policy initiatives. But even if they gained no immediate action in that realm, they could still attempt to build personal bonds that they could leverage in the future. When the Queen departed Norwich, her final words were: "I haue laid vp in my breast such good wil, as I shall neuer forget Norwich" (*JN2*, 817). The reason her words were so carefully recorded is that they implied that a future benefit had accrued to the city. They suggest that a store of royal capital had been "laid vp" that Norwich might draw from in the future. The Queen's pledge to "neuer forget Norwich" suggested not only that the monarch would *remember* her time in the city, but that she would therefore *not neglect* Norwich in the days to come.

In the 1560s and 1570s, royal progress visits gave cities the opportunity to engage with the Queen and her retinue in ceremonial dialogues about pressing local issues. In these decades, Elizabeth made some forty visits to urban centers—nine of which are among the most elaborate and well-documented of her reign. Yet these ceremonial encounters were fleeting. In the second half of her reign, the Queen made only twenty-two visits to cities, almost all in close proximity to London.[13] In large part, Elizabethan progresses were curtailed by the threat of Spanish invasion in the 1580s and by the aging Queen's desire to travel shorter distances in the 1590s. The factors that had produced such fruitful civic dialogues in the 1560s and 1570s had also changed. Early in her reign, the Queen was eager to consolidate her rule, build consensus, and cultivate the devotion of her people. She therefore embarked on long progresses where she could go out among her people to see and be seen. These encounters gave civic hosts an unparalleled opportunity to "speak" to the Queen—both literally and through the entertainments they devised. These moments were particularly advantageous for post-Reformation cities that were consolidating their local authority, gaining additional powers from the Crown, and actively negotiating their relationship to the center. For the week of a royal visit, these cities had not only the ear but the eyes and mind of the reigning monarch.

Such opportunities were less frequent later in her reign, when "Elizabeth became a much less public queen" and made fewer attempts to "mix with her people."[14] When she visited Oxford in 1592—the only well-documented civic visit after 1578—the dynamic felt much different. Elizabeth cancelled the academic disputes that had been prepared for her, aggrandized her own learned authority, and endorsed an acceptance of the status quo.[15] She appeared much less interested in dialogue, ceremonial or otherwise. It may be that by her thirty-fourth year on the throne, the Queen was more authoritative or had less need to build consensus. Or perhaps her relationships with urban centers were more fixed, or her policy priorities more established and less in need of negotiation. These are all reasons why a dialogue might have been less productive. The real change from the first part of her reign was that these civic dialogues were themselves less likely to occur, and for the simple reason that the older Queen was less likely to be physically present in a provincial city. The royal presence, more than anything, was the key catalyst for the memorable civic pageants of the 1560s and 1570s. In choosing to enter a city as its guest, the Queen gave her hosts the opportunity to shape her understanding of the city. They responded by imaginatively embracing the occasion and deploying the rich components of civic pageantry to speak to their royal visitors about the things that mattered to them most.

NOTES

INTRODUCTION

1. William Lambarde, *A Perambulation of Kent,* ed. Richard Church (Bath, UK: Adams and Dart, 1970), 355. The reasons for the bridge's decline seemingly stemmed from a lack of initiative and/ or authority. Lambarde records that "the landes contributarie to the repaire thereof were not called to the charge" and that "the revenewe [was] converted to private uses" (355). For a more detailed explanation, see James M. Gibson, "Rochester Bridge, 1530–1660," in *Traffic and Politics: The Construction and Management of Rochester Bridge, AD 43–1993,* ed. Nigel Yates and James M. Gibson (Woodbridge, Suffolk: Boydell Press, 1994), 109–29.
2. This far-reaching act "marked the start of a new administrative system for the bridge that lasted until the twentieth century." Gibson, "Rochester Bridge," 130.
3. Lambarde, *Perambulation of Kent,* 354–55.
4. Ibid., 353.
5. For a full list of bridge commission members see Gibson, "Rochester Bridge," 126–27.
6. Gibson, "Rochester Bridge," 127.
7. Quoted in *John Nichols's "The Progresses and Public Processions of Queen Elizabeth I": A New Edition of the Early Modern Sources,* vol. 2, 1572–1578, ed. Elizabeth Goldring, Faith Eales, Elizabeth Clarke, Jayne Elisabeth Archer (Oxford: Oxford University Press, 2014), 81. Unless otherwise specified, I will rely on this set of volumes as the chief primary account of the Queen's visits to the towns discussed. I am indebted to the work of the scholars who edited the documents for individual locations: Oxford by Sarah Knight, Canterbury by David J. Crankshaw, Worcester by Gabriel Heaton, and Norwich by Matthew Woodcock. Citations of the primary material will use the abbreviation "*JN1*" for volume 1 and "*JN2*" for volume 2 alongside page numbers in the text, while citations of editorial comments will merit separate footnotes.
8. This is true in the same way that Renaissance Venice embraced waterborne pageantry for the very reason that water was such a crucial part of its self-definition. See Evelyn Korsch, "Renaissance Venice and the Sacred-Political Connotations of Waterborne Pageants," *Waterborne Pageants and Festivities in the Renaissance: Essays in Honour of J. R. Mulryne,* ed. Margaret Shewring (Burlington, VT: Ashgate, 2013), 81.
9. See for example, William Leahy, *Elizabethan Triumphal Processions* (Burlington, VT: Ashgate, 2005); Judith M. Richards, *Elizabeth I* (New York: Routledge, 2012); and Lisa Hopkins, *Queen Elizabeth I and Her Court* (New York: St. Martin's Press, 1990).
10. Mary Hill Cole, *The Portable Queen: Elizabeth I and the Politics of Ceremony* (Amherst: University of Massachusetts Press, 1999), 32.
11. Ibid., 32.
12. Figures from the two preceding sentences are based on Cole's extremely useful appendix "Chronology of Royal Visits and Progresses" in *The Portable Queen,* 180–202.
13. Rosemary O'Day, *Longman Companion to the Tudor Age* (New York: Longman, 1996), 164.
14. Robert Tittler, *The Reformation and the Towns in England* (Oxford: Clarendon Press, 1998), 150.
15. O'Day reports that there were about 500–600 market towns, and I am indebted to her for the three categories of towns discussed in this paragraph. O'Day, *Longman Companion,* 164–65. Tittler gives similar population ranges for market towns in the period. Robert Tittler, *Architecture and*

Power: The Town Hall and the English Urban Community, c. 1500–1640 (Oxford: Clarendon Press, 1991), 19.

16. Peter Clark, "Introduction," The Cambridge Urban History of Britain, Vol. II, ed. Peter Clark (Cambridge: Cambridge University Press, 2000), 2.

17. O'Day, Longman Companion, 164.

18. Ibid. 164. Penry Williams calls them "substantial towns," though he agrees on both the number and population figures. Penry Williams, Later Tudors: England 1547–1603 (Oxford: Clarendon Press, 1995), 177.

19. O'Day notes that they typically "had more than one market and often specialised in particular products." Longman Companion, 164. Penry Williams notes their more "complex structure of government." The Later Tudors, 177.

20. Williams and Clark concur on these five. Later Tudors, 177; "Introduction," 27. O'Day leaves out Newcastle—since it only began to develop late in the sixteenth century—and adds Salisbury and Coventry. Longman Companion, 164.

21. O'Day, Longman Companion, 164.

22. Clark, "Introduction," 27.

23. Sybil M. Jack, Towns in Tudor and Stuart Britain (New York: St. Martin's Press, 1996), 173.

24. Alan Dyer, Decline and Growth in English Towns, 1400–1640 (Houndmills, Basingstoke: Macmillan, 1991), 55.

25. Clark, "Introduction," 3. See also Williams, Later Tudors, 177.

26. See Williams, Later Tudors, 177–78; Jack, Towns in Tudor and Stuart Britain, 200–201; and Dyer, Decline and Growth, 54–56. These scholars are responding to Clark and Slack's highly influential thesis that there was widespread urban decline in the early modern period. See Peter Clark and Paul Slack, English Towns in Transition, 1500–1700 (New York: Oxford University Press, 1976). Dyer in particular thinks that this view is overly pessimistic and instead argues for overall economic stability and population growth during 1540 to 1600.

27. Dyer, Decline and Growth, 55; Jack, Towns in Tudor and Stuart Britain, 200; Williams, Later Tudors, 178.

28. Williams, Later Tudors, 178.

29. Jack, Towns in Tudor and Stuart Britain, 200; Williams, Later Tudors, 178.

30. A. L. Rowse, England of Elizabeth, 2nd ed. (Madison: University of Wisconsin Press, 2003), 188.

31. See Williams, for instance, on the differing fortunes of provincial capitals, medium-sized towns, and small market towns. Later Tudors, 178–80.

32. See his chapter on "The Drive for Local Autonomy, c. 1540s–1560s," in Tittler, Reformation and the Towns, 149–81. Much of this paragraph is indebted to him.

33. Tittler, Reformation and the Towns, 9; Tittler, Architecture and Power, 121.

34. Tittler, Reformation and the Towns, 9; Tittler, Architecture and Power, 81–88.

35. Catherine Patterson, Urban Patronage in Early Modern England: Corporate Boroughs, the Landed Elite, and the Crown, 1580–1640 (Stanford, CA: Stanford University Press, 1999), 10. See also Rowse, The England of Elizabeth, 195–96.

36. Tittler, Reformation and the Towns, 161.

37. Ibid., 162.

38. Jack, Towns in Tudor and Stuart Britain, 74–89.

39. Tittler, Architecture and Power, 75–76; Tittler, Reformation and the Towns, 166–75; see also Rowse, England of Elizabeth, 198; and Clark, "Introduction," 14.

40. Tittler, Reformation and the Towns, 9.

41. Ibid., 10.

42. Ibid., 179; Williams, Later Tudors, 184.

43. Patterson, Urban Patronage, 4; Jack, Towns in Tudor and Stuart Britain, 120.

44. Tittler, Reformation and the Towns, 9.

45. Ibid., 9.

46. Tittler, Architecture and Power, 102.

47. Tittler, Reformation and the Towns, 252, 305–34.

48. Ibid., 272–79.

49. Lorraine Attreed, *The King's Towns: Identity and Survival in Late Medieval English Boroughs* (New York: Peter Lang, 2001), 2, 4.

50. Patterson, *Urban Patronage*, 4. Although Patterson is mainly concerned with the years 1580 to 1640, she notes that these processes had already begun earlier in the sixteenth century.

51. Jack, *Towns in Tudor and Stuart Britain*, 120.

52. Williams, *The Later Tudors*, 186.

53. Ian A. Archer, "Politics and Government, 1540–1700," *The Cambridge Urban History of Britain, Vol. II*, ed. Peter Clark (Cambridge: Cambridge University Press, 2000), 240.

54. Patterson, *Urban Patronage*, 2, 3.

55. Ibid., 7.

56. Attreed, *The King's Towns*, 7–9; Patterson, *Urban Patronage*, 181–88; Rosemary Horrox, "Urban Patronage in the Fifteenth Century," in *Patronage, the Crown, and the Provinces*, ed. Ralph A. Griffiths (Gloucester: Alan Sutton, 1981), 145–46.

57. Patterson, *Urban Patronage*, 180.

58. Ibid., 166–69.

59. Ibid., 170.

60. Horrox, "Urban Patronage," 148, 152.

61. Ibid., 150–51.

62. Williams, *The Later Tudors*, 132.

63. Michael Barraclough Pulman, *The Elizabethan Privy Council in the Fifteen-Seventies* (Berkeley: University of California Press, 1971), 62.

64. Christopher Haigh, *Elizabeth I* (New York: Longman, 2001), 108.

65. Williams, *The Later Tudors*, 124, 129.

66. Ibid., 124.

67. Haigh, *Elizabeth I*, 121–24.

68. Horrox, "Urban Patronage," 149.

69. Patterson, *Urban Patronage*, 29–30. Bristol went a step further in formalizing this function by passing an ordinance in 1570 that their High Steward must not only be a Privy Councilor, but one who is "commonly attending upon the Cowrte abowte the Queenes person." Maureen Stanford, ed., *The Ordinances of Bristol: 1506–1598* (Bristol: Bristol Record Society, 1990), 40.

70. Horrox, "Urban Patronage," 158.

71. Ibid., 151.

72. Patterson, *Urban Patronage*, 25–26.

73. Ibid., 170.

74. Jack, *Towns in Tudor and Stuart Britain*, 139.

75. Ibid., 142.

76. Felicity Heal, *Hospitality in Early Modern England* (Oxford: Clarendon Press, 1990), 302, 307–9.

77. Lorraine Attreed, "The Politics of Welcome: Ceremonies and Constitutional Development in Later Medieval English Towns," in *City and Spectacle in Medieval Europe*, ed. Barbara A. Hanawalt and Kathryn L. Reyerson (Minneapolis: University of Minnesota Press, 1994), 209.

78. Daryl Palmer, *Hospitable Performances: Dramatic Genre and Cultural Practices in Early Modern England* (West Lafayette, IN: Purdue University Press, 1992), 4, 22. See my Worcester chapter for a fuller treatment of hospitality in this context.

79. Patterson, *Urban Patronage*, 19; Heal, *Hospitality in Early Modern England*, 307.

80. Patterson, *Urban Patronage*, 16.

81. Attreed, "The Politics of Welcome," 213.

82. Cole, *The Portable Queen*, 173.

83. Patrick Collinson, "Court and Country," in "Elizabeth I," *Oxford Dictionary of National Biography website*, 2012, paragraphs 10–13, accessed March 8, 2019.

84. Jayne Archer and Sarah Knight, "Elizabetha Triumphans," in *The Progresses, Pageants, and Entertainments of Queen Elizabeth I*, ed. Jayne Archer, Elizabeth Goldring, Sarah Knight (New York:

Oxford University Press, 2007), 4. See Felicity Heal's article in this volume: "Giving and Receiving on Royal Progress," 46–61.

85. Cole, *The Portable Queen*, 43.

86. However, the next sentence of the account laments that "bothe were promised by his officers, but nothing deliuered" (*JN2*, 41).

87. Collinson, "Court and Country" in "Elizabeth I," *Oxford Dictionary*, paragraph 2, accessed March 8, 2019. See also Haigh, *Elizabeth I*, 121–24.

88. See Christopher Hibbert, *The Virgin Queen: Elizabeth I, Genius of the Golden Age* (Reading, MA: Addison-Wesley, 1991), 136–38.

89. Haigh, *Elizabeth I*, 180, 186, 192; Hopkins, *Queen Elizabeth I and Her Court*, 136; Richards, *Elizabeth I*, 133.

90. Jean Wilson, *Entertainments for Elizabeth I* (Totowa, NJ: Rowman & Littlefield, 1980), 9.

91. Heal, "Giving and Receiving," 47.

92. David Bergeron, *English Civic Pageantry: 1558–1642*, rev. ed. (Tempe: Arizona State University, 2003), 3.

93. Cole, *The Portable Queen*. Cole's main argument is that the Queen used the "dislocating confusion" of the royal progress as a calculated strategy to "preserve her independence" (10). However, her chapter on "Civic Hosts" explores how towns used the occasion of the Queen's visit to frame requests for economic aid.

94. Archer, Goldring, Knight, eds., *The Progresses, Pageants, and Entertainments of Queen Elizabeth I*. See also two other collections that are mostly Continental in focus: Margaret Shewring, ed., *Waterborne Pageants and Festivities in the Renaissance: Essays in Honour of J. R. Mulryne* (Burlington, VT: Ashgate, 2013); and J. R. Mulryne, ed., *Ceremonial Entries in Early Modern Europe: The Iconography of Power* (Burlington, VT: Ashgate, 2015). Focusing lower down the social scale, Leahy looks at the extent to which the "common people" were successfully interpellated. Leahy, *Elizabethan Triumphal Processions*.

95. Peter Arnade, *Realms of Ritual: Burgundian Ceremony and Civic Life in Late Medieval Ghent* (Ithaca, NY: Cornell University Press, 1996); Margit Thøfner, *A Common Art: Urban Ceremonial in Antwerp and Brussels during and after the Dutch Revolt* (Zwolle: Waanders Publishers, 2007).

96. Neil Murphy, *Ceremonial Entries, Municipal Liberties and the Negotiation of Power in Valois France, 1328–1589* (Boston, MA: Brill, 2016); Michael Wintroub, *A Savage Mirror: Power, Identity, and Knowledge in Early Modern France* (Stanford: Stanford University Press, 2006). See also Nicolas Russell and Helene Visentin, ed., *French Ceremonial Entries in the Sixteenth Century* (Toronto: Centre for Reformation and Renaissance Studies, 2007).

97. Wintroub, *A Savage Mirror*, 11.

98. In creating a new post-Reformation political culture, urban elites grafted secular rituals onto the older, more religious ceremonials rather than making a clean break. Even pre-Reformation practices like the Corpus Christi processional lasted in some places into the 1570s. Tittler, *The Reformation and the Towns*, 248–52, 329, 333. Similarly, Alexandra Johnston discusses the aspects of medieval religious processionals that got co-opted into pageantry. "Introduction," in *Civic Ritual and Drama*, ed. Alexandra Johnston and Wim Hüsken (Atlanta, GA: Rodopi, 1997), 13. See also Bergeron, *English Civic Pageantry*, 6–7.

99. See Cole, *The Portable Queen*, 17–18.

100. Cole, *The Portable Queen*, 18; Bergeron, *English Civic Pageantry*, 128.

101. Bergeron, *English Civic Pageantry*, 17–18.

102. Ibid., 18–19. For a modern edition of Richard Mulcaster's account, see Germaine Warkentin, ed., *The Queen's Majesty's Passage and Related Documents* (Toronto: Centre for Reformation and Renaissance Studies, 2004).

103. Bergeron, *English Civic Pageantry*, 126.

104. Ibid., 126. Though Ann K. Lancashire suggests that these shows may have appeared some fifty years earlier. See "Continuing Civic Ceremonies of 1530s London," *Civic Ritual and Drama*, ed. Alexandra Johnston and Wim Hüsken (Atlanta, GA: Rodopi, 1997), 9–10.

105. Bergeron, *English Civic Pageantry*, 128–32.

106. I am indebted to Bergeron for my description of this pageant as well as for the connections with royal entries and Lord Mayors' Shows discussed later in the paragraph. *English Civic Pageantry,* 126–30, 133, 139–40.

107. Barbara Hanawalt and Kathryn Reyerson, "Introduction," in *City and Spectacle in Medieval Europe,* ed. Barbara A. Hanawalt and Kathryn L. Reyerson (Minneapolis: University of Minnesota Press, 1994), ix.

108. J. R. Mulryne, "Introduction: Ceremony and the Iconography of Power," *Ceremonial Entries in Early Modern Europe,* 1.

109. Nicolas Russell and Helene Visentin, "The Multilayered Production of Meaning in Sixteenth-Century French Ceremonial Entries," *French Ceremonial Entries,* 16.

110. Mulryne, "Introduction," *Ceremonial Entries in Early Modern Europe,* 2.

111. Russell and Visentin, "Multilayered Production of Meaning," 17.

112. Murphy, *Ceremonial Entries, Municipal Liberties,* 11.

113. See Richard Cooper, "The Theme of War in French Renaissance Entries," *Ceremonial Entries,* 15–36.

114. Murphy, *Ceremonial Entries, Municipal Liberties,* 21–23.

115. Ibid., 12. Those festival books that were translated were typically rendered in Italian. Russell and Visentin, "Multilayered Production of Meaning," 19.

116. William Kemp, "Transformations in the Printing of Royal Entries during the Reign of Francois I: The Role of Geofroy Tory," *French Ceremonial Entries,* 113. For a list of other printed accounts of French entries circa 1531 to 1632, see Margaret M. McGowan, "The French Royal Entry in the Renaissance: The Status of the Printed Text," *French Ceremonial Entries,* 50–52.

117. Murphy, *Ceremonial Entries, Municipal Liberties,* 9.

118. Thøfner, *A Common Art,* 25.

119. For this paragraph's account of these two ceremonies, I am indebted to Thøfner, *A Common Art,* 54, 60–66.

120. Examples include Neptune riding a whale, Mount Parnassus and the Cave of Discord, a seahorse, the giant Druon, and an elephant. Many of these floats were reused in the 1582 entry of the Duke of Anjou, with images of them appearing in an associated festival book. Thøfner reprints these images in *A Common Art,* 60–62, 65.

121. Thøfner discusses how some of these floats addressed the tensions surrounding the 1566 pageants. *A Common Art,* 67–68.

122. Johnston, "Introduction," 9.

123. Ibid. 13–14.

124. Bergeron, *English Civic Pageantry,* 2.

125. Cole, *The Portable Queen,* 17.

126. Ibid., 16–17.

127. Mulryne, "Introduction," *Ceremonial Entries in Early Modern Europe,* 6.

128. Russell and Visentin, "Multilayered Production of Meaning," 17.

129. McGowan, "French Royal Entry," 31.

130. J. R. Mulryne, "Introduction: Making Space for Festival," in *Architectures of Festival in Early Modern Europe,* ed. J. R. Mulryne, Krista de Jonge, Pieter Martens, and R.L.M. Morris (New York: Routledge, 2018), 3.

131. Mulryne, "Introduction," *Ceremonial Entries in Early Modern Europe,* 6.

132. Norwich's 1578 entry featured a triumphal arch, positioned at the entrance to the city market.

133. Bergeron, *English Civic Pageantry,* 52.

134. Janette Dillon, *The Language of Space in Court Performance, 1400–1625* (Cambridge: Cambridge University Press, 2010), 21.

135. Murphy, *Ceremonial Entries, Municipal Liberties,* 9–10. As a result, Murphy goes on to explain, town leaders continued to perform spectacle, but came to increasingly entrust their messages to formal petitions and the more direct exchange of greeting speech and gift (11).

136. Bergeron, *English Civic Pageantry,* 2.

137. Ibid., 17.

138. See Murphy, *Ceremonial Entries, Municipal Liberties.* In her treatment of the ceremonial conventions that structured progress interactions, Cole refers to a specific part of the entry when some towns "petition[ed]" the Queen with "a major request." *The Portable Queen,* 107, 126.

139. Heal, "Giving and Receiving," 53. "Instead," says Heal, "they approached the councillors travelling with the Queen, or persuaded the local bishop to speak on their behalf" (53). While I do plan to emphasize towns' appeals to potential patrons who might provide access to the center, I also want to explore how the pageants themselves attempt to speak to both the Queen and her retinue.

140. In *Portable Queen,* Cole devotes a section of a chapter to "Requests for Economic Aid." However, of the nine or so towns discussed, only three (Rye, Folkestone, and Sandwich) seem to have submitted actual petitions—and all of these were for assistance with silted-up harbors.

141. Kathleen Ashley, "Introduction," in *Moving Subjects: Processional Performance in the Middle Ages and the Renaissance,* ed. Kathleen Ashley and Wim Hüsken (Atlanta, GA: Rodopi, 2001), 13.

142. Cole, *Portable Queen,* 124.

143. Hanawalt and Reyerson, "Introduction," xiv–xv.

144. Ashley, "Introduction," 13.

145. Russell and Visentin, "Multilayered Production of Meaning," 15.

146. Dillon, *Language of Space,* 6, 48. See also Cole, who argues that movement, positioning, and space were as important as scripts in conveying meaning in royal progresses. *The Portable Queen,* 121–24. For a useful overview of the "spatial turn" that began in the 1990s as well as the ways in which space is both historically constituted and reflective of power and social relations, see Michel Pauly and Martin Scheutz, "Space and History as Exemplified by Urban History Research," in *Cities and Their Spaces: Concepts and Their Use in Europe,* ed. Michel Pauly and Martin Scheutz (Koln: Bohlau, 2014), 15–28.

147. Dillon, *Language of Space,* 49.

148. Pauly and Scheutz, "Space and History," 16; Hester Lees-Jeffries, "Location as Metaphor in Queen Elizabeth's Coronation Entry (1559): *Veritas Temporis Filia,*" in *Progresses, Pageants, and Entertainments,* ed. Archer, Goldring, and Knight, 66.

149. Malcolm Smuts and George Gorse, "Introduction," in *The Politics of Space: European Courts ca. 1500–1750,* ed. Marcello Fantoni, George Gorse, and Malcolm Smuts (Rome: Bulzoni Editore, 2009), 19–24.

150. Tittler, *Architecture and Power,* 105–21.

151. Dillon, *Language of Space,* 49.

152. Smuts and Gorse, "Introduction," 13–15.

153. Dillon, *Language of Space,* 5, 17.

154. Ashley, "Introduction," 7, 12.

155. Mulryne, "Introduction," *Architectures of Festival,* 9. See also Ashley, "Introduction," 17.

156. See, for example, the account of the Queen's 1566 visit to Coventry (*JN*1, 462).

157. Ashley, "Introduction," 21.

158. Bergeron, *English Civic Pageantry,* 12.

159. Mulryne, "Introduction," *Ceremonial Entries in Early Modern Europe,* 6.

160. Mulryne, "Introduction," *Architectures of Festival,* 2.

161. See Martina Frank, "From Ephemeral to Permanent Architecture: The Venetian Palazzo in the Second Half of the Seventeenth Century," in *Architectures of Festival,* 119–38.

162. See Marten Snickare, "A Productive Conflict: The Colosseum and Early Modern Religious Performance," *Architectures of Festival,* 11–26.

163. Mulryne, "Introduction," *Architectures of Festival,* 9.

164. Thøfner, *A Common Art,* 16–18. Quotes in the next three sentences are from pages 24, 17, and 18.

165. Thøfner, *A Common Art,* 24.

166. See Jack, *Towns in Tudor and Stuart Britain,* 4.

167. Tittler, *Reformation and the Towns,* 254.

168. Tittler, *Architecture and Power,* 93.

169. Thøfner, *A Common Art,* 12, 14, 20.

170. Johnston, "Introduction," 7.
171. Bristol and Norwich get the most attention, probably because they have left the most detailed surviving accounts, including a high proportion of "literary" elements. Other towns tend to get mentioned in larger works on pageantry or royal progresses, if at all. In *Portable Queen*, Cole does draw from the existing records of most English towns, but she does so in the service of tracing larger practices and conventions rather than giving systematic treatments of particular towns.
172. Mulryne, "Introduction," *Ceremonial Entries in Early Modern Europe*, 1. As Russell and Visentin put it: "In order to understand ceremonial entries fully we must take into account both their cultural and political context" because "different elements that compose the entry assume their full meaning only when viewed in the context in which they are inscribed." "Multilayered Production of Meaning," 18, 21.
173. Williams, *Later Tudors*, 246.
174. See Richards, *Elizabeth I*, 87.
175. Keith Randell, *Elizabeth I and the Government of England* (London: Hodder & Stoughton, 1994), 45–46. See also Haigh, *Elizabeth I*, 126–27. Randall has pointed out that the "orthodox" view of the mid-Elizabethan period has, however, been challenged by revisionist historians (131–32).
176. Haigh, *Elizabeth I*, 204.
177. Russell and Visentin, "Multilayered Production of Meaning," 16–18.
178. Natalie Mears, *Queenship and Political Discourse in the Elizabethan Realms* (Cambridge: Cambridge University Press, 2005), 6.
179. For example, Williams's treatment of this period features chapters on France, Spain, the Netherlands, and Ireland in this period but is largely silent on domestic issues. *Later Tudors*, 265–99.
180. Wallace T. MacCaffrey, *Queen Elizabeth and the Making of Policy, 1572–1588* (Princeton, NJ: Princeton University Press, 1981), 459.
181. Ibid., 460.
182. Helen Castor's new biography gives useful treatment of all of these domestic issues, including the events of the Northern Rebellion. *Elizabeth I: A Study in Insecurity* (London: Penguin, 2018).
183. Cole, *Portable Queen*, 11, 33–34.
184. Ibid., 22–24.
185. Figures based on Cole's "Chronology of Royal Visits and Progresses" in *Portable Queen*, 180–202.
186. While more than just a market town, Sandwich was in decline because of its silting harbor, and its population got as low as 1,500 in the decade before the Queen's visit. Helen Clarke, Sarah Pearson, Mavis E. Mate, and Keith Parfitt, *Sandwich, The 'Completest Medieval Town in England': A Study of the Town and Port from its Origins to 1600* (Oxford: Oxbow Books, 2010), 231.
187. It is thus overly simplistic to say of town welcome speeches that "the sentiments are so similar, the wording at times identical, that one suspects there was a model version of the speech, sent out by the Council or passed around." Haigh, *Elizabeth I*, 189.
188. Hibbert, *The Virgin Queen*, 138.
189. Cole, *Portable Queen*, 72–74, 99.
190. Ibid., 103.
191. Thøfner, *Common Art*, 24, 56, 73.
192. Norwich is a good example of such heterogeneity.
193. Cole, *Portable Queen*, 115. Coventry 1566 is a notable exception, which Cole analyzes in detail (116–20).
194. Dillon, *Language of Space*, 5, 14; Palmer, *Hospitable Performances*, 125–28.
195. Palmer, *Hospitable Performances*, 119–21.
196. Murphy, *Ceremonial Entries, Municipal Liberties*, 13.
197. Palmer, *Hospitable Performances*, 20.
198. The account in Worcester's Chamber Order Book does refer the reader to further details regarding "the effecte" of these pageant speeches, but these notes have been lost (*JN2*, 343–44).
199. Bernard Garter, *The Ioyfull Receyuing of the Queenes Most Excellent Maiestie into Hir Highnesse Citie of Norwich* (London: Henry Bynneman, 1578).

200. Bergeron, *English Civic Pageantry*, 10.

201. Examples of the former include the Ordinances of the Common Council (Bristol), the Chamber Order Book (Worcester), and the Norwich Assembly Proceedings Book. Examples of the latter include the Mayor's Audit's (Bristol) and The Accompts of Master Christofer Dighton Hygh Baylyff (Worcester).

202. Murphy, *Ceremonial Entries, Municipal Liberties*, 16.

203. See William Boys, *Collection for an History of Sandwich in Kent* (Canterbury: Simmons, Kirkby, and Jokes, 1792); and Valentine Green, *The History and Antiquities of the City and Suburbs of Worcester* (London: W. Bulmer & Co., 1796).

204. John Nichols, *The Progresses and Public Processions of Queen Elizabeth I, among Which Are Interspersed Other Solemnities, Public Expenditures, and Remarkable Events during the Reign of That Illustrious Princess, Collected from Original Manuscripts, Scarce Pamphlets, Corporation Records, Parochial Registers, etc., etc., Illustrated with Historical Notes* (London: Society of Antiquaries, 1823).

205. Elizabeth Goldring, Faith Eales, Elizabeth Clarke, and Jayne Elisabeth Archer, eds., *John Nichols's "The Progresses and Public Processions of Queen Elizabeth I": A New Edition of the Early Modern Sources*, 3 vols. (Oxford: Oxford University Press, 2014).

206. The first in Canterbury Cathedral archives. The second and third in relation to Sandwich but at Kent Library and History Centre in Maidstone. The fourth at the Worcester Archive and Archaeology Service. See Bibliography for full citations.

207. Ursula Priestley, *The Great Market: A Survey of Nine Hundred Years of Norwich Provision Market* (Norwich: Centre for East Anglian Studies, 1987); Jewson, C. B., *History of the Great Hospital* (Norwich: Great Hospital, 1966); Helen Sutermeister, *The Norwich Blackfriars: A History and Guide to St. Andrew's and Blackfriar's Halls* (Norwich: City of Norwich, 1977).

208. For example, I met with Nicholas Groves in Norwich to learn more about the surviving tomb monuments of religious refugees. He is the author of *The Medieval Churches of the City of Norwich* (Norwich Heritage Economic and Regeneration Trust, 2010). In Canterbury, I interviewed Margaret Sparks about the appearance and layout of the Elizabethan cathedral. She is the author of *Canterbury Cathedral Precincts: A Historical Survey* (2007).

209. See Pulman, *Elizabethan Privy Council*, chapters seven to twelve for a full description of these wide-ranging activities.

210. The remainder of this paragraph is drawn from Pulman, *Elizabethan Privy Council*, 137–38, 135, 139.

211. Ibid., 62.

212. Williams, *Later Tudors*, 134; Pulman, *Elizabethan Privy Council*, 62.

213. Haigh, *Elizabeth I*, 87–100.

214. Cole, *Portable Queen*, 36.

215. MacCaffrey, *Queen Elizabeth and the Making of Policy*, 436.

216. Ibid., 432; Williams, *Later Tudors*, 134; Collinson, "The Shaping and Testing of the Elizabethan Regime, 1558–1572" in "Elizabeth I," *Oxford Dictionary*, paragraph 12, accessed March 8, 2019.

217. Haigh, *Elizabeth I*, 84.

218. Ibid., 84.

219. Randell, *Elizabeth I and the Government of England*, 46; see also Haigh, *Elizabeth I*, 110–12; and MacCaffrey, *Queen Elizabeth and the Making of Policy*, 440–57; though the latter two place less emphasis on the role of Walsingham.

220. Haigh, *Elizabeth I*, 110.

221. MacCaffrey, *Queen Elizabeth and the Making of Policy*, 443. Leicester was high steward of Bristol, Andover, Reading, Abingdon, New Windsor, Kings Lynn, and Great Yarmouth (443).

222. Pulman, *Elizabethan Privy Council*, 20.

223. Ibid., 34.

CHAPTER ONE: OXFORD, 1566

1. Penry Williams treats 1564 to 1568 as "the years of peace." *The Later Tudors: England, 1547–1603* (Oxford: Clarendon Press, 1995), 246–53.

2. Of her previous four progresses, only the 1561 one was longer (at sixty-eight days). However, this progress was largely confined to counties (like Essex and Hertfordshire) that were adjacent to London. See Mary Hill Cole, *The Portable Queen: Elizabeth I and the Politics of Ceremony* (Amherst: University of Massachusetts, 1999), 206, 180–81.

3. John R. Elliott Jr., Alan H. Nelson, Alexandra F. Johnston, and Diana Wyatt, eds., *Records of Early English Drama: Oxford (henceforth REED: Oxford)*, vol. 2 (Toronto: University of Toronto Press, 2004), 584.

4. Ibid., 591.

5. Quoted in Elliot, *REED: Oxford,* 591.

6. Ibid., 597.

7. L. W. B. Brockliss, *The University of Oxford: A History* (New York: Oxford University Press, 2016), 167.

8. Elliot, *REED: Oxford,* 585–86.

9. Ibid., 587–88.

10. Brockliss, *University of Oxford,* 158, 139.

11. John Newman, "The Physical Setting: New Building and Adaptation," in *The History of the University of Oxford,* vol. 3, ed. James McConica (Oxford: Clarendon Press, 1986), 597.

12. Ibid., 598–99.

13. J. M. Fletcher, "The Faculty of Arts," in *History of the University,* 198–99, 160.

14. Claire Cross, "Oxford and the Tudor State from the Accession of Henry VIII to the Death of Mary," *History of the University,* 117.

15. For more on university governance, see Cross, "Oxford and the Tudor State," 117–18; Elliot, *REED: Oxford,* 597–98; Penry Williams, "Elizabethan Oxford: State, Church, and University," *History of the University,* 400–5; Brockliss, *University of Oxford,* 143.

16. Elliot, *REED: Oxford,* 588.

17. Newman, "Physical Setting," 615, 597.

18. Helen M. Jewell, *Education in Early Modern England* (New York: St. Martin's Press, 1998), 110–11.

19. Brockliss, *University of Oxford,* 151.

20. For more details, see Brockliss, *University of Oxford,* 184–201; Loach, "Reformation Controversies," 381–84; Williams, "Elizabethan Oxford," 405–15.

21. For the first four, see James McConica, "The Rise of the Undergraduate College," in *History of the University,* 1–66. For the primacy of arts, see Fletcher, "Faculty of Arts," 160–64. For changes in internal governance, see Williams, "Elizabethan Oxford," 403.

22. Fletcher, "Faculty of Arts," 175.

23. James D. Tracy, *Erasmus of the Low Countries* (Berkeley: University of California Press, 1996), 25.

24. McConica, "Rise of the Undergraduate," 66. For his part, Erasmus "hailed [Corpus Christi] as a great advance for humane literature and classical studies" (66–67).

25. Ibid., 30.

26. Brockliss, *University of Oxford,* 131.

27. Ibid., 131.

28. Eleanor Rosenberg, *Leicester: Patron of Letters* (New York: Columbia University Press, 1955), 118; James McConica, "Elizabethan Oxford: The Collegiate Society," in *History of the University,* 730–31.

29. Fletcher, "The Faculty of Arts," 174, 176–77.

30. Ibid., 193–94.

31. McConica, "Rise of the Undergraduate," 58, 60, 66, 44.

32. Fletcher, "Faculty of Arts," 159.

33. Ibid., 158.

34. Jewell, *Education in Early Modern England,* 111.

35. Fletcher, "Faculty of Arts," 175.

36. Ibid., 160.

37. McConica, "Elizabethan Oxford," 701.

38. Brockliss, *University of Oxford,* 240–52.

39. McConica, "Elizabethan Oxford," 701–11.

40. Ibid., 712–16, 730–31.

41. Fletcher, "Faculty of Arts," 181.

42. Brockliss, *University of Oxford*, 158.

43. See McConica, "Rise of the Undergraduate," 1–66.

44. Michael Van Cleave Alexander, *The Growth of English Education, 1348–1648: A Social and Cultural History* (University Park: Penn State University Press, 1990), 157.

45. Alexander, *Growth of English Education*, 157, 171.

46. Brockliss, *University of Oxford*, 137. Quotes in the succeeding two sentences are also from Brockliss, 161.

47. Ibid., 137. Brockliss provides a number of reasons, ranging from differences in feeder schools to the desire of the landed elite to assert their status over the new moneyed classes (137, 162).

48. Alexander, *Growth of English Education*, 157.

49. Brockliss, *University of Oxford*, 232.

50. Ibid., 252.

51. See McConica, "Rise of the Undergraduate" and "Elizabethan Oxford," 66, 693–95.

52. Brockliss, *University of Oxford*, 252.

53. James McConica, "Studies and Faculties: Introduction," in *History of the University*, 153. McConica puts the figure somewhere between 1,015 and 1,150 students. The primary cause of this decline was probably religious instability. Not only had the Reformation halted the study of canon law, it had created "unsettled religious conditions" during the reigns of Henry VIII, Edward VI, and Mary, so that "young men naturally avoided this controversial and even dangerous field." Rosenberg, *Leicester*, 120.

54. Brockliss, *University of Oxford*, 226.

55. McConica, "Elizabethan Oxford," 729; Alexander, *Growth of English Education*, 171.

56. Jewell, *Education in Early Modern England*, 112; Brockliss, *University of Oxford*, 162–63.

57. In the 1580s, only 25 to 30 percent of all first-year students at Oxford went on to earn the B.A. McConica, "Studies and Faculties" 156; Elliot, *REED: Oxford*, 599; Brockliss, *University of Oxford*, 238.

58. McConica, "Elizabethan Oxford," 689–90; Alexander, *Growth of English Education*, 174.

59. Alexander, *Growth of English Education*, 172–73.

60. Ibid., 173.

61. McConica, "Elizabethan Oxford," 689.

62. Alexander, *Growth of English Education*, 172.

63. Brockliss, *University of Oxford*, 161. Stone is quoted in Alexander, *Growth of English Education*, 172.

64. McConica, "Rise of the Undergraduate," 1.

65. Brockliss, *University of Oxford*, 151.

66. Brockliss, *University of Oxford*, 152; McConica, "Elizabethan Oxford," 730.

67. Brockliss, *University of Oxford*, 152; McConica, "Elizabethan Oxford," 730.

68. Cross, "Oxford and the Tudor State," 119, 122.

69. Ibid., 125.

70. Williams, "Elizabethan Oxford," 434–39.

71. Ibid., 435–38.

72. G. E. Aylmer, "The Economics and Finances of the Colleges and University, c. 1530–1640," *History of the University*, 522.

73. Ibid., 522.

74. Brockliss, *University of Oxford*, 167.

75. For example, the new St. John's College and Trinity College took over buildings of the disbanded monastic colleges of St. Bernhard's and Durham College, respectively. Brockliss, *University of Oxford*, 167.

76. G. E. Aylmer notes that "general appeals to old members for help were as yet unknown." "Economics and Finances," 523.

77. Elliot, *REED: Oxford*, 587.

78. Carl I. Hammer, Jr., "Oxford Town and Oxford University," *History of the University*, 92.

79. Ibid., 94. The previous and succeeding sentence are both drawn from Hammer, 94, 93.

80. Brockliss, *University of Oxford*, 191.

81. Ibid., 191. Their numbers varied depending on college leadership and the relative strictness of religious discipline.

82. Ibid., 192.

83. Alexander, *Growth of English Education*, 165.

84. Williams, "Elizabethan Oxford," 402.

85. Ibid., 402.

86. Brockliss, *University of Oxford*, 148.

87. Elliot, *REED: Oxford*, 597.

88. Williams, "Elizabethan Oxford," 401. The remainder of this paragraph (excepting the final sentence) draws from Williams, 424–26, 440.

89. Cross, "Oxford and the Tudor State," 149.

90. Williams, "Elizabethan Oxford," 440.

91. Ibid., 440.

92. Ibid., 425.

93. James Binns, "Abraham Hartwell, Herald of the New Queen's Reign. The *Regina Literata* (London, 1565)" in *Ut Granum Sinapis: Essays on Neo-Latin Literature in Honour of Jozef Ijsewijn*, ed. Gilbert Tournoy and Dirk Sacre (Leuven: Leuven University Press, 1997), 293. See also Rosenberg, *Leicester*, 116–27.

94. Cole, *Portable Queen*, 138–40.

95. Linda Shenk, "Turning Learned Authority into Royal Supremacy: Elizabeth I's Learned Persona and Her University Orations," in *Elizabeth I: Always Her Own Free Woman*, ed. Carole Levin, Jo Eldridge Carney, and Debra Barrett-Graves (Burlington, VT: Ashgate, 2003), 84–87.

96. Siobhan Keenan, "Spectator and Spectacle: Royal Entertainments at the Universities in the 1560s," in *The Progresses, Pageants, and Entertainments of Queen Elizabeth I*, ed. Jayne Elisabeth Archer, Elizabeth Goldring, and Sarah Knight (New York: Oxford University Press, 2007), 98.

97. Campion, a Catholic, eventually left Oxford (and England) for Douai, became a Jesuit, and returned to England in 1580 (where he was shortly thereafter arrested and executed). Humphrey was a proto-Puritan leader during the Vestiarian Controversy of the mid-1560s.

98. Keenan, "Spectator and Spectacle," 101. Cambridge performed a biblical history play with reformist implications and an "unscripted show attacking transubstantiation." Keenan, "Spectator and Spectacle," 92–94.

99. Jennifer Loach, "Reformation Controversies," *History of the University*, 385.

100. Elizabeth Goldring, Faith Eales, Elizabeth Clarke, Jayne Elisabeth Archer, eds., *John Nichols's "The Progresses and Public Processions of Queen Elizabeth": A New Edition of the Early Modern Sources*, vol. 1, *1533 to 1571* (Oxford: Oxford University Press, 2014), 529–30. I will rely on this edition for the various accounts of the Queen's visit to Oxford that are referenced in this chapter. Subsequent citations of primary material will use the abbreviation "*JN1*" alongside page numbers in the text, while citations of editorial comments will merit separate footnotes.

101. Those not on Robinson's list include Throckmorton, Tamworth, Mountjoy, Seymour (*JN1*, 637); Chandos, Carsle, Heymunde, "and others" (*JN1*, 471).

102. For comparison, fourteen nobles and courtiers accompanied the Queen to both Croydon (in 1574) and Worcester (in 1575), while some twenty were present when Lord Burghley hosted the Queen at Theobalds in 1583. Cole, *Portable Queen*, 41.

103. See Christopher Hibbert, *The Virgin Queen: Elizabeth I, Genius of the Golden Age* (New York: Addison-Wesley, 1991), 141.

104. Keenan, "Spectator and Spectacle," 96, 98.

105. "Doctor Whyte" was Thomas White, who had been Vice Chancellor 1562 to 1564.

106. Keenan, "Spectator and Spectacle," 96.

107. Patrick Collinson, "Elizabeth I," *Oxford Dictionary of National Biography* website, 2012, paragraph 7, accessed March 8, 2019.

108. Simon Adams, "Robert Dudley, Earl of Leicester," *Oxford Dictionary of National Biography* website, 2008, paragraph 2, accessed March 8, 2019.

109. Biographical information for this and the succeeding two paragraphs is based primarily on the *Oxford Dictionary of National Biography* website, accessed September 2, 2019; the Tudor Place website, accessed September 2, 2019, https://www.tudorplace.com.ar; and the book Arthur E. Kinney and Jane A. Lawson, eds., *Titled Elizabethans: A Directory of Elizabethan Court, State, and Church Officers, 1558–1603,* (New York: Palgrave Macmillan, 2014).

110. Knollys and Rutland may have spent time at Oxford, while Northampton possibly attended Cambridge.

111. Alexander, *Growth of English Education,* 173.

112. Both of these young aristocrats were connected to Cecil's household via his position as head of the Court of Wards.

113. Collinson, "Elizabeth I," par. 8.

114. Quoted by Thomas Warton in Goldring, Eales, Clarke, Archer, *John Nichols's,* 86–87.

115. Collinson, "Elizabeth I," par. 9.

116. Rosenberg, *Leicester,* 140–42.

117. Ibid., 117–21.

118. Collinson, "Elizabeth I," par. 11.

119. Adams, "Robert Dudley," par. 2.

120. J. W. Binns, *Intellectual Culture in Elizabethan and Jacobean England: The Latin Writings of the Age* (Leeds: Francis Cairns, 1990), 36. For example, university officials dressed as the nine muses hung a Hercules tapestry at her lodging and performed a play by Plautus. Shenk, "Turning Learned Authority," 84.

121. Binns, "Abraham Hartwell," 303.

122. Binns, *Intellectual Culture,* 36.

123. Leah Marcus, Janel Mueller, and Mary Beth Rose, eds., *Elizabeth I: Collected Works* (Chicago: University of Chicago Press, 2000), 88. For the conventional interpretation that Elizabeth is referring to the founding of a college, see Binns, "Abraham Hartwell," 302; and Hibbert, *Virgin Queen,* 141.

124. For a full discussion of this work, see Binns, "Abraham Hartwell."

125. Rosenberg, *Leicester,* 124.

126. Ibid., 124.

127. The Queen's visit to Oxford was supposed to occur in 1565, but had to be postponed a year because of an outbreak of plague.

128. Rosenberg, *Leicester,* 124–25.

129. Ibid., 126.

130. Binns, *Intellectual Culture,* 3, 393.

131. McConica, "Elizabethan Oxford," 699–700.

132. Brockliss, *University of Oxford,* 235.

133. Ibid., 235.

134. Binns, *Intellectual Culture,* 298. The remainder of this paragraph draws directly from Binns, 3, 8–9, 393–94, 9, 7.

135. All three plays have now been lost. For a discussion of their content, see Keenan, "Spectator and Spectacle."

136. The Queen was absent on the first night, but the nobles in attendance "commended the same so highlie to the Queene that her Grace sayde shee woulde lose no more sporte for the good reporte shee heard of their doinges" and was in attendance all of the subsequent nights (*JN1*, 476). The collapsing wall killed two people and injured two others; the Queen responded sympathetically by sending "her owne surgions to helpe them" (*JN1*, 477).

137. Elliot, *REED: Oxford,* 603.

138. Binns, *Intellectual Culture,* 120. Material in the succeeding two sentences is from Binns, 121, 120.

139. McConica, "Elizabethan Oxford," 652.

140. Keenan, "Spectator and Spectacle," 101.
141. Ibid., 98.
142. Ibid., 98.
143. McConica, "Elizabethan Oxford," 652.
144. The five declamations were delivered by Christ Church orator Roger Marbeck, Oxford mayor Thomas Williams, New College fellow Robert Deale, Greek professor Giles Lawrence, and Magdalen orator Thomas Kingsmill. The written speeches were put in the Queen's hands by two of the young men in the crowd of bachelors outside St. Aldate's church (*JN*1, 640).
145. Fletcher, "The Faculty of Arts," 193.
146. Ibid., 194.
147. Ibid., 194.
148. Binns, *Intellectual Culture,* 297–98.
149. Ibid., 46–59.
150. Ibid., 46.
151. Goldring, Eales, Clarke, Archer, *John Nichols's,* 546. The collected verse includes acrostics, propositions, prosopopoeia, and poems in sapphic meter
152. Binns, *Intellectual Culture,* 47.
153. For instance, Bereblock devotes a full eleven pages (of his twenty-nine-page account) to describing these disputations.
154. Natural Philosophy was studied by candidates for the M.A., while Law, Medicine, and Divinity were the three subjects that Oxford students could earn doctoral degrees in.
155. Goldring, Eales, Clarke, Archer, *John Nichols's,* 483.
156. Fletcher, "Faculty of Arts," 169–70. See this source for more detail about academic exercises sketched out in this paragraph.
157. Ibid., 181–83, 190–92.
158. Ibid., 191, 193.
159. These topics have been translated from the Latin in the footnotes of Windsor's account in Goldring, Eales, Clarke, Archer, *John Nichols's,* 478, 482, 484.
160. Elliot, *REED: Oxford,* 594.
161. Geoffrey Tyack, *Oxford: An Architectural Guide* (New York: Oxford University Press, 1998), 34; Elliot, *REED: Oxford,* 593.
162. Newman, "The Physical Setting," 599.
163. Ibid., 599.
164. See Goldring, Eales, Clarke, Archer, *John Nichols's,* 487.
165. Shenk, "Turning Learned Authority into Royal Supremacy," 85.
166. Ibid., 85.
167. These lines are found in a slightly different version of the speech than the one supplied by Miles Windsor's account. See Marcus et al., *Elizabeth I: Collected Works,* 91.
168. Aylmer, "Economics and Finances," 533.
169. Brockliss, *University of Oxford,* 167.
170. One of the short-term solutions hit on by a number of colleges was to house additional students by converting the attics of existing buildings into "cocklofts." Aylmer, "Economics and Finances," 548.
171. Brockliss, *University of Oxford,* 181–82.
172. Ibid., 169, 175.
173. Newman, "Physical Setting," 616–33.
174. Brasenose was founded by William Smith, Bishop of Lincoln; Corpus Christi by Richard Foxe, Bishop of Winchester; and Cardinal College by Thomas Wolsey, Archbishop of York. The non-clerical exception to the pre-Reformation foundations is Balliol, which was established by the prominent northern landowner John Balliol.
175. Felicity Heal, *Of Prelates and Princes: A Study of the Economic and Social Position of the Tudor Episcopate* (New York: Cambridge University Press, 1980).

176. Alexander, *Growth of English Education,* 180.
177. Despite this trend, the next college founded at Oxford (and, as it turned out, the only one founded during Elizabeth's reign) was Jesus College in 1571. It did have a clerical founder, though Hugh Price was also a wealthy lawyer.
178. Marcus, *Elizabeth I: Collected Works,* 88.
179. Louise Durning argues convincingly that the manuscript housed in the Bodleian Library (MS. Bodl. 13 Part A i-iv, 1–21) is indeed the presentation copy that was presented to the Queen. *Queen Elizabeth's Book of Oxford,* ed. Louise Durning (Oxford: Bodleian Library, 2006), 10, 35. Durning's 2006 edited edition includes an introduction, a facsimile of the manuscript, translations from the Latin and Hebrew, and detailed notes.
180. For a discussion of these three genres, see Durning's introduction in *Queen Elizabeth's Book of Oxford,* 12, 22, 29.
181. Durning, *Queen Elizabeth's Book of Oxford,* 15.
182. Throughout the early modern period, Exeter continued to recruit and attract students from the West Country.
183. Goldring, Eales, Clarke, Archer, *John Nichols's,* 512.
184. Neale's methodology is something of a hybrid. He starts with the six largest and wealthiest colleges and then follows a roughly topographical track around the city before ending with the final three colleges outside the city walls. But another college outside the city walls—Magdalen—is discussed third rather than saved for this section, whereas the ecclesiastical/secular dichotomy is followed throughout.
185. Goldring, Eales, Clarke, Archer, *John Nichols's,* 510.
186. Durning, *Queen Elizabeth's Book of Oxford,* 15, 17.
187. John Cavell and Brian Kennett, *A History of Sir Roger Manwood's School, Sandwich, 1563–1963, with a Life of the Founder* (London: Cory, Adams, and Mackay, 1963), 15, 191.
188. Durning, *Queen Elizabeth's Book of Oxford,* 17. Subsequent quotes in the paragraph are from 19–21, 29, 32.
189. Ibid., 113–14.
190. Ibid., 113–14.
191. For example, Parr is recorded as lodging "in Christechurche in the Chamber nexte the gate on the southe syde" (469n125). Magdalen and Merton were also used to house the visitors.
192. Including New College on Monday and Merton on Thursday (*JN1,* 533, 539).
193. Keenan, "Spectator and Spectacle," 94. According to Cole, the latter was a matching annuity of forty pounds specifically "for the college to erect buildings." *Portable Queen,* 115.
194. Tyack, *Oxford,* 71.
195. Judith Curthoys, *The Stones of Christ Church* (London: Profile Books, 2017), 71.
196. Tyack, *Oxford,* 76–77.
197. Keenan, "Spectator and Spectacle," 96.
198. Curthoys, *Stones of Christ Church,* 44.
199. Durning, *Queen Elizabeth's Book of Oxford,* 102.
200. Tyack, *Oxford,* 75.
201. These were the ones in Greek, Hebrew, and Theology. G. D. Duncan, "Public Lectures and Professorial Chairs," *History of the University* 345.
202. Judith Curthoys, *The Cardinal's College: Christ Church, Chapter and Verse* (London: Profile Books, 2012), 68.
203. Indeed, the Queen actually served as the Christ Church visitor in ecclesiastical matters. Williams, "Elizabethan Oxford," 404.
204. Curthoys, *The Stones of Christ Church,* 78.
205. Ibid., 89–91.
206. Ibid., 45, 48–49.
207. Ibid., 71.

208. Quoted in James Ferguson and Jan Morris, *Christ Church Oxford: A Brief History and Guide* (Oxford: Christ Church College, 2011), 70.
209. Durning, *Queen Elizabeth's Book of Oxford*, 102.
210. Ibid., 102.
211. Keenan, "Spectator and Spectacle," 97.
212. Ibid., 96.
213. McConica, "Elizabethan Oxford," 657–62.
214. Williams, "Elizabethan Oxford," 426.
215. Ibid., 426–27.
216. Ibid., 427.
217. Durning, *Queen Elizabeth's Book of Oxford*, 13.
218. Rosenberg, *Leicester*, 132, 127.
219. Shenk, "Turning Learned Authority into Royal Supremacy," 78–79.
220. Ibid., 84.
221. These words are actually a paraphrase of the Queen excusing such opinions, but the speakers themselves make similar caveats over the course of the debates. See, for instance, 535, 541, 543.
222. Quoted in Shenk, "Turning Learned Authority into Royal Supremacy," 88.
223. Ibid., 79–80.
224. This seems to be yet another gesture modeled on what was done at Cambridge in 1564, when seventeen degrees were awarded to noblemen. Oxford also extended honorary degrees to visiting Cambridge masters—another way of affirming "that fraternal relationship that exists between us" (*JN1*, 664).
225. Brockliss, *University of Oxford*, 183.
226. Binns, "Abraham Hartwell," 303.
227. Both Windsor and Bereblock attribute the choice to these men (*JN1*, 488, 663), though Robinson says that the recipients were decided by "the Chancellor and three or four Doctors" (*JN1*, 544).
228. Elliot, *REED: Oxford*, 587.
229. Rosenberg, *Leicester*, 127.
230. Lines 1–4. This poem is not included in Goldring, Eales, Clarke, Archer, *John Nichols's*, though it is reproduced in Durning's *Queen Elizabeth's Book of Oxford* (40) and translated from Latin into English (79) by Sarah Knight.
231. Ibid., 79, lines 8–10.
232. The latter quote is from Goldring, Eales, Clarke, Archer, *John Nichols's*, 588.
233. Written in Hebrew, the poem is perhaps intended to serve as one of the "fruits" of Neale's regius professorship. It is reproduced in Durning, *Queen Elizabeth's Book of Oxford* (76–78) and translated from Hebrew into English (98–99) by Helen Spurling. All subsequent quotations in this paragraph are from page 98.
234. Rosenberg, *Leicester*, 116.
235. Keenan, "Spectator and Spectacle," 102.
236. Brockliss, *University of Oxford*, 158.
237. Rosenberg, *Leicester*, 132.
238. Ibid., 132.
239. Keenan, "Spectator and Spectacle," 102.
240. Hammer, "Oxford Town and Oxford University," 93.
241. Keenan, "Spectator and Spectacle," 101. The principal founder was Hugh Price, a Welsh lawyer and clergyman. Jesus College was the first Protestant foundation at Oxford and the only new college founded during Elizabeth's reign.
242. Alexander, *Growth of English Education*, 173; McConica, "Elizabethan Oxford," 689.
243. Brockliss, *University of Oxford*, 168.
244. Ibid., 176–77.

245. Williams, "Elizabethan Oxford," 400–405. The remainder of this paragraph is also drawn from Williams, 402, 434–39.
246. Ibid., 440.

CHAPTER TWO: SANDWICH, 1573

1. Penry Williams, *The Later Tudors: England 1547–1603* (Oxford: Clarendon Press, 1995), 253–65.
2. "During the northern tensions of 1569 . . . she remained around London before heading south on progress into Hampshire. In the aftermath of rebellion, the next year's itinerary kept her mostly in Buckinghamshire and Bedfordshire, while in 1571 she had only a brief progress in Essex and Hertfordshire." Mary Hill Cole, *The Portable Queen: Elizabeth I and the Politics of Ceremony* (Amherst: University of Massachusetts Press, 1999), 33.
3. Cole, *Portable Queen,* 33.
4. Williams, *Later Tudors,* 260.
5. Helen C. Bentwich, *History of Sandwich* (1971; repr. Sandwich: Sandwich Local History Society, 1995), 43.
6. The Privy Council was viewed as something of problem-solver for the localities, and was involved in the fixing of roads, scouring of rivers, and (from 1579) the repairing of Dover's harbor. See Michael Barraclough Pulman, *The Elizabethan Privy Council in the Fifteen-Seventies* (Berkeley: University of California Press, 1971), 137–39.
7. J. R. Mulryne, "Introduction: Ceremony and the Iconography of Power," in *Ceremonial Entries in Early Modern Europe: The Iconography of Power,* ed. J. R. Mulryne (Burlington, VT: Ashgate, 2015), 1.
8. Helen Clarke, *Discover Medieval Sandwich: A Guide to its History and Buildings* (Oxford: Oxbow Books, 2012), 2.
9. Clarke, *Discover Medieval Sandwich,* 2.
10. Bentwich, *History of Sandwich,* 9.
11. Clarke, *Discover Medieval Sandwich,* 2.
12. Bentwich, *History of Sandwich,* 9.
13. Clarke, *Discover Medieval Sandwich,* 31.
14. For a more detailed description of the Cinque Ports and their privileges, see Bentwich, *History of Sandwich,* 15–22.
15. Ibid., 24.
16. Clarke, *Discover Medieval Sandwich,* 24. As early as 1300, the council was divided into "positions that still have their modern equivalents, such as the treasurer (finance), the serjeant (law and order), the warden for orphans (social services) and the common weigher (trading standards)" (24). As Clarke explains, the jurats were essentially a "small coterie of rich merchants," whereas "less affluent townsmen" could serve in the common council (79).
17. Bentwich, *History of Sandwich,* 35. This convoy of ships called at Sandwich annually from about the mid-fourteenth century to the mid-fifteenth century (35).
18. Ibid., 35.
19. Clarke, *Discover Medieval Sandwich,* 31.
20. Ibid., 32.
21. Bentwich, *History of Sandwich,* 35.
22. Thirty times between 1383 and 1453, fleets assembled in Sandwich Haven. Ships were also repaired here, with "carpenters and other labourers being dispatched to the port specifically for this purpose." Helen Clarke et al., *Sandwich, The 'Completest Medieval Town in England,': A Study of the Town and Port from its Origins to 1600* (Oxford: Oxbow, 2010), 162.
23. Although Dover was a bit closer than the 60 km separating Sandwich and Calais, Dover's harbor "was man-made, small and exposed, more suited to single vessels than to flotillas." Clarke, *Discover Medieval Sandwich,* 45.
24. Bentwich, *History of Sandwich,* 36.

25. Ibid., 36.

26. The silting was by nature a gradual process, so it is hard to pinpoint exactly when it began. Clarke says "mid 1400s" (*Discover Medieval Sandwich*, 40), whereas Bentwich puts it closer to 1500 (*History of Sandwich*, 36). Both of these authors provide a more detailed discussion of contributing factors that I only briefly trace in this paragraph (see Clarke 3–6, and Bentwich 43–45).

27. Bentwich, *History of Sandwich*, 36. As Bentwich notes, these visits had already become more sporadic since 1457.

28. Not only did trade volume dip, but the "luxury goods that had been the mainstay of the port's commerce in the previous two centuries had been replaced by less valuable or exotic cargoes." Clarke, *Sandwich*, 130.

29. Clarke, *Discover Medieval Sandwich*, 62.

30. Estimates are from Clarke, *Sandwich*, 136, 137, 231.

31. Ibid., 162–63.

32. Ibid., 163.

33. Lucy Toulmin Smith, ed., *The Itinerary of John Leland in or about the Years 1535–1543*, vol. 4 (Carbondale: Southern Illinois University Press, 1964), 62.

34. William Lambarde, *A Perambulation of Kent*, ed. Richard Church (Bath, UK: Adams and Dart, 1970), 118.

35. William Camden, *Britannia* (London: George Bishop & John Norton, 1610), 342.

36. Clarke, *Sandwich*, 127–28.

37. See Clarke, *Discover Medieval Sandwich*, 62.

38. On the 1548 proposal, see Clarke, *Sandwich*, 128. As for Dover, Lambarde reports that Henry VIII spent £63,000 on a new pier, and that more recently Elizabeth had "bestowed great favours of hir owne gift" and taken other actions "towards the reliefe of this decaied Harborow." *Perambulation of Kent*, 123–24. These improvements were principally carried out by William Brooke, Lord Cobham—who was Lord Warden of the Cinque Ports from 1558 to 1597 and resident at Dover Castle—and largely completed by 1595.

39. Clarke et al. estimate that Sandwich's total population had climbed back to 2,500 by 1565 and may even have reached 5,000 by 1575 (*Sandwich*, 231). However, within two decades, many of the Strangers had departed for larger immigrant communities in Canterbury, Norwich, or London or had returned to the Low Countries (Clarke, *Discover Medieval Sandwich*, 93; *Records of Early English Drama: Kent*, vol. 1, ed. James M. Gibson (Toronto: University of Toronto Press, 2002), xlv (hereafter in the notes *REED: K1*).

40. This Year Book, also known as the New Red Book, contains official town records for the years 1568 to 1582 and is currently housed in the Kent Library and History Centre in Maidstone (KLHC) SA/AC 5. A transcript of the section covering the Queen's 1573 visit—including the aforementioned visit narrative as well as seven entries on the town's preparations in the two months leading up to the visit—appears in *Records of Early English Drama: Kent*, vol. 2, ed. James M. Gibson (Toronto: University of Toronto Press, 2002), 853–59 (hereafter *REED: K2*). Citations of the primary material will use the abbreviation "*K1*" for volume 1 and "*K2*" for volume 2 alongside page and line numbers in the text, while citations of editorial comments will merit separate footnotes. Another modern edition of the Year Book account can be found in Elizabeth Goldring, Faith Eales, Elizabeth Clarke, and Jayne Elisabeth Archer, eds., *John Nichols's "The Progresses and Public Processions of Queen Elizabeth I": A New Edition of the Early Modern Sources*, vol. 2, 1572–1578 (Oxford University Press, 2014), 87–90—though it does not include the entries on the town's preparations.

41. Cole, *Portable Queen*, 107.

42. David N. Klausner, ed., *Records of Early English Drama: Herefordshire, Worcestershire* (Toronto: University of Toronto Press, 1990), 441.

43. Daryl Palmer, *Hospitable Performances: Dramatic Genre and Cultural Practices in Early Modern England* (West Lafayette, IN: Purdue University Press, 1992), 125–28.

44. The recent publication of Helen Clarke et al.'s archaeological and historical study of the town—

Sandwich, The "Completest Medieval Town in England": A Study of the Town and Port from its Origins to 1600 (Oxford: Oxbow, 2010)—makes this task much easier. In the pages that follow, I rely heavily on this book for my knowledge of the fabric, layout, and landmarks of the Elizabethan town.

45. Ibid., 150.

46. Ibid., 150.

47. Ibid., 150, 153. It is unclear if the drawbridge was still extant in the 1570s. However, Sandown Gate had been re-beautified with bricks in 1538 (150) and in 1566 "a metalled surface 16 feet . . . wide and suitable for horses and carriages was laid [on its roadway], using cobbles and shingle" (235). In short, it would have been something of a "showpiece" gate for the Queen to see. Three days later, Elizabeth's departure through Canterbury Gate would provide a close encounter with Sandwich's other heavily fortified gate.

48. Subsequent details in this paragraph about the Bulwark, the artillery piece, and the Barbican are drawn from Clarke, *Sandwich,* 154–55, 158–59.

49. That these were largely vertical elements fits with Janette Dillon's observation that pageant construction often "prioritize[ed] the vertical plane." *The Language of Space in Court Performance,* 1400–1625 (Cambridge: Cambridge University Press, 2010), 22. In Sandwich's case, emphasizing the vertical helped make its civic spaces seem larger and more imposing.

50. Ibid., 19, 28.

51. Clarke, *Sandwich,* 235.

52. Cole, *Portable Queen,* 101.

53. Felicity Heal, *The Power of Gifts: Gift-Exchange in Early Modern England* (Oxford University Press, 2014), 3–19.

54. Cole records the following gift amounts for different towns and cities: Great Yarmouth £16, Saffron Walden £19, 3 shillings, Northampton £26, Cambridge £36, Litchfield £40, Worcester £50, 17 shillings, 2 pence. Canterbury, by comparison, gave Elizabeth £30 in a 16 shillings purse when she visited it later in her 1573 progress. *Portable Queen,* 101.

55. Both cities gave gifts worth £100. Cole, *Portable Queen,* 101.

56. Largely owing to the fact that such gifts generally "constituted the largest expense attached to a royal visit." Cole, *Portable Queen,* 101. See Cole's list of towns and their approximate total expenditures on 103–4.

57. In Strand Street alone, there are some seventeen surviving houses that were constructed between circa 1450 and circa 1600. Clarke, *Discover Medieval Sandwich,* 64.

58. This location, according to Clarke et al., "was probably on the west corner of Upper Strand Street and Quay Lane." *Sandwich,* 233.

59. It is worth noting that the two houses on High Street were not on the way to the Queen's lodging, and thus represent a conscious detour. After the welcome ceremony, the Queen had to backtrack down High Street to return to Strand Street.

60. Dillon, *Language of Space,* 28, 31.

61. KLHC 10/19/113.

62. John Cavell and Brian Kennett, *A History of Sir Roger Manwood's School* (London: Cory, Adams, and Mackay, 1963), 13. One of the formative events in Manwood's courtly career was his participation in a 1561 Inner Temple entertainment, the *Masque of Desire and Beauty,* in which he acted alongside both Robert Dudley and Christopher Hatton. See Sybil M. Jack, "Sir Roger Manwood," *Oxford Dictionary of National Biography website,* 2004–2016, paragraph 3, accessed November 15, 2016.

63. In 1562, the Queen granted Manwood the royal manor of Hackington (just outside of Canterbury), which thereafter became his primary residence. Both John and Thomas Manwood served as mayors, jurats, and MPs for Sandwich. Cavell and Kennett, *Sir Roger Manwood's School,* 19, 21.

64. Ibid., 12.

65. Ibid., 3. A number of manuscripts in the KLHC attest to Manwood's legal activities in this period on behalf of the town, including a collection of customs and precedents compiled by Manwood in the 1570s KLHC, Sa/LC4.

66. Jack, "Sir Roger Manwood," *Oxford Dictionary,* paragraph 3, accessed November 15, 2016.

67. KLHC Nr/CPc25.

68. According to Cole, "In general, the desire of civic hosts to preserve a corporate image of communal solidarity . . . curbed the divisive tongues of local officials." *Portable Queen*, 115. See also Mulryne, who discusses the "common voice" that such ceremonial occasions fostered. "Introduction," 1.

69. Thus, in Sandwich at least, disparate civic groups were galvanized by a common local concern rather than by (as Gordon Kipling writes) the physical presence or *corpus mysticum* of the visiting monarch. *Enter the King: Theatre, Liturgy, and Ritual in the Medieval Civic Triumph* (Oxford: Clarendon Press, 1998), 45–46.

70. Clarke, *Discover Medieval Sandwich*, 62.

71. Since the disappearance of Manwood House, the "King's Lodging" appellation now refers to a different house—46 Strand Street—in the immediate area. It is unclear whether this misapplication is due to confusion or simply to the unwillingness to lose such a tangible marker of a royal visit.

72. Anne Somerset, *Elizabeth I* (New York: St. Martin's, 1991), 15.

73. For the exact site of the former Manwood House, see map in Clarke, *Sandwich*, 246.

74. Ibid., 215–16.

75. Ibid., 160–61, 215–16. In the sixteenth century, "vessels were able to load and unload at specified sites along a stretch of town and coast up to roughly 1 mile . . . long" (234).

76. David Harris Sacks and Michael Lynch, "Ports 1540–1700," in *The Cambridge Urban History of Britain*, vol. 2, ed. Peter Clark (Cambridge: Cambridge University Press, 2008), 388. Other southeastern headports were London, Chichester, and Southampton. Even though these designations were "made for the administrative convenience of the customs, rather than exclusively for their economic significance" (387), headport status still necessarily increased the economic activity of the town.

77. Clarke, *Sandwich*, 128–29.

78. Ibid., 129.

79. It is tempting to imagine that her host, Roger Manwood, might have himself made this point.

80. According to Dillon, "A royal entry is above all a performance in motion where the performance space is correspondingly in motion." *Language of Space*, 28.

81. Clarke, *Sandwich*, 242.

82. Clarke, *Discover Medieval Sandwich*, 17.

83. The Queen almost certainly saw the exterior of St. Mary's parish church, as it was directly across the street from Manwood House. However, there is no indication that she went inside.

84. Margaret Shewring, "Introduction," in *Waterborne Pageants and Festivities in the Renaissance: Essays in Honour of J. R. Mulryne*, ed. Margaret Shewring (Burlington, VT: Ashgate, 2013), 6.

85. See Evelyn Korsch, "Renaissance Venice and the Sacred-Political Connotations of Waterborne Pageants" in *Waterborne Pageants*, 81.

86. Mulryne is characterizing Margaret Shewring's article, "The Iconography of Populism: Waterborne Entries to London for Anne Boleyne (1533), Catherine of Braganza (1662), and Elizabeth II (2012)" in "Introduction," in *Ceremonial Entries*, 10.

87. David Bergeron, *English Civic Pageantry: 1558–1642*, rev. ed. (Tempe: Arizona State University, 2003), 7. For more on the blending of history and myth in civic pageantry, see Sara Trevisan, "The Golden Fleece of the London Drapers' Company: Politics and Iconography in Early Modern Lord Mayor's Shows" in *Ceremonial Entries*, 245.

88. The Year Book mentions these weaving "scaffoldes" directly in relation to the Queen's departure on Thursday morning, though they may also have featured during her arrival and/or at other times during her visit.

89. "Bays were tissues fabricated with the use of carded wool: says were crossed tissues made with the threads of combed wool." Clarke, *Sandwich*, 298.

90. While it was not unusual for children to appear in Elizabethan civic pageants—they would also participate in Bristol in 1574, Worcester in 1575, and Norwich in 1578—their presence at Sandwich seems particularly resonant.

91. The banquet was hosted by mayor Gilbert's wife and "[her] Sisters the Iurates wyves" (*K2*, 858:37).

92. Schoolroom dimensions estimated from the floorplan in Clarke, *Sandwich*, 241. Though some 90 percent of Sandwich houses had a hall (*K2, 257*), most of these (based on the numerous floorplans throughout *Sandwich*) range in size from 150 to 600 square feet—compared to the schoolroom's estimated 1,056 square feet.

93. The schoolroom even exceeded the size of the fifteenth-century Court Hall in St. Peter's Churchyard, which measured around 44 by 21, or 924 square feet.

94. Canterbury, Tonbridge, Maidstone, Sevenoaks, Tenterden, and Wye. Based on appendix list in A. Monroe Stowe, *English Grammar Schools in the Reign of Queen Elizabeth* (New York: Teacher's College, Columbia University, 1908), 157–68.

95. Ibid., 157–68.

96. Robert Tittler, *Architecture and Power: The Town Hall and the English Urban Community c. 1500–1640* (Oxford: Oxford University Press, 1991), 4.

97. During Elizabeth's reign, some 130 new schools were added to an estimate of 230 pre-existing ones. Although the Queen was not directly responsible for all of these school foundations, she did "give considerable support to educational causes," including her reestablishment of the famed Westminster School in 1560. Michael Van Cleave Alexander, *The Growth of English Education, 1348–1648* (University Park: Pennsylvania State University Press, 1990), 185–86.

98. In fact, Manwood himself may well have arranged this particular entertainment as a way of demonstrating to the Queen that he had made the sort of "public benefaction" that was expected from those who had received her royal favor. See Cavell and Kennett, *Sir Roger Manwood's School*, 15, 191.

99. Cavell and Kennett, *Sir Roger Manwood's School*, 16.

100. Bentwich, *History of Sandwich*, 77.

101. Alexander, *Growth of English Education*, 185; Bentwich, *History of Sandwich*, 77.

102. Stowe, *English Grammar Schools*, 14. Parker's correspondence also reveals that he visited Sandwich in person and was "struck by the local enthusiasm for the project." Cavell and Kennett, *Sir Roger Manwood's School*, 19.

103. Stowe, *English Grammar Schools*, 14.

104. According to Bentwich, the mayor and jurats were the school's governors, the vicar of St. Clement's Church was schoolmaster, and the pupils were selected by the master and two jurats (*History of Sandwich*, 78–80). Meanwhile, Manwood collected land rents and paid school expenses (J. Howard Brown, *Elizabethan Schooldays* [Oxford: Basil Blackwell, 1933], 6) and also set up scholarships for boys from the school at Lincoln College, Oxford and Caius College, Cambridge (Bentwich, *History of Sandwich*, 79).

105. See Clarke, *Sandwich*, 123, 127–28.

106. Kathleen Ashley, "Introduction," in *Moving Subjects: Processional Performance in the Middle Ages and the Renaissance*, ed. Kathleen Ashley and Wim Hüsken (Atlanta, GA: Rodopi, 2001), 14.

107. Unfortunately, this document has not survived.

108. Korsch, "Renaissance Venice," 79.

109. KLHC Sa/LC4, 85–86. This three-page document is in the aforementioned collection of customs and precedents compiled by Manwood in the 1570s.

110. Clarke, *Sandwich*, 229.

CHAPTER THREE: CANTERBURY, 1573

1. Felicity Heal, "The Archbishops of Canterbury and the Practice of Hospitality," *Journal of Ecclesiastical History* 33, no. 4 (October 1982): 545–46.

2. Ibid., 545–46.

3. Ibid., 544.

4. Rosemary O'Day, *The Debate on the English Reformation* (New York: Methuen, 1986), 173.

5. Felicity Heal, *Hospitality in Early Modern England* (New York: Oxford University Press, 1990), 263.

6. Ibid., 265.

7. Felicity Heal, *Of Prelates and Princes: A Study of the Economic and Social Position of the Tudor Episcopate* (Cambridge: Cambridge University Press, 1980), 259.

8. Ibid., 259.

9. Heal, "Archbishops of Canterbury," 560.

10. Patrick Collinson, quoted in O'Day, *Debate on the English Reformation*, 181.

11. Matthew Parker, *Correspondence of Matthew Parker*, ed. John Bruce and Thomas Perowne (Cambridge: Cambridge University Press, 1853), 208.

12. For details of Parker's household in 1563, see Parker, *Correspondence*, 175–76, 195. Patrick Collinson, "The Protestant Cathedral, 1541–1660," in *A History of Canterbury Cathedral*, ed. Patrick Collinson, Nigel Ramsay, Margaret Sparks (Oxford: Oxford University Press, 1995), 175.

13. V. J. K. Brook, *A Life of Archbishop Parker* (Oxford: Clarendon Press, 1962), 343.

14. Ibid., 343.

15. David Crankshaw and Alexandra Gillespie, "Matthew Parker," in *Oxford Dictionary of National Biography*, vol. 42 (Oxford: Oxford University Press, 2004), 724.

16. O'Day, *Debate on the English Reformation*, 167.

17. Crankshaw and Gillespie, "Matthew Parker," 714; Bowker quoted in O'Day, *Debate on the English Reformation*, 171.

18. Heal, *Of Prelates*, 212.

19. Ibid., 204, 219–20, 232. Heal characterizes "concealed lands" as "parcels of chantry land or forgotten corners of monastic property" (232).

20. O'Day discusses this practice, though she concludes that its frequency has been exaggerated. *Debate on the English Reformation*, 174–75.

21. Keith Randell, *Elizabeth I and the Government of England* (London: Hodder & Stoughton, 1994), 27; Heal, *Of Prelates*, 248. See also Patrick Carter, "'Certain, Continual, and Seldom Abated': Royal Taxation of the Elizabethan Church," in *Belief and Practice in Reformation England*, ed. Susan Wabuda and Caroline Litzenberger (Brookfield, VT: Ashgate, 1998), 94–112.

22. Heal, *Of Prelates*, 245.

23. O'Day, *Debate on the English Reformation*, 178.

24. Heal, *Of Prelates*, 244. Many of the financial details described in this paragraph are supported by Susan Doran and Christopher Durston, *Princes, Pastors and People: The Church and Religion in England, 1529–1689* (New York: Routledge, 2003), 129–31.

25. Heal, "Archbishops of Canterbury," 548.

26. Ibid., 553. This "'minimalist' view of wealth and secular involvement" can also be found among some early Elizabethan bishops like Jewel and Parkhurst. See Heal, *Of Prelates*, 216, 321.

27. Susan Doran, *Elizabeth I and Religion, 1558–1603* (New York: Routledge, 1994), 34.

28. Whitgift was actually chosen by Parker to respond on behalf of the Church. Both Donald Joseph McGinn (*The Admonition Controversy* [New Brunswick, NJ: Rutgers University Press, 1949]) and W. J. Sheils (*The English Reformation, 1530–1570* [New York: Longman, 1989]) have synthesized key passages from these texts (quoted below).

29. McGinn, *Admonition Controversy*, 289.

30. Sheils, *English Reformation*, 107.

31. Ibid., 108.

32. McGinn, *Admonition Controversy*, 286.

33. Ibid., 289.

34. Simon Adams, "Robert Dudley," in *Oxford Dictionary of National Biography*, vol. 10 (Oxford University Press, 2004), 99.

35. Brett Usher, *William Cecil and Episcopacy, 1559–1577* (Burlington, VT: Ashgate, 2003), book jacket.

36. For examples, see Doran, *Elizabeth I and Religion*, 36; Judith M. Richards, *Elizabeth I* (New York: Routledge, 2012), 106.

37. Caroline Litzenberger, "Defining the Church of England: Religious Change in the 1570s," in *Belief*

and Practice in Reformation England, ed. Susan Wabuda and Caroline Litzenberger (Brookfield, VT: Ashgate, 1998), 141–42.

38. Brook, *Life of Archbishop Parker,* 115, 164, 338.

39. Crankshaw and Gillespie, "Matthew Parker," 716.

40. Ibid., 717.

41. Parker, *Correspondence,* 280.

42. Individual documents discussed at length in Brook, *Life of Archbishop Parker.* David Crankshaw criticizes Parker for "becoming increasingly fixated upon the idea of introducing change by canon," claiming "that was the source of many of his problems, because it necessarily brought the queen into the frame." "Ecclesiastical Statesmanship in England in the Age of Reformation," in *Sister Reformations:The Reformation in Germany and in England,* ed. Dorothea Wendebourg (Tubingen: Mohr Siebeck, 2010), 302.

43. Doran, *Elizabeth I and Religion,* 36.

44. Parker, *Correspondence,* 429. Of course, it is also possible to put some of the blame for this state of affairs on Parker himself. For example, Penry Williams writes that the Archbishop was not a "dynamic" leader and that he was "at odds with the leading councillors and almost morbidly suspicious of them." *The Later Tudors: England 1547–1603* (Oxford: Clarendon Press, 1995), 277.

45. Crankshaw and Gillespie, "Matthew Parker," 720.

46. Parker, *Correspondence,* 418–19.

47. Ibid., 426.

48. Heal, *Of Prelates,* 326.

49. Litzenberger, "Defining the Church of England," 137; Heal, *Of Prelates,* 318.

50. Parker, *Correspondence,* 454.

51. Michael Barraclough Pulman, *The Elizabethan Privy Council in the Fifteen-Seventies* (Berkeley: University of California Press, 1971), 130, 18.

52. Parker's letters of these dates accompanied and introduced these four texts. *Correspondence,* 424–26, 436.

53. Elizabeth Goldring, Faith Eales, Elizabeth Clarke, and Jayne Elisabeth Archer, eds., *John Nichols's "The Progresses and Public Processions of Queen Elizabeth I: A New Edition of the Early Modern Sources,"* vol. 2, 1572–1578 (Oxford: Oxford University Press, 2014), 56.

54. Vivienne Sanders, "The Household of Archbishop Parker and the Influencing of Public Opinion," *Journal of Ecclesiastical History* 34, no. 4 (October 1983): 539–40. Examples of such texts include chronicles by Matthew Paris, "who had written against the iniquities of the medieval papacy," and a letter by Anglo-Saxon Bishop Aelfric "which spoke out against the idea of a bodily presence in the sacrament" (538).

55. Parker, *Correspondence,* 424.

56. Ibid., 424.

57. It was Nichols who first suggested that the "Discourse of Dover" may refer to a Latin tract that Darell composed about castles in Kent. Both Lambarde and Camden quote from Darell in the sections of their work on Dover, and part of the manuscript was translated and printed by Alexander Campbell in 1786 as *The History of Dover Castle.* Given Darell's ties to Canterbury Cathedral, his work would certainly have been accessible to Parker.

58. John M. Adrian, *Local Negotiations of English Nationhood, 1570–1680* (New York: Palgrave Macmillan, 2011), 52–53.

59. William Lambarde, *A Perambulation of Kent* (Bath, UK: Adams and Dart, 1970), 188, 147, 197, 259, 261.

60. Ibid., 250, 258.

61. Possibly as few as fifty copies. Goldring, Eales, Clarke, Archer, *John Nichols's,* vol. 2, 64. John Josselyn, Parker's antiquarian friend and Latin secretary, probably played a big role in the research and writing of this book. Sanders, "The Household of Archbishop Parker," 536.

62. Brook, *Life of Archbishop Parker,* 324.

63. Parker, *Correspondence,* 425.

64. Heal, *Of Prelates,* 245.

65. Parker, *Correspondence,* 426.

66. Ibid., 425.

67. Ibid., 425.

68. Matthew Parker, *De Antiquitate Britannicae Ecclesiae* (London: John Day, 1572). Presentation copy to Queen Elizabeth I. British Library, shelf mark C.24.b.8.

69. Parker, *Correspondence,* 441.

70. Heal, *Hospitality,* 271.

71. Parker, *Correspondence,* 436–37.

72. Probably composed by Josselyn, the Latin *Matthaeus* was included in some copies of the *De Antiquitate.* The sections relevant to the Queen's visit in 1573 have been translated and printed in Goldring, Eales, Clarke, Archer, *John Nichols's,* vol. 2, 69–83. Citations of the primary material will use the abbreviation "*JN2*" alongside page numbers in the text, while citations of editorial comments will merit separate footnotes.

73. Heal, "Archbishops of Canterbury," 560. See Veronika Sandbichler on scale and extravagance as a deliberate strategy—the "aesthetics of overpowering"—in German pageantry. "Elements of Power in Court Festivals of Habsburg Emperors in the Sixteenth Century" in *Ceremonial Entries in Early Modern Europe: The Iconography of Power* ed. J. R. Mulryne (Burlington, VT: Ashgate, 2015), 174.

74. Goldring, Eales, Clarke, Archer, *John Nichols's,* vol. 2, 63.

75. Ibid., 57.

76. Lambarde, *Perambulation of Kent,* 276.

77. For instance, in 1608, Robert Cecil, "was using 'the ruins' as a stone quarry for his extensive building schemes elsewhere." Margaret Sparks, "The Abbey Site 1538–1997," in *The English Heritage Book of St. Augustine's Abbey, Canterbury,* ed. Richard Gem (London: B. T. Batsford, 1997), 148.

78. The royal palace had been leased out to Lord Cobham in 1564, with the stipulation that the Queen still had rights of usage if the occasion ever arose.

79. Parker, *Correspondence,* 442.

80. Cole, *Portable Queen,* 86.

81. "Map of Barton Farm . . . ," Canterbury Cathedral Archives, CCA-Map149.

82. See Sparks, "The Abbey site," 146–47.

83. William Camden, *Britannia* (London: George Bishop & John Norton, 1610), 337.

84. William Somner, *Antiquities of Canterbury* (Wakefield, UK: EP Publishing, 1977), 32.

85. Tim Tatton-Brown, "The Buildings and Topography of St. Augustine's Abbey, Canterbury," *Journal of the British Archaeological Association* 144, no. 1 (1991): 73.

86. R. J. E. Boggis, *A History of St. Augustine's College, Canterbury* (Canterbury: Cross & Jackson, 1907), 126. The remaining details of this paragraph are indebted to Boggis, 128–33.

87. Tatton-Brown, "Buildings and Topography," 73.

88. Boggis, *History of St. Augustine's,* 119.

89. J. Rady, T. Tatton-Brown, and J. A. Bowen, "The Archbishop's Palace, Canterbury," *Journal of the British Archaeological Association* 144, no. 1 (1991): 1.

90. Brook, *Life of Archbishop Parker,* 142.

91. Ibid., 142.

92. Heal, "Archbishops of Canterbury," 557; Brook, *Life of Archbishop Parker,* 143.

93. Heal, "Archbishops of Canterbury," 557.

94. Rady, Tatton-Brown, and Bowen, "Archbishop's Palace," 14.

95. Parker, *Correspondence,* 475.

96. Rady, Tatton-Brown, and Bowen, "Archbishop's Palace," 7. For reconstructed drawings of the palace, see pages 7 and 13. Most of the remaining details in this paragraph and the next are taken from Francis Woodman, *The Architectural History of Canterbury Cathedral* (London: Routledge, 1981), 134–35; and Tim Tatton-Brown, "The Archbishop's Palace," pamphlet (Canterbury: Canterbury Archaeological Trust, 1986).

97. Woodman, *Architectural History of Canterbury Cathedral*, 135.
98. Details in the paragraph are from Rady, Tatton-Brown, and Bowen, "Archbishop's Palace," 47.
99. Ibid., 14.
100. Tim Tatton-Brown, *Lambeth Palace: A History of the Archbishops of Canterbury and their Palaces* (London: SPCK, 2000), 66–67. These items at Lambeth included "a paire of virginalls" and a Hans Holbien portrait of Archbishop Warham that now hangs in the Louvre (66). For an analysis of how the Earl of Leicester used the furnishings at Kenilworth (particularly his portraits and maps) to advance his agenda during a 1575 progress visit, see Elizabeth Goldring, "Portraiture, Patronage, and the Progresses: Robert Dudley, Earl of Leicester and the Kenilworth Festivities of 1575," in *The Progresses, Pageants, and Entertainments of Queen Elizabeth I*, ed. Jayne Archer, Elizabeth Goldring, Sarah Knight (New York: Oxford University Press, 2007).
101. Tatton-Brown, *Lambeth Palace*, 68.
102. Parker, *Correspondence*, 443.
103. Brook, *Life of Archbishop Parker*, 319.
104. Heal, "Archbishops of Canterbury," 560.
105. Parker, *Correspondence*, 420–21.
106. Brook, *Life of Archbishop Parker*, 144.
107. Goldring, Eales, Clarke, Archer, *John Nichols's*, vol. 2, 77.
108. Indeed, the *Matthaeus* reports, "After the Queen left Canterbury, the Archbishop invited many guests from the town and from neighbouring parishes, to the remainder of the provisions, which . . . he had amassed for the Queen's arrival: he received his guests generously, and provided continuous and hearty meals for the paupers (82).
109. Parker, *Correspondence*, 475.
110. Ibid., 442.
111. Camden, *Britannia*, 337.
112. Somner, *Antiquities of Canterbury*, 50, 93–101.
113. Camden, *Britannia*, 337.
114. Margaret Sparks, personal interview with the author, October 6, 2015. The area probably earned this appellation because the tombs of Henry IV, Joan of Navarre, and the Black Prince all occupied this part of the cathedral.
115. Ibid.
116. Camden, *Britannia*, 337.
117. Parker, *Correspondence*, 475.
118. Goldring, Eales, Clarke, Archer, *John Nichols's*, vol. 2, 62.
119. Doran, *Elizabeth I and Religion*, 24.
120. Stanford Lehmberg, *The Reformation of Cathedrals: Cathedrals in English Society, 1485–1603* (Princeton, NJ: Princeton University Press, 1988), 155.
121. Brook, *Life of Archbishop Parker*, 165–66.
122. Parker, *Correspondence*, 442.
123. Brook, *Life of Archbishop Parker*, 166.
124. She suggests that through her church attendance on the progress, "Elizabeth lent her ceremonial support to the religious settlement" and that she sought to "create a dual image of royal and religious authority." Cole, *Portable Queen*, 140–41.
125. Brook, *Life of Archbishop Parker*, 318.
126. Collinson, "Protestant Cathedral," 154.
127. Ibid., 156.
128. Lehmberg, *Reformation of Cathedrals*, 269.
129. Collinson, "Protestant Cathedral," 157.
130. Ibid., 156.
131. Goldring, Eales, Clarke, Archer, *John Nichols's*, vol. 2, 78.

132. Lehmberg, *Reformation of Cathedrals*, 182.

133. Parker, *Correspondence*, 443.

134. Lehmberg, *Reformation of Cathedrals*, 268.

135. Brook, *Life of Archbishop Parker*, 252–54, 319–22, 239.

136. Parker, *Correspondence*, 442.

137. Felicity Heal, *The Power of Gifts: Gift-Exchange in Early Modern England* (Oxford University Press, 2014).

138. Ibid., 97.

139. Goldring, Eales, Clarke, Archer, *John Nichols's*, vol. 2, 79.

140. For this and the subsequent sentence, see Heal, *Power of Gifts*, 97, 107–08. Heal notes that the trend of giving elaborate jewels instead of plate was introduced by Robert Dudley and began to show up from 1574 onward. Thus, Parker was ahead of the curve.

141. Heal, *Power of Gifts*, 55–56.

142. All three secondary quotes in this paragraph are from Heal, *Power of Gifts*, 157, 18, 158.

143. Ibid., 158.

144. Parker, *Correspondence*, 443.

145. Heal, *Power of Gifts*, 48.

146. Ibid., 111–15.

147. Ibid., 46–48.

148. John Strype, *The Life and Acts of Matthew Parker* Vol. II (Oxford, 1821), 177.

149. Goldring, Eales, Clarke, Archer, *John Nichols's*, vol. 2, 79.

150. The book's full title is *An Exposition of Salomons Booke, called Ecclesiastes or the Preacher* (London: John Day, 1573).

151. Goldring, Eales, Clarke, Archer, *John Nichols's*, vol. 2, 80. The quarto version was first published in 1569 as *The Holi Bible*.

152. Cranmer's prologue had first appeared in the 1540 Great Bible (the revised edition of the first authorized English Bible).

153. The only thing that appears to be missing is Cranmer's prologue.

154. For more on the relationship between Parker and John Day, see Elizabeth Evenden, *Patents, Pictures and Patronage: John Day and the Tudor Book Trade* (Aldershot: Ashgate, 2008), 105–17.

155. Brook, *Life of Archbishop Parker*, 309.

156. Crankshaw and Gillespie, "Matthew Parker," 720.

157. Patrick Collinson, *The Elizabethan Puritan Movement* (Berkeley: University of California Press, 1967), 152.

158. Heal, *Of Prelates*, 318.

159. Doran and Durston, *Princes, Pastors and People*, 133.

160. See Doran and Durston, *Princes, Pastors and People*, 130.

CHAPTER FOUR: BRISTOL, 1574

1. Mary Hill Cole, *The Portable Queen: Elizabeth I and the Politics of Ceremony* (Amherst: University of Massachusetts Press, 1999), 23.

2. Numerous city records provide details of the Queen's visit, including those contained in the *Mayor's Audits*, the *Ordinances of the Common Council*, the *Great White Book*, *Ricart's Calendar*, and *Adams' Chronicle of Bristol*. In 1576, Thomas Churchyard published a full textual account of the speeches and pageant devices that he devised for the occasion in *The firste parte of Churchyardes chippes*. Fortunately, the relevant passages from all of these sources have been conveniently printed in Mark C. Pilkinton, ed., *Records of Early English Drama: Bristol* (Toronto: University of Toronto Press, 1997) (hereafter *REED: Bristol* in the notes). Citations of the primary material will use the abbreviation "*RB*" alongside page and line numbers (where applicable), while citations of editorial

comments will merit separate footnotes. Another modern edition of some of these sources can be found in Elizabeth Goldring, Faith Eales, Elizabeth Clarke, and Jayne Elisabeth Archer, eds., *John Nichols's "The Progresses and Public Processions of Queen Elizabeth I": A New Edition of the Early Modern Sources*, vol. 2, 1572–1578 (Oxford: Oxford University Press, 2014). However, it does not include the *Mayor's Audits* and Churchwarden's accounts, both of which I draw from in the discussion that follows.

3. Population and wealth rankings are derived from Patrick Carter, "Historical Background" in Pilkinton, *REED: Bristol*, xiii.

4. See David Harris Sacks, *The Widening Gate: Bristol and the Atlantic Economy, 1450–1700* (Berkeley: University of California Press, 1991).

5. C. E. McGee, "Mysteries, Musters, and Masque: The Import(s) of Elizabethan Civic Entertainments" in *The Progresses, Pageants, and Entertainments of Queen Elizabeth I*, ed. Jayne Elisabeth Archer, Elizabeth Goldring, Sarah Knight (Oxford: Oxford University Press, 2007), 107.

6. These expenditures are listed in minute detail in the *Mayor's Audits* in Pilkinton, *REED: Bristol*, 84–89.

7. According to David Bergeron, the 1574 entertainments at Bristol are the first time "in this historical period we can be certain about the identity of the deviser of entertainment," *English Civic Pageantry: 1558–1642*, rev. ed. (Tempe: Arizona State University, 2003), 31.

8. David Harris Sacks, "Celebrating Authority in Bristol, 1475–1640" in *Urban Life in the Renaissance*, ed. Susan Zimmerman and Ronald F. E. Weissman (Newark: University of Delaware Press, 1989), 209. David Bergeron's discussion of the Bristol pageants is more balanced but still stresses those aspects of the entertainments that praise and affirm the Queen, *English Civic Pageantry*, 30–34.

9. Cole (in *The Portable Queen*, 109–10) is one of the few commentators to consider the meaning of the Bristol pageants from the city's perspective. However, she interprets the pageants through the lens of Bristol's concern with international trade, a focus that I will depart from markedly.

10. Pilkinton, *REED: Bristol*, 91.

11. Most of the changes involved an increase in the number of aldermen and sheriffs, and the addition of the office of recorder. For more on the development of civic government in this period, see Peter Fleming and Kieran Costello, *Discovering Cabot's Bristol: Life in the Medieval and Tudor Town* (Tiverton, Devon: Redcliffe, 1998), 21–30.

12. Carter, "Historical Background" in Pilkinton, *REED: Bristol*, xiv.

13. For a fuller account of this episode, see Fleming and Costello, *Discovering Cabot's Bristol*, 49–51.

14. Martha Skeeters, *Community and Clergy: Bristol and the Reformation c. 1530–c.1570* (Oxford: Clarendon Press, 1993), 9–10.

15. Skeeters, *Community and Clergy*, 125.

16. Ibid., 128.

17. Ibid., 135.

18. Lindsay Boynton, *The Elizabethan Militia: 1558–1638* (Toronto: University of Toronto Press, 1967), 58.

19. Ibid., 58–59.

20. Penry Williams, *The Council in the Marches of Wales under Elizabeth I* (Cardiff: University of Wales Press, 1958), 198.

21. According to Williams, "It is doubtful how far this exemption extended. According to a document in B.M. additional MS. 25,244, the city was still under the Council's jurisdiction for personal actions and Crown pleas at a later date." Ibid., 198.

22. K. J. Kesselring, *The Northern Rebellion of 1569: Faith, Politics, and Protest in Elizabethan England* (Houndmills, Basingstoke: Palgrave Macmillan, 2007). I follow Kesselring in his emphasis on the rebellion as being religious (rather than political) in focus and popular (rather than aristocratic) in scope.

23. Ibid., 3.

24. Boynton, *Elizabethan Militia*, 63–64.

25. Ibid., 73–81.

26. Kesselring, *Northern Rebellion,* 3. The author also discusses other factors—the decline of the cloth trade, poor harvests, enclosures, increasing vagrancy—that exacerbated the situation and contributed to the Crown's heightened concern with order and rebellion (11–16).

27. Jonathan Barry, "Area Surveys 1540–1840: South-West" in *The Cambridge Urban History of Britain,* vol. 2, ed. Peter Clark (Cambridge: Cambridge University Press), 87.

28. Details in this paragraph of Leicester's appointment and subsequent patronage are from John Latimer, *Sixteenth-Century Bristol* (Bristol: J. W. Arrowsmith, 1908), 52–53.

29. Ibid., 52.

30. A. L. Rouse, *The England of Elizabeth,* rev. ed. (Madison: University of Wisconsin Press, 2003), 199.

31. Ibid., 199.

32. Though Chandos died in 1573, shortly before the Queen's visit.

33. While Leicester was in attendance, it is not clear if Pembroke was at Bristol. One would expect Pembroke (as Lord Lieutenant) to be there, but he was to host the Queen at Wilton near the end of the progress (September 3–6), so he may well have been in Wiltshire preparing for her visit.

34. Michael Barraclough Pulman, *The Elizabethan Privy Council in the Fifteen-Seventies* (Berkeley: University of California Press, 1971), 22, 196.

35. Ibid., 119–23.

36. Burghley's diary and Leicester's correspondence confirm that both were on the 1574 progress. See Goldring, Eales, Clarke, and Archer, *John Nichols's,* vol. 2, 222–25. Burghley also mentions the Earl of Oxford's being at Bristol, and the mayor's audits refer to the Earl of Lincoln (Pilkinton, *REED: Bristol,* 87). Walsingham's journal confirms his presence. See Marion E. Colethorpe, "The Elizabethan Court Day by Day: 1574," *Folgerpedia* website, 2017, 23, accessed March 5, 2020, https://folgerpedia.folger.edu/mediawiki/media/images_pedia_folgerpedia_mw/5/54/ECDbD_1574.pdf.

37. Pulman, *Elizabethan Privy Council,* 34.

38. Churchyard's military career began in the 1540s, and his published works were frequently devoted to recounting (and probably exaggerating) his battlefield exploits. He was thus a well-known soldier-poet. It is also worth noting that Churchyard was himself a native of Shrewsbury—another town on the Welsh Marches. See the excellent *Dictionary of Literary Biography* article (in vol. 132) by Carmel Gaffney for more about this versatile and interesting writer.

39. Pilkinton, *REED: Bristol,* 91.

40. Ibid., 92

41. In her short discussion of the Bristol pageant, Boynton notes the "lavish expenditure on gunpowder," asserting that "being so expensive at this period it was normally doled out in meager quantities," *Elizabethan Militia,* 116.

42. The city was also willing to accept the dangers associated with handling large amounts of gunpowder. According to *Adams' Chronicle,* on August 13 (the day before the Queen's arrival), some gunpowder that was being stored in St. Thomas Street exploded, killing ten people. During the mock battle, a similar number of people were "burnt by misfortune with gunpowder in Treenemills," *Adams's Chronicle of Bristol* (Bristol: J. W. Arrowsmith, 1910), 114.

43. Boynton, *Elizabethan Militia,* 115, 14.

44. Contemporary sources confirm that the soldiers were indeed "city men." *Adams' Chronicle* notes that the mock battles were "performed by the best experienced men in martiall practice about this Cittie," Pilkinton, *REED: Bristol,* 92. They were also, as previously noted, clothed in the city uniform.

45. The speeches are not simply, as John Latimer would later write, "tedious rhymed twaddle by a man named Churchyard." *Sixteenth-Century Bristol,* 61.

46. Churchyard reports that "all . . . three drue theyr swords whan it was named," showing that "the hoel staet is reddie to defend (agaynst all dissencions) a pesable Prince," Pilkinton, *REED: Bristol,* 95; 13–14.

47. The final speaker at St. John's Gate was supposed to be Obedient Goodwill, though his lines were unable to be delivered because "time was so far spent." The text of this short speech echoes Gratulation in proclaiming "what deep desier [the city residents] have, / To spend their goods, their lands, & livs, her staet in peace to save," Pilkinton, *REED: Bristol,* 97; 19–20.

48. Skeeters, *Community and Clergy,* 125.

49. Indeed, as a part of her ongoing emphasis on building religious conformity, Elizabeth had one month earlier "ordered the establishment of a special commission for ecclesiastical causes within the dioceses of Bristol and Gloucester," Cole, *Portable Queen,* 141.

50. Ricart describes it as "a greate large forte standinge in trenemill meade" on the other side of the River Avon, Pilkinton, *REED: Bristol,* 91.

51. Latimer, *Sixteenth-Century Bristol,* 73–74. These rebellions, led by the Earl of Desmond, occurred in the province of Munster in 1569–1573 and again in 1579–1583.

52. Ibid., 74.

53. Ibid., 74.

54. The city seems to have realized the importance of this effect, as it (ironically) brought in a professional soldier from the outside to achieve it. According to the *Mayor's Audits* in *REED: Bristol,* the city paid a Captain John Shute to come from Windsor and be "generall of all the armye," Pilkinton, *REED: Bristol,* 86, 88.

55. Margit Thøfner, *A Common Art: Urban Ceremonial in Antwerp and Brussels during and after the Dutch Revolt* (Zwolle: Waanders Publishers, 2007), 76–77.

56. Many of these practices are made visible only because of the unusually extensive financial records (the *Mayor's Audits*) that have survived at Bristol. These accounts, reprinted in Pilkinton, *REED: Bristol,* provide revealing details about the preparations and expenditures of the city as it prepared for the Queen's visit.

57. Latimer, *Sixteenth-Century Bristol,* 38.

58. In 1572, a small building "for practice of shooting with guns with bullets" had even been constructed in the marsh, *Adams's Chronicle of Bristol,* 113.

59. Though the mayor's audits do not list a progress-specific payment, the waits were paid the following month (September) for "the rent of their howse" and for "their ffee," Pilkinton, *REED: Bristol,* 89.

60. Latimer, *Sixteenth-Century Bristol,* 38.

61. Mary E. Williams, *Civic Treasures of Bristol* (Bristol: City of Bristol, 1984), 42.

62. Ibid., 45.

63. The sixteenth-century scabbard was replaced in 1953 but is still stored in the Council House in Bristol. I am grateful to David Clark and Peter Ockman for allowing me to view the scabbard.

64. "The Phoenix and the Pelican: two portraits of Elizabeth I, c. 1575" National Portrait Gallery website, accessed March 3, 2020, https://www.npg.org.uk/research/programmes /making-art-in-tudor-britain/the-phoenix-and-the-pelican-two-portraits-of-elizabeth-i-c .1575.php.

65. J. F. Nicholls and John Taylor, *Bristol Past and Present,* vol. 1 (Bristol: J. W. Arrowsmith, 1881), 254.

66. See Maureen Stanford, ed., *The Ordinances of Bristol: 1506–1598* (Bristol: Bristol Record Society, 1990), ix–x. For example, in 1563 they are enjoined to wear scarlet gowns on certain festival days, and from 1570 they were required to wear "black velvet tippets" when going to or coming from a council meeting and when they accompanied the mayor to sermons, burials, and weddings.

67. Latimer, *Sixteenth-Century Bristol,* 37–38, 49.

68. Stanford, *Ordinances of Bristol,* 58–59.

69. See Latimer, *Sixteenth-Century Bristol,* 44–45.

70. Ibid., 53.

71. Both actions are recorded in Stanford, *Ordinances of Bristol,* xii, 60–62.

72. Fletcher "rarely visited" and was translated to Worcester in 1593, with the bishopric remaining

vacant for the next ten years until 1603. From the city's perspective, this relative "freedom from direct episcopal oversight" was definitely an improvement. Carter, "Historical Background," in Pilkinton, *REED: Bristol*, xxv.

73. Latimer mentions an episode in 1586 in which the Council of the Marches tried to "assume suzerainty over Bristol," but he also declares that it resulted in the city being able to "put a final end to the Lord President's pretensions." *Sixteenth-Century Bristol*, 35.

74. Williams, *The Council in the Marches*, 201.

75. Sacks, *The Widening Gate*, 209. For a detailed account see "Ricart's Calendar," in Pilkinton, *REED: Bristol*, 177–78.

76. Carter, "Historical Background," in Pilkinton, *REED: Bristol*, xliv.

77. See Latimer, *Sixteenth-Century Bristol*, 52–53.

78. The charter's main goal was to increase the number of aldermen from six to twelve. Carter, "Historical Background," in Pilkinton, *REED: Bristol*, xiv. Latimer discusses the role of both men and notes that Walsingham "proved a . . . trustworthy friend" in forwarding the suit. *Sixteenth-Century Bristol*, 76–77.

79. There were popular rebellions in each decade from the 1530s to the 1560s, but none in the last thirty-four years of Elizabeth's reign.

80. David Harris Sacks and Michael Lynch, "Ports 1540–1700," in *Cambridge Urban History*, 400, 390, 398. For additional details on Bristol's economic growth and development, see Sacks, *Widening Gate*.

81. Sacks and Lynch, "Ports 1540–1700," 384.

CHAPTER FIVE: WORCESTER, 1575

1. Mary Hill Cole, *The Portable Queen: Elizabeth I and the Politics of Ceremony* (Amherst: University of Massachusetts Press, 1999), 33. Details for the next three sentences are derived from Cole's useful appendices, 188–89, 206.

2. Ibid., 24. The others were in 1566, 1574, and 1578.

3. Ibid., 23.

4. Based on the annual figure provided by Alan D. Dyer in *The City of Worcester in the Sixteenth Century* (Leicester: Leicester University Press, 1973), 216. Cole provides figures—all in the £45–90 range—for Southampton, Lichfield, Gloucester, and Canterbury. *Portable Queen*, 103.

5. Ute Engel, *Worcester Cathedral: An Architectural History* (Chichester: Phillimore, 2007), 17; Eric Kerridge, *Textile Manufacture in Early Modern England* (Manchester: Manchester University Press, 1985), 182.

6. Lucy Toulmin Smith, ed., *The Itinerary of John Leland in or about the years 1535–1543*, vol. 2 (Carbondale: Southern Illinois University Press, 1964), 91. Dyer largely confirms Leland's claim, *City of Worcester*, 94.

7. G. D. Ramsay, *The English Woolen Industry, 1500–1750* (London: Macmillan, 1982), 29.

8. Kerridge, *Textile Manufacture*, 20–21.

9. Thomas Habington, *A Survey of Worcestershire*, vol. 2 (Oxford: James Parker & Co., 1895), 427. Printed from a seventeenth-century manuscript.

10. Kerridge, *Textile Manufacture*, 21.

11. Paul Slack, "Great and Good Towns 1540–1700" in *Cambridge Urban History of Britain*, vol. 2, ed. Peter Clark (Cambridge: Cambridge University Press, 2008), 357.

12. Ibid., 357.

13. Alan D. Dyer, "The Economy of Tudor Worcester" in *University of Birmingham Historical Journal*, 10, no. 2 (1966), 124; Slack, "Great and Good Towns," 358.

14. Dyer, *City of Worcester*, 96.

15. Ramsay, *English Woolen Industry*, 29.

16. Ibid., 28–29. Dyer concludes that "Worcester was the biggest of the surviving urban textile centers by the later sixteenth century," *City of Worcester*, 128.

17. Kerridge, *Textile Manufacture*, 181.

18. Dyer, "Economy of Tudor Worcester," 127.

19. Kerridge, *Textile Manufacture*, 182; Dyer, *City of Worcester*, 225.

20. Ramsay, *English Woolen Industry*, 29.

21. Dyer, "Economy of Tudor Worcester," 129.

22. Ibid.

23. David Loades, *England's Maritime Empire: Seapower, Commerce, and Policy, 1490–1690* (New York: Longman, 2000), 54.

24. For a detailed account of this complex episode, see G. D. Ramsay, *The Queen's Merchants and the Revolt of the Netherlands: The End of the Antwerp Mart, Part II* (Manchester: Manchester University Press, 1986).

25. Ramsay, *Queen's Merchants*, 180, 13, 127.

26. Ramsay, *English Woolen Industry*, 39.

27. Ibid., 51.

28. Dyer, "Economy of Tudor Worcester," 129; Dyer, *City of Worcester*, 106.

29. Joel Benson, *Changes and Expansion in the English Cloth Trade in the Seventeenth Century* (Lewiston, NY: Edwin Mellen Press, 2002), 12.

30. This paragraph—including the quoted sections—is indebted to Ramsay, *English Woolen Industry*, 23, 40–41, 72, 46.

31. Ramsay, *English Woolen Industry*, 58.

32. Benson, *Changes and Expansion*, 19.

33. Ramsay, *Queen's Merchants*, 162.

34. Dyer, *City of Worcester*, 215.

35. Ramsay, *English Woolen Industry*, 62.

36. Dyer, *City of Worcester*, 214–15.

37. Dyer, "Economy of Tudor Worcester," 130.

38. Dyer, *City of Worcester*, 15, 193, 210–11, 195–96.

39. Ibid., 213. One of the few exceptions was Sir John Bourne from nearby Battenhall, who was Secretary of State for Queen Mary I. He was "the only local man to achieve great national power at a time when the city was anxious to acquire the maximum assistance from high places to further its application for a new charter" (214).

40. Dyer, *City of Worcester*, 201–2, 213.

41. Ibid., 213.

42. Ibid., 193.

43. *John Nichols's "The Progresses and Public Processions of Queen Elizabeth I": A New Edition of the Early Modern Sources*, vol. 2, ed. Elizabeth Goldring, Faith Eales, Elizabeth Clarke, and Jayne Elisabeth Archer (Oxford: Oxford University Press, 2014), 351. Subsequent primary quotations from the Queen's visit to Worcester will come from this volume and will use the abbreviation "*JN2*" alongside page numbers in the text, while citations of editorial comments will merit separate footnotes.

44. Dyer, *City of Worcester*, 48–49, 217, 221.

45. Ibid., 48, 163–64.

46. Dyer says that Bell's depiction is "unreliable" and that "pleas of disastrous impoverishment and impending ruin are very common in this period in complaints to the central government," *City of Worcester*, 109. In contrast, Mary Hill Cole takes Bell's statement at face value, *Portable Queen*, 111. For a more general assessment of Worcester's economy in the sixteenth century—"the textile manufacturers and merchants prospered in a modest but solid way"—see Penry Williams, *The Later Tudors: England 1547–1603* (Oxford: Clarendon Press, 1995), 179.

47. Ramsay, *Queen's Merchants*, 177.

48. Ibid., 143–45.

49. Nigel Baker and Richard Holt, *Urban Growth and the Medieval Church: Gloucester and Worcester* (Burlington, VT: Ashgate, 2004), 338–39.

50. Habington, *Survey of Worcestershire*, 418.
51. Thomas Buchanan-Dunlop, *William and Francis Bell* (Worcester: Buchanan-Dunlop, 1949), 4. Buchanan-Dunlop quotes heavily from *The Testament of William Bell*, which was written by Bell in 1587 and eventually annotated and published by his son Arthur in 1632. The quote above is from one of these annotations.
52. Felicity Heal, *Hospitality in Early Modern England* (New York: Oxford University Press, 1990), 302, 307–9, 339, 302, 20–21.
53. Dyer, *City of Worcester*, 220, 209.
54. Worcester had six main civic offices: two bailiffs, two aldermen, and two chamberlains. In 1575, Christopher Dighton was high bailiff (who essentially functioned as the mayor). Dighton had been an MP for Worcester in 1572, so he had an especially good sense of the macro issues facing the clothing industry. Though he was primarily a vintner, he seems to have dabbled in cloth, and his son is listed as a member of the company of clothiers in a 1596 account book. Worcestershire Archive and Archaeology, x705:232/5955/1.
55. Cole, *Portable Queen*, 123–25.
56. When the Queen visited a cathedral town, it was not unusual for the presiding bishop to host. See, for example, Canterbury, Norwich, Salisbury, and Winchester.
57. Bullingham had been born in Worcester circa 1512 and was only one of four (out of seventy-six) Elizabethan bishops who were natives of the cities that were the seats of their dioceses. His brother had been high bailiff in the 1560s and M.P. for the city in 1571, and his sister was married to Christopher Dighton, the current high bailiff. The epitaph on Bullingham's tomb in Worcester Cathedral—"Here:Born:Here:Bishop:Buried:Here"—attests to his strong sense of local place.
58. The preparations described in the Chamber Order Book reveal that these maces were regilded prior to the Queen's arrival (338).
59. Heal, *Hospitality*, 302.
60. This number is based on Dyer's earlier estimate of the number of freemen in the city, taking corresponding population increases into account, *City of Worcester*, 176.
61. For more on the role of color, costume, and banners in processional performance, see Kathleen Ashley, "Introduction" in *Moving Subjects: Processional Performance in the Middle Ages and the Renaissance*, ed. Kathleen Ashley and Wim Hüsken (Atlanta, GA: Rodopi, 2001), 19–20.
62. These processions had survived in Worcester into the mid-sixteenth century, as recently as 1566, Dyer, *City of Worcester*, 249.
63. Ashley, "Introduction," *Moving Subjects*, 16.
64. See Heal, *Hospitality*, 301–7, for links between hospitality and honor.
65. Daryl Palmer, *Hospitable Performances: Dramatic Genre and Cultural Practices in Early Modern England* (West Lafayette, IN: Purdue University Press, 1992), 4.
66. Ibid., 3, 22.
67. Felicity Heal, "Giving and Receiving on Royal Progress" in *The Progresses, Pageants, and Entertainments of Queen Elizabeth I*, ed. Jayne Archer, Elizabeth Goldring, Sarah Knight (New York: Oxford University Press, 2007), 52.
68. Ibid., 52.
69. Cole, *Portable Queen*, 132.
70. Ibid., 127.
71. Ibid., 101.
72. Ibid., 101.
73. Felicity Heal, *The Power of Gifts: Gift Exchange in Early Modern England* (New York: Oxford University Press, 2014), 5–6.
74. Ibid., 18.
75. Ibid., 17.
76. Heal, *Hospitality*, 16.
77. Palmer, *Hospitable Performances*, 6.

78. Jayne Archer and Sarah Knight, "Elizabetha Triumphans" in *Progresses, Pageants, and Entertainments*, 4.

79. Dyer, *City of Worcester*, 193.

80. For these three functions of the Privy Council, see Michael Barraclough Pulman, *The Elizabethan Privy Council in the Fifteen-Seventies* (Berkeley: University of California Press, 1971), 75, 189, 139–41.

81. Ibid., 148.

82. W. J. Tighe, "Courtiers and Politics in Elizabethan Herefordshire: Sir James Croft, His Friends and Foes," *The Historical Journal* 32, no. 2 (1989): 259.

83. Ibid., 261.

84. P. W. Hasler, "Sir James Croft," *History of Parliament* website, 1981, accessed March 15, 2016, https://www.historyofparliamentonline.org/volume/1558-1603/member/croft-sir-james-1518-90.

85. Tighe, "Courtiers and Politics," 265.

86. He was therefore a much safer potential patron than someone like John Habington, who, while Cofferer to Queen Elizabeth and also a member of the Privy Council, had his primary estate at Hindlip, some three miles north of the city.

87. Cole, *Portable Queen*, 102.

88. Heal, *Power of Gifts*, 58.

89. Lorraine Attreed, *The King's Towns: Identity and Survival in Late Medieval English Boroughs* (New York: Peter Lang, 2001), 6.

90. These gifts are not recorded in the narrative, but the record of expenses later specifies that "Ipocras [was] geven to the Lordes & others of the privie councell" (*JN2*, 356).

91. While painting the Queen's arms was a typical practice of civic hosts and a conventional way to express welcome and loyalty (Cole, *Portable Queen*, 101), the practice seems to have special resonance for Worcester's attempt to associate the city with royalty.

92. "King John and Worcester," Worcester Cathedral Library and Archive website, accessed February 8, 2016, https://worcestercathedrallibrary.blogspot.com/2012/02.

93. For example, in 1209. "King John and Magna Carta: Christianity and Culture," Worcester Cathedral exhibit, September 2015.

94. The quotes in the preceding two sentences are from Engel, *Worcester Cathedral*, 199, 207.

95. Descriptions of the two tombs are from Engel, *Worcester Cathedral*, 208, 184.

96. "King John and Magna Carta" exhibit.

97. Engel, *Worcester Cathedral*, 207, 211, 217.

98. Phillip Lindley, "Worcester and Westminster: The Figure-Sculpture of Prince Arthur's Chapel" in *Arthur Tudor, Prince of Wales: Life, Death and Commemoration*, ed. Steven Gunn and Linda Monckton (Rochester, NY: Boydell Press, 2009), 149.

99. Lindley, "Worcester and Westminster," 155.

100. Ibid., 157–58, 155.

101. Engel, *Worcester Cathedral*, 218.

102. Lindley, "Worcester and Westminster," 154.

103. Heal, "Giving and Receiving," 53.

104. Heal, *Power of Gifts*, 41.

105. Ibid., 41–42.

106. Palmer, *Hospitable Performances*, 22.

CHAPTER SIX: NORWICH, 1578

1. The 1576 progress was similar to other 1570s progresses in its length—seventy-five days—but it was restricted to the counties near London.

2. She crossed into Suffolk for a few days during the 1561 progress but had never set foot in Norfolk.

3. Elizabeth Goldring, Faith Eales, Elizabeth Clarke, and Jayne Elisabeth Archer, eds., *John Nichols's "The Progresses and Public Processions of Queen Elizabeth I": A New Edition of the Early Modern Sources*, vol. 2, 1572–1578 (Oxford: Oxford University Press, 2014), 779.

4. John Pound, *Tudor and Stuart Norwich* (Chichester: Phillimore, 1988), 19.

5. "The City Walls Walks," Explore Norwich: Walking Trails, the Norwich Society website, accessed May 26, 2021, https://www.thenorwichsociety.org.uk/explore-norwich/the-city-walls-walks.

6. Penelope Corfield, "East Anglia," in *The Cambridge Urban History of Britain*, vol. 2, ed. Peter Clark (Cambridge: Cambridge University Press, 2000), 38.

7. Peter Clark, "Introduction," *Cambridge Urban History*, 27.

8. Helen Hoyte, *The Strangers of Norwich* (Norwich: Red Herring, 2017), 2–3.

9. Goldring, Eales, Clarke, Archer, *John Nichols's*, 779.

10. David Galloway, ed., *Records of Early English Drama: Norwich 1540–1642* (Toronto: University of Toronto Press, 1984), xvii (hereafter cited as *REED*).

11. A. Hassell Smith, *County and Court: Government and Politics in Norfolk, 1558–1603* (Oxford: Clarendon Press, 1974), 18.

12. Laura Hunt Yungblut, *Strangers Settled Here amongst Us* (New York: Routledge, 1996), 106.

13. Yungblut, *Strangers Settled*, 107.

14. Galloway, *REED*, xvi.

15. William Hudson and John Cottingham, eds., *The Records of the City of Norwich*, vol. 2, (Norwich: Jarrold & Sons, 1910), 332–33.

16. William John Charles Moens, *The Walloons and their Church at Norwich, 1565–1832* (Lymington: Huguenot Society of London, 1888), 18.

17. Barbara Green and Rachel Young, *Norwich: The Growth of a City* (Norfolk: Norfolk Museums Service, 1981), 23; Ursula Priestley, *The Fabric of Stuffs: The Norwich Textile Industry from 1565* (Norwich: Centre of East Anglian Studies, 1990), 11.

18. Scott Oldenburg, *Alien Albion: Literature and Immigration in Early Modern England* (Toronto: University of Toronto Press, 2014), 8.

19. Ibid., 4.

20. Yungblut, *Strangers Settled*, 30.

21. The two main groups are typically identified as the Dutch and the (French-speaking) Walloons.

22. Yungblut, *Strangers Settled*, 30.

23. Ibid., 3, 90.

24. Ibid., 36, 102.

25. Priestley, *Fabric of Stuffs*, 10; Bernard Cottret, *The Huguenots in England: Immigration and Settlement, c. 1550–1700* (New York: Cambridge University Press, 1991), 57.

26. Yungblut, *Strangers Settled*, 30; Frank Meeres, *A History of Norwich* (Chichester: Phillimore, 1998), 65. The most detailed treatment of the refugees who came to Norwich is Meeres's well-researched *The Welcome Stranger: Dutch, Walloon and Huguenot Incomers to Norwich, 1550–1750* (Norwich: Lasse Press, 2018), though he tends to emphasize the Strangers' overall integration rather than the problems they encountered in the first few decades after their arrival.

27. Green and Young, *Norwich*, 23.

28. Pound, *Tudor and Stuart Norwich*, 58; Yungblut, *Strangers Settled*, 53.

29. Yungblut, *Strangers Settled*, 52.

30. Ibid., 58–59, 112.

31. James Wentworth Day, *Norwich through the Ages* (Ipswich: East Anglian Magazine, 1976), 64; Priestley, *Fabric of Stuffs*, 10.

32. Priestley, *Fabric of Stuffs*, 10.

33. Yungblut, *Strangers Settled*, 54.

34. Ibid., 7, 51–52.

35. Quoted in Oldenburg, *Alien Albion*, 48.

36. Yungblut, *Strangers Settled*, 45.

37. Ibid., 50.

38. Pound, *Tudor and Stuart Norwich*, 57. As Helen Hoyte puts it: "Some members of the Council did not share the Mayor's enthusiasm for inviting rivals," *Strangers of Norwich*, 12. The restrictions (discussed in the text) that greeted the Strangers on their arrival may well have been made to "satisfy the [dissenting] Council members" (16).

39. Moens, *Walloons and their Church*, ii.

40. Ibid., 19–20.

41. John T. Evans, *Seventeenth-Century Norwich: Politics, Religion, and Government, 1620–1690* (Oxford: Clarendon Press, 1979), 63–64.

42. According to Pound, only 14 percent of the freemen of the city were textile workers, *Tudor and Stuart Norwich*, 59–60. See also Green and Young, *Norwich* 24.

43. Green and Young, *Norwich*, 24. Grocers account for half of the mayors during this period.

44. Ibid., 23.

45. Moens, *Walloons and their Church*, 19.

46. Yungblut, *Strangers Settled*, 48–49.

47. Priestley, *Fabric of Stuffs*, 10.

48. Moens, *Walloons and their Church*, 29.

49. Priestley, *Fabric of Stuffs*, 10.

50. Ibid., 10; Moens, *Walloons and their Church*, 29.

51. Moens, *Walloons and their Church*, 30.

52. Ibid., 29, 20.

53. Ibid., 80; Green and Young, *Norwich* 23.

54. Meeres, *History of Norwich*, 65.

55. Cottret, *Huguenots in England*, 61; Priestley, *Fabric of Stuffs*, 11.

56. Yungblut, *Strangers Settled*, 37.

57. Pound, *Tudor and Stuart Norwich*, 58.

58. Ibid., 24; Patrick Collinson, "Europe in Britain: Protestant Strangers and the English Reformation," in *From Strangers to Citizens: The Integration of Immigrant Communities in Britain, Ireland and Colonial America, 1550–1750*, ed. Randolph Vigne and Charles Littleton (London: Huguenot Society of Great Britain and Ireland, 2001), 61.

59. Yungblut, *Strangers Settled*, 55; Cottret, *Huguenots in England*, 58.

60. Green and Young, *Norwich*, 25; see also Paul Slack, "Great and Good Towns 1540–1700," in *Cambridge Urban History of Britain*, 357. According to Helen Hoyte, it took about twenty years for the Norwich cloth trade to return to former levels of prosperity. *Strangers of Norwich*, 25, 62.

61. Green and Young, *Norwich*, 23. The Strangers did not begin to instruct the natives in their new methods until the 1570s and 1580s, and even then it was chiefly in relation to bays. They were particularly slow in passing along the techniques they used for fulling and scouring. Pound, *Tudor and Stuart Norwich*, 58.

62. Oldenburg, *Alien Albion*, 9, 45.

63. Moens, *Walloons and their Church*, 25.

64. Cottret, *Huguenots in England*, 71.

65. Ibid., 72.

66. Collinson, "Europe in Britain," 60.

67. According to Yungblut, "This could indeed have been a cause of native jealousy, for the conformity required of them by the Church of England either was not applied to the aliens, or was applied very loosely." *Strangers Settled*, 45.

68. Ibid., 46, 59, 87.

69. Ibid., 87.

70. Cottret, *Huguenots in England*, 57.

71. Yungblut, *Strangers Settled*, 25–27.

72. Brian Ayers, *Book of Norwich* (London: English Heritage, 1994), 96.

73. Only in Norwich and Canterbury did the Stranger communities maintain their own police forces. Cottret, *The Huguenots in England*, 62. For more on the Norwich Strangers' innovative system of poor relief, see Laura Hunt Yungblut, "'Mayntayninge the indigente and nedie': The Institutionalization of Social Responsibility in the Case of the Resident Alien Communities in Elizabethan Norwich and Colchester," in *From Strangers to Citizens*, 101–2.

74. A 1590 inventory of a recently deceased Stranger, Vincentianna Heytes, lists clothing that includes "1 duytsch cloak, one flemish cloak for a woman, two duch hattes" and "a duch houdde." Quoted in Hoyte, *Strangers of Norwich*, 48.

75. Moens, *Walloons and their Church*, iii.

76. Cottret, *Huguenots in England*, 57.

77. Moens, *Walloons and their Church*, 72.

78. Ibid., 73.

79. Hoyte, *Strangers of Norwich*, 67.

80. Moens, *Walloons and their Church*, 33.

81. Ibid., 38.

82. Corfield, "East Anglia," 39.

83. Moens, *Walloons and their Church*, 72.

84. Oldenburg, *Alien Albion*, 48.

85. Yungblut, *Strangers Settled*, 45.

86. Oldenburg, *Alien Albion*, 15.

87. Pound posits an even higher proportion of Strangers in 1578: some 6,000 out of a total population of 14,000 to 15,000. *Tudor and Stuart Norwich*, 28.

88. Galloway, *REED*, xxiii.

89. Ibid., xxv.

90. Moens, *Walloons and their Church*, 20, 37; Hudson and Cottingham, *Records of the City of Norwich*, 184.

91. Hudson and Cottingham, *Records of the City of Norwich*, 184; Moens, *Walloons and their Church*, 79.

92. Yungblut, *Strangers Settled*, 47–49.

93. Hudson and Cottingham, *Records of the City of Norwich*, 183.

94. Ibid., 184.

95. Moens, *Walloons and their Church*, 30.

96. The examples in this paragraph are drawn from Moens, *Walloons and their Church*, 77, 79–80.

97. Yungblut, *Strangers Settled*, 15–16; Oldenburg, *Alien Albion*, 8; Cottret, *Huguenots in England*, 50.

98. Hoyte, *Strangers of Norwich*, 12, 36.

99. Ibid., 16–17.

100. Yungblut, *Strangers Settled*, 48.

101. Moens, *Walloons and their Church*, 37, 78.

102. Ibid., 74.

103. Oldenburg attributes a similar range of motives to London Strangers in the period. *Alien Albion*, 13.

104. These two examples of Strangers' complaints are from Moens, *Walloons and their Church*, 28, 80.

105. Ibid., 77.

106. Ibid., 78.

107. Frank Meeres, "Records Relating to the Strangers at the Norfolk Record Office," *Dutch Crossing* 38, no. 2 (July 2014): 151.

108. Noel Currer-Briggs and Royston Gambier, *Huguenot Ancestry* (Chichester: Phillimore, 1985), 48.

109. Meeres, *Welcome Stranger*, 118, 120.

110. Ibid., 163.

111. The registers for St. Michael-at-Plea, St. James Pockthorpe, and St. Michael Coslany all record burials of Strangers between the years 1567 and 1579. Meeres, "Records Relating to the Strangers," 147–48.

112. Ibid., 149. Another surviving monument—that of Jacques de Hem, who died in 1603—can be seen in the church of St. Michael-at-Plea.

113. Yungblut, *Strangers Settled*, 55.

114. Priestley, *Fabric of Stuffs*, 9, 11.

115. Hudson and Cottingham, *Records of the City of Norwich*, 185–86. For a 1573 example, see Meeres, "Records Relating to the Strangers," 139.

116. Priestley, *Fabric of Stuffs*, 11.

117. Cottret, *Huguenots in England*, 63. See Yungblut on the medieval origin of and specifics regarding "hostage," *Strangers Settled*, 67–68, 103.

118. Moens, *Walloons and their Church*, i.

119. Cottret, *Huguenots in England*, 64.

120. Moens, *Walloons and their Church*, 41.

121. Ibid., i.

122. Ibid., , 41. One of these letters is in the Norfolk Record Office: NCR 17d/9.

123. Aldrich in 1558 and 1570, Suckling in 1572, Peck in 1573, and Wood in 1569. Robert Suckling was the grandfather of the cavalier poet Sir John Suckling.

124. Sotherton was mayor in 1565, Greene in 1571, Layer in 1576, and Some in 1574. Greene may have been the father of the Elizabethan writer Robert Greene.

125. Basil Cozens-Hardy and Ernest A. Kent, *The Mayors of Norwich: 1403 to 1835* (Norwich: Jarrold & Sons, 1938), 60.

126. Ibid., 61.

127. Moens, *Walloons and their Church*, ii.

128. Not only was the Mayor's Court involved with the Strangers' affairs as a body, individual members had also worked closely with the community. Peck, Suckling, and Cullie had helped create the 1571 Book of Orders, while Aldrich had helped revise the orders in 1574.

129. In Norwich, the mayor was "supreme in all civic affairs" and "presid[ed] over all . . . city functions." Galloway, *REED*, xx. Cozens-Hardy and Kent confirm that Wood "was responsible for the arrangments of all the pageants that were performed." *Mayors of Norwich*, 59.

130. Goldring, Eales, Clarke, Archer, *John Nichols's*, 779–83.

131. Ibid., 783.

132. Ibid., 722.

133. Galloway, *REED*, 297.

134. Felicity Heal, *Hospitality in Early Modern England* (Oxford: Clarendon Press, 1990), 322–38.

135. In Norwich, these events ranged from medieval guild processions during Corpus Christi to pageantry associated with the annual feast (and guild) of St. George to the contemporary public ceremony for inaugurating the new mayor. Ursula Priestley, *The Great Market: A Survey of Nine Hundred Years of the Norwich Provisional Market* (Norwich: Centre for East Anglian Studies, 1987), 13–16. Norwich also had its own city waits from at least 1408. These musicians were given their own liveries, banners, and badges, and were employed by the corporation to play at festivals, feasts, and other momentous events; they were thus another feature of the city's investment in civic pageantry and ceremony. See George Stephen, *The Waits of the City of Norwich through Four Centuries to 1790* (Norwich: Goose & Son, 1933).

136. Mary Hill Cole, *The Portable Queen: Elizabeth I and the Politics of Ceremony* (Amherst: University of Massachusetts Press, 2000), 115. Jayne Archer and Sarah Knight, "Elizabetha Triumphans," in *The Progresses, Pageants, and Entertainments of Queen Elizabeth I*, ed. Jayne Archer, Elizabeth Goldring, and Sarah Knight (New York: Oxford University Press, 2007), 4; in this same volume, see C. E. McGee's article, "Mysteries, Musters, and Masques: The Import(s) of Elizabethan Civic Entertainments," 104–21.

137. See Herman du Toit for a general discussion of the ways in which pageantry can create unity, promote pluralism and tolerance, initiate newcomers, educate and assimilate, and create imaginary affiliations. "Introduction," in *Pageants and Processions: Images and Idiom as Spectacle*, ed. Herman du Toit (Newcastle upon Tyne: Cambridge Scholars, 2009), xiii–xv.

138. Oldenburg, *Alien Albion*, 4–5.

139. Whereas Oldenburg (*Alien Albion*, 8–9) posits coherence around religion, shared economic crafts, and domestic relations, I emphasize the role of the Queen as a unifying focus.

140. Goldring, Eales, Clarke, Archer, *John Nichols's*, 779. Cole also reads the Norwich pageants primarily in terms of the Queen's responses to Catholic and Puritan factions. *Portable Queen*, 141–44.

141. As Woodcock points out, both "were prominent concerns that were discussed by the Council during the progress and also find their way into speeches and shows staged for Elizabeth when she reached Norwich." Woodcock also summarizes Patrick Collinson's view that the Queen and Privy Council differed on the issues of both Puritan nonconformity and military aid, and that each used the events of the 1578 progress to try to influence each others' views. *John Nichols's*, 710.

142. Day, *Norwich through the Ages*, 67–69. See also Priestley, who speaks of the "heart-felt but interminable orations of her loyal Norwich subjects" (*Great Market*, 14) and Sylvia Haymon's description of "a barrage" of labored verses and pedestrian imagery "to which the Queen, during her 6 days' stay, was to be subjected to without mercy." *Norwich* (Harmondsworth, Middlesex: Longman, 1973), 110, 114.

143. McGee, "Mysteries, Musters, and Masque," 118.

144. Zillah Dovey, *An Elizabethan Progress: The Queen's Journey into East Anglia, 1578* (Stroud, Gloucester: Alan Sutton, 1996), 63–87.

145. For textual history, see *John Nichols's*, 715, 777; see also Galloway, *REED*, 243–44. For more information on Thomas Churchyard, see Matthew Woodcock's recent biography *Thomas Churchyard: Pen, Sword, and Ego* (Oxford: Oxford University Press, 2016). Biographical details on Garter are more scant. Mark Eccles identifies him as a poet who published *Two English Lovers* (1565) and *A New Year's Gift* (1579). The records indicate that he lived in London and was a scrivener by profession. He was born in 1533, so he would have been forty-five at the time of the Queen's visit. His connections to Norwich are unknown. "Brief Lives: Tudor and Stuart Authors," *Studies in Philology* 79, no. 4 (Fall 1982): 54.

146. Bernard Garter's and Thomas Churchyard's accounts serve as the primary texts for my analysis of the Norwich pageants. Both are found in Elizabeth Goldring, Faith Eales, Elizabeth Clarke, and Jayne Elisabeth Archer, eds., *John Nichols's "The Progresses and Public Processions of Queen Elizabeth I": A New Edition of the Early Modern Sources*, vol. 2, 1572–1578 (Oxford: Oxford University Press, 2014). Subsequent citations of primary material will use the abbreviation "*JN2*" alongside page numbers in the text, while citations of editorial comments will merit separate footnotes.

147. Dovey, *Elizabethan Progress*, 17.

148. For example, Monday's appearance of Mercury (beneath the Queen's window) to preview the coming entertainments, Tuesday's dialogue between Cupid and Philosophy (called "The Shew of Chastitie"), Thursday's "Shew of Manhode and Dezart" featuring Beauty, Good Favor, and Good Fortune, and Friday's Show of Fairies. The location and timing of Churchyard's devices are often spontaneously altered to fit the circumstances of the weather and the Queen's movements (e.g. 727, 737, 748), suggesting their more generalized nature.

149. Churchyard reports that he arrived three weeks early, "deuising and studying the best I coulde for the Citie" (721). Thursday's "Show of Manhood" explores the seemingly topical theme of the dangers of disunity.

150. Gurgunt did not walk all the way to Harford Bridge, but instead broke away and took up his position just outside the city walls (*JN2*, 787). This suggests that he was included in the procession purely for the benefit of the city spectators.

151. This speech was actually "not vttered" because of a sudden shower of rain, but Garter's account prints it in its entirety (*JN2*, 790–93).

152. For more on King Gurgunt, see *John Nichols's*, 787n1012.

153. Oldenburg, *Alien Albion*, 6.

154. Goldring, Eales, Clarke, Archer, *John Nichols's The Progresses*, 791n1031.

155. Hoyte positions the stage just inside the city gate. *Strangers of Norwich*, 51, 59. However, Garter says "then passed she forward, through Saint Stephens streete, where the first Pageant was placed" (*JN2*, 792)—which implies that the stage was set up somewhere further along St. Stephen's Street. One possibility is the open area—later known as St. Stephen's Plain—where St. Stephen's Street, Westlegate, Rampant Horse Street, and Red Lion Street all merged. Richard Lane, *The Plains of Norwich* (Dereham, Norfolk: The Larks Press, 1999), 65.

156. While it is known that the Strangers participated in the pageant, it is unknown if they were the *only* participants. Blomefield refers to it as the "artisan-Strangers pageant," and Nancy Ives suggests that Strangers had creative control over the pageant to the point of designing and painting the set. "Strangers and Others in St. Stephens, Norwich, in the 1570s," talk given at the Norfolk Family History Society, February 2002, 16. Norfolk Records Office: MC 3015, Box 18. However, both Hoyte and Priestley imagine that the Strangers were invited to join native textile craftsmen in exhibiting cloth works to the Queen (*Strangers of Norwich*, 51; *Fabric of Stuffs*, 11, respectively). Either way, it is remarkable that the Strangers were either given a sole voice or put on equal footing with native textile workers. Priestley says that the Strangers' participation in this pageant shows their growing integration (*Fabric of Stuffs*, 11), whereas I argue that such participation helped *cause* this integration.

157. Ives, "Strangers and Others," 12.

158. Ibid., 30–31.

159. In the Middle Ages, White Lion Street was called Sadler's Row (and later Lorimer's Row—since harnesses and straps were also sold here) before acquiring its present street name.

160. Dimensions from Priestley, *Great Market*, 8. In the late Middle Ages and early modern period, Norwich's market was even larger than it is today; its open space extended westward (beyond St. Peter Mancroft) all the way to Rampant Horse Street.

161. Sybil M. Jack, *Towns in Tudor and Stuart Britain* (New York: St. Martin's Press, 1996), 8; Priestley, *Great Market*, 13.

162. The church was "largely financed by the City's merchants" circa 1430 to 1455. It also had close connections to the city market: historically, all stallholders had prerogatives of marriage and burial in the church and its churchyard. *A Market for Our Times: A History of Norwich Provision Market* (Norwich: Norwich Heritage Projects, 2010), 13.

163. Ibid., 12.

164. Priestley, *Great Market*, 12.

165. Oldenburg, *Alien Albion*, 50.

166. Cottret, *Huguenots in England*, 61.

167. For example, city leaders worked to assuage Strangers' concerns about Tipper's Grant by communicating with the immigrants via their churches.

168. For example, they used the former preaching nave, which became known as St. Andrew's Hall, as a space for assemblies and banquets. In 1544, the first mayor's feast was held here; subsequently, some twenty guilds held their annual feasts in the hall. Meanwhile, the Blackfriars chancel became a chapel for the use of the city corporation and guilds. Michael Shaw, *The Norwich Blackfriars: A History and Guide to the Friary* (Norwich: Parke Sutton, n.d.), 12–15.

169. At the same time, the smaller, French-speaking Walloon population was granted (by Bishop John Parkhurst) the use of the Bishop's Chapel in the cathedral complex.

170. Indeed, the Dutch congregation would continue to worship at Blackfriars until well into the nineteenth century.

171. Hoyte, *Strangers of Norwich*, 35; Shaw, *Norwich Blackfriars*, 14; Helen Sutermeister, *The Norwich Blackfriars: A History and Guide to St. Andrew's and Blackfriar's Halls* (Norwich: City of Norwich, 1977), 13.

172. Aside from the associations mentioned above, this section of the city also included the so-called Stranger's Hall (where some of the original 1565 Strangers were reputedly lodged), Anthony de Solempne's printing press (in Dove Street), and some of the local churches that the Strangers were beginning to attend (e.g. St. Michael-at-Plea and St. John Maddermarket).

173. Robert Suckling's hall and residence were right across the street from the southern side of the complex. Thomas Sotherton and Thomas Layer had large houses down Wymer Street in the direction of St. Benet's Gate. All three buildings are still extant. The location of Thomas Peck's house is unknown, but it may well have adjoined St. Andrew's churchyard, a stone's throw to the south. Goldring, Eales, Clarke, Archer, *John Nichols's, 722n833.*

174. Kathleen Ashley, "Introduction," in *Moving Subjects: Processional Performance in the Middle Ages and the Renaissance,* ed. Kathleen Ashley and Wim Hüsken (Atlanta, GA: Rodopi, 2001), 17; J. R. Mulryne, "Introduction: Making Space for Festival," in *Architectures of Festival in Early Modern Europe,* ed. J. R. Mulryne, Krista de Jonge, Pieter Martens, and R. L. M. Morris (New York: Routledge, 2018), 3.

175. That Modert formally presented a cup to the Queen on behalf of the Strangers adds credence to the speculation there was a large group of Dutch Strangers assembled alongside him.

176. Ellie Phillips and Isla Fay, *Health and Hygiene in Early Modern Norwich* (Norwich: Norfolk Record Society, 2013), 10.

177. C. B. Jewson, *History of the Great Hospital* (Norwich: Great Hospital, 1966), 24.

178. Ibid., 22–24.

179. Ibid., 26.

180. Haymon, *Norwich,* 105. Such poor relief programs were not entirely altruistic. As Phillips and Fay suggest, the city knew that "poverty and ill-health . . . would inevitably cause a financial disaster." *Health and Hygiene,* 12. The city leaders' interest in "searching and correcting" the poor has also been tied to Norwich's status as an early center of Puritanism. Yungblut, "'Mayntayninge,'" 103.

181. Galloway, *REED,* xvii. Yungblut, "'Mayntayninge,'" 99. According to Paul Slack, Norwich was also the earliest of the major provincial cities to establish a poor rate and one of the earliest to establish a workhouse (preceded only by Oxford and Salisbury). "Great and Good Towns," 367.

182. Galloway, *REED,* xvii.

183. The latter would seem to invite special application to Norwich's own "Strangers," though Limbert alludes to these ancient writers rather than quoting them directly.

184. Phillips and Fay, *Health and Hygiene,* xi, 11. Most of the information included in this paragraph is indebted to pages 8–14 of this source.

185. The hospital also managed an endowment (by Archbishop Matthew Parker) that annually supported three scholars at Corpus Christi, Cambridge, ibid., 13.

186. Ibid., 8.

187. City aldermen automatically became members and common councilors had the right to do so. The outgoing mayor became the new head of the company. "Snap: The Story of the Dragons of Norwich" (Norwich: St. George Colegate, 2015), 4.

188. Phillips and Fay, *Health and Hygiene,* 14.

189. Carole Rawcliffe, *Medicine for the Soul: The Life, Death and Resurrection of an English Medieval Hospital: St. Giles, Norwich, c.* 1249–1550 (Stroud, Gloucester: Alan Sutton, 1999), plate 27 caption.

190. Ibid., plate 26 caption.

191. As Yungblut observes, "Only a small proportion arrived with substantial possessions, either due to the circumstances of their departure from their homelands or to their belief that their migration was temporary." "'Mayntayninge,'" 100.

192. This paragraph's description of the Strangers' poor relief is drawn from Yungblut, "'Mayntayninge,'" 101, 103–4.

193. Ibid., 102–3.

194. Hudson and Cottingham, *Records of the City of Norwich,* 332–33.

195. Ives, "Strangers and Others," 30.

196. Significantly, the first pageant was set up within St. Stephen's parish. For more information on its location, see chap. 6, n. 155.

197. Cottret, *Huguenots in England,* 60. In fact, says Cottret, "when the Crown attempted to assimilate the Strangers in the 1630s it encountered the worst possible opposition on the part of the refugees" (60).

198. Oldenburg, *Alien Albion,* 12.

199. Unfortunately for Churchyard, rain prevented the Queen from riding. In the event, Churchyard partially transformed Thursday's "Shew of Nimphs" into Friday's "Shew of Fairies."

200. Broken music is also specified in the abovementioned musical epilogue to the second pageant (JN2, 799). Indeed, music featured prominently in entertainments throughout the week: at St. Stephen's Gate, in the second pageant, at Peck's door, and so on. Its prominence probably owes something to the availability of the Norwich city waits; however, music is also an apt emblem of the type of internal harmony that the city seems keen to promote.

201. Cottret, Huguenots in England, 60.

202. Garter includes both the Latin original and English translation in his published account. He titles it: "Mr. Limberts Oration, which had bin rehearsed at hir Graces departing, but that she set late forward in hir Progresse" (JN2, 821). Along with the Mayor's second oration, Limbert's second oration was supposed to be delivered after the Queen had exited out of St. Giles's Gate and traveled two miles to Earlham Bridge—the outer boundary of the city's liberties and thus the place where the city said its final farewell (JN2, 815, 817). Dovey conjectures that Limbert may have originally intended to deliver his oration as the Queen left the Bishop's Palace to begin her departure, Elizabethan Progress, 84.

203. See also the first few lines of the City of Norwich's speech in the second pageant, which provides additional examples of friendship and succor, including Castor and Pollux, Hercules and Theseus, Nisus and Euryalus, and Penelope and Ulysses (JN2, 795).

204. Many of the orations are actually in Latin. Whereas at Oxford, the function of Latin orations was to display humanistic learning, at Norwich Latin may have been chosen because it was a lingua franca that many English, Dutch, and French would have had in common. By delivering the Dutch Minister's Oration in Latin, Modert ensured that both the royal visitors and the educated Norwich citizens understood its message (much more so than if it had been spoken in Dutch).

205. Hudson and Cottingham, Records of the City of Norwich, 192.

206. Ibid., 192–93.

207. Ibid., 189, 190. The groups were of eight and eleven people. In both groups, exceptions were made to allow select people to stay: "a yonge maid" and her two children in the first group; a family of five that had come from Sandwich with a certificate of good behavior from the Sandwich mayor. While Meeres reads this incident as showing that "the city was becoming more wary of refugees" (Welcome Stranger, 46), the city here seems to be drawing a distinction between resident Strangers and newly arrived immigrants.

208. Hudson and Cottingham, Records of the City of Norwich, 193.

209. Ibid., 193–94.

210. It may also be that as they became more acculturated into their adopted city, the Norwich Strangers were beginning to see themselves as distinct from other religious refugees from the Continent. In 1581, conflict broke out with a group of newly arrived Strangers from Canterbury. According to the Mayor's Court (which stepped in to broker peace), the groups "doth most unnaturallye contend one agaynste the other, grevouselye defaminge and sclaunderinge one another." Moens, Walloons and their Church, 41.

211. Ibid., 41. Wright accused four prominent Strangers of "selling goods by retail and defrauding her Majesty's customs" (45).

212. Hudson and Cottingham, Records of the City of Norwich, 191.

213. Ibid., 195. In 1587, the city used "monye collected for the seallyng of their commodities" to assist the Dutch. In 1589, they used a combination of "the benevolence of well affected persons" and the "treasurey of this citie" to help the Walloons.

214. Priestley, Fabric of Stuffs, 10. Some Strangers had attained the freedom earlier—e.g. the printer Anthony de Solempne in 1570—but only in 1598 could they do so on the same terms as natives. Green and Young, Norwich, 23; Meeres, History of Norwich, 65.

215. Pound, Tudor and Stuart Norwich, 60.

216. Ibid., 60.
217. Meeres, *Welcome Stranger*, 163. Meeres writes that these children are "among the earliest examples of [the] merging of the incomer community with the native-born community," which he then traces throughout the seventeenth century.
218. Cottret, *Huguenots in England*, 74.
219. Ibid., 74.
220. Oldenburg, *Alien Albion*, 69.
221. Cottret, *Huguenots in England*, 76.
222. Hudson and Cottingham, *Records of the City of Norwich*, 186. The Dutch congregation was given £19, while the Walloons received £11.
223. Moens, *Walloons and their Church*, 44.
224. Given the context and themes of the pageant, the Queen's gesture seems to go well beyond Dovey's suggestion that "Perhaps the Queen had been touched by the immigrants' gift of a cup on the previous Tuesday." *Elizabethan Progress*, 86.
225. Hudson and Cottingham, *Records of the City of Norwich*, 186.

CONCLUSION

1. Black pears are edible, but only after they have been stored for several months and then cooked— both of which factors mitigate against spontaneous plucking and eating.
2. Since five of the six case studies treat of cities (with only Sandwich having town status), I will predominantly use the term "city" rather than "town" in this conclusion.
3. Hester Lees-Jeffries, "Location as Metaphor in Queen Elizabeth's Coronation Entry (1559): *Veritas Temporis Filia*," ed. Jayne Archer, Elisabeth Goldring, Sarah Knight, in *Progresses, Pageants, and Entertainments of Queen Elizabeth I* (New York: Oxford University Press, 2007), 66.
4. Margit Thøfner, *A Common Art: Urban Ceremonial in Antwerp and Brussels during and after the Dutch Revolt* (Zwolle: Waanders Publishers, 2007), 76–77.
5. Ibid., 77.
6. David Bergeron, *English Civic Pageantry: 1558–1642*, rev. ed., (Tempe: Arizona State University, 2003), 6–7.
7. Elizabeth Goldring, Faith Eales, Elizabeth Clarke, and Jayne Elisabeth Archer, eds., *John Nichols's "The Progresses and Public Processions of Queen Elizabeth I": A New Edition of the Early Modern Sources*, vol. 1 (Oxford: Oxford University Press, 2014), 465.
8. J. R. Mulryne, "Introduction: Making Space for Festival," in *Architectures of Festival in Early Modern Europe*, ed. J. R. Mulryne, Krista de Jonge, Pieter Martens, and R. L. M. Morris (New York: Routledge, 2018), 5, 3.
9. Kathleen Ashley, "Introduction" in *Moving Subjects: Processional Performance in the Middle Ages and the Renaissance*, ed. Kathleen Ashley and Wim Hüsken (Atlanta, GA: Rodopi, 2001), 13.
10. Ibid., 14.
11. Most takeaways in this category are from the four cities where urban leaders actually hosted, though Oxford and Canterbury also offer some interesting insights.
12. Mary Hill Cole, *The Portable Queen: Elizabeth I and the Politics of Ceremony* (Amherst: University of Massachusetts Press, 1999), 126.
13. See Cole's "Chronology of Royal Visits and Progresses" in *Portable Queen*, 180–202.
14. Christopher Haigh, *Elizabeth I* (New York: Longman, 2001), 204.
15. See my discussion of Elizabeth's 1592 visit at the end of chapter one, which draws from Linda Shenk's insightful article, "Turning Learned Authority into Royal Supremacy: Elizabeth I's Learned Persona and Her University Orations" in *Elizabeth I: Always Her Own Free Woman*, ed. Carole Levin, Jo Eldridge Carney, and Debra Barrett-Graves (Burlington, VT: Ashgate, 2003).

BIBLIOGRAPHY

INTRO/GENERAL

Archer, Ian A. "Politics and Government 1540–1700." In Clark, *Cambridge Urban History,* 235–62.

Archer, Jayne Elisabeth, Elizabeth Goldring, and Sarah Knight, ed. *The Progresses, Pageants, and Entertainments of Queen Elizabeth I.* New York: Oxford University Press, 2007.

Archer, Jayne Elisabeth and Sarah Knight. "Elizabetha Triumphans." In Archer, Goldring, and Knight, *Progresses, Pageants,* 1–23.

Arnade, Peter. *Realms of Ritual: Burgundian Ceremony and Civic Life in Late Medieval Ghent.* Ithaca, NY: Cornell University Press, 1996.

Ashley, Kathleen and Wim Hüsken, ed. *Moving Subjects: Processional Performance in the Middle Ages and the Renaissance.* Atlanta, GA: Rodopi, 2001.

Attreed, Lorraine. *The King's Towns: Identity and Survival in Late Medieval English Boroughs.* New York: Peter Lang, 2001.

Attreed, Lorraine. "The Politics of Welcome: Ceremonies and Constitutional Development in Later Medieval English Towns." In Hanawalt and Reyerson, *City and Spectacle,* 208–34.

Barry, Jonathan. "Area Surveys 1540–1840: South-West." In Clark, *Cambridge Urban History,* 67–92.

Bergeron, David. *English Civic Pageantry: 1558–1642.* Rev. ed. Tempe: Arizona State University, 2003.

Castor, Helen. *Elizabeth I: A Study in Insecurity.* London: Penguin, 2018.

Clark, Peter, ed. *The Cambridge Urban History of Britain.* Vol. 2, 1540–1840. Cambridge: Cambridge University Press, 2000.

Clark, Peter and Paul Slack. *English Towns in Transition 1500–1700.* New York: Oxford University Press, 1976.

Cole, Mary Hill. *The Portable Queen: Elizabeth I and the Politics of Ceremony.* Amherst: University of Massachusetts Press, 1999.

Collinson, Patrick. "Elizabeth I." *Oxford Dictionary of National Biography* online. 2012.

Cooper, Richard. "The Theme of War in French Renaissance Entries." In Mulryne, *Ceremonial Entries in Early Modern Europe,* 15–36.

Corfield, Penelope. "Area Surveys 1540–1840: East Anglia." In Clark, *Cambridge Urban History*, 31–48.

Dean, Lucinda H. S. "Making the Best of What They Had: Adaptations of Indoor and Outdoor Space for Royal Ceremony in Scotland c. 1214–1603." In Mulryne, de Jonge, Martens, and Morris, *Architectures of Festival*, 99–118.

Dillon, Janette. *The Language of Space in Court Performance, 1400–1625.* Cambridge: Cambridge University Press, 2010.

Dyer, Alan. *Decline and Growth in English Towns, 1400–1640* (Basingstoke: Macmillan, 1991).

Fantoni, Marcello, George Gorse, and Malcolm Smuts, ed. *The Politics of Space: European Courts ca. 1500–1750.* Rome: Bulzoni Editore, 2009.

Frank, Martina. "From Ephemeral to Permanent Architecture: The Venetian Palazzo in the Second Half of the Seventeenth Century." In Mulryne, de Jonge, Martens, and Morris, *Architectures of Festival*, 119–38.

Gibson, James M. "Rochester Bridge, 1530–1660." In *Traffic and Politics: The Construction and Management of Rochester Bridge AD 43–1993*, edited by Nigel Yates and James M. Gibson, 107–60. Woodbridge, Suffolk: Boydell Press, 1994.

Goldring, Elizabeth. "Portraiture, Patronage, and the Progresses: Robert Dudley, Earl of Leicester and the Kenilworth Festivities of 1575." In Archer, Goldring, and Knight, *Progresses, Pageants*, 163–88.

Haigh, Christopher. *Elizabeth I.* New York: Longman, 2001.

Hanawalt, Barbara and Kathryn Reyerson, eds. *City and Spectacle in Medieval Europe.* Minneapolis: University of Minnesota Press, 1994.

Heal, Felicity. *Hospitality in Early Modern England.* Oxford: Clarendon Press, 1990.

Heal, Felicity. "Giving and Receiving on Royal Progress." In Archer, Goldring, and Knight, *Progresses, Pageants*, 46–61.

Hibbert, Christopher. *The Virgin Queen: Elizabeth I, Genius of the Golden Age.* Reading, MA: Addison-Wesley, 1991.

Hopkins, Lisa. *Queen Elizabeth I and Her Court.* New York: St. Martin's Press, 1990.

Horrox, Rosemary. "Urban Patronage in the Fifteenth Century." In *Patronage, the Crown, and the Provinces*, edited by Ralph A. Griffiths, 145–61. Gloucester: Alan Sutton, 1981.

Jack, Sybil M. *Towns in Tudor and Stuart Britain.* New York: St. Martin's Press, 1996.

Johnston, Alexandra F. and Wim Hüsken, ed. *Civic Ritual and Drama.* Atlanta, GA: Rodopi, 1997.

Lancashire, Ann K. "Continuing Civic Ceremonies of 1530s London." In Johnston and Hüsken, *Civic Ritual and Drama*, 81–106.

Kemp, William. "Transformations in the Printing of Royal Entries during the Reign of Francois I: The Role of Geofroy Tory." In Russell and Visentin, *French Ceremonial Entries*, 111–32.

Korsch, Evelyn. "Renaissance Venice and the Sacred-Political Connotations of Waterborne Pageants." In Shewring, *Waterborne Pageants*, 1–8.

Leahy, William Leahy. *Elizabethan Triumphal Processions.* Burlington, VT: Ashgate, 2005.

Lees-Jeffries, Hester. "Location as Metaphor in Queen Elizabeth's Coronation Entry (1559): *Veritas Temporis Filia*." In Archer, Goldring, and Knight, *Progresses, Pageants*, 65–85.

MacCaffrey, Wallace T. *Queen Elizabeth and the Making of Policy, 1572–1588*. Princeton, NJ: Princeton University Press, 1981.

McGee, C. E. "Mysteries, Musters, and Masque: The Import(s) of Elizabethan Civic Entertainments." In Archer, Goldring, and Knight, *Progresses, Pageants*, 104–21.

McGowan, Margaret M. "The French Royal Entry in the Renaissance: The Status of the Printed Text." In Russell and Visentin, *French Ceremonial Entries*, 29–54.

Mears, Natalie. *Queenship and Political Discourse in the Elizabethan Realms*. Cambridge: Cambridge University Press, 2005.

Mulryne, J. R., Krista de Jonge, Pieter Martens, and R. L. M. Morris, ed. *Architectures of Festival in Early Modern Europe: Fashioning and Re-fashioning Urban and Courtly Space*. New York: Routledge, 2018.

Mulryne, J. R., ed. *Ceremonial Entries in Early Modern Europe: The Iconography of Power*. Burlington, VT: Ashgate, 2015.

Murphy, Neil. *Ceremonial Entries, Municipal Liberties and the Negotiation of Power in Valois France, 1328–1589*. Boston, MA: Brill, 2016.

O'Day, Rosemary. *The Longman Companion to the Tudor Age*. New York: Longman, 1996.

Palmer, Daryl. *Hospitable Performances: Dramatic Genre and Cultural Practices in Early Modern England*. West Lafayette, IN: Purdue University Press, 1992.

Patterson, Catherine. *Urban Patronage in Early Modern England: Corporate Boroughs, the Landed Elite, and the Crown, 1580–1640*. Stanford: Stanford University Press, 1999.

Pauly, Michel and Martin Scheutz, ed. *Cities and Their Spaces: Concepts and Their Use in Europe*. Koln: Bohlau, 2014.

Pulman, Michael Barraclough. *The Elizabethan Privy Council in the Fifteen-Seventies*. Berkeley: University of California Press, 1971.

Randell, Keith. *Elizabeth I and the Government of England*. London: Hodder & Stoughton, 1994.

Richards, Judith M. *Elizabeth I*. New York: Routledge, 2012.

Rowse, A. L. *The England of Elizabeth*. 2nd ed. Madison, University of Wisconsin Press, 2003.

Russell, Nicolas and Helene Visentin. "The Multilayered Production of Meaning in Sixteenth-Century French Ceremonial Entries." In *French Ceremonial Entries in the Sixteenth Century*, edited by Nicolas Russell and Helene Visentin, 15–27. Toronto: Centre for Reformation and Renaissance Studies, 2007.

Sandbichler, Veronika. "Elements of Power in Court Festivals of Habsburg Emperors in the Sixteenth Century." In Mulryne, *Ceremonial Entries in Early Modern Europe*, 167–88.

Shewring, Margaret, ed. *Waterborne Pageants and Festivities in the Renaissance: Essays in Honour of J. R. Mulryne*. Burlington, VT: Ashgate, 2013.

Shewring, Margaret. "The Iconography of Populism: Waterborne Entries to London for Anne Boleyne (1533), Catherine of Braganza (1662), and Elizabeth II (2012)." In Mulryne, *Ceremonial Entries in Early Modern Europe,* 221–44.

Slack, Paul. "Great and Good Towns 1540–1700." In Clark, *Cambridge Urban History,* 347–76.

Snickare, Marten. "A Productive Conflict: The Colosseum and Early Modern Religious Performance." In Mulryne, de Jonge, Martens, and Morris, *Architectures of Festival,* 11–26.

Thøfner, Margit. *A Common Art: Urban Ceremonial in Antwerp and Brussels during and after the Dutch Revolt.* Zwolle: Waanders Publishers, 2007.

Tittler, Robert. *Architecture and Power: The Town Hall and the English Urban Community c. 1500–1640.* Oxford: Clarendon Press, 1991.

Tittler, Robert. *The Reformation and the Towns in England.* Oxford: Clarendon Press, 1998.

Trevisan, Sara. "The Golden Fleece of the London Drapers' Company: Politics and Iconography in Early Modern Lord Mayor's Shows." In Mulryne, *Ceremonial Entries in Early Modern Europe,* 245–66.

Williams, Penry. *The Later Tudors: England 1547–1603.* Oxford: Clarendon Press, 1995.

Wilson, Jean. *Entertainments for Elizabeth I.* Totowa, NJ: Rowman & Littlefield, 1980.

Wintroub, Michael. *A Savage Mirror: Power, Identity, and Knowledge in Early Modern France.* Stanford: Stanford University Press, 2006.

OXFORD

Adams, Simon. "Robert Dudley, Earl of Leicester." *Oxford Dictionary of National Biography* website. 2008.

Alexander, Michael Van Cleave. *The Growth of English Education, 1348–1648: A Social and Cultural History.* University Park: Penn State University Press, 1990.

Aylmer, G. E. "The Economics and Finances of the Colleges and University, c. 1530–1640." In McConica, *History of the University.* Vol. 3, 521–58.

Binns, James. "Abraham Hartwell, Herald of the New Queen's Reign. The *Regina Literata* (London, 1565)." In *Ut Granum Sinapis: Essays on Neo-Latin Literature in Honour of Jozef Ijsewijn,* edited by Gilbert Tournoy and Dirk Sacre, 292–304. Leuven: Leuven University Press, 1997.

Binns, J. W. *Intellectual Culture in Elizabethan and Jacobean England: The Latin Writings of the Age.* Leeds: Francis Cairns, 1990.

Brockliss, L. W. B. *The University of Oxford: A History.* New York: Oxford University Press, 2016.

Cross, Claire. "Oxford and the Tudor State from the Accession of Henry VIII to the Death of Mary." In McConica, *History of the University.* Vol. 3, 117–49.

Curthoys, Judith. *The Cardinal's College: Christ Church, Chapter and Verse.* London: Profile Books, 2012.

Curthoys, Judith. *The Stones of Christ Church*. London: Profile Books, 2017.

Duncan, G. D. "Public Lectures and Professorial Chairs." In McConica, *History of the University*. Vol. 3, 335–61.

Ferguson, James and Jan Morris. *Christ Church Oxford: A Brief History and Guide*. Oxford: Christ Church College, 2011.

Fletcher, J. M. "The Faculty of Arts." In McConica, *History of the University*. Vol. 3, 157–99.

Hammer, Jr., Carl I. "Oxford Town and Oxford University." In McConica, *History of the University*. Vol. 3, 69–116.

Heal, Felicity. *Of Prelates and Princes: A Study of the Economic and Social Position of the Tudor Episcopate*. New York: Cambridge University Press, 1980.

Jewell, Helen M. *Education in Early Modern England*. New York: St. Martin's Press, 1998.

Keenan, Siobhan. "Spectator and Spectacle: Royal Entertainments at the Universities in the 1560s." In Archer, Goldring, and Knight, *Progresses, Pageants*, 86–103.

Kinney, Arthur and Jane A. Lawson, ed. *Titled Elizabethans: A Directory of Elizabethan Court, State, and Church Officers, 1558–1603*. New York: Palgrave Macmillan, 2014.

Loach, Jennifer. "Reformation Controversies." In McConica, *History of the University*. Vol. 3, 363–96.

McConica, James, ed. *The History of the University of Oxford*. Vol. 3, *The Collegiate University*. Oxford: Clarendon Press, 1986.

McConica, James. "The Rise of the Undergraduate College." In McConica, *History of the University*. Vol. 3, 1–68.

McConica, James. "Elizabethan Oxford: The Collegiate Society." In McConica, *History of the University*. Vol. 3, 645–732.

McConica, James. "Studies and Faculties: Introduction." In McConica, *History of the University*. Vol. 3, 151–56.

Newman, John. "The Physical Setting: New Building and Adaptation." In McConica, *History of the University*. Vol. 3, 597–633.

Rosenberg, Eleanor. *Leicester: Patron of Letters*. New York: Columbia University Press, 1955.

Shenk, Linda. "Turning Learned Authority into Royal Supremacy: Elizabeth I's Learned Persona and Her University Orations." In *Elizabeth I: Always Her Own Free Woman*. Edited by Carole Levin, Jo Eldridge Carney, and Debra Barrett-Graves, 78–96. Burlington, VT: Ashgate, 2003.

Tracy, James D. *Erasmus of the Low Countries*. Berkeley: University of California Press, 1996.

Tyack, Geoffrey. *Oxford: An Architectural Guide*. New York: Oxford University Press, 1998.

Williams, Penry. "Elizabethan Oxford: State, Church, and University." In McConica, *History of the University*. Vol. 3, 397–440.

SANDWICH

Bentwich, Helen C. *History of Sandwich*. Sandwich: Sandwich Local History Society, 1975.

Brown, J. Howard. *Elizabethan Schooldays*. Oxford: Basil Blackwell, 1933.

Cavell, John and Brian Kennett. *A History of Sir Roger Manwood's School, Sandwich, 1563–1963, with a Life of the Founder*. London: Cory, Adams, and Mackay, 1963.

Clarke, Helen. *Discover Medieval Sandwich: A Guide to its History and Buildings*. Oxford: Oxbow Books, 2012.

Clarke, Helen, Sarah Pearson, Mavis E. Mate, and Keith Parfitt. *Sandwich, The 'Completest Medieval Town in England': A Study of the Town and Port from its Origins to 1600*. Oxford: Oxbow Books, 2010.

Heal, Felicity. *The Power of Gifts: Gift-Exchange in Early Modern England*. Oxford University Press, 2014.

Jack, Sybil M. "Sir Roger Manwood." *Oxford Dictionary of National Biography* website. 2004–2016.

Kipling, Gordon. *Enter the King: Theatre, Liturgy, and Ritual in the Medieval Civic Triumph*. Oxford: Clarendon Press, 1998.

Somerset, Anne. *Elizabeth I*. New York: St. Martin's, 1991.

Stowe, A. Monroe. *English Grammar Schools in the Reign of Queen Elizabeth*. New York: Teacher's College, Columbia University, 1908.

CANTERBURY

Adrian, John M. *Local Negotiations of English Nationhood 1570–1680*. New York: Palgrave Macmillan, 2011.

Boggis, R. J. E. *A History of St. Augustine's College, Canterbury*. Canterbury: Cross & Jackson, 1907.

Brook, V. J. K. *A Life of Archbishop Parker*. Oxford: Clarendon Press, 1962.

Carter, Patrick. "'Certain, Continual, and Seldom Abated': Royal Taxation of the Elizabethan Church." In *Belief and Practice in Reformation England*, edited by Susan Wabuda and Caroline Litzenberger, 94–112. Brookfield, VT: Ashgate, 1998.

Collinson, Patrick. *The Elizabethan Puritan Movement*. Berkeley: University of California Press, 1967.

Collinson, Patrick. "The Protestant Cathedral, 1541–1660." In *A History of Canterbury Cathedral*, edited by Patrick Collinson, Nigel Ramsay, and Margaret Sparks, 154–203. Oxford: Oxford University Press, 1995.

Crankshaw, David and Alexandra Gillespie. "Matthew Parker." In *Oxford Dictionary of National Biography*, vol. 42. Oxford: Oxford University Press, 2004.

Crankshaw, David. "Ecclesiastical Statesmanship in England in the Age of Reformation." In *Sister Reformations: The Reformation in Germany and in England*, edited by Dorothea Wendebourg, 271–303. Tubingen: Mohr Siebeck, 2010.

Doran, Susan. *Elizabeth I and Religion* 1558–1603. New York: Routledge, 1994.

Doran, Susan and Christopher Durtson. *Princes, Pastors and People: The Church and Religion in England* 1529–1689. New York: Routledge, 2003.

Evenden, Elizabeth. *Patents, Pictures and Patronage: John Day and the Tudor Book Trade.* Aldershot: Ashgate, 2008.

Heal, Felicity. "The Archbishops of Canterbury and the Practice of Hospitality." *Journal of Ecclesiastical History* 33 no. 4 (October 1982): 544–63.

Lehmberg, Stanford. *The Reformation of Cathedrals: Cathedrals in English Society, 1485–1603.* Princeton, NJ: Princeton University Press, 1988.

Litzenberger, Caroline. "Defining the Church of England: Religious Change in the 1570s." In *Belief and Practice in Reformation England,* edited by Susan Wabuda and Caroline Litzenberger, 137–53. Brookfield, VT: Ashgate, 1998.

McGinn, Donald Joseph. *The Admonition Controversy.* New Brunswick, NJ: Rutgers University Press, 1949.

O'Day, Rosemary. *The Debate on the English Reformation.* New York: Methuen, 1986.

Rady, J., Tim Tatton-Brown, and J. A. Bowen. "The Archbishop's Palace, Canterbury: Excavations and Building Recording Works from 1981 to 1986." *Journal of the British Archaeological Association* 144 (1991): 1–60.

Sanders, Vivienne. "The Household of Archbishop Parker and the Influencing of Public Opinion." *Journal of Ecclesiastical History* 34 no. 4 (October 1983): 534–47.

Sheils, W. J. *The English Reformation* 1530–1570. New York: Longman, 1989.

Sparks, Margaret. "The Abbey Site 1538–1997." In *The English Heritage Book of St. Augustine's Abbey, Canterbury,* edited by Richard Gem, 143–61. London: B.T. Batsford, 1997.

Strype, John. *The Life and Acts of Matthew Parker.* Vol. 2. Oxford: Oxford, 1821.

Tatton-Brown, Tim. *Lambeth Palace: A History of the Archbishops of Canterbury and Their Palaces.* London: Society for Promoting Christian Knowledge, 2000.

Tatton-Brown, Tim. "The Buildings and Topography of St. Augustine's Abbey, Canterbury." *Journal of the British Archaeological Association* 144 (1991): 61–91.

Usher, Brett. *William Cecil and Episcopacy,* 1559–1577. Burlington, VT: Ashgate, 2003.

Woodman, Francis. *The Architectural History of Canterbury Cathedral.* London: Routledge, 1981.

BRISTOL

Boynton, Lindsay. *The Elizabethan Militia: 1558–1638.* Toronto: University of Toronto Press, 1967.

Fleming, Peter and Kieran Costello. *Discovering Cabot's Bristol: Life in the Medieval and Tudor Town.* Tiverton, Devon: Redcliffe, 1998.

Gaffney, Carmel. "Thomas Churchyard." *Gale Literature: Dictionary of Literary Biography* 132 (1993): 73–80.

Kesselring, K. J. *The Northern Rebellion of 1569: Faith, Politics, and Protest in Elizabethan England.* Basingstoke: Palgrave Macmillan, 2007.

Latimer, John. *Sixteenth-Century Bristol.* Bristol: J.W. Arrowsmith, 1908.

Nicholls, J. F., and John Taylor. *Bristol Past and Present*, vol. 1. Bristol: J.W. Arrowsmith, 1881.

Sacks, David Harris. "Celebrating Authority in Bristol, 1475–1640." In *Urban Life in the Renaissance*, edited by Susan Zimmerman and Ronald F. E. Weissman, 187–223. Newark: University of Delaware Press, 1989.

Sacks, David Harris. *The Widening Gate: Bristol and the Atlantic Economy, 1450–1700.* Berkeley: University of California Press, 1991.

Skeeters, Martha. *Community and Clergy: Bristol and the Reformation c. 1530—c. 1570.* Oxford: Clarendon Press, 1993.

Williams, Mary E. *Civic Treasures of Bristol.* Bristol: City of Bristol, 1984.

Williams, Penry. *The Council in the Marches of Wales under Elizabeth I.* Cardiff: University of Wales Press, 1958.

WORCESTER

Baker, Nigel and Richard Holt. *Urban Growth and the Medieval Church: Gloucester and Worcester.* Burlington, VT: Ashgate, 2004.

Benson, Joel. *Changes and Expansion in the English Cloth Trade in the Seventeenth Century.* Lewiston, NY: Edwin Mellen Press, 2002.

Dyer, Alan D. *The City of Worcester in the Sixteenth Century.* Leicester: Leicester University Press, 1973.

Dyer, Alan D. "The Economy of Tudor Worcester." *University of Birmingham Historical Journal* 10 no. 2 (1966): 117–36.

Engel, Ute. *Worcester Cathedral: An Architectural History.* Chichester: Phillimore, 2007.

Gunn, Steven and Linda Monckton, ed. *Arthur Tudor, Prince of Wales: Life, Death and Commemoration.* Rochester, NY: Boydell Press, 2009.

Hasler, P. W. "Sir James Croft." History of Parliament. Accessed June 14, 2021. https://www.historyofparliamentonline.org/volume/1558-1603 /member/croft-sir-james-1518-90.

Kerridge, Eric. *Textile Manufacture in Early Modern England.* Manchester: Manchester University Press, 1985.

Loades, David. *England's Maritime Empire: Seapower, Commerce, and policy, 1490–1690.* New York: Longman, 2000.

Ramsay, G. D. *The English Woolen Industry, 1500–1750.* London: Macmillan, 1982.

Ramsay, G. D. *The Queen's Merchants and the Revolt of the Netherlands: The End of the Antwerp Mart, Part II.* Manchester: Manchester University Press, 1986.

Tighe, W. J. "Courtiers and Politics in Elizabethan Herefordshire: Sir James Croft, His Friends and Foes." *The Historical Journal* 32, no. 2 (June 1989): 257–79.

NORWICH

Ayers, Brian. *Book of Norwich.* London: English Heritage, 1994.

Collinson, Patrick. "Europe in Britain: Protestant strangers and the English Reformation." In *From Strangers to Citizens: the Integration of Immigrant Communities in Britain, Ireland and Colonial America, 1550–1750*, edited by Randolph Vigne and Charles Littleton, 57–67. London: Huguenot Society of Great Britain and Ireland, 2001.

Cottret, Bernard. *The Huguenots in England: Immigration and Settlement c. 1550–1700*. New York: Cambridge University Press, 1991.

Cozens-Hardy, Basil and Ernest A. Kent. *The Mayors of Norwich: 1403 to 1835*. Norwich: Jarrold & Sons, 1938.

Currer-Briggs, Noel and Royston Gambier. *Huguenot Ancestry*. Chichester: Phillimore, 1985.

Day, James Wentworth. *Norwich through the Ages*. Ipswich: East Anglian Magazine, 1976.

Dovey, Zillah. *An Elizabethan Progress: The Queen's Journey into East Anglia, 1578*. Stroud, Gloucester: Alan Sutton, 1996.

Eccles, Mark. "Brief Lives: Tudor and Stuart Authors." *Studies in Philology* 79, no. 4 (Fall 1982): 1–135.

Evans, John T. *Seventeenth-Century Norwich: Politics, Religion, and Government, 1620–1690*. Oxford: Clarendon Press, 1979.

Green, Barbara and Rachel Young. *Norwich: the Growth of a City*. Norfolk: Norfolk Museums Service, 1981.

Haymon, Sylvia. *Norwich*. Harmondsworth, Middlesex: Longman, 1973.

Hoyte, Helen. *The Strangers of Norwich*. Norwich: Red Herring, 2017.

Ives, Nancy. "Strangers and Others in St. Stephens, Norwich, in the 1570s," talk given at the Norfolk Family History Society. February 2002. Norfolk Records Office, MC 3015, Box 18.

Jewson, C. B. *History of the Great Hospital*. Norwich: Great Hospital, 1966.

Lane, Richard. *The Plains of Norwich*. Dereham, Norfolk: The Larks Press, 1999.

Meeres, Frank. *A History of Norwich*. Chichester: Phillimore, 1998.

Meeres, Frank. "Records Relating to the Strangers at the Norfolk Record Office" *Dutch Crossing* 38, no. 2 (July 2014): 132–53.

Meeres, Frank. *The Welcome Stranger: Dutch, Walloon and Huguenot Incomers to Norwich 1550–1750*. Norwich: Lasse Press, 2018.

Moens, William John Charles. *The Walloons and their Church at Norwich, 1565–1832*. Lymington: Huguenot Society of London, 1888.

Norwich Heritage Projects. *A Market for Our Times: A History of Norwich Provision Market*. Norwich: Norwich Heritage Projects, 2010.

Oldenburg, Scott. *Alien Albion: Literature and Immigration in Early Modern England*. Toronto: University of Toronto Press, 2014.

Phillips, Ellie and Isla Fay. *Health and Hygiene in Early Modern Norwich*. Norwich: Norfolk Record Society, 2013.

Pound, John. *Tudor and Stuart Norwich*. Chichester: Phillimore, 1988.

Priestley, Ursula. *The Fabric of Stuffs: The Norwich Textile Industry from 1565*. Norwich: Centre of East Anglian Studies, 1990.

Priestley, Ursula. *The Great Market: A Survey of Nine Hundred Years of Norwich Provision Market*. Norwich: Centre for East Anglian Studies, 1987.

Rawcliffe, Carole. *Medicine for the Soul: The Life, Death and Resurrection of an English Medieval Hospital: St. Giles, Norwich, c.* 1249–1550. Stroud, Gloucester: Alan Sutton, 1999.

Smith, A. Hassell. *County and Court: Government and Politics in Norfolk,* 1558–1603. Oxford: Clarendon Press, 1974.

Stephen, George. *The Waits of the City of Norwich through 4 Centuries to* 1790. Norwich: Goose & Son, 1933.

Sutermeister, Helen. *The Norwich Blackfriars: A History and Guide to St. Andrew's and Blackfriar's Halls.* Norwich: City of Norwich, 1977.

du Toit, Herman, ed. *Pageants and Processions: Images and Idiom as Spectacle.* Newcastle upon Tyne: Cambridge Scholars, 2009.

Woodcock, Matthew. *Thomas Churchyard: Pen, Sword, and Ego.* Oxford: Oxford University Press, 2016.

Yungblut, Laura Hunt. *Strangers Settled Here amongst Us.* New York: Routledge, 1996.

Yungblut, Laura Hunt. "'Mayntayninge the Indigente and Nedie': The Institutionalization of Social Responsibility in the Case of the Resident Alien Communities in Elizabethan Norwich and Colchester." In *From Strangers to Citizens: The Integration of Immigrant Communities in Britain, Ireland and Colonial America,* 1550–1750, edited by Randolph Vigne and Charles Littleton, 99–105. London: Huguenot Society of Great Britain and Ireland, 2001.

PRIMARY

Adams, William. *Adams's Chronicle of Bristol,* edited by Francis Fox. Bristol: J. W. Arrowsmith, 1910.

Camden, William. *Britannia.* London: George Bishop & John Norton, 1610.

Churchyard, Thomas. *A Discourse of the Queenes Maiesties entertainement in Suffolk and Norffolk.* London: Henry Bynneman, 1578.

Durning, Louise, ed. *Queen Elizabeth's Book of Oxford.* Oxford: Bodleian Library, 2006.

Elizabeth I. *Elizabeth I: Collected Works,* edited by Leah Marcus, Janel Mueller, and Mary Beth Rose. Chicago: University of Chicago Press, 2000.

Elliot Jr., John R., Alan H. Nelson, Alexadra F. Johnston, and Diana Wyatt, ed. *Records of Early English Drama: Oxford,* Vol. 2. Toronto: University of Toronto Press, 2004.

Galloway, David, ed. *Records of Early English Drama: Norwich* 1540–1642. Toronto: University of Toronto Press, 1984.

Garter, Bernard. *The Ioyful Receyuing of the Queenes most excellent Maiestie into hir Highnesse Citie of Norwich.* London: Henry Bynneman, 1578.

Gibson, James M., ed. *Records of Early English Drama: Kent.* Vol. 2. Toronto: University of Toronto Press, 2002.

Goldring, Elizabeth, Faith Eales, Elizabeth Clarke, and Jayne Elisabeth Archer, eds. *John Nichols's "The Progresses and Public Processions of Queen Elizabeth I": A New Edition of the Early Modern Sources.* Vol. 1 & 2. Oxford: Oxford University Press, 2014.

Habington, Thomas. *A Survey of Worcestershire*. Vol. 2. Oxford: James Parker & Co., 1895.

Hudson, William and John Cottingham, ed. *The Records of the City of Norwich*. Vol. 2. Norwich: Jarrold & Sons, 1910.

Klausner, David N., ed. *Records of Early English Drama: Herefordshire, Worcestershire*. Toronto: University of Toronto Press, 1990.

Lambarde, William. *A Perambulation of Kent*. Edited by Richard Church. Bath, UK: Adams and Dart, 1970.

Leland, John. *The Itinerary of John Leland in or about the Years 1535–1543*. Vol. 4. Edited by Lucy Toulmin Smith. Carbondale: Southern Illinois University Press, 1964.

Luther, Martin. *An Exposition of Salomons Booke, Called Ecclesiastes or the Preacher. Translated by* Anonymous. London: John Day, 1573.

Mulcaster, Richard. *The Queen's Majesty's Passage & Related Documents*. Edited by Germaine Warkentin. Toronto: Centre for Reformation and Renaissance Studies, 2004.

Parker, Matthew. *Correspondence of Matthew Parker*. Edited by John Bruce and Thomas Perowne. Cambridge: Cambridge University Press, 1853.

Parker, Matthew. *De Antiquitate Britannicae Ecclesiae*. London: John Day, 1572. Presentation copy to Queen Elizabeth I. British Library, General Reference Collection, shelfmark C.24.b.8.

Pilkinton, Mark C., ed. *Records of Early English Drama: Bristol*. Toronto: University of Toronto Press, 1997.

Somner, William. *Antiquities of Canterbury*. Wakefield, UK: E.P. Publishing, 1977.

Speed, John. *Theatre of the Empire of Great Britain*. London: John Dawson, 1627.

Stanford, Maureen, ed. *The Ordinances of Bristol 1506–1598*. Bristol: Bristol Record Society, 1990.

Kent Library and History Centre, Maidstone

Nr/CPc25 "Letter from Roger Manwood, Henry Cobham and others concerning their efforts to obtain the repair of all their havens by Act of Parliament." October 26, 1566.

Sa/LC4 "A miscellaneous volume of customs and precedents . . . c. 1571 with additions . . . compiled by Roger Manwood and Robert Alcock . . . (the town's counsels)."

Sa/LC4, 85–86 "Report on Sandwich Haven, 1574, in the form of answers by commissioners to articles of enquiry."

SA/AC 5 "Sandwich Year Book, also known as the New Red Book."

10/19/113 "Inventory of the goods of Roger Manwood late of Sandwich, Jurat, taken . . . Dec. 21, 1590."

Canterbury Cathedral Archives

CCA-Map/49   "Map of Barton Farm, St. Paul's Canterbury, showing St.
Augustine's abbey, the deer park, the Sandwich and Dover
Roads, St. Paul's and St. Lawrence's hospital." 1550–1650.

CCA-DCc-ChAnt   "Catalog description of grant for land for Sandwich school,"
/S/253   sent from the dean and chapter of Canterbury Cathedral to
Roger Manwood of Hackington.

Worcestershire Archive and Archaeology (Worcester)

x705:232/5955/1   "The names of the high members and officers of the
corporation of weavers, walkers and clothiers . . . in the city
of Worcester in anno dom 1596."

Norfolk Record Office (Norwich)

NCR 17d/9   "The Book of Dutch and Walloon Strangers."

MC 3015, Box 18   Nancy Ives, "Strangers and Others in St. Stephens, Norwich,
in the 1570s," talk given at the Norfolk Family History Society,
February 2002.

INDEX